FISH TALES

FISH TALES

Timeless and Compelling Stories of Anglers and Fish

EDITED AND WITH AN INTRODUCTION BY

LAMAR UNDERWOOD

Essex, Connecticut

An imprint of Globe Pequot, the trade division of The Rowman & Littlefield Publishing Group, Inc.
4501 Forbes Blvd., Ste. 200
Lanham, MD 20706
www.rowman.com

Distributed by NATIONAL BOOK NETWORK

British Library Cataloguing in Publication Information available

Library of Congress Cataloging-in-Publication Data
Names: Underwood, Lamar, editor. Title: Fish tales : timeless and compelling stories of anglers and fish / edited and with an introduction by Lamar Underwood.
Description: Essex, Connecticut : Lyons Press, an imprint of Globe Pequot, the trade division of The Rowman & Littlefield Publishing Group, Inc., [2023] | Includes bibliographical references.
Identifiers: LCCN 2022061510 (print) | LCCN 2022061511 (ebook) | ISBN 9781493071975 (cloth ; alk. paper) | ISBN 9781493071982 (electronic)
Subjects: LCSH: Fishing. | Fishing—Anecdotes.
Classification: LCC SH441 .F493 2023 (print) | LCC SH441 (ebook) | DDC 799.1—dc23/eng/20230109
LC record available at https://lccn.loc.gov/2022061510
LC ebook record available at https://lccn.loc.gov/2022061511

∞™ The paper used in this publication meets the minimum requirements of American National Standard for Information Sciences—Permanence of Paper for Printed Library Materials, ANSI/NISO Z39.48-1992.

CONTENTS

Contents

INTRODUCTION

Lamar Underwood

AS EVERY EXPERIENCED ANGLER CAN TELL YOU, FISHING IS OFTEN A serious waiting game. Your lure, or baited hook, is in the water, lost from sight in a shadowed pool or amid tumbling whitewater currents. *This is the place* your mind screams. But the moment drifts on—no action or sound enhance the scene. Your expectations begin to crumble as the lure or bait goes unmolested. Either they're not biting, or, God forbid, they're not here!

The *Fish Tales* book you're reading now has no "waiting game" moments. Each chapter will plunge you into fishing in print that has a felt life. You will be reliving experiences that invoke William Faulkner's famous quote, "The past is not dead. It's not even past."

As a bonus, you can count on the fact that fishing with other anglers will bring you a treasure trove of skills, intuition, and hard-core how-to you'll put to use somewhere in your upcoming days on the water.

You'll find it all here—from angling scholars like Ernest ("Matching the Hatch") Schwiebert, to simple fishing-for-action with Ernest Hemingway baiting his hook with live grasshoppers or worms.

Fishing is a diverse experience. From the tiny creek at the end of a country lane, where your "rod" is often a tree limb cut with your pocket-knife, to mysterious ocean depths so far away that they might as well be on the moon as far as you're concerned, the panorama of fishing includes tiny sunfish and marlin over 1,000 pounds. This book has it all, with every story driven by a common thread: a passion for fishing.

The other day, while wandering through some of the lesser-known regions of angling literature, I stumbled across the following little gem by John M. Dickie in the Preface of his anthology *Great Angling Stories*, published in England and Scotland (the edition I have in hand is 1953, but the book obviously was first published much earlier):

"Against books on sport," writes John Dickie, "the charge may often be laid that they depend too little on merit, too much on a bond of sympathy between author and reader."

Hello! Mr. Dickie hasn't merely thrown down the gauntlet: He has smacked me across the face with it.

Now, my experiences in both books and magazines have taught me that the editor's chair is often an uneasy one, but Dickie's observation is so much on the mark that he positively has me squirming. How many times, I must ask myself, have I rushed some work into print, in fact heralded its coming with gushes of praise, simply because it was authored by "one of the boys"? Or because the subject matter struck a warm and familiar chord? What's the harm of a little lame and undistinguished prose between friends?

Further words by John Dickie provide a positive answer to this dilemma. Of the anthology he has edited, he notes: "But angling is a fair literature and no stories have here been included which do not possess, quite apart from their subject, intrinsic literary worth."

Let's hear that again: "intrinsic literary worth." Now there's a benchmark to live up to, and I am going to attempt to do exactly that in this volume of stories, just as John Dickie did in his superb book.

While poking through the works of a lifetime of reading about fishing in preparation for this book, I was struck more than once by a trend that emerged in the eighties and nineties of angling stories, mostly fly fishing, that linked the sport to self-discovery. Words like "saving the soul," "inner peace," "inner compass"—expressions of gooey sentimentality of that sort—begin to appear in dust jacket and magazine cover blurb copy.

Perhaps I am weird, or just plain lucky, but I am quite sure I began to love fishing, and reading about fishing, when I was so young that I had not yet blundered, fumbled, and, in general, screwed up enough to need spiritual cleansing. The reason I sometimes had trouble sleeping the night before a big fishing trip was the sheer excitement of anticipating catching fish and seeing the places where fish lived. Both prospects aroused (and still do!) in me a yearning so deep and part of my psyche that quite honestly I have little desire to trace its origins to its sources. Perhaps, as the scientific-minded might point out, the trigger that says "Let's go fishing" might be traced to some distant hunter-gatherer ancestor who stood at the mouth of the cave every day and wondered where he was going to find something to eat. Perhaps thousands of years have left that spark alive in only a few of us, people like you and me, and not the guy down the street. But for me there is no mystery in the fact that the fish I buy at the market can never replace the fish that I pulled from the edge of the sea and now lies on the cutting board, ready for broiling. Were the reverse true, that because I can buy fish I will cease all fishing myself, I would become an emotional basket case, asking myself, "What happened to you, boy?"

Of course, fishing for food is only part of the story. The freezer will only hold so much; there are only so many fish dinners one can eat. Still, we press on, eager as ever, armed with new tactics and equipment to meet any angling challenge. Because it's fun, damn it!

This is the point in the story where "catch-and-release" comes on stage. Either because the freezer is stuffed, or because of dwindling numbers that need protection in certain places, "catch-and-release" fishing becomes as natural to many sensible anglers as yelling, "Got one!" And it works. We are seeing many cases—in trout fishing especially—where resources would be dwindling or wiped out completely were it not for catch-and-release.

One type of angler I do not want in the boat with me or at the fishing camp where I'm staying is the emotional idiot who fishes to prove something. He's got to catch the most and the biggest. Always! The successes or disappointments of others mean nothing to him. Scratch this guy deep enough and you'll find a miserable bastard who isn't fishing for food or pleasure, but for some weird and dark obsession to excel.

Now don't think I'm saying there's something wrong with catching big fish, or a lot of fish. No sir! I'm right in there pitching to do both, but there are boundaries and limits I respect. And I will always hope I'm the kind of good buddy whose eyes and ears are open to seeing your big one, hearing about your twenty-fish day and the story about the lunker that wrapped you around a limb and broke off.

The time I have spent reading about fishing has always been as important a part of my fishing enjoyment as the time spent with a rod in my hand. But I do not pretend to have unearthed and read every single gem of angling literature. As much as I yearn to live up to the promise of making this book a great reading experience, I am quite certain my selections will not always be the ones the reader would have chosen, given the opportunity. My decisions were guided by several considerations beyond sheer literary merit. One of the most important was to not stumble blindly into focusing on one type of fishing at the expense of others. Obviously, fishing is so diverse that its literature can never be captured in a single book, no matter how ambitious. Entire libraries are needed, and indeed have been built and stocked for just such a project. The astute reader will no doubt have titles in mind that he or she feels should have been included here. And if you are keenly disappointed by the absence of one of your personal favorites, then I regret not serving you better.

It is my hope that the pages ahead will take you fishing in two kinds of places: Those like the ones you have never fished but would like to try, and those like the ones you have fished and enjoy remembering. Places like cold rivers where you will start out by looking for trout but will also truly lift up your eyes unto the hills and remember how fortunate you are to be there; dark pockets under old oaks where bigmouth bass lurk; estuaries where iron-muscled steelhead and salmon are fresh from the throbbing ocean currents; on some sandy beach where the green waves are slashed by slashes of striped bass and bluefish; out on the blue water of the Gulf Stream where your trolled baits barely scratch the surface of the domain roamed by marlin and tuna; and on the tidal flats where the thin clear pushes of water give the fishing for tarpon, bonefish, and permit the visual drama of hunting.

You'll find all kinds of fishing here. And all kinds of fishermen. They have wonderful stories to tell you. You'll especially enjoy them on those long winter evenings when real fishing seems a distant promise. Throw another log on the fire, get your favorite chair and lamp just right, and hope everybody in the house will leave you alone. The fact that the stories have "intrinsic literary worth" won't bother you at all. I guarantee it!

CHAPTER ONE

The Bass Doctor

Generations of Experience in Two Parts

by James A. Henshall, MD

**PART ONE: THE FIGHTING QUALITIES OF LARGEMOUTH
BLACK BASS**

*In a lifetime of editing, writing, and fishing, I've never come across a more
controversial statement than this gem by Dr. Henshall, writing on the large-
mouth black bass: "Inch for inch, and pound for pound, he is the gamest fish
that swims."*

The quote from Dr. Henshall's Book of the Black Bass *(1881), has not
only survived over these many years, it has often been referenced and pointed
out by modern-era writers, such as my friend the late Grits Gresham in his*
The Complete Book of Bass Fishing. *Dr. Henshall has even been called "The
father of bass fishing in America" by many scribes.*

*If your personal opinion, like mine, leads you to thinking that Dr. Hen-
shall was wrong and lacked experience that should have made him think twice
about his statement, get ready for a jolt. Twenty-five years later, in his book*
Bass, Pike, Perch and Others, *Henshall doubles down on his opinion. As
you shall see in this excerpt from that book, he goes in-your-face to repeat his
previous statement. He also compares largemouth bass to smallmouth, calling
the contest on fighting qualities a draw.*

Be aware that Dr. Henshall was no novice. His angling experiences ranged from salmon to tarpon. His books reflect that experience and form a foundation for his observations.

In another chapter in this book we have Dr. Henshall on more bass lore in an excerpt from Favorite Fish and Fishing. *In his many observations and bass and bass fishing, he never backs down from his original statement on how bass put up a fight.*

AS A GAME-FISH THE BLACK-BASS HAS COME INTO HIS INHERITANCE. As the French say, he has arrived. With the special tools and tackle now furnished for his capture, he has proved my aphorism. "Inch for inch, and pound for pound, he is the gamest fish that swims." When I ventured this opinion twenty-five years ago, there were no special articles made for his capture except the Kentucky reel and the McGinnis rod, twelve feet long and fifteen ounces in weight. In awarding the palm as a game-fish to the black-bass, I do so advisedly, in the light of ample experience with all other game-fishes, and without prejudice, for I have an innate love and admiration for all, from the lovely trout of the mountain brook to the giant tarpon of the sea.

In the application of so broad and sweeping an assertion each and every attribute of a game-fish must be well considered: his habitat; his aptitude to rise to the fly; his struggle for freedom; his manner of resistance; his weight as compared with other game-fishes; and his excellence as a food-fish, must be separately and collectively considered and duly and impartially weighed. His haunts are amid most charming and varied scenes. Not in the silent and solemn solitudes of the primeval forests, where animated Nature is evidenced mainly in swarms of gnats, black-flies, and mosquitoes; nor under the shadows of grand and lofty mountains, guarded by serried ranks of pines and firs, but whose somber depths are void of feathered songsters. However grand, sublime, and impressive such scenes truly are, they do not appeal profoundly to the angler. He must have life, motion, sound. He courts Nature in her more communicative moods, and in the haunts of the black-bass his desires are realized. Wading down the rippling stream, casting his flies hither and yon, alert for the responsive tug, the sunlight is filtered through overhanging trees, while the thrush, blackbird, and cardinal render the air vocal with sweet sounds, and his rival, the kingfisher, greets him with vibrant voice. The summer breeze, laden with the scent of woodland blossoms, whispers among the leaves, the wild bee flits by on droning wing, the squirrel barks defiantly, and the tinkle of the cow-bell is mellowed in the distance. I know of such streams in the mountain valleys of West Virginia, amid the green rolling hills of Kentucky and Tennessee, and in the hill country where Missouri and Arkansas meet.

The aptitude of the black-bass to rise to the artificial fly is not questioned by the twentieth-century angler, though it was considered a matter of doubt by many anglers during the last quarter of the nineteenth. The doubt was mainly owing to a lack of experience, for fly-fishing for black-bass was successfully practiced in Kentucky as early, certainly, as 1845. I have before me a click reel made in 1848 by the late Mr. J. L. Sage, of Lexington, Kentucky, especially for fly-fishing. I have also seen his fly-rod made by him about the same time, and used by him for many years on the famous bass streams of that state. And I might say, in passing, that black-bass bait-fishing, as an art, originated in Kentucky a century ago. George Snyder, of Paris, Kentucky, when president of the Bourbon County Angling Club, made the first multiplying reel for casting the minnow, in 1810, and as early as 1830 many such reels were used in that state. The rods employed by those pioneers of black-bass fishing were about ten feet long, weighing but several ounces, cut from the small end of a Mississippi cane, with the reel lashed to the butt. They used the smallest Chinese "sea-grass" lines, or home-made lines of three strands of black sewing-silk twisted together. Those old disciples of Walton would have been shocked, could they have seen the heavy rods and coarse lines that are still used in some sections, for their own tackle was as light, if not so elegant, as any made at the present day.

Another quality in a game-fish is measured by his resistance when hooked and by his efforts to escape. I think no fish of equal weight exhibits so much finesse and stubborn resistance, under such conditions, as the black-bass. Most fishes when hooked attempt to escape by tugging and pulling in one direction, or by boring toward the bottom, and if not successful in breaking away soon give up the unequal contest. But the black-bass exhibits, if not intelligence, something akin to it, in his strategical maneuvers. Sometimes his first effort is to bound into the air at once and attempt to shake out the hook, as if he knew his misfortune came from above. At other times he dashes furiously, first in one direction, then in another, pulling strongly meanwhile, then leaps into the air several times in quick succession, madly shaking himself with open jaws. I have seen him fall on a slack line, and again by using his tail as a lever and the water as a fulcrum, throw himself over a taut line, evidently with the intent to break it or tear out the hook. Another clever ruse is to wind the line around a root or rock, and still another is to embed himself in a clump of water-weeds if permitted to do so. Or, finding it useless to pull straight away, he reverses his tactics and swims rapidly toward the angler, shaking himself and working his jaws, meanwhile, as if he knew that with a slack line he would be more apt to disengage the hook.

I have never known a black-bass to sulk like the salmon by lying motionless on the bottom. He is never still unless he succeeds in reaching a bed of weeds. He is wily and adroit, but at the same time he is brave and valiant. He seems to employ all the known tactics of other fishes, and to add a few of his own in his gallant fight for freedom.

As a food-fish there is, in my estimation, but one fresh-water fish that is better, the whitefish of the Great Lakes. Its flesh is white, firm, and flaky, with a fine savor, and a juicy, succulent quality that is lacking with most other fresh-water fishes. About the spawning period, especially in fish from weedy ponds, it is somewhat musky or muddy in flavor, like other fishes in similar situations; but by skinning the fish instead of scaling it much of that unpleasant feature is removed.

***

In fly-fishing it is imperative to strike as soon as the bass seizes the fly, otherwise he ejects it at once, if not hooked by a taut line, for he is conscious of the deception as soon as the fly is taken into his mouth. With natural bait it is different. The bass first seizes the minnow crosswise or tail first, turns it in his mouth, and swallows it head first. This takes a little time. Usually he holds it in his mouth and bolts away from other fish, or rushes toward a secure hiding-place—hence the vigorous initial dash and taking of line. If stopped before being hooked, he gives several tugs in quick succession, when he should be given line slowly. The angler, with thumb on the spool of the reel, can feel every motion of the fish. When he pulls steadily and strongly and increases his speed, the hook should be driven in by striking in the opposite direction to his course, or upward. A vigorous "yank" is not needed. With the strained line a movement of the tip of the rod a foot or two is sufficient with a sharp hook.

If fishing from a boat, where the angler is more apt to be seen, it should be kept in deep water and the casts made toward the haunts of the bass in shallow water. Should the hooked bass break water on a long line, the slight straightening of the bent rod that ensues will tend to keep it taut, and there is nothing more to do. On a short line, however (the bend of the rod being maintained), he should be followed back to the water by a slight lowering of the tip, but it should again be raised as soon as he touches the water. The critical moment is when he is apparently standing on his tail, shaking himself, with wide-opened jaws. If he is given any slack line at this time, the hook is likely to be thrown out.

Lowering the tip to a leaping fish is a good old rule when done understandingly. It has been ridiculed by some anglers who do not seem to have a clear conception of it. They claim that by lowering the tip it gives sufficient slack line to enable the fish to free himself. But if the rod is bent, as it should be, the simple lowering of the tip with a short line merely relieves it somewhat from the weight of the fish; there is no slack line, nor could there be unless the rod is lowered until it is perfectly straight, which no wide-awake angler would permit. As the fish is in the air but a second or two, the careless angler simply does nothing, which is, perhaps, the best thing that could happen for him.

***

As to the much-mooted subject of the gameness of the large-mouth bass I have no hesitation in saying, from an experience of nearly forty years, covering all sections of the country, that where the two species coexist there is no difference in their game qualities. The large-mouth is fully the equal of the small-mouth where they are exposed to the same conditions. Many anglers profess to think otherwise, but their deductions are drawn from a comparison of the two species when subject to totally different environment; for it is altogether a matter of environment and not of physical structure or idiosyncrasy that influences their game qualities. A small-mouth bass in a clear, rocky stream, highly aerated as it must be, is, as a matter of course, more active than a large-mouth bass in a quiet, weedy pond.

With others the opinion is merely a matter of prejudice or hearsay, a prejudice that is, indeed, difficult to account for. It does not make the small-mouth bass a gamer fish by disparaging the large-mouth. As I have said elsewhere, if the large-mouth bass is just as game as the small-mouth, the angler is just that much better off. As prejudice and ignorance go hand in hand, we are not surprised when we hear persons—I do not style them anglers—call the small-mouth the "true" black-bass, implying that the large-mouth is not a black-bass, but is, as they often say, the Oswego bass, which is, of course, absurd. I am glad to add, however, that the prejudice against the large-mouth bass is dying out among observant anglers, who know that a trout in a clear stream is more vigorous than one in a weedy, mucky pond.

From my own experience I am prepared to say that the large-mouth bass is more to be relied on in rising to the fly than the small-mouth, which fact should be taken into consideration when the gameness of the two species is compared. The remarks concerning fly-fishing for the small-mouth bass are also applicable to the large-mouth, as both are fished for in the same way, and with the same tackle, except that the rod may be a little heavier. For the large bass of the Gulf states the rod should be fully eight ounces in weight, and the flies a trifle larger, on hooks Nos. 2 to 6; otherwise the tackle should be the same.

PART TWO: THE BLACK BASS: THE GAMEFISH OF THE PEOPLE

Down in southeast Georgia, where I spent much of my boyhood, "dinner" was the meal you ate in the middle of the day. And the fish everybody called a "trout" was actually a largemouth bass.

To back me up, I have no less an authority than Dr. James A. Henshall in his book Favorite Fish and Fishing. *In that book, published many years after his famous* Book of the Black Bass, *Dr. Henshall shares wisdom and observations that are timeless and vivid.*

BLACK-BASS FISHING! THESE ARE WORDS TO CONJURE WITH. WHAT pleasurable emotions they call up! To the superannuated angler the words are fraught with retrospective reflections of the keenest enjoyment, while they cause the soul of the new hand to become obsessed with pleasures yet to come—pleasures rendered brighter by the rosy tint of anticipation.

With the first blossoms of spring the thoughts of many men, both old and young, turn lightly to love—the love of angling. And as the leaves unfold, and the birds begin their wooing, and the streams become clear, the premonitory symptoms of the affection are manifested in a rummaging of drawers and lockers for fly-books and tackle boxes, and the critical examination of rods and reels, and in the testing of lines and leaders. These preliminaries are the inevitable harbingers of the advent of the angling season, when black bass are leaping gayly from the waters after their enforced hibernation in the gloom and seclusion of the deep pools.

And when the encroachment of age or rheumatism forbids wading the stream, one can still sit in a boat on a quiet lake and enjoy to the full the delight and fascination of "bass fishing." What farmer's boy in the Middle West does not look forward to a Saturday when the ground is too wet to plow or plant, when he can repair to the creek or pond with his rude tackle and realize his fond dreams of fishing for black bass! And when such a day arrives, as it is sure to do, how he hurries through the chores, and with what sanguine hope he digs for angle-worms in the garden, or nets crawfish or minnows in the brook, each one good for at least one "sockdolager" of a bass. For it sometimes happens that a bass will take a wriggling earth-worm or a "soft craw" when it will not deign to notice the choicest minnow or the most cunningly devised artificial fly. And the country lad always knows just where an old "whopper" of a bronze-back black bass has his lair beneath the roots of a big tree, or under the ledge of a moss-grown rock. To do future battle with such a one has engrossed his thoughts by day and his dreams by night, ever since the Christmas tree for him bore such fruit as a linen line, a red and green float and a dozen fishhooks.

The triumphal march of a Roman warrior, with captives chained to his chariot wheels, entering the gates of the Eternal City with a blare of trumpets and the applause of the multitude, was an event to fill his soul with just pride—but it descends to the level of vainglory and mediocrity when compared with the swelling heart of the lad as he enters the farm-house kitchen with two or three old "lunkers" of black bass strung on a willow withe. Many times during his homeward march had he halted to admire the scale armor and spiny crests of his captive knights!

And then to an appreciative audience he relates, in a graphic manner, how this one seized a minnow, and that one a crawfish, and the other one a hellgramite—and how often each one leaped from the water, and how high it jumped—and how the "ellum" rod bent and twisted as the large one tried to regain the hole under the big rock—and how the good line cut the water in curving reaches and straight lines as another one forged toward the sunken roots of the old sycamore. And then came the climax, as, with pride and regret struggling for mastery, and "suiting the action to the word and the word to the action," he tells again the old, old story of how the biggest of all, a regular "snolligoster," shook out the hook and got away!

In the years to come, will that lad exult over the capture of a mighty tuna or giant tarpon with as much genuine joy and enthusiasm as over that string of bass? Well, hardly. And as the boy is father to the man, and as we are all but children of larger growth, the black-bass angler never outlives that love and enthusiasm of his younger days—younger only as reckoned by the lapse of years.

Although the black bass, as a game fish, has come into his own only during the last two or three decades, black-bass fishing is older than the Federal Union. The quaint old naturalist, William Bartram, the "grandfather of American ornithology," in 1764, described, minutely, "bobbing" for black bass in Florida, there, as in all the Southern States, called "trout"—a name bestowed by the English colonists owing to its gameness. While black-bass fishing is comparatively a recent sport in the Eastern States, it was practiced in Kentucky, Tennessee, and southern Ohio before the end of the eighteenth century. In 1805 George Snyder, the inventor of the Kentucky reel, was president of the Bourbon County

Angling Club at Paris, Kentucky. Fly-fishing was practiced as early as 1840 on the Elkhorn and Kentucky rivers by Mr. J. L. Sage and others. His click reel, made by himself, is now in my possession; and George Snyder's own reel, made in 1810, a small brass multiplying reel running on garnet jewels, is still in the possession of his grandson at Louisville.

The black bass is now an acknowledged peer among game fishes, and taking him by and large excels them all, weight for weight. The generic term black bass, as here used, includes both the large-mouth bass and the small-mouth bass. The two species are as much alike as two peas in a pod, the most striking difference between them being that one has a larger mouth and larger scales than the other. When subject to the same conditions and environment, they are equal in game qualities. The habits of the two species are similar, though the large-mouth bass is more at home in ponds and weedy waters than the small-mouth bass, which prefers running streams and clear lakes. Their natural food is crawfish, for which their wide mouths and brush-like teeth are well adapted, though they do not object to an occasional minnow or small frog.

Owing to the wide distribution of black bass, fishing for it is universal. It is no less enjoyed by the rustic youth with peeled sapling rod and crawfish bait than by the artistic angler with slender wand and fairy-like flies. While black-bass fishing was known and practiced in the Ohio Valley from the earliest years of the nineteenth century, as just stated, our angling books for three-fourths of the century contained but little, if anything, about the black bass, as they were mostly compilations from English authors. The only exception were the books of Robert B. Roosevelt, an uncle of the President, who fished for black bass in Canada about 1860. At the present day there are more articles of fishing tackle made especially for black bass than for all other game fishes combined. This is proof that it is the most popular and, all things considered, the best game fish of America.

Salmon fishing, the grandest sport in the curriculum of angling, is now an expensive luxury. There is but little free water readily accessible, for all the best pools are in the possession of wealthy clubs. The bold leap of the salmon, when hooked, the exciting play of the fish on the rod, and the successful gaffing, are as so many stanzas of an epic poem. Trout fishing is a summer idyl. The angler wades the merry stream while the leaves whisper and rustle overhead, the birds chirp and sing, the insects drone and hum, the cool breeze fans his cheek, as he casts his feathery lures, hither and yon, in eager expectation of a rise.

Black-bass fishing combines, in a measure, the heroic potentialities of salmon fishing with the charms of trout fishing. The leap of the bass is no less exciting than that of the salmon, and is oftener repeated, while in stream fishing the pastoral features of trout fishing are experienced and enjoyed.

The leap of a hooked fish is always an exciting episode to the angler with red blood in his veins—exciting because as an offset to its probable capture there is the very possible contingency of its escape by throwing out the hook, or by breaking away. So with each leap of the bass the hopes and fears of the angler are constantly exercised, while his pulses quicken and his enthusiasm is aroused. Game fishes often leap a few inches above the surface in play, or to catch a low-flying insect; but when hooked they vault to a height commensurate with their agility and muscular ability. They do not leap so high, however, as is commonly supposed.

A tarpon will leap six feet high, but the cero, or Florida kingfish, will leap higher, for it is the greatest vaulter of them all. The ladyfish executes a series of short, whirling leaps that puzzle the eye to follow—it is the gamest fish for its size in salt water. The leap of the flying-fish is sustained for a long distance by its wing-like pectoral fins, on the principle of the aëroplane, though its sole motive power is probably derived from its tail before leaving the water. The salt-water mullet is an expert jumper, leaping often in play, but when pursued by an enemy its leaps are higher and longer than would be expected from its size. The brook trout, pike, and mascalonge seldom leap when hooked, though the steelhead trout and grayling both leap nearly as often as the black bass in their efforts to dislodge the hook. The leap of the salmon is a long, graceful curve, as it heads up stream. Once, while playing my first salmon, on the Restigouche, many years ago, my taut line was leading straight down the stream, when I caught sight of a salmon over my shoulder and above me, leaping from the surface, which, to my surprise, proved to be my hooked fish—the line making a long detour in the swift water.

I have heard many anglers declare that a black bass could leap five feet high, when as a matter of fact they leap but a few inches, usually, and occasionally one, or at most three feet, though I think two feet nearer the limit. By an examination of Mr. A. Radcliffe Dugmore's photograph, [Editor's note: This comment refers to Henshall's original book and text.] reproduced herewith, it will readily be seen that the leaps are not very high ones. A black bass is in the air but a second or two, and to catch him in the act as Mr. Dugmore has done must be considered a wonderful achievement. The picture shows the bass returning to the water, with either the head or the shoulders at, or beneath, the surface, while the displaced water at his point of emergence still shows plainly—standing up, as it were. This proves that the bass regains the surface as soon as the displaced water, or rather before the upheaved water finds its level, which could not be the case were the leaps three or four feet high.

Why does a hooked bass leap from the water? This question is sometimes raised, though the answer is plain. He leaps into the air to endeavor to dislodge the hook; this he tries to do by violently shaking his body, with widely extended jaws. He does not "shake his head," as is often said, for having no flexible neck, his head can only be thrown from side to side by the violent contortions of his body, often using the water as a fulcrum, when he appears to be standing on his tail. A dog or a cat will shake its head vigorously to eject some offending substance from the mouth, and a bass does the same thing; but as he cannot shake his body to the extent required beneath the surface, owing to the resistance of the water, he leaps above it. And if he succeeds in throwing out the hook he disappears beneath the surface and is seen no more; his object in leaping has been accomplished.

Usually, it is only surface-feeding fishes that leap when hooked. Bottom-feeding fishes bore toward the bottom or struggle in mid-water. Every fish has its characteristic way of resisting capture, but any fish is more easily subdued if kept on the surface by the skill of the angler and the use of good and trustworthy tackle.

The manner of taking a bait also varies considerably with different fishes; and the character of their teeth is a good guide to what they feed on. For instance, the cunner and sheepshead are expert bait stealers. With their incisor teeth their habit is to pinch off barnacles and other mollusks from their attachment to rocks and old timbers, and so they nip off the clam or crab bait from the hook with but little disturbance. A trout takes a fly or bait with a vigorous snap, without investigation as to its nature, and a black bass does much the same, giving immediate and unmistakable notice to the angler that there is "something doing."

CHAPTER TWO

Bright Rivers

by Nick Lyons

I had the great pleasure of publishing Nick Lyons's stories in Sports Afield *before I had ever clapped eyes on the man. Getting to know Nick personally was a bonus I never expected back in the early seventies when I purchased "The Legacy" and made it a cornerstone piece in one of the issues launching my six-year editorship of the magazine.*

A lot of water has flowed down the trout rivers since then, and a lot of prose has flowed by Nick's old Royal standard typewriter, which he clings to like a man holding a lifebuoy, flaunting the electronic whiz-bang writing aids of today. I can say quite honestly that every Nick Lyons article and book has always pleased me immensely with its sheer readability. The talent I saw in the work of Nick Lyons in the first manuscript of his I ever read has been manifested time and time again in the enormous body of work he has produced, which includes everything from criticism in the New York Times *to essays in* Fly Fisherman *magazine. Everything from describing the sheer utter heartbreak of being a rejected writer to describing the temporary heartbreak of fishing a rejected dry fly.*

The Nick Lyons story is excerpted from the first section of the book Bright Rivers, *published by Lippincott in 1977. Here, my friends, is what fishing is all about—especially a long-awaited fishing trip to someplace very special. The journey begins in downtown New York, "where the game for the big green is played," as Nick describes the setting. But ahead lie Bright Rivers, and all that they promise.*

Downtown, where the game for the big green is played, I go to a meeting that lasts eight hours. After the first ten minutes, I feel the tightening in my chest. I begin to doodle; I scribble out a meaningless note and pass it to someone I know across the table, because I've seen executives in the movies do that. I look for the windows, but they're hidden behind heavy, brocaded draperies so that the air conditioning will take—anyway, we're in the back of the hotel so even if the windows were open, I'd only see the backs of other buildings. Everyone is talking with pomp and edge; I jot down Evelyn Waugh's observation, "that neurosis people mistake for energy." I drink two glasses of ice water. I speak like a good boy, when spoken to.

Suddenly I begin to sweat. I've been in this windowless room for fifteen years. I have been a juggler, flinging my several lives high and carelessly into the air, never catching them, barely feeling one as it touches my hand. Nine to five I am here; then a salt stick on the subway and five hours in the classroom; then I am the fastest ghostwriter in the East, becoming a lawyer one week, an expert on Greece the next, then an adopted girl searching for the blood link. When there is time, after midnight, I write high-toned scholarship—on Chrétien de Troyes and Thomas Nashe and William Ellery Channing and Saint Augustine—and shaggy-fish stories; or I prepare a lecture on "The Generosity of Whitman." A smorgasbord, my life. Five hours of sleep and back at 'em again, the ghost who is not what he seems, back at meetings like this one, dreaming.

I say my piece in front of all these important men as enthusiastically as I can. These are the rules of the game. Part of what I say—a few words—has to do with rivers. From my words I catch their briefest warbling sound, like the faint rush of wind among the leaves, or a rushing faucet, and when I sit down, there in the back of the hotel, with the windows covered by heavy drapes and the smoke from cigars (mine among them) thick around our heads, as strategies unfold and campaigns thicken, I see a glimpse of them, inside. Deep within me they uncoil.

Rivers.

Bright green live rivers.

The coil and swoop of them, their bright dancing riffles and their flat dimpled pools at dusk. Their changes and undulations, each different flowing inch of them. Their physics and morphology and entomology and soul. The willows and alders along their banks. A particular rock the size of an igloo. Layers of serrated slate from which rhododendron plumes like an Inca headdress, against which the current rushes, eddies. The quick turn of a yellow-bellied trout in the lip of the current. Five trout, in loose formation, in a pellucid backwater where I cannot get at them. A world. Many worlds.

> . . . oft, in lonely rooms, and 'mid the din
> Of towns and cities . . .

as Wordsworth said in "Tintern Abbey," about a nature he felt but never really saw,

> . . . I have owed to them
> In hours of weariness, sensations sweet,
> Felt in the blood, and felt along the heart. . . .

Yes, I owe rivers that. And more. They are something wild, untamed—like that Montana eagle riding a thermal on extended wings, high above the Absaroka mountain pasture flecked with purple lupine. And like the creatures in them: quick trout with laws we can learn, sometimes, somewhat.

I do not want the qualities of my soul unlocked only by this tense, cold, gray, noisy, gaudy, grabby place—full of energy and neurosis and art and antiart and getting and spending—in which that business part of my life, at this time in my life, must of necessity be lived. I have other needs as well. I have other parts of my soul.

Nothing in this world so enlivens my spirit and emotions as the rivers I know. They are necessities. In their clear, swift or slow, generous or coy waters, I regain my powers; I find again those parts of myself that have been lost in cities. Stillness. Patience. Green thoughts. Open eyes. Attachment. High drama. Earthiness. Wit. The Huck Finn I once was. Gentleness. "The life of things." They are my perne within the whirling gyre.

Just knowing they are there, and that their hatches will come again and again according to the great natural laws, is some consolation to carry with me on the subways and into the gray offices and out onto upper Broadway at night.

Rivers have been brought to me by my somewhat unintelligible love of fishing. From the little Catskill creek in which I gigged my first trout to the majestic rivers of the West—the Madison, the Yellowstone, the Big Hole, the Snake—fishing has been the hook. And in the pursuit of trout I have found much larger fish.

"Must you actually fish to enjoy rivers?" my friend the Scholar asks.

It is difficult to explain but, yes, the *fish* make every bit of difference. They anchor and focus my eye, rivet my ear.

And could this not be done by a trained patient lover of nature who did not carry a rod?

Perhaps it could. But fishing is my hinge, the "oiléd ward" that opens a few of the mysteries for me. It is so for all kinds of fishermen, I suspect, but especially so for fly-fishermen, who live closest to the seamless web of life in rivers. That shadow I am pursuing beneath the amber water is a hieroglyphic: I read its position, watch its relationship to a thousand other shadows, observe its steadiness and purpose. That shadow is a great glyph, connected to the darting swallow overhead; to that dancing cream caddis fly near the patch of alders; to the little cased caddis larva on the streambed; to the shell of the hatched stone fly on the rock; to the contours of the river, the velocity of the flow, the chemical composition and temperature of the water; to certain vegetable life called plankton that I cannot see; to the mill nine miles upstream and the reservoir into which the river flows—and, oh, a thousand other factors, fleeting and solid and telling as that shadow. Fishing makes me a student of all this—and a hunter.

Which couldn't be appreciated unless you fish?

Which mean more to me because I do. Fishing makes rivers my corrective lens; I see differently. Not only does the bird taking the mayfly signify a hatch, not only does the flash of color at the break of the riffle signify a fish feeding, but my powers uncoil inside me and I must determine which insect is hatching and what feeding pattern the trout has established. Then I must properly equip myself and properly approach the fish and properly present my imitation. I am engaged in a hunt that is more than a hunt, for the objects of the hunt are mostly to be found within myself, in the nature of my response and action. I am on a Parsifalian quest. I must be scientist, technician, athlete, perhaps even a queer sort of poet.

The Scholar smiles wanly and says, "It all sounds like rank hedonism. And some cultism. With some mumbo jumbo thrown in."

Yes, I am out to pleasure myself, though sometimes after I've been chewed by no-see-ums until I'm pocked like a leper you wouldn't think that. There is a physical testing: the long hours at early morning, in bright sun, or at dusk; casting until your arm is like lead and your legs, from wading against the stiff current, are numb. That is part of the quest: to cleanse through exertion.

And the cultism and mumbo jumbo?

Some of trout fishing has become that, perhaps always was that. It is a separate little world, cunningly contrived, with certain codes and rules and icons. It is not a religion, though some believers make it such, and it is less than an art. But it has qualities of each. It touches heart and head; it demands and builds flexibility and imagination; it is not easy. I come to rivers like an initiate to holy springs. If I cannot draw from them an enduring catechism or from their impulses even very much about "moral evil and of good," they still confer upon me the beneficence of the only deity I have been able to find. And when the little world becomes too cunningly contrived? Wit helps.

My friend the Scholar says he is not a puritan or a moralist but that it seems to him it would be more satisfying to make something that would last—a book, a poem, a cabinet, a wooden bowl—than merely to fish well. He quotes Cézanne, from a letter, after a day of fishing: "All this is easier than painting but it does not lead far."

Not hardly. Not very far at all. Except that this may be precisely where I want it to lead. Let the world lead far—as one should frame it to do; let art last long and lead far and to form. Let a few other human activities lead far, though most of them lead us up a tree or up the asshole of the world. Let fly-fishing be temporary and fleeting and inconsequential. I do not mind.

Enough. Enough.

Too much theory and this pleasant respite from the north Broadway renaissance and gray offices will become an extravagant end that leads too far. Fishing is nothing if not a pastime; it would be hell if I did it all the time.

Beyond the dreams and the theories, there are the days when a close friend will pick me up at dawn on my deserted city block and we will make the long drive together, talking, connected, uncoiling, until we reach our river for the day. It is a simple adventure we are undertaking; it is a break from the beetle-dull routine, a new start, an awakening of the senses, a pilgrimage.

Flooded with memories and expectations, we take out our rods, suit up in waders and vest, special fish hats and nets, arrange flies and leaders, and take to the woods. Each article of equipment, each bit of gear in our ritualistic uniform, is part of the act. The skunk cabbage is thrusting up, lush and green-purple out of the moist brown mulch of last year's leaves; we flush a white-tailed deer that bounds off boldly; we see the pale-green buds pressing out of the birch branches. "Spring has come again," says Rilke. "The earth is like a little child who knows poems by heart—many, so many." We wonder whether the Hendricksons will or will not hatch at midday. We have our hopes.

With rivers as with good friends, you always feel better for a few hours in their presence; you always want to review your dialogue, years later, with a particular pool or riffle or bend, and to live back through layers of experience. We have been to this river before and together. We have much to relive.

Then we are on the river. It is still there. So much is perishable, impermanent, dispensable today, so much is gobbled up by industry and housing and the wanton surge of people, we half thought it might be gone, like that river we used to fish in Dutchess County, now bludgeoned by tract homes and industrial plants and trailers, now littered and warm and dead. Trout are yardsticks; they are an early warning system like the canary in the mine—when they go, what will happen to the rest of the planet, to the quality of life?

Yes, this river is still there, still alive, still pregnant with possibility.

"There's a swirl," I say, pointing.

"I saw one upstream, too."

"A few flies are coming off, see?"

"Yes, we're going to make a day of it."

My pulse quickens, the long gray city winter vanishes. In a moment we separate and belong to the river and to its mysteries, to its smooth glides and pinched bends, to the myriad sweet problems that call forth total concentration, that obviate philosophy.

Yes, these are Hendricksons, *Ephemerella subvaria*, and the hatch, on schedule, is just beginning. I am by profession neither an angler nor a scientist but there's always more pleasure in knowing than in not knowing. I take the lower pool and spot four good trout, poised high in the clear, flat water, waiting for the duns to hatch in the riffles and float down. By tilting my head close to the surface, I can see them, like little sailboats, drifting down. Two, three, there's another. Not many yet. A couple of birds are working, dipping and darting; against the light sky above the treeline I pick out one mayfly, watch it flutter, watch a swallow swoop, hesitate, and take it. What looks so pastoral is violent; it is, only on a smaller, more civilized scale, a horde of bluefish slashing a bunker school to bits, leaving blood and fin and head everywhere, to be picked up by the ravenous sea birds. The bites are cleaner here: the birds and trout take a whole creature in one mouthful.

Then back to the river. There are circles below me; the fish are feeding steadily. Shall I fish above or below them? They are so still, so firmly established in an irregular row across the channel in that clear flat water, that I elect the road less traveled and decide to fish down to them on a slack line—this way I won't have to cast over their backs.

It is delicate work, but I know that this year I have an excellent imitation of the natural fly, that my 5X leader is light enough, and that I've done just enough slack-line downstream casting to manage. Fishing is cumulative, though you don't learn all of it, ever.

I position myself carefully on the bank—it would be fatal to wade above such fish—strip about forty feet of line from my reel, and false cast twice.

My rod jerks backward. I've hung my fly in that low brush.

The interruption of the music, like the needle hitting a scratch on a recording of the Brandenburg Concerto, irritates madly but is not final.

When I return, the fish are still feeding, more steadily now, even rhythmically.

My cast lands well above the fish, and my fly floats without drag a few feet short of their feeding station before the line tightens; a little V forms behind the fly and it goes under.

I retrieve the fly slowly, unwilling to ruffle the surface until there are no more than ten feet of line still in the water, then cast again. The fly floats freely and I hold my breath. This time it will go far enough. It's two feet upstream of the first fish; I'm still holding my breath; the snake in the line unwinds and begins to straighten, slowly, then faster; I lean forward to give it another foot, another few inches; I watch the fish move slightly, turn toward the fly, inspect it, nose up to it, and then the fly drags and the fish turns away.

A deep breath.

Two more casts: one that quarters the river too amply and causes the fly to drag within two feet; another that floats properly but gets there a second after the trout has taken a natural. Then a good cast, a good float, and the fish pivots and takes, feels the hook, jumps twice, and burrows across and upstream. It's thirteen inches and not strong enough to cause much mischief; anyway, after the strike, after I have successfully gulled this creature from another element, linked my brain to its brain, I am less interested. After a few minutes I have the fish near my bank, lean down and twitch the hook free, and it is gone, vigorously—sleek and spotted and still quick.

When I've taken the slime off the fly and air-dried it, I notice that most of the fish have left their stations; only one fish is working in the pool now, across the main current, in a little backwater. It will require a different approach, a different strategy. I take fully five minutes to work my way downstream along the bank, into the water, and across to the other side, moving slowly so as not to disturb the life of the river. I am only its guest. The fish is still working when I get there.

I am directly below the trout now and can see only the periodic circles about forty feet above me. I don't want to put the fly line over it, and

I know its actual feeding position in the water will be at least several feet above the mark of the rise form, which is floating downstream and is the final mark of his deliberate inspection ritual. I elect to cast into the edge of the main current above the fish and hope the fly will catch an eddying current and come down into the trout's position. The cast is good. Squinting, I watch the fly float down, then free of, the fast center current and my fly line hug the nearly dead water. There is an electric moment when the circle forms. My arm shoots up. The fish has taken the fly solidly and feels like a good one. It does not jump but bores into its little pool, then into the current; then it gets below me. I slip, recover, and begin to edge downstream, the fish stripping line from the reel now, boiling at the surface twice, then coming upstream quickly while I raise the rod high and haul in line to keep the fish from slipping the hook.

A little later I release the fish from the net, turning it out—a beautiful seventeen-inch brown.

I take two more fish, smaller ones, in the riffle below the pool, then head upstream again to where the first fish were feeding, approaching the spot from below. The hatch has peaked and is tapering now; the late-afternoon chill of late April has set in and I feel it for the first time. One fish is still feeding but I cannot, in six or seven casts, raise it, and finally it stops.

I breathe deeply and take out a pipe. There may be a spinner fall in another hour but I am exhausted. The river is placid, calm now. No fish are rising. The drama is over; the actors have retired to the wings. I have been caught for two hours in an intensely sensual music, and I want to stop, perhaps for the day—to smoke the pipe now, watch that squirrel in the oak, look for deer tracks and chipmunk holes. The city has become a bad dream, a B movie I once saw that violates my imagination by returning at odd moments. Most of the world would be bored by these past two hours. Most of the world? Most of the world is polluting the rivers, making the worse appear the better cause, peacocking, grating on each other's ears, gouging, putting their fingers on others' souls or their hands in the wrong pockets, scheming, honking, pretending, politicking, small-talking, criticizing.

"Is that *all* you find?" I hear the Scholar ask me.

"Nope. But there's a damned lot of it."

"You're a misanthrope, a hater of cities," he says. "You claim to love gentleness but ..."

I don't especially want to answer his questions now so I look back at the river. We invented the non sequitur for just such moments.

Yes, we have made a day of it. Two, three hours sandwiched in. Little enough. But deep. And durable. And more than a day's worth. We've earned memories—full and textured—that live now in our very marrowbones, that make us more alive. Our thoughts will be greener, our judgments perhaps sharper, our eyes a bit brighter. We live day to day with little change in our perceptions, but I never go to a river that I do not see newly and freshly, that I do not learn, that I do not find a story.

On the way home I still feel the tug of the river against my thighs, and in my mind's eye I can see that largest rising trout, the neat circle when it took a natural, the quick dramatic spurt—electric through my whole body—when it took my fly and I felt its force. And I wondered why I had not raised that last fish.

It was not the ultimate river, the ultimate afternoon; it was not so exquisite as a Keatsian moment frozen and anguished because it would not last. There will be others—never equal, always discretely, sharply different. A thousand such moments. Days when, against all expectation, the river is dead; days when it is generous beyond dreams.

A luxury? A mere vacation?

No, those rivers are more. They are my Pilgrim Creek and Walden Pond, however briefly. Those rivers and their bounty—bright and wild—touch me and through me touch every person whom I meet. They are a metaphor for life. In their movement, in their varied glides, runs, and pools, in their inevitable progress toward the sea, they contain many of the secrets we seek to understand about ourselves, our purposes. The late Roderick Haig-Brown said, "Were it not for the strong, quick life of rivers, for their sparkle in the sunshine, for the cold grayness of them under rain and the feel of them about my legs as I set my feet hard down on rocks or sand or gravel, I should fish less often." Amen. When such rivers die, as so many have, so too dies an irretrievable part of the soul of each of the thousands of anglers who in their waters find deep, enduring life.

CHAPTER THREE

Fishing Tips You Can Count On

by Lamar Underwood

These tips are from the book 1001 Fishing Tips *I did for Skyhorse Press in 2010. Tips like these come and go, but these have stayed with me over many years. They work! Trust me, and you'll see for yourself.*

IT'S A FACT: YOU MIGHT BE FISHING DEAD WATER!

It happened in the 1950s and '60s. Two great events came along that changed bass fishing forever. ("Ruined it!" some disenchanted stalwarts proclaim.) The Carl Lowrance's "fish finder" underwater tracking device was invented and Buck Perry began preaching the gospel of bass following migration routes from shoreline shallows into deeper water away from the banks at varying distances. Bass migrate! Like ducks and geese leaving for the winter. THERE ARE SELDOM ANY BASS ALONG THE BANKS WHERE YOU'VE BEEN FISHING! That was Perry's sermon. ". . . might just as well have been fishing in your bathtub," Buck Perry is reported as saying in Grits Gresham's classic *Complete Book of Bass Fishing* (1966).

BELIEVE IT OR NOT, BASS MIGRATE EVERY DAY!

Buck Perry, the Spoonplug inventor and pioneer bass tactic innovator, believed (and has been proven right) that bass were along the shorelines only during brief periods every day, mostly early and late. Anglers who thought the bass "weren't hitting," were mistaken, Perry believed. They "weren't hitting" because, in Perry's words, they weren't there. The "Fish Finders" and the technology of electronic devices and sophisticated boats and motors, coupled with the new knowledge of fishing "honey holes" out in the vast waters of the lakes and reservoirs, led not only to tournaments and halcyon days for cashing in on exploding tackle demands, but to the notion that would have made our grandfathers faint: "Turn you back on the shore . . . get out in the lake . . . that's where the fish are."

IT'S NOT JUST "LUCK"

It happens all the time: two men in a boat, one keeps catching fish, the other doesn't, even though they're using the same lures or bait. The reason may not be luck, as Grits Gresham explains in his *Complete Book of Bass Fishing* (1966): "It may be the way he casts, how he retrieves, or even the way he has the lure attached to his line."

GET THAT HOOK OUT!

It can happen at any time: You're hooked! Past the barb! You've got to get the thing out, and you don't want to head in for first aid or docs. What to do? Well, this system works like magic. But you've got to have some nerve to pull it off. First press down on the eye of the hook. Next, wrap a piece of string or cloth around the curve of the hook. Finally, while pressing down hard on the eye give the shank a quick jerk. Put some antiseptic on the wound and go back to fishing. Caveat: Don't try this when hooked in vulnerable areas like the face. If you want to see technique done visually before you try it, Google the words "fish hook removal." That will take you to several sites.

FORCEPS, PLEASE!

If you're fishing without forceps or a tool to remove your hook from a fish's mouth, you're just making things hard for yourself.

FLY FISHING RULE ONE!

"Regardless the rig—streamer, nymph, dry—strive to make each cast different. Lengthen the cast, move a step or two, change the angle, change the retrieve, etc. The *only* exceptions are when casting to visible fish—rising, feeding, resting underneath cover, whatever."

—Chuck Robbins, noted author and fly-fishing guide

HOW AN EXPERT PLAYS BIG TROUT

"Let a large trout get his head down and he will dictate the fight, but keep his head up and he cannot run effectively. You will quickly realize how much easier it is to control a fish on the surface, and to bring the battle to a rapid conclusion."

—John Goddard, *A Fly Fisher's Reflections* (2002)

WHERE TO FISH EARLY, PRE-SPAWN BASS

Expect largemouth bass to be moving onto flats and lake edges that catch the sun early and often. (They're as tired of Old Man Winter as you are.) Fish the headwaters where rivers and creeks flow into impounds. These tributaries will warm up before the main, cold lake waters. Bass move into the areas fed by the warming flow of waters. Be there to meet them with swim baits, such as Berkley's soft-plastic Gulp Minnows and Mann's Hard-Nosed Jerkbait. There are many other swim bait choices to check out at Cabelas or Bass Pro. Many experienced and well-known anglers prefer crankbaits for this type fishing. I do not. I've found they're tough to fish with the slow action I want at this time of the year. Fish swim baits very, very slowly.

BEST BET FOR MIXED BAG ACTION

For a mixed-bag springtime catch of crappie, bluegill, perch, walleye, bass—you name it!—fish a ⅛-oz. or ¼-oz. jig, sweetened with a minnow hooked through the lip, and use a sliding bobber at your preferred depth. Experiment to find the depth where you're getting strikes, then pulls, and fun that make you feel like a kid again.

DON'T WASTE TIME ON TOP-WATER

Despite some scattered exceptions, it's a mistake to spend your fishing hours searching for top-water action in early spring. Sure, we all want top-water when we can get it, but on these first cold spring outings, I'll take action and fish, thank you very much.

IT'S WOOLY BUGGERS FOR SPRING TROUT

When there's no hatch to match, and the water is running high, cold, and off-color—and you're on fly-fishing-only water—you can bet your day's fishing on the olive wooly bugger fished slowly as deep as necessary. Choose a bead-head model large enough to get down to the fish. You may prefer the jazzed-up crystal bugger, but make no mistake: Nothing catches spring trout like a well-fished wooly bugger. And I repeat: Olive is the color you want.

CHANGE LOCATIONS AND BAITS OFTEN

"Be persistent, vary your lures, colors, and baits, keep them moving, and do not spend more than 15 minutes in one location unless you are catching fish. Do these things, and you'll increase your chances for success."

—Oklahoma Department of Wildlife Conservation,
Reservoir Fishing Tips

TURNING "NIBBLES" INTO BITES

"When a fish nibbles indecisively or shows only a lackadaisical interest, I start withdrawing my lure with tantalizing twitches to make him think he is about to lose it."

—Havilah Babcock, *Tales of Quails 'N Such* (1951)

HOW TO FISH JIGS FOR SPRING BASS ON POINTS

Bass expert and lure-maker, the late Tom Mann Jr., explains his favorite way to fish points in early spring: "If I'm fishing 15 to 25 feet of water, I use a 6/7-oz. leaded-headed jig. If I'm fishing shallower than this, I use a

5/16-oz. jig. In clear water I like a brown jig with a black twin-tail grub. In stained water, I reverse the colors, going with a black jib and a brown grub."

—Wade L. Bourne, *Structure Basics: A Complete Guide to Bass Hideouts* (1999)

Seeing Trout: Rule One

"Perhaps the most common factor that betrays the trout is its movement. So imprint this upon your mind: *movement equals fish.*"

—John Goddard and Brian Clarke, *Understanding Trout Behavior* (2001)

Weeds: The Trout Stream Signpost

Weeds in trout streams are like signposts that say, "Fish here!" Weeds not only provide cover for the trout, but for the food the trout needs to live.

Foggy Weather Fishing: Forget About It!

I have never, anywhere, anytime, been able to catch fish when dense fog covers the water. My choice is to wait until it clears, or at least starts to clear.

Finding Those "Migrating" Bass

Like it or not, the big reservoir and lake dilemma of bass moving away from the shoreline at various times of the day is very real. Buck Perry was perhaps the "first"—or certainly one of the "first"—anglers to focus on catching these wandering fish, but others soon followed. The late Grits Gresham, destined to become a TV personality as well as top writer, discussed the "migrating" bass in one of the first major books published on bass fishing in the modern era, his *Complete Book of Bass Fishing* (1966). Grits, a good friend, pointed out the discoveries of Buck Perry and went on to add, "Bass spend most of their time in deep water, in schools, and in a very restricted area—their sanctuary. That sanctuary is most often found in the deepest water of a lake or immediately adjacent to it." Grits said such sanctuaries could be found on bars, ridges, or reefs, or even clean spots in the lake bottom, and that bass would be moving along a regular underwater highway toward this spot twice a day. Expect to find the migration route along a ridge, with the sanctuary occurring at a break in the ridge—a fairly level spot somewhere along the ridge, "below 20 feet if the water is that deep."

No Hatch to Match? It's Time for Nymphs

Advice for fishing *western* rivers from a top guide and author: "Lacking a hatch it's tough to beat a pair of nymphs rigged five or six feet or so below a strike indicator. Limited to just two patterns, a #10 Pat's Rubber Legs and a similar-sized red San Juan Worm would be my picks. Though my nymph box contains a good selection of bead-head and standard nymph patterns—Prince Pheasant Tail, Hare's Ear, Micro-May, Bloody Mary, Copper John, etc., in a variety of sizes and variations."

—Chuck Robbins, noted author and fly-fishing guide

Barbless Hooks: How to Know They're Legal

There are so many trout streams today that require barbless hooks, anglers need to be doubly on the alert to make sure the flies they are using in these waters are legal. Even after the barb has been mashed down with pliers, the hook may not pass the test. What tests? Fishermen in many states are confused over this issue and are asking for legal guideposts. One state, Arkansas, spells out its definition in the 2007 *Trout Guidebook* as, "Crimped completely, the hook is smooth and will not snag when passed through cloth." That sounds pretty clear. If it will not pass through cloth without snagging, it's not legal. Until a better uniform definition comes along, that one sounds reasonable.

They're *Not Hitting* Because They're *Not There!*

As pointed out elsewhere in this book, when a stretch of shoreline that has been producing good fishing suddenly goes cold, the usual angling lament is, "They've stopped biting." Other stretches of shoreline are deemed to be poor because they seldom or never produce fish. The key thing to remember about the "good" stretches of shoreline is that when the fish "aren't biting," they probably have moved out along their migration routes to deeper water. Turning your back on the shoreline and exploring outside water, using charts, electronics, and local knowledge (if it is available), should lead to better catches when they're "not biting" along your favorite, dependable shorelines.

THOSE IMPORTANT "SCATTER POINTS"

The areas along bass "migration routes" where the bass break away from their schools and begin fanning out individually along the shoreline are called "scatter points." Think of them as exits off the turnpikes. Grits Gresham points out in his *Complete Book of Bass Fishing* (1966), "Big bass school in tighter groups than do the yearlings, and they are especially reluctant to move past the scatter point. They seldom do so, in fact, in any numbers." That's exactly why you seldom find the real lunkers along the shoreline, and why big catches can be made if the school can be located in deeper water.

FLOAT FISHING'S TOP TIP

In float fishing, whether the boat is moving slowly or whipping right along, you'll have much more success with this simple tip: While fishing out a cast, be eyeing the water ahead where you're going to *make your next cast*. You'll be ready to make a good cast into a likely pocket instead of making a quick, clumsy, indecisive chunk that goes to barren water.

NYMPH FISHING MADE EASY

The greatest discovery in the history of fly fishing—as far as float-fishing guides in the high-country West have discovered—is nymph fishing. Not the classic nymph fishing of most American trout streams, spawned from English experts like Frank Sawyer and co., but using a couple of nymphs tied in tandem below a strike indicator that floats on the surface. Said "strike indicator"—they come in all different shapes and sizes—is nothing more than an elaborate "bobber." Picture this: You started out years and years ago fishing with a bobber. Now, you've got the money and time to book a top guide on one of Montana's top streams, like the Big Horn or Beaverhead, and you're floating along in the raft chunking out a stretch of fly line (yes "chunking" is the right word, not "casting") with a couple of weighted nymphs tied to a "bobber"—aka "strike indicator"—riding the current. OK, you're having fun, catching trout. I have no problem with that. As long as you see the irony.

Watch Your Step, Stop Spooking Trout

I watched a guy wading into the Missouri River, his rod and fly ready. Clearly, he was looking out in the current, where several rainbows were rising in a nice pod. What he didn't realize, or take time to discover, was that there were many more fish holding in the current right by the shore. He waded into them, intent on the distant pod. The fish bolted away, taking the pod fish with them. It pays to not be in such a hurry. Look trout water over very carefully before wading ahead.

Polaroid Glasses: The Absolute Essential

No matter what kind of fishing you do, you shouldn't be out there without wearing glasses. Just too many hooks flying around. The glasses you're wearing should be Polaroids. They cut the glare, and you can see what's happening in the water. You can buy economy models that cost $20 to $50. With some of these, you may feel as if you need two pair, one with the dark lenses for bright days, and one with the lighter lenses for dull days. Personally, I like the more expensive models with copper photochromatic lenses. They adjust to any light all day long. Cost is around $130 to $160 for the really good ones.

Surf Fishing's Scouting Report

Next to seeing fish breaking and knowing exactly where the action is (instead of guessing where it might eventually happen) try to get a look at your stretch of beach at extreme low tides. Study where even the smallest cuts and channels show on the bottom. That's where you're more likely to get strikes when the waves move in, bringing the fish with them on a rising tide.

WADING STAFFS MAKE SENSE

Falling down while wading and fishing isn't funny—on any kind of water, small creeks, or big rivers. You'll get hurt, break some tackle, or at least get wet, possibly very, very wet. Small streams have rocks, slippery and rounded. Large rivers have powerful currents, and sometimes, as a bonus, slippery and rounded rocks. If you're a geezer, you already know darn well you need a wading staff. If you're coming onto geezer age, you're probably thinking about using one. If you're young and strong, you probably think wading staffs are for geezers only. Wading staffs, clipped to your fly vest, whether homemade or purchased, make life so easy. If your legs are in the least unsteady, try using one. You'll never go wade-fishing again without it.

CHAPTER FOUR

Just for Openers

by Tom Hennessey

If you happen to be caught in a dangerous outdoor crisis, facing death in tumul-tuous rivers, blizzards, or even bear attacks, having a Maine man by your side might be your best hope.

I'm fortunate to say I've never faced such trials by nature, but a Maine man whose companionship I've counted on and enjoyed most over many years was Tom Hennessey. As outdoor editor of the Bangor Daily News *and a free-lance writer and artist, Tom earned the respect of thousands who appreciated his skills in reporting what was happening and sharing the know-how needed in the Maine outdoors. For myself, he was a companion whose presence made every hour afield a treasure trove of memories.*

Even though Tom passed away three years ago, he is still very much alive in the hearts of all who knew him, and all who feel the kinship of his writings and paintings. Tom was the embodiment of the spirit of Maine outdoors. Con-sider the agenda: grouse and woodcock, smallmouth bass, landlock and Atlantic salmon, ducks and geese, snowshoe rabbits, whitetail deer, moose, and black bear. Tom knew how to deal with whatever conditions the Maine outdoor life pushed his way. He was a complete outdoorsman, who put much of what he knew and felt down on paper in words and pictures.

This is the first of two Tom Hennessey contributions in this book, both taken from his book Feathers 'n Fins *(Amwell Press, 1989).*

ACCORDING TO THE CALENDAR, MARCH 20 WAS THE FIRST DAY OF spring. Not so. The sports pages claimed spring arrived April 2 with the opening games of the baseball season. Not so. Spring arrived on April 1, the long-awaited and much-anticipated "opening day" of Maine's open-water fishing season.

With the exception of brooks and streams and the races below dam spillways, open water was scarcer than stars at sunup. On April 1, however, it didn't make much difference. If the Lord ever created a prettier opening day he must have kept it for himself. The warmth of the sun steamed fields patchy with snow and silvered the wings of crows coursing a sky of brilliant blue. Already the marooning buds of maples are staining the winter gray of hardwooded hills, and in the low places cedars and spruces are spattered white with pussy willows.

I figure it was the kind of day that moved Mark Twain to philosophize, "When a man goes fishing he may not realize it isn't fish he's after."

It took a while, but the wisdom of the years—or just plain years—finally convinced me that opening-day fishing is, at best, a ritual. A ceremony that affords the opportunity to officially kick the departing drawers of Ol' Man Winter and, at the same time, embrace the promises of springtime.

Many are the memories that are shined up in the minds of fishermen at the mention of opening day. Foremost, of course, are reflections of days now distant when a battered steel telescoping rod was the only "fishin' pole" you owned. That weighty wand was, no doubt, replete with cracked and chipped agate guides, and a grip and reel seat that could be reversed. For sure the tip section had a kink in it.

Clamped to the rod was a nickel-plated Ocean City or South Bend reel whose dented and wobbly discs uttered a tiny stutter when line was stripped off or reeled in. The reel was also equipped with an anti-backlash level wind—which didn't mean a thing—and a click drag that didn't work. The all-purpose line wound onto that which was, I'll bet, purchased at the hardware store for about 35 cents or thereabouts. It came coiled on a card bearing the brand name "Fisherman's Pal," or something equally as fetching.

Unimpressive as it was, that outfit accounted for a lot of fish. With just the tip extended you could thread your way through the crowds of alders that gather along trout brooks. By extending the rod to half its length, and by thumbing the reel so it wouldn't overrun, you could heave a plug or spoon far enough to snag a pickerel or a bass. With that rattly relic at full length you could, surprisingly, put a fly pretty close to where you wanted it. You may have trolled for salmon and togue with that telescope rod. Certainly you plug fished for perch with it, and jigged suckers and alewives when the runs were on.

Usually opening day meant trout fishing on ice-rimmed brooks that beckoned from the still-snowy woods. Worms were dug around old sink spouts and septic tanks. The mother lode, though, was the steaming mound of manure beneath a cow barn. On the eve of opening, the reel received an additional drop of oil. A slice biscuit was stuck together with peanut butter, wrapped in waxed paper, and stuffed into a jacket pocket. Another pocket carried a card of snelled hooks, a tin of split shot sinkers, and a plastic box containing spinners of silver and gold and maybe a red-dotted white one—just in case. A raid on the refrigerator produced a plastic bag of carrots that was quickly emptied. Such containers were just right for carrying six or eight "brookies." Creels looked good on calendars, but even a small one seemed like a laundry basket in thickets that clutched and clawed at you. Last but not least was a sharp jackknife weighting a pants pocket.

Dawn of that long-awaited day found you hiking down the train tracks to try your luck in the brook, broad-shouldered with run-off, that raced beneath the trestle. Crossing open fields and pastures, you mushed through granular snow. Within the chilling shadows of the woods, you walked on crust. Quietly you approached the brook. Cautiously you edged onto its snowy banks. Carefully your eyes followed the flash of the spinner as the swift current swept the baited barb into a dark, foam-flecked pool. It looked trouty. It sounded trouty. It even felt trouty—but not a touch.

Knowing that trout are sluggish in cold water, you fished slowly, probing each pool and rippling run several times. Honeycombed overhangs caved in beneath you and filled your boots with crystals of snow and mud. A fresh young alder tossed your hat into the brook, and a twig so slender you'd think it couldn't support a snowflake speared perfectly a loop of line and refused to let go.

Optimism, however, springs eternal in the heart of a fisherman. Right where the current laughed at the stony stare of an ancient ledge, you felt the tapping tug of the season's first fish. Now it may be that a lot of years later you put the hook into marlin and sailfish out on the Gulf Stream, or tangled with ill-tempered tarpon or bonefish on the scorching flats of the Florida Keys. But tell me, friend, did any of those piscatorial pleasures compare to the first rod-bending strike of a brook trout on a years-ago opening day?

With a flip of your wrist you arced the trout through the alders and onto the snow where, as it shook free of the hook, you tackled that eight-inch speckled treasure before it could flop back into the brook. In your hand the olive-hued orange-finned brookie felt as firm and cold as an icicle.

When you had fished all the way to where the brook curled beneath a log bridge and spilled into an ice-soldered pond, you had managed to snag three trout—the biggest being a nine-incher. There you emptied your boots before trudging the tote road out to the train tracks. It would be well after dark when you arrived home. The hounds would greet you as only hounds can, and your supper would be on a plate in the oven with an upside-down plate covering it. You were cold, wet, and a little tired, but you didn't pay any mind to the remarks about the trout not being big enough to feed the cat.

Naturally, no one knew about the copy-cat conversation that you carried on with an owl in the damp, smudgy dusk, or the wedge of geese you heard gossiping with the wind. And if I remember right, you didn't mention any of it, either.

CHAPTER FIVE

Hemingway's Many-Hearted Fox River

by Nick Lyons

This story originally appeared in the June 1997 issue of National Geographic *magazine. It was accompanied by photographs by Jay Dickman over several pages of graphic splendor showing trout fishing and trout streams of Michigan's Upper Peninsula. Nick included the story in his book* Fishing Stories *(Skyhorse Publishing, 2014).*

Stated quite simply, Nick Lyons's story is one of the best-written fishing stories I've ever presented to readers in my long editing history. It has everything one could hope for: mood, atmosphere, fishing action, and literary insights. Nick's story comes to these pages through his gracious permission, for which I am grateful.

Yes, this is the same Nick Lyons who founded Lyons Press (now owned by Rowman and Littlefield). Nick has spent a lifetime teaching, publishing, editing, and writing. His most recent book is the critically acclaimed memoir Fire in the Straw: Notes on Inventing a Life *(Arcade, 2020).*

While I have no intention of letting this introduction spoil what's ahead in Nick's article, some basic background might help you enjoy the story to its fullest.

Ernest Hemingway's short story "Big Two-Hearted River" (actually a long, long short story but not a full novella) first appeared in his In Our Time *collection of stories in 1925. Since then the story has been reprinted many times and is one of the most discussed fishing stories in American literature. He began writing the story in Paris in 1923, completing what he called "Part 1."*

He put the tale aside for journalism assignments, then returned to it in 1924, completing "Part 2" while still living in Paris.

The big-game fishing photos and tales about Ernest Hemingway wrestling with fish like marlin and tuna, or striking a hero pose on the docks beside the monster fish, are misleading. They are from the years during and after the time when he was writing his second novel, A Farewell to Arms. *While writing* A Farewell to Arms *in Key West after moving there from Paris, Hemingway's innate angling passion morphed from trout to the biggest fish that swim. With the help of Key West locals, he began catching "dock" fish like groupers, then moved on up the food chain to sailfish and marlin. As his income and big-game fishing connections improved he moved into the world of big-game fishing and boats. By the time* The Old Man and the Sea *came along, articles about Hemingway seldom referenced the gentle world of trout fishing. The trout and experiences of his youth were left behind, and he began his "trademark" identification, "Papa Hemingway."*

He had come far from his youth, when he had fished for trout with buddies in Michigan's Upper Peninsula. Back then, he signed his letters "Ernie."

In the Green Hills of Africa, *describing his Paris youth and the rejections he endured, Hemingway wrote: "(all the stories back in the mail through a slot in the sawmill door with notes of rejection that would never call them stories but always anecdotes, sketches, coates, etc. They did not want them.)"*

Reading that, one wonders: Was "Big Two-Hearted River" rejected by Field & Stream, Sports Afield, Outdoor Life? *We'll never know, but in May 1954 editor Hugh Grey at* Field & Stream *published the entire "Big Two-Hearted" story, with superb illustrations by artist Bob Kuhn.*

LATE SEPTEMBER IN MICHIGAN'S UPPER PENINSULA CAN BE A TIME OF gray mists and steady rain. The deciduous trees—maple, aspen, crabapple, birch—have begun to turn; but in a wet year, their colors are less brilliant, more muted: umber, ochre, russet, mustard yellow rather than gold, gaudy orange, and vermillion. At gas stations you see fifty-pound bags of carrots, dried corn, and rutabagas, piled five or six high, used for baiting black bear and whitetail deer. The blackflies of June and July are gone; the few mosquitoes near the river are enough to verify that reports of their size and ferociousness were not far-fetched. After a year of heavy rains, the trees were only beginning to turn when I came; it rained all week; the rivers were still high, some as much as several feet.

The Fox River near the town of Seney is several feet fuller than it should be in September and the fishing has been slow. Anyway, the bear and grouse seasons have opened. In more than a week of driving every day from Seney to the blackstump fields of the Kingston Plains, to Stanley Lake at the head of the Little Fox River, the sky has rarely changed from its somber Payne's gray, but I have watched the maples and birch along the Fox Road turn slowly, the sweet fern grow from faded green to tawny red. I have seen Canada geese silhouetted against the ashen sky, two bald eagles, a couple of ruffed grouse, and a dozen whitetail deer— always at dusk, one fording the river. No fly fishermen. Only a handful of men who use spinning rod and bait, all concentrated at the eight campsites and state access points on the main river. Two Fox regulars, Howard and Dean, brothers who live downstate, have been taking brook trout on worms; they come up every year, camp in the grove of sleek recreation vehicles at the Seney Municipal Campground just north of town, and love to catch native brookies. It is a happy ritual for them and they tell me that they can take their limits anytime they choose; they are forthright, workingmen, not the kind to brag.

Over the years I have heard of a dozen young writers who made the pilgrimage to fish the river Ernest Hemingway fished, and used for his remarkable story "Big Two-Hearted River"—taking the resonant name of a nearby river to suggest life and death, perhaps, and also, I think, a generosity of spirit. A few pilgrims, including Hemingway's eldest son, Jack, fished the main stem of the Two-Hearted River, thirty miles northeast of Seney, in error; those who have come out of curiosity or homage to the Fox, as I first did in the late 1950s, have been less impressed by the trout than by the blackflies and mosquitoes. From June through August the blackflies and mosquitoes are prodigious, legendary.

In a week of hard fishing I caught more nostalgia than trout. One look at the tangled river above Seney, choked with tag alder trees, and I glumly put my fly rod back into its aluminum case and set up a spinning outfit. I tied on a favorite lure from my teens, the silver C. P. Swing, size #3. With it, I cast into the deeper pools at the few pullouts, where the state has built fences and paths to stabilize the soft sand banks; in the flat below the old railroad bridge; as close always, to the many deadfalls as I dared. I lost a scant seventeen lures and caught a handful with brookies—all with parr marks, bright as jewels and not much larger. Then I found a place where a grassy bank left room for casting a fly and began to fish with my long rod and Jay-Dave Hopper tied by Jay. I'd cast up and across, against the omnipresent tag alder branches on the opposite bank. I'd try to find slight indentations into which I could pitch my fly, allowing me to float the hopper into the trouty shade, out of sight, and keep it free-floating until it dragged in the slick glides. I liked having the fly rod in my hand again, and I cast well and finished the water well but took only one eight-inch brookie.

As the week wore on I learned more about this difficult, even inhospitable river, of a kind I had not fished in many years. And I tried—in the steady, cold rain—to scrape the patina of time away to find the underpainting, a river and a young man more than three-quarters of a century ago.

Seney, the town through which the Fox flows, and the place-name that positively identifies the river Nick Adams fished, has 185 residents these days. There are a couple of gas stations, motels, a bar, two family restaurants that serve pasties and good plain food with lots of gravy, stores only sparsely stocked in September. A Mennonite family runs the Golden Grill and the grocery attached to it and sells, with the necessities, inspirational books, cards, and key holders. Welding, truss business, woods work, and tourism are how most people earn their living here. Seney is now mainly a brief stop on the arrow-straight M-28 that bisects the Upper Peninsula. It is hard to imagine that a hundred years ago it was a notoriously rough and lawless town, officially founded in 1881, growing like "an ugly and poisonous toadstool," the fulcrum for fifteen lumber camps that cut the great white pine forests and floated logs to Seney or, downriver, Thompson and Manistique. Much of the lumber used to rebuild Chicago after the Great Fire of 1871 came from the Seney area.

The town had twenty-odd saloons, two huge brothels and smaller ones at the outskirts, and it catered to tough lumbermen with names like Snag Jaw, Pig Foot, Pump Handle Joe, Wiry Jim, and Silver Jack. It was a raw, violent place, where an ear sometimes got chewed off in a fight, with 3,000 permanent residents and double that number in the spring.

While the lumber companies were decimating the great white pine forests, the town burned in 1891 and then again in 1895. Little remains except the contents of a one-room museum assiduously assembled since the early 1970s by C. R. St. Martin, the town supervisor, and his wife, Myrtle, and pilings in the river from dams built to store water that was later used to run logs downriver. Only in the little graveyard just south of town is there one of the last hints of the town that was. It is a simple inscription on a white wooden gravemarker:

CHAS DEWEY
Killed Age 33 Fighten

Seney and its history of violence and eventual demise are important to Hemingway's story; he starts there, and the burned-over country reflects Nick's nearly bankrupt emotions. But the river is the heart of the story, and I went directly to the iron railroad bridge, even as Nick Adams did, as soon as I reached the town. I knew the river would not be the same long before I stood where Nick stood more than seventy-five years earlier and looked down at the "clear, brown water." You don't even wade in the same river twice on the same day. The river was smooth and quick, still tea-colored from the tannic acid it picks up in the bogs, from the decomposition of pine and cedar needles, and it brushes up against the same black bridge pilings. I stood for a long time but could see no trout holding on the sand-ridged bottom. Surely the water—even in this month of high water—was not deep enough to hold the head of trout Nick describes, no doubt because sand and silt had filled it in, a process begun in the 1890s, when timbering sent the soft sand banks crumbling into the river. And the process had been accelerated by poor management in the 1950s, a period when motorboats were permitted on the river. I doubt if the boulders and pebbles Nick saw were ever in this sand-bottomed river; he plucked them, as he did whatever else he needed, from other rivers he had fished. Looking down from the bridge, I was looking at several rivers—the one Hemingway fished, the one fished by Nick in the story, and the one below me; only aesthetically was it of less importance where Hemingway had been than the discrete world he created in his story.

In a few moments I took one of the five grasshoppers I had caught by hand in the high grasses between the road and the bridge and dropped it into the river below the bridge. The hopper kicked and twisted on the flat surface, floated without movement, kicked a bit more, and then drifted the length of the pool, undisturbed. The others followed it and went downstream, equally undisturbed; another dozen went into the Fox at various points upstream, and not one was taken. For those first few hours, I thought I was fishing a halfhearted little river.

In September 1919, Hemingway fished the Fox with two friends, Jock Pentecost and Al Walker, for a week. Though there are a dozen theories about where they camped, their base was probably no more than a mile or so upriver and from there they ranged above the confluence with the Little Fox, eight miles northwest. In a letter Hemingway wrote on September 15 describing the trip, he says that the three of them caught some two hundred trout, mostly on live grasshoppers, wantonly shot at deer with a .22, and that he lost a fish big enough to break his hook at the shank. And then, late in 1923 in Paris, he started a story called first "Black River," then "Big Two-Hearted River."

"We got off the train at Seney," that first draft began, and then he changed the "We" to "They." Jock and Al are in the fragment, by name. They lift "the bundle of tents and bedding out of the cinders" where the baggageman had thrown them, and look around. Hemingway describes the burned remnants of the town, the hotel "almost level with the ground," its limestone "chipped and split by the fire," the ironwork melted. It is good reporting, but he cannot find the imaginative energy to leave Seney and, after several pages, stops this version. Then in a 100-page handwritten draft of the story he wrote on and off in 1924, finishing it in high summer, he came to the river at once and, despite some long false sections that he eventually cut, never left it. For the river is the great heart of the story. But is it the Fox? "I made it all up," he told Gertrude Stein in August when he showed her the draft, "so I see it all."

In brief, the story is a vivid, detailed drama in which the young man, quite alone, gets off the train at a burned-out town called Seney, takes a day-long walk upriver, camps, and the next day, with ritual care, fishes with live grasshoppers. He catches a small trout that he releases, two decent fish that he kills, and loses a big one—the "thrill of the loss" too much for him. Then he decides that to fish in the swamp would be a "tragic adventure" and heads back to camp. Nothing—and everything—has happened.

By his deliberate movements, we realize that the young man has come to the woods—as many fishermen do—for some form of rejuvenation; we realize he is carrying some unidentified mental baggage, dislocation, and that by slowly setting up his camp, preparing his own beans and spaghetti, and the next day rigging his fly rod and fishing, he is regaining some measure of control over himself, imputing order to his life. He brings certain skills: how to read a river, the techniques of fishing. He loves to fish. The story starts late, after traumatic events have happened to Seney and Nick, and ends abruptly when he decides he will not fish the swamp, where he has less control. "There were plenty of days coming when he could fish the swamp." He knows his limits.

It is a remarkable story—fresh, understated, crisp, elliptical, earthy, full of innocence and love of country, and oddly as suspenseful as a good detective story. Much later, in *A Moveable Feast*, Hemingway said, "The story was about coming back from the war but there was no mention of the war in it."

Though Hemingway changed the Fox River, along with the country around it, to fit the precise needs of the story, a river called the Fox very much remains, and it has the raw and mysterious spirit of the river Nick Adams fished. The whole Upper Peninsula still contains pockets of wilderness, vast stretches of raw and barely compromised country.

The Fox today is still the color of tea, from the swamps it drains. There are still old logjams, with velvet moss and grasses growing from them, plastered with maple leaves. There are Jack pine deadfalls everywhere, their spiked branches like a Maginot Line to protect the river from canoers, float-tubers, even fishermen. Often, the bottom and midwater of pools are booby-trapped with tangled branches and snags—or are too soft with silt to dare wade. The quick river plays against the tangle of trees and creates riffles and eddies, and so do the pilings from old dams, bridges, and conservation deflectors the river has mostly reclaimed. In the distance you can see stands of yellowing birch and aspen, the brighter red of a few maples; and you can always see random clusters of conifers defoliated by insects or fire—skeletal, ghostly, still straight. The land is mostly sand-loam plains, with pockets of muck or bog or hardpan, covered with pine and tamarack needles and sweet fern, dotted with an occasional late black-eyed Susan, high grasses, sweet gale. There is not one as in the story, but a hundred of them, each dangerous, each—for Hemingway's purposes—a "moveable" swamp, each as threatening to a sixty-four-year-old writer as to a twenty-one-year-old boy back from the war. And everywhere there are tag alders, the low-growing, weedlike trees that proliferate after the cuttings and burnings brought sun to the moist plains near the river; often they extend three or four feet into the river, making wading and casting impossible. The river runs under the branches and then, as it bends, the river appears to vanish into a maze of browning alder leaves and angled pines. It is a difficult, overhung, and very trouty river.

Eventually I fished hardest well below the town, where the river is wilder, shallower, as it flows through cattail bogs and tamarack swamps, dotted with maples and elm. There I found several worn spots in the marsh and thicket where bait fishermen have set up shop. There was barely room to lean out for a quick underhand cast, a single thrust directly across and slightly upstream. It was an old skill for me, and I could soon send the lure to the opposite bank with some ease, flutter it back a foot, reel backward a turn or two so it dropped lower in the water, flutter it again. I had switched, on local advice, to a Panther Martin; on the same local advice I soon affixed a small worm I found by lifting a log. On my seventh cast a fish flashed at it in the deep water downstream and against the near bank. I could see little more than that the fish was large. I cast again, to the same spot across the river, and negotiated the lure so it went back into the same eddy. There was no response this time, so I lifted the lure with a swift movement for another cast. And then, a foot below the surface, coming quickly, I saw a head emerge from the undercut bank, and one of the largest wild brookies I have ever seen, nineteen or twenty inches' worth, lunged at the lure and nicked the worm. I saw the whole of it—its solid girth, dark flanks, huge head. And then it was gone and, on repeated casts, would not come to the lure again.

I sat on the wet bank, shaking a little, smiling, and listened to the susurrant hum of water against the deadfalls, of the riffles as the smooth river bent and went out of sight. There are tales told at the Seney party store of secret pools and trout measured by hands spread half a yard apart. Local young men, rugged and evasive, walk far back into the tag alder swamps, camp for several nights, and come out with their limit of wild brook trout, twelve to twenty inches—plump wild brookies, their flanks a smooth dark silver gray. With mottled back and bright red markings. Clearly the river can provide excellent fishing, but only to those who have private routes in—below Seney, upriver from the town, through the swamps that protect the "spreads" on the East Branch and below Seney, up the East Branch, which may hold the better fish. The fishermen take faintly marked trails or make their own, often through high grasses, marshland, and bog. They are rightly covetous of their hard-won knowledge, and they rightly resent those who blaze trails, cut the tag alders and fallen hardwoods that make penetration by foot or canoe difficult. It is not a river to be fished quickly.

Howard and Dean tell me that they caught bigger trout in the 1940s when they first came up, that the fish were smaller and fewer in the 1950s, and that it is better now than it's been in twenty years. They use flies downstate, only live bait here. They come for the wild brookies. And there is one man in his late eighties who fished the Fox before Hemingway came; his father tied him to that same railroad bridge in 1913 and he caught his first fish, eight brook trout, on a cane pole in no time at all. He used to get nine or ten fish out of one hole, he reports; now he's lucky to get one. He still fishes when he can, but he thinks the river has been raped too often.

But the fish are there, thanks to friends like Dick St. Martin, who pressed the state to make the Fox a Scenic Wild River recently, and thanks to sensible, well-educated men like Steve Scott, a biologist and the district fisheries program manager. He has seen photographs of tables loaded with the sixteen- to twenty-inch brook trout, from the turn of the century, and he knows that a few of the better fishermen today can still take a limit of twelve- to twenty-inch brook trout. He broods about the river, about whether the limit of ten fish is too great (he and I think it is, even for an area where local folk still insist on living off the land), whether boats ought to be allowed on the river, how to prevent (with sediment traps) more sand from collecting on the bottom, how many fish to stock; though there is an excellent natural reproduction, the state does supplemental stocking of Assinica brook trout in the main river—12,000 in 1996. It all costs money—and there are limits to that. Scott is pleased that, since 1989, the Fox has been part of the Michigan Natural Rivers Program. He is pleased that there is enough gravel for natural reproduction; enough sculpin, minnows, crayfish, caddis, mayflies, and stoneflies for food; that there is no winterkill. The river has a lot going for it—the groundwater that feeds it, which keeps the temperature under sixty-eight degrees Fahrenheit; the deadfalls that provide cover; even the tag alders that provide shade and make access so difficult. He is pleased that the Fox, in both of its branches, but especially the East Branch, is a river capable of yielding quality fishing for wild brookies, decent numbers of big fish like the three-pounder he recently shocked. He worries about use and overuse, crowds and publicity, and the mandate to provide quality fishing against the conflicting demands made on it. He says, puckishly, that "the best fishing is in May and June—when the mosquitoes and blackflies are worst."

Each day there was a bit more gold and crimson in the birch and maples along the Fox River Road. On my last day, looking out across the burnt-over Kingston Plains, littered with black stumps a hundred years old, preserved when fire-struck pitch preserved them, I thought about the old second-growth pine, the grasshoppers. It was not hard, beneath the patina of the years, to imagine Hemingway up here with Jock and Al, finding the Little Fox "lousy with them," camping out, ranging over country just as wild now as it was then—and Hemingway being brawny young Hemingway with youth to burn, which he did, and Nick Adams being skittish of swamps. Nor was it hard to imagine the young man in Paris who had not yet (in his words) begun to trade on his talent, writing about what he knew and loved best, trout fishing in wild country.

In front of me, next to a stand of blueberries, there is a black stump, stark against the failing vermillion sun in the west. It looks solid as oak. I touch it gently. The crust is firm, the century-old cinders soft beneath my fingers. I touch it again and the stump, like an old memory or stale cake, crumbles in my hand to black dust. But inside is a core of fresh pine, preserved all these years by the pitch.

Chapter Six

Big Two-Hearted River

by Ernest Hemingway

In the preceding chapter, Nick Lyons told us all about Ernest Hemingway's long short story "Big Two-Hearted River." Here's the complete story, told in two parts, just as it was first published in 1925. Hemingway at some point experimented with the ending, with the story's "Nick" having thoughts about art and literature. He abandoned the revisions and stuck with the original story you see here. You can check out his temporary revisions in the book The Nick Adams Stories *(Scribners, 1972). One of the important things to remember about the Hemingway story is the work and sweat Nick had to put into carrying his food and gear. This was long, long before the lightweight choices of today's camping equipment and meals.*

PART I

The train went on up the track out of sight, around one of the hills of burnt timber. Nick sat down on the bundle of canvas and bedding the baggage man had pitched out of the door of the baggage car. There was no town, nothing but the rails and the burned-over country. The thirteen saloons that had lined the one street of Seney had not left a trace. The foundations of the Mansion House hotel stuck up above the ground. The stone was chipped and split by the fire. It was all that was left of the town of Seney. Even the surface had been burned off the ground.

Nick looked at the burned-over stretch of hillside, where he had expected to find the scattered houses of the town and then walked down the railroad track to the bridge over the river. The river was there. It swirled against the log spiles of the bridge. Nick looked down into the clear, brown water, colored from the pebbly bottom, and watched the trout keeping themselves steady in the current with wavering fins. As he watched them they changed their positions by quick angles, only to hold steady in the fast water again. Nick watched them a long time.

He watched them holding themselves with their noses into the current, many trout in deep fast moving water, slightly distorted as he watched far down through the glassy convex surface of the pool, its surface pushing and swelling smooth against the resistance of the log-driven piles of the bridge. At the bottom of the pool were the big trout. Nick did not see them at first. Then he saw them at the bottom of the pool, big trout looking to hold themselves on the gravel bottom in a varying mist of gravel and sand, raised in spurts by the current.

Nick looked down into the pool from the bridge. It was a hot day. A kingfisher flew up the stream. It was a long time since Nick had looked into a stream and seen trout. They were very satisfactory. As the shadow of the kingfisher moved up the stream, a big trout shot upstream in a long angle, only his shadow marking the angle, then lost his shadow as he came through the surface of the water, caught the sun, and then, as he went back into the stream under the surface, his shadow seemed to float down the stream with the current, unresisting, to his post under the bridge where he tightened facing up into the current.

Nick's heart tightened as the trout moved. He felt all the old feeling.

He turned and looked down the stream. It stretched away, pebbly-bottomed with shallows and big boulders and a deep pool as it curved away around the foot of a bluff.

Nick walked back up the ties to where his pack lay in the cinders beside the railway track. He was happy. He adjusted the pack harness around the bundle, pulling straps tight, slung the pack on his back, got his arms through the shoulder straps and took some of the pull off his shoulders by leaning his forehead against the wide band of the tump-line. Still, it was too heavy. It was much too heavy. He had his leather rod-case in his hand and leaning forward to keep the weight of the pack high on his shoulders he walked along the road that paralleled the railway track, leaving the burned town behind in the heat, and then turned off around a hill with a high, fire-scarred hill on either side onto a road that went back into the country. He walked along the road feeling the ache from the pull of the heavy pack. The road climbed steadily. It was hard work walking up-hill. His muscles ached and the day was hot, but Nick felt happy. He felt he had left everything behind, the need for thinking, the need to write, other needs. It was all back of him.

From the time he had gotten down off the train and the baggage man had thrown his pack out of the open car door things had been different. Seney was burned, the country was burned over and changed, but it did not matter. It could not all be burned. He knew that. He hiked along the road, sweating in the sun, climbing to cross the range of hills that separated the railway from the pine plains.

The road ran on, dipping occasionally, but always climbing. Nick went on up. Finally the road after going parallel to the burnt hillside reached the top. Nick leaned back against a stump and slipped out of the pack harness. Ahead of him, as far as he could see, was the pine plain. The burned country stopped off at the left with the range of hills. On ahead islands of dark pine trees rose out of the plain. Far off to the left was the line of the river. Nick followed it with his eye and caught glints of the water in the sun.

There was nothing but the pine plain ahead of him, until the far blue hills that marked the Lake Superior height of land. He could hardly see them, faint and far away in the heat-light over the plain. If he looked too steadily they were gone. But if he only half-looked they were there, the far off hills of the height of land.

Nick sat down against the charred stump and smoked a cigarette. His pack balanced on the top of the stump, harness holding ready, a hollow molded in it from his back. Nick sat smoking, looking out over the country. He did not need to get his map out. He knew where he was from the position of the river.

As he smoked, his legs stretched out in front of him, he noticed a grasshopper walk along the ground and up onto his woolen sock. The grasshopper was black. As he had walked along the road, climbing, he had started many grasshoppers from the dust. They were all black. They were not the big grasshoppers with yellow and black or red and black wings whirring out from their black wing sheathing as they fly up. These were just ordinary hoppers, but all a sooty black in color. Nick had wondered about them as he walked, without really thinking about them. Now, as he watched the black hopper that was nibbling at the wool of his sock with its fourway lip, he realized that they had all turned black from living in the burned-over land. He realized that the fire must have come the year before, but the grasshoppers were all black now. He wondered how long they would stay that way.

Carefully he reached his hand down and took hold of the hopper by the wings. He turned him up, all his legs walking in the air, and looked at his jointed belly. Yes, it was black too, iridescent where the back and head were dusty.

"Go on, hopper," Nick said, speaking out loud for the first time, "Fly away somewhere."

He tossed the grasshopper up into the air and watched him sail away to a charcoal stump across the road.

Nick stood up. He leaned his back against the weight of his pack where it rested upright on the stump and got his arms through the shoulder straps. He stood with the pack on his back on the brow of the hill looking out across the country, toward the distant river and then struck down the hillside away from the road. Underfoot the ground was good walking. Two hundred yards down the hillside the fire line stopped. Then it was sweet fern, growing ankle high, to walk through, and clumps of jack pines; a long undulating country with frequent rises and descents, sandy underfoot and the country alive again.

Nick kept his direction by the sun. He knew where he wanted to strike the river and he kept on through the pine plain, mounting small rises to see other rises ahead of him and sometimes from the top of a rise a great solid island of pines off to his right or his left. He broke off some sprigs of the heathery sweet fern, and put them under his pack straps. The chafing crushed it and he smelled it as he walked.

He was tired and very hot, walking across the uneven, shadeless pine plain. At any time he knew he could strike the river by turning off to his left. It could not be more than a mile away. But he kept on toward the north to hit the river as far upstream as he could go in one day's walking.

For some time as he walked Nick had been in sight of one of the big islands of pine standing out above the rolling high ground he was crossing. He dipped down and then as he came slowly up to the crest of the ridge he turned and made toward the pine trees.

There was no underbrush in the island of pine trees. The trunks of the trees went straight up or slanted toward each other. The trunks were straight and brown without branches. The branches were high above. Some interlocked to make a solid shadow on the brown forest floor. Around the grove of trees was a bare space. It was brown and soft underfoot as Nick walked on it. This was the over-lapping of the pine needle floor, extending out beyond the width of the high branches. The trees had grown tall and the branches moved high, leaving in the sun this bare space they had once covered with shadow. Sharp at the edge of this extension of the forest floor commenced the sweet fern.

Nick slipped off his pack and lay down in the shade. He lay on his back and looked up into the pine trees. His neck and back and the small of his back rested as he stretched. The earth felt good against his back. He looked up at the sky, through the branches, and then shut his eyes. He opened them and looked up again. There was a wind high up in the branches. He shut his eyes again and went to sleep.

Nick woke stiff and cramped. The sun was nearly down. His pack was heavy and the straps painful as he lifted it on. He leaned over with the pack on and picked up the leather rod-case and started out from the pine trees across the sweet fern swale, toward the river. He knew it could not be more than a mile.

He came down a hillside covered with stumps into a meadow. At the edge of the meadow flowed the river. Nick was glad to get to the river. He walked upstream through the meadow. His trousers were soaked with the dew as he walked. After the hot day, the dew had come quickly and heavily. The river made no sound. It was too fast and smooth. At the edge of the meadow, before he mounted to a piece of high ground to make camp, Nick looked down the river at the trout rising. They were rising to insects come from the swamp on the other side of the stream when the sun went down. The trout jumped out of water to take them. While Nick walked through the little stretch of meadow alongside the stream, trout had jumped high out of water. Now as he looked down the river, the insects must be settling on the surface, for the trout were feeding steadily all down the stream. As far down the long stretch as he could see, the trout were rising, making circles all down the surface of the water, as though it were starting to rain.

The ground rose, wooded and sandy, to overlook the meadow, the stretch of river and the swamp. Nick dropped his pack and rod-case and looked for a level piece of ground. He was very hungry and he wanted to make his camp before he cooked. Between two jack pines, the ground was quite level. He took the ax out of the pack and chopped out two projecting roots. That leveled a piece of ground large enough to sleep on. He smoothed out the sandy soil with his hand and pulled all the sweet fern bushes by their roots. His hands smelled good from the sweet fern. He smoothed the uprooted earth. He did not want anything making lumps under the blankets. When he had the ground smooth, he spread his three blankets. One he folded double, next to the ground. The other two he spread on top.

With the ax he slit off a bright slab of pine from one of the stumps and split it into pegs for the tent. He wanted them long and solid to hold in the ground. With the tent unpacked and spread on the ground, the pack, leaning against a jackpine, looked much smaller. Nick tied the rope that served the tent for a ridge-pole to the trunk of one of the pine trees and pulled the tent up off the ground with the other end of the rope and tied it to the other pine. The tent hung on the rope like a canvas blanket on a clothes line. Nick poked a pole he had cut up under the back peak of the canvas and then made it a tent by pegging out the sides. He pegged the sides out taut and drove the pegs deep, hitting them down into the ground with the flat of the ax until the rope loops were buried and the canvas was drum tight.

Across the open mouth of the tent Nick fixed cheese cloth to keep out mosquitoes. He crawled inside under the mosquito bar with various things from the pack to put at the head of the bed under the slant of the canvas. Inside the tent the light came through the brown canvas. It smelled pleasantly of canvas. Already there was something mysterious and homelike. Nick was happy as he crawled inside the tent. He had not been unhappy all day. This was different though. Now things were done. There had been this to do. Now it was done. It had been a hard trip. He was very tired. That was done. He had made his camp. He was settled. Nothing could touch him. It was a good place to camp. He was there, in the good place. He was in his home where he had made it. Now he was hungry.

He came out, crawling under the cheese cloth. It was quite dark outside. It was lighter in the tent.

Nick went over to the pack and found, with his fingers, a long nail in a paper sack of nails, in the bottom of the pack. He drove it into the pine tree, holding it close and hitting it gently with the flat of the ax. He hung the pack up on the nail. All his supplies were in the pack. They were off the ground and sheltered now.

Nick was hungry. He did not believe he had ever been hungrier. He opened and emptied a can of pork and beans and a can of spaghetti into the frying pan.

"I've got a right to eat this kind of stuff, if I'm willing to carry it," Nick said. His voice sounded strange in the darkening woods. He did not speak again.

He started a fire with some chunks of pine he got with the ax from a stump. Over the fire he stuck a wire grill, pushing the four legs down into the ground with his boot. Nick put the frying pan on the grill over the flames. He was hungrier. The beans and spaghetti warmed. Nick stirred them and mixed them together. They began to bubble, making little bubbles that rose with difficulty to the surface. There was a good smell. Nick got out a bottle of tomato catchup and cut four slices of bread. The little bubbles were coming faster now. Nick sat down beside the fire and lifted the frying pan off. He poured about half the contents out into the tin plate. It spread slowly on the plate. Nick knew it was too hot. He poured on some tomato catchup. He knew the beans and spaghetti were still too hot. He looked at the fire, then at the tent, he was not going to spoil it all by burning his tongue. For years he had never enjoyed fried bananas because he had never been able to wait for them to cool. His tongue was very sensitive. He was very hungry. Across the river in the swamp, in the almost dark, he saw a mist rising. He looked at the tent once more. All right. He took a full spoonful from the plate.

"Chrise," Nick said, "Geezus Chrise," he said happily.

He ate the whole plateful before he remembered the bread. Nick finished the second plateful with the bread, mopping the plate shiny. He had not eaten since a cup of coffee and a ham sandwich in the station restaurant at St. Ignace. It had been a very fine experience. He had been that hungry before, but had not been able to satisfy it. He could have made camp hours before if he had wanted to. There were plenty of good places to camp on the river. But this was good.

Nick tucked two big chips of pine under the grill. The fire flared up. He had forgotten to get water for the coffee. Out of the pack he got a folding canvas bucket and walked down the hill, across the edge of the meadow, to the stream. The other bank was in the white mist. The grass was wet and cold as he knelt on the bank and dipped the canvas bucket into the stream. It bellied and pulled hard in the current. The water was ice cold. Nick rinsed the bucket and carried it full up to the camp. Up away from the stream it was not so cold.

Nick drove another big nail and hung up the bucket full of water. He dipped the coffee pot half full, put some more chips under the grill onto the fire and put the pot on. He could not remember which way he made coffee. He could remember an argument about it with Hopkins, but not which side he had taken. He decided to bring it to a boil. He remembered now that was Hopkins's way. He had once argued about everything with Hopkins. While he waited for the coffee to boil, he opened a small can of apricots. He liked to open cans. He emptied the can of apricots out into a tin cup. While he watched the coffee on the fire, he drank the juice syrup of the apricots, carefully at first to keep from spilling, then meditatively, sucking the apricots down. They were better than fresh apricots.

The coffee boiled as he watched. The lid came up and coffee and grounds ran down the side of the pot. Nick took it off the grill. It was a triumph for Hopkins. He put sugar in the empty apricot cup and poured some of the coffee out to cool. It was too hot to pour and he used his hat to hold the handle of the coffee pot. He would not let it steep in the pot at all. Not the first cup. It should be straight Hopkins all the way. Hop deserved that. He was a very serious coffee maker. He was the most serious man Nick had ever known. Not heavy, serious. That was a long time ago. Hopkins spoke without moving his lips. He had played polo. He made millions of dollars in Texas. He had borrowed carfare to go to Chicago, when the wire came that his first big well had come in. He could have wired for money. That would have been too slow. They called Hop's girl the Blonde Venus. Hop did not mind because she was not his real girl. Hopkins said very confidently that none of them would make fun of his real girl. He was right. Hopkins went away when the telegram came. That was on the Black River. It took eight days for the telegram to reach him. Hopkins gave away his .22 caliber Colt automatic pistol to Nick. He gave his camera to Bill. It was to remember him always by. They were all going fishing again next summer. The Hop Head was rich. He would get a yacht and they would all cruise along the north shore of Lake Superior. He was excited but serious. They said good-bye and all felt bad. It broke up the trip. They never saw Hopkins again. That was a long time ago on the Black River.

Nick drank the coffee, the coffee, according to Hopkins. The coffee was bitter. Nick laughed. It made a good ending to the story. His mind was starting to work. He knew he could choke it because he was tired enough. He spilled the coffee out of the pot and shook the grounds loose into the fire. He lit a cigarette and went inside the tent. He took off his shoes and trousers, sitting on the blankets, rolled the shoes up inside the trousers for a pillow and got in between the blankets.

Out through the front of the tent he watched the glow of the fire, when the night wind blew on it. It was a quiet night. The swamp was perfectly quiet. Nick stretched under the blanket comfortably. A mosquito hummed close to his ear. Nick sat up and lit a match. The mosquito was on the canvas, over his head. Nick moved the match quickly up to it. The mosquito made a satisfactory hiss in the flame. The match went out. Nick lay down again under the blankets. He turned on his side and shut his eyes. He was sleepy. He felt sleep coming. He curled up under the blanket and went to sleep.

PART II

In the morning the sun was up and the tent was starting to get hot. Nick crawled out under the mosquito netting stretched across the mouth of the tent, to look at the morning. The grass was wet on his hands as he came out. He held his trousers and his shoes in his hands. The sun was just up over the hill. There was the meadow, the river and the swamp. There were birch trees in the green of the swamp on the other side of the river.

The river was clear and smoothly fast in the early morning. Down about two hundred yards were three logs all the way across the stream. They made the water smooth and deep above them. As Nick watched, a mink crossed the river on the logs and went into the swamp. Nick was excited. He was excited by the early morning and the river. He was really too hurried to eat breakfast, but he knew he must. He built a little fire and put on the coffee pot. While the water was heating in the pot he took an empty bottle and went down over the edge of the high ground to the meadow. The meadow was wet with dew and Nick wanted to catch grasshoppers for bait before the sun dried the grass. He found plenty of good grasshoppers. They were at the base of the grass stems. Sometimes they clung to a grass stem. They were cold and wet with the dew, and could not jump until the sun warmed them. Nick picked them up, taking only the medium sized brown ones, and put them into the bottle. He turned over a log and just under the shelter of the edge were several hundred hoppers. It was a grasshopper lodging house. Nick put about fifty of the medium browns into the bottle. While he was picking up the hoppers the others warmed in the sun and commenced to hop away. They flew when they hopped. At first they made one flight and stayed stiff when they landed, as though they were dead.

Nick knew that by the time he was through with breakfast they would be as lively as ever. Without dew in the grass it would take him all day to catch a bottle full of good grasshoppers and he would have to crush many of them, slamming at them with his hat. He washed his hands at the stream. He was excited to be near it. Then he walked up to the tent. The hoppers were already jumping stiffly in the grass. In the bottle, warmed by the sun, they were jumping in a mass. Nick put in a pine stick as a cork. It plugged the mouth of the bottle enough, so the hoppers could not get out and left plenty of air passage.

He had rolled the log back and knew he could get grasshoppers there every morning.

Nick laid the bottle full of jumping grasshoppers against a pine trunk. Rapidly he mixed some buckwheat flour with water and stirred it smooth, one cup of flour, one cup of water. He put a handful of coffee in the pot and dipped a lump of grease out of a can and slid it sputtering across the hot skillet. On the smoking skillet he poured smoothly the buckwheat batter. It spread like lava, the grease spitting sharply. Around the edges the buckwheat cake began to firm, then brown, then crisp. The surface was bubbling slowly to porousness. Nick pushed under the browned under surface with a fresh pine chip. He shook the skillet sideways and the cake was loose on the surface. I won't try and flop it, he thought. He slid the chip of clean wood all the way under the cake, and flopped it over onto its face. It sputtered in the pan.

When it was cooked Nick regreased the skillet. He used all the batter. It made another big flapjack and one smaller one.

Nick ate a big flapjack and a smaller one, covered with apple butter. He put apple butter on the third cake, folded it over twice, wrapped it in oiled paper and put it in his shirt pocket. He put the apple butter jar back in the pack and cut bread for two sandwiches.

In the pack he found a big onion. He sliced it in two and peeled the silky outer skin. Then he cut one half into slices and made onion sandwiches. He wrapped them in oiled paper and buttoned them in the other pocket of his khaki shirt. He turned the skillet upside down on the grill, drank the coffee, sweetened and yellow brown with the condensed milk in it, and tidied up the camp. It was a nice little camp.

Nick took his fly rod out of the leather rod-case, jointed it, and shoved the rod-case back into the tent. He put on the reel and threaded the line through the guides. He had to hold it from hand to hand, as he threaded it, or it would slip back through its own weight. It was a heavy, double tapered fly line. Nick had paid eight dollars for it a long time ago. It was made heavy to lift back in the air and come forward flat and heavy and straight to make it possible to cast a fly which has no weight.

Nick opened the aluminum leader box. The leaders were coiled between the damp flannel pads. Nick had wet the pads at the water cooler on the train up to St. Ignace. In the damp pads the gut leaders had softened and Nick unrolled one and tied it by a loop at the end to the heavy fly line. He fastened a hook on the end of the leader. It was a small hook; very thin and springy.

Nick took it from his hook book, sitting with the rod across his lap. He tested the knot and the spring of the rod by pulling the line taut. It was a good feeling. He was careful not to let the hook bite into his finger.

He started down to the stream, holding his rod, the bottle of grasshoppers hung from his neck by a thong tied in half hitches around the neck of the bottle. His landing net hung by a hook from his belt. Over his shoulder was a long flour sack tied at each corner into an ear. The cord went over his shoulder. The sack flapped against his legs.

Nick felt awkward and professionally happy with all his equipment hanging from him. The grasshopper bottle swung against his chest. In his shirt the breast pockets bulged against him with the lunch and his fly book.

He stepped into the stream. It was a shock. His trousers clung tight to his legs. His shoes felt the gravel. The water was a rising cold shock.

Rushing, the current sucked against his legs. Where he stepped in, the water was over his knees. He waded with the current. The gravel slid under his shoes. He looked down at the swirl of water below each leg and tipped up the bottle to get a grasshopper.

The first grasshopper gave a jump in the neck of the bottle and went out into the water. He was sucked under in the whirl by Nick's right leg and came to the surface a little way down stream. He floated rapidly, kicking. In a quick circle, breaking the smooth surface of the water, he disappeared. A trout had taken him.

Another hopper poked his head out of the bottle. His antennae wavered. He was getting his front legs out of the bottle to jump. Nick took him by the head and held him while he threaded the slim hook under his chin, down through his thorax and into the last segments of his abdomen. The grasshopper took hold of the hook with his front feet, spitting tobacco juice on it. Nick dropped him into the water.

Holding the rod in his right hand he let out line against the pull of the grasshopper in the current. He stripped off line from the reel with his left hand and let it run free. He could see the hopper in the little waves of the current. It went out of sight.

There was a tug on the line. Nick pulled against the taut line. It was his first strike. Holding the now living rod across the current, he brought in the line with his left hand. The rod bent in jerks, the trout pumping against the current. Nick knew it was a small one. He lifted the rod straight up in the air. It bowed with the pull.

He saw the trout in the water jerking with his head and body against the shifting tangent of the line in the stream.

Nick took the line in his left hand and pulled the trout, thumping tiredly against the current, to the surface. His back was mottled the clear, water-over-gravel color, his side flashing in the sun. The rod under his right arm, Nick stooped, dipping his right hand into the current. He held the trout, never still, with his moist right hand, while he unhooked the barb from his mouth, then dropped him back into the stream.

He hung unsteadily in the current, then settled to the bottom beside a stone. Nick reached down his hand to touch him, his arm to the elbow under water. The trout was steady in the moving stream, resting on the gravel, beside a stone. As Nick's fingers touched him, touched his smooth, cool, underwater feeling he was gone, gone in a shadow across the bottom of the stream.

He's all right, Nick thought. He was only tired.

He had wet his hand before he touched the trout, so he would not disturb the delicate mucus that covered him. If a trout was touched with a dry hand, a white fungus attacked the unprotected spot. Years before when he had fished crowded streams, with fly fishermen ahead of him and behind him, Nick had again and again come on dead trout, furry with white fungus, drifted against a rock, or floating belly up in some pool. Nick did not like to fish with other men on the river. Unless they were of your party, they spoiled it.

He wallowed down the stream, above his knees in the current, through the fifty yards of shallow water above the pile of logs that crossed the stream. He did not rebait his hook and held it in his hand as he waded. He was certain he could catch small trout in the shallows, but he did not want them. There would be no big trout in the shallows this time of day.

Now the water deepened up his thighs sharply and coldly. Ahead was the smooth dammed-back flood of water above the logs. The water was smooth and dark; on the left, the lower edge of the meadow; on the right the swamp.

Nick leaned back against the current and took a hopper from the bottle. He threaded the hopper on the hook and spat on him for good luck. Then he pulled several yards of line from the reel and tossed the hopper out ahead onto the fast, dark water. It floated down towards the logs, then the weight of the line pulled the bait under the surface. Nick held the rod in his right hand, letting the line run out through his fingers.

There was a long tug. Nick struck and the rod came alive and dangerous, bent double, the line tightening, coming out of water, tightening, all in a heavy, dangerous, steady pull. Nick felt the moment when the leader would break if the strain increased and let the line go.

The reel ratcheted into a mechanical shriek as the line went out in a rush. Too fast. Nick could not check it, the line rushing out, the reel note rising as the line ran out.

With the core of the reel showing, his heart feeling stopped with the excitement, leaning back against the current that mounted icily his thighs, Nick thumbed the reel hard with his left hand. It was awkward getting his thumb inside the fly reel frame.

As he put on pressure the line tightened into sudden hardness and beyond the logs a huge trout went high out of water. As he jumped, Nick lowered the tip of the rod. But he felt, as he dropped the tip to ease the strain, the moment when the strain was too great; the hardness too tight. Of course, the leader had broken. There was no mistaking the feeling when all spring left the line and it became dry and hard. Then it went slack.

His mouth dry, his heart down, Nick reeled in. He had never seen so big a trout. There was a heaviness, a power not to be held, and then the bulk of him, as he jumped. He looked as broad as a salmon.

Nick's hand was shaky. He reeled in slowly. The thrill had been too much. He felt, vaguely, a little sick, as though it would be better to sit down.

The leader had broken where the hook was tied to it. Nick took it in his hand. He thought of the trout somewhere on the bottom, holding himself steady over the gravel, far down below the light, under the logs, with the hook in his jaw. Nick knew the trout's teeth would cut through the snell of the hook. The hook would imbed itself in his jaw. He'd bet the trout was angry. Anything that size would be angry. That was a trout. He had been solidly hooked. Solid as a rock. He felt like a rock, too, before he started off. By God, he was a big one. By God, he was the biggest one I ever heard of.

Nick climbed out onto the meadow and stood, water running down his trousers and out of his shoes, his shoes squlchy. He went over and sat on the logs. He did not want to rush his sensations any.

He wriggled his toes in the water, in his shoes, and got out a cigarette from his breast pocket. He lit it and tossed the match into the fast water below the logs. A tiny trout rose at the match, as it swung around in the fast current. Nick laughed. He would finish the cigarette.

He sat on the logs, smoking, drying in the sun, the sun warm on his back, the river shallow ahead entering the woods, curving into the woods, shallows, light glittering, big water-smooth rocks, cedars along the bank and white birches, the logs warm in the sun, smooth to sit on, without bark, gray to the touch; slowly the feeling of disappointment left him. It went away slowly, the feeling of disappointment that came sharply after the thrill that made his shoulders ache. It was all right now. His rod lying out on the logs, Nick tied a new hook on the leader, pulling the gut tight until it grimped into itself in a hard knot.

He baited up, then picked up the rod and walked to the far end of the logs to get into the water, where it was not too deep. Under and beyond the logs was a deep pool. Nick walked around the shallow shelf near the swamp shore until he came out on the shallow bed of the stream.

On the left, where the meadow ended and the woods began, a great elm tree was uprooted. Gone over in a storm, it lay back into the woods, its roots clotted with dirt, grass growing in them, rising a solid bank beside the stream. The river cut to the edge of the uprooted tree. From where Nick stood he could see deep channels, like ruts, cut in the shallow bed of the stream by the flow of the current. Pebbly where he stood and pebbly and full of boulders beyond; where it curved near the tree roots, the bed of the stream was marly and between the ruts of deep water green weed fronds swung in the current.

Nick swung the rod back over his shoulder and forward, and the line, curving forward, laid the grasshopper down on one of the deep channels in the weeds. A trout struck and Nick hooked him.

Holding the rod far out toward the uprooted tree and sloshing backward in the current, Nick worked the trout, plunging, the rod bending alive, out of the danger of the weeds into the open river. Holding the rod, pumping alive against the current, Nick brought the trout in. He rushed, but always came, the spring of the rod yielding to the rushes, sometimes jerking under water, but always bringing him in. Nick eased downstream with the rushes. The rod above his head he led the trout over the net, then lifted.

The trout hung heavy in the net, mottled trout back and silver sides in the meshes. Nick unhooked him; heavy sides, good to hold, big undershot jaw, and slipped him, heaving and big sliding, into the long sack that hung from his shoulders in the water.

Nick spread the mouth of the sack against the current and it filled, heavy with water. He held it up, the bottom in the stream, and the water poured out through the sides. Inside at the bottom was the big trout, alive in the water.

Nick moved downstream. The sack out ahead of him, sunk, heavy in the water, pulling from his shoulders.

It was getting hot, the sun hot on the back of his neck.

Nick had one good trout. He did not care about getting many trout. Now the stream was shallow and wide. There were trees along both banks. The trees of the left bank made short shadows on the current in the forenoon sun. Nick knew there were trout in each shadow. In the afternoon, after the sun had crossed toward the hills, the trout would be in the cool shadows on the other side of the stream.

The very biggest ones would lie up close to the bank. You could always pick them up there on the Black. When the sun was down they all moved out into the current. Just when the sun made the water blinding in the glare before it went down, you were liable to strike a big trout anywhere in the current. It was almost impossible to fish then, the surface of the water was blinding as a mirror in the sun. Of course, you could fish upstream, but in a stream like the Black, or this, you had to wallow against the current and in a deep place, the water piled up on you. It was no fun to fish upstream with this much current.

Nick moved along through the shallow stretch watching the banks for deep holes. A beech tree grew close beside the river, so that the branches hung down into the water. The stream went back in under the leaves. There were always trout in a place like that.

Nick did not care about fishing that hole. He was sure he would get hooked in the branches.

It looked deep though. He dropped the grasshopper so the current took it under water, back in under the overhanging branch. The line pulled hard and Nick struck. The trout threshed heavily, half out of water in the leaves and branches. The line was caught. Nick pulled hard and the trout was off. He reeled in and holding the hook in his hand, walked down the stream.

Ahead, close to the left bank, was a big log. Nick saw it was hollow; pointing up river the current entered it smoothly, only a little ripple spread each side of the log. The water was deepening. The top of the hollow log was gray and dry. It was partly in the shadow.

Nick took the cork out of the grasshopper bottle and a hopper clung to it. He picked him off, hooked him and tossed him out. He held the rod far out so that the hopper on the water moved into the current flowing into the hollow log. Nick lowered the rod and the hopper floated in. There was a heavy strike. Nick swung the rod against the pull. It felt as though he were hooked into the log itself, except for the live feeling.

He tried to force the fish out into the current. It came, heavily.

The line went slack and Nick thought the trout was gone. Then he saw him, very near, in the current, shaking his head, trying to get the hook out. His mouth was clamped shut. He was fighting the hook in the clear flowing current.

Looping in the line with his left hand, Nick swung the rod to make the line taut and tried to lead the trout toward the net, but he was gone, out of sight, the line pumping. Nick fought him against the current, letting him thump in the water against the spring of the rod. He shifted the rod to his left hand, worked the trout upstream, holding his weight, fighting on the rod, and then let him down into the net. He lifted him clear of the water, a heavy half circle in the net, the net dripping, unhooked him and slid him into the sack.

He spread the mouth of the sack and looked down in at the two big trout alive in the water.

Through the deepening water, Nick waded over to the hollow log. He took the sack off, over his head, the trout flopping as it came out of water, and hung it so the trout were deep in the water. Then he pulled himself up on the log and sat, the water from his trousers and boots running down into the stream. He laid his rod down, moved along to the shady end of the log and took the sandwiches out of his pocket. He dipped the sandwiches in the cold water. The current carried away the crumbs. He ate the sandwiches and dipped his hat full of water to drink, the water running out through his hat just ahead of his drinking.

It was cool in the shade, sitting on the log. He took a cigarette out and struck a match to light it. The match sunk into the gray wood, making a tiny furrow. Nick leaned over the side of the log, found a hard place and lit the match. He sat smoking and watching the river.

Ahead the river narrowed and went into a swamp. The river became smooth and deep and the swamp looked solid with cedar trees, their trunks close together, their branches solid. It would not be possible to walk through a swamp like that. The branches grew so low. You would have to keep almost level with the ground to move at all. You could not crash through the branches. That must be why the animals that lived in swamps were built the way they were, Nick thought.

He wished he had brought something to read. He felt like reading. He did not feel like going on into the swamp. He looked down the river.

A big cedar slanted all the way across the stream. Beyond that the river went into the swamp.

Nick did not want to go in there now. He felt a reaction against deep wading with the water deepening up under his armpits, to hook big trout in places impossible to land them. In the swamp the banks were bare, the big cedars came together overhead, the sun did not come through, except in patches; in the fast deep water, in the half light, the fishing would be tragic. In the swamp fishing was a tragic adventure. Nick did not want it. He did not want to go down the stream any further today.

He took out his knife, opened it and stuck it in the log. Then he pulled up the sack, reached into it and brought out one of the trout. Holding him near the tail, hard to hold, alive, in his hand, he whacked him against the log. The trout quivered, rigid. Nick laid him on the log in the shade and broke the neck of the other fish the same way. He laid them side by side on the log. They were fine trout.

Nick cleaned them, slitting them from the vent to the tip of the jaw. All the insides and the gills and tongue came out in one piece. They were both males; long gray-white strips of milt, smooth and clean. All the insides clean and compact, coming out all together. Nick tossed the offal ashore for the minks to find.

He washed the trout in the stream. When he held them back up in the water they looked like live fish. Their color was not gone yet. He washed his hands and dried them on the log. Then he laid the trout on the sack spread out on the log, rolled them up in it, tied the bundle and put it in the landing net. His knife was still standing, blade stuck in the log. He cleaned it on the wood and put it in his pocket.

Nick stood up on the log, holding his rod, the landing net hanging heavy, then stepped into the water and splashed ashore. He climbed the bank and cut up into the woods, toward the high ground. He was going back to camp. He looked back. The river just showed through the trees. There were plenty of days coming when he could fish the swamp.

Chapter Seven

The Royal Purple Game of the Sea

by Zane Grey

To the average reader, the name Zane Grey conjures up immediate visions of shelves of Western novels. Excellent and popular Western novels with romantic names like Riders of the Purple Sage, Last of the Plainsmen, *and* Heritage of the Desert, *to name only three of scores. But among the hundreds of thousands of words Grey wrote in his lifetime (1872–1939), nine entire volumes were devoted to his deep passion for fishing. This excerpt is taken from his* Tales of Fishes, *first published in 1919.*

Zane Grey literally cut his angling teeth on bass and other fish in the Delaware River and other nearby Pennsylvania and New Jersey streams he fished as a youngster. He never lost his love of freshwater fishing, but the enormous royalties of his Westerns eventually fed his growing passion for big-game fishing—marlin, swordfish, sailfish, and sharks—searching for the big ones outside the reefs. In those distant times, there were very few commercial operations and local knowledge. Grey became a trailblazer, a pioneer of big-game fishing around the world in places like Tahiti and New Zealand.

In this story, Grey describes early pursuits of one of the great gladiators of the sea, the swordfish.

To the great majority of anglers it may seem unreasonable to place swordfishing in a class by itself—by far the most magnificent sport in the world with rod and reel. Yet I do not hesitate to make this statement and believe I can prove it.

The sport is young at this writing—very little has been written by men who have caught swordfish. It was this that attracted me. Quite a number of fishermen have caught a swordfish. But every one of them will have something different to tell you and the information thus gleaned is apt to leave you at sea, both metaphorically and actually. Quite a number of fishermen, out after yellowtail, have sighted a swordfish, and with the assistance of heavy tackle and their boatmen have caught that swordfish. Some few men have caught a small swordfish so quickly and easily that they cannot appreciate what happened. On the other hand, one very large swordfish, a record, was caught in an hour, after a loggy rolling about, like a shark, without leaping. But these are not fighting swordfish. Of course, under any circumstances, it is an event to catch a swordfish. But the accidents, the flukes, the lucky stabs of the game, do not in any sense prove what swordfishing is or what it is not.

In August 1914, I arrived at Avalon with tuna experience behind me, with tarpon experience, and all the other kinds of fishing experience, even to the hooking of a swordfish in Mexico. I am inclined to confess that all this experience made me—well, somewhat too assured. Any one will excuse my enthusiasm. The day of my arrival I met Parker, the genial taxidermist of Avalon, and I started to tell him how I wanted my swordfish mounted. He interrupted me: "Say, young fellow, you want to catch a swordfish first!" One of the tuna boatmen gave me a harder jolt. He said: "Well, if you fish steadily for a couple of weeks, maybe you'll get a strike. And one swordfish caught out of ten strikes is good work!" But Danielson was optimistic and encouraging, as any good boatman ought to be. If I had not been fortunate enough to secure Captain Dan as my boatman, it is certain that one of the most wonderful fishing experiences on record would have fallen to some other fisherman, instead of to me.

We went over to Clemente Island, which is thirty-six miles from Catalina Island. Clemente is a mountain rising out of the sea, uninhabited, lonely, wild, and beautiful. But I will tell about the island later.

The weather was perfect, the conditions were apparently ideal. I shall never forget the sight of the first swordfish, with his great sickle-shaped tail and his purple fin. Nor am I likely to forget my disappointment when he totally ignored the flying-fish bait we trolled before him.

That experience was but a forerunner to others just like it. Every day we sighted one or more swordfish. But we could not get one to take hold. Captain Dan said there was more chance of getting a strike from a swordfish that was not visible rolling on the surface. Now a flying-fish bait makes a rather heavy bait to troll; and as it is imperative to have the reel free running and held lightly with the thumb, after a few hours such trolling becomes hard work. Hard as it was, it did not wear on me like the strain of being always ready for a strike. I doubt if any fisherman could stand this strain.

In twenty-one days I had seen nineteen swordfish, several of which had leaped playfully, or to shake off the remoras—parasite, blood-sucking little fish—and the sight of every one had only served to increase my fascination. By this time I had realized something of the difficult nature of the game, and I had begun to have an inkling of what sport it might be. During those twenty-one days we had trolled fifteen hundred miles, altogether, up and down that twenty-five-mile coast of rugged Clemente. And we had trolled round these fish in every conceivable way. I cannot begin to describe my sensations when we circled round a swordfish, and they grew more intense and acute as the strain and suspense dragged. Captain Dan, of course, was mostly dominated by my feeling. All the same, I think the strain affected him on his own account.

Then one day Boschen came over to Clemente with Farnsworth— and let me explain, by the way, that Boschen is probably the greatest heavy tackle fisherman living. Boschen would not fish for anything except tuna or swordfish, and up to this visit to Clemente he had caught many tuna, but only one swordfish, a *Xiphias*. This is the broadbill, or true, swordfish; and he is even rarer, and certainly larger and fiercer, than the Marlin, or roundbill, swordfish. This time at Clemente, Boschen caught his first Marlin and it weighed over three hundred pounds, leaped clear into the air sixty-three times, and gave a spectacular and magnificent surface fight that simply beggared description.

It made me wild to catch one, of like weight and ferocity. I spent several more endless days in vain. Then on the twenty-fifth day, way off the east end of Clemente, we sighted a swordfish with a tail almost pink. He had just come to those waters and had not yet gotten sunburnt.

We did not have to circle round him! At long distance he saw my bait, and as he went under I saw he had headed for it. I remember that I shook all over. And when I felt him take that bait, thrill on thrill electrified me. Steadily the line ran off the reel. Then Captain Dan leaned over and whispered, hoarsely:

"When you think he's had enough throw on your drag and strike. Then wind quick and strike again. . . . Wind and strike! Keep it up till he shows!"

Despite my intense excitement, I was calm enough to follow directions. But when I struck I felt no weight at all—no strain on the line. Frantically I wound and jerked—again and again! I never felt him at all. Suddenly my line rose—and then, bewilderingly near the boat, when I was looking far off, the water split with a roar and out shot a huge, gleaming, white-and-purple fish. He blurred in my sight. Down he went with a crash. I wound the reel like a madman, but I never even half got up the slack line. The swordfish had run straight toward the boat. He leaped again, in a place I did not expect, and going down, instantly came up in another direction. His speed, his savageness, stunned me. I could not judge of his strength, for I never felt his weight. The next leap I saw him sling the hook. It was a great performance. Then that swordfish, finding himself free, leaped for the open sea, and every few yards he came out in a clean jump. I watched him, too fascinated to count the times he broke water, but he kept it up till he was out of sight on the horizon.

At first Captain Dan took the loss harder than I took it. But gradually I realized what had happened, and, though I made a brave effort to be game and cheerful, I was sick. It did seem hard that, after all those twenty-five days of patience and hope and toil, I could not have hooked the swordfish. I see now that it was nothing, only an incident, but I shall never forget the pang.

That day ended my 1914 experience. The strain had been too hard on me. It had taken all this time for me to appreciate what swordfishing might be. I assured Captain Dan I would come back in 1915, but at the time he did not believe me. He said:

"If you hadn't stuck it out so long I wouldn't care. Most of the fishermen try only a few days and never come back. Don't quit now!"

***

But I did go back in 1915. Long ago on my lonely desert trips I learned the value of companions and I dreaded the strain of this swordfishing game. I needed some one to help lessen it. Besides that, I needed snapshot pictures of leaping swordfish, and it was obvious that Captain Dan and I would have our hands full when a fish got hooked. We had music, books, magazines—everything that could be thought of.

Murphy, the famous old Avalon fisherman and tackle-maker, had made me a double split-bamboo rod, and I had brought the much-talked-of B-Ocean reel. This is Boschen's invention—one he was years in perfecting. It held fifteen hundred feet of No. 24 line. And I will say now that it is a grand reel, the best on the market. But I did not know that then, and had to go through the trip with it, till we were both tired out. Lastly, and most important, I had worked to get into condition to fight swordfish. For weeks I rowed a boat at home to get arms and my back in shape, and especially my hands. Let no fisherman imagine he can land a fighting swordfish with soft hands!

So, prepared for a long, hard strain, like that of 1914, I left Avalon hopeful, of course, but serious, determined, and alive to the possibilities of failure.

I did not troll across the channel between the islands. There was a big swell running, and four hours of it gave me a disagreeable feeling. Now and then I got up to see how far off Clemente was. And upon the last of these occasions I saw the fins of a swordfish right across our bow. I yelled to Captain Dan. He turned the boat aside, almost on top of the swordfish. Hurriedly I put a bait on my hook and got it overboard, and let the line run. Then I looked about for the swordfish. He had gone down.

It seemed then that, simultaneously with the recurrence of a peculiar and familiar disappointment, a heavy and powerful fish viciously took my bait and swept away. I yelled to Captain Dan:

"He's got it!" . . .

Captain Dan stopped the engine and came to my side. "No!" he exclaimed.

Then I replied, "Look at that line!" . . .

It seemed like a dream. Too good to be true! I let out a shout when I hooked him and a yell of joy when he broke water—a big swordfish, over two hundred pounds. What really transpired on Captain Dan's boat the following few moments I cannot adequately describe. Suffice to say that it was violent effort, excitement, and hilarity. I never counted the leaps of the swordfish. I never clearly saw him after that first leap. He seemed only a gleam in flying spray. Still, I did not make any mistakes.

At the end of perhaps a quarter of an hour the swordfish quit his surface work and settled down to under-water fighting, and I began to find myself. Captain Dan played the phonograph, laughed, and joked while I fought the fish. My companions watched my rod and line and the water, wide-eyed and mute, as if they could not believe what seemed true.

In about an hour and a half the swordfish came up and, tired out, he rolled on the top of the great swells. But he could not be drawn near the boat. One little wave of his tail made my rod bend dangerously. Still, I knew I had him beaten, and I calculated that in another hour, perhaps, I could lead him alongside.

Then, like thunder out of a clear sky, something went wrong with the great B-Ocean reel. It worked hard. When a big swell carried the swordfish up, pulling out line, the reel rasped.

"It's freezing on you!" shouted Captain Dan, with dark glance.

A new reel sometimes clogs and stops from friction and heat. I had had von Hofe and other reels freeze. But in this instance, it seemed that for the reel to freeze would be simply heartbreaking. Well—it froze, tight as a shut vise! I sat there, clutching the vibrating rod, and I watched the swordfish as the swells lifted him. I expected the line to break, but, instead, the hook tore out.

Next day we sighted four swordfish and tried in vain to coax one to bite.

Next day we sighted ten swordfish, which is a record for one day. They were indifferent.

The next three. The next one, with like result. The next day no fish were sighted, and that fact encouraged Captain Dan.

The next day, late in the afternoon, I had a strike and hooked a swordfish. He leaped twice and threw the hook.

The next day I got eleven jumps out of another before he gracefully flung the hook at the boat.

The next day, a big swordfish, with a ragged purple fin, took my bait right astern of the boat and sounded deep. I hooked him. Time and time again I struck with all my might. The fish did not seem to mind that. He swam along with the boat. He appeared very heavy. I was elated and curious.

"What's he going to do?" I kept asking Captain Dan.

"Wait!" he exclaimed.

After six minutes the swordfish came up, probably annoyed by the hook fast in him. When he showed his flippers, as Captain Dan called them, we all burst out with wonder and awe. As yet I had no reason to fear a swordfish.

"He's a whale!" yelled Captain Dan.

Probably this fish measured eight feet between his dorsal fin and the great curved fluke of his tail, and that would make his total length over twelve feet.

No doubt the swordfish associated the thing fast in his jaw with the boat, for he suddenly awoke. He lifted himself, wagging his sword, showing his great silvery side. Then he began to thresh. I never felt a quarter of such power at the end of a line. He went swift as a flash. Then he leaped sheer ahead, like a porpoise, only infinitely more active. We all yelled. He was of great size, over three hundred, broad, heavy, long, and the most violent and savage fish I ever had a look at. Then he rose half–two-thirds out of the water, shaking his massive head, jaws open, sword sweeping, and seemed to move across the water in a growing, boiling maelstrom of foam. This was the famous "walking on his tail" I had heard so much about. It was an incredible feat. He must have covered fifty yards. Then he plunged down, and turned swiftly in a curve toward the boat. He looked threatening to me. I could not manage the slack line. One more leap and he threw the hook. I found the point of the hook bent. It had never been embedded in his jaw. And also I found that his violent exercise had lasted just one minute. I wondered how long I would have lasted had the hook been deep-set.

Next day I had a swordfish take my bait, swim away on the surface, showing the flying-fish plainly between his narrow beak, and after fooling with it for a while he ejected it.

Next day I got a great splashing strike from another, without even a sight of the fish.

Next day I hooked one that made nineteen beautiful leaps straightaway before he got rid of the hook.

And about that time I was come to a sad pass. In fact, I could not sleep, eat, or rest. I was crazy on swordfish.

Day after day, from early morning till late afternoon, aboard on the sea, trolling, watching, waiting, eternally on the alert, I had kept at the game. My emotional temperament made this game a particularly trying one. And every possible unlucky, unforeseen, and sickening thing that could happen to a fisherman had happened. I grew morbid, hopeless. I could no longer see the beauty of that wild and lonely island, nor the wonder of that smooth, blue Pacific, nor the myriad of strange sea-creatures. It was a bad state of mind which I could not wholly conquer. Only by going at it so hard, and sticking so long, without any rests, could I gain the experience I wanted. A man to be a great fisherman should have what makes Stewart White a great hunter—no emotions. If a lion charged me I would imagine a million things. Once when a Mexican *tigre*, a jaguar, charged me I—But that is not this story. Boschen has the temperament for a great fisherman. He is phlegmatic. All day—and day after day—he sits there, on trigger, so to speak, waiting for the strike that will come. He is so constituted that it does not matter to him how soon or how late the strike comes. To me the wait, the suspense, grew to be maddening. Yet I stuck it out, and in this I claim a victory, of which I am prouder than I am of the record that gave me more swordfish to my credit than any other fisherman has taken.

On the next day, August 11th, about three o'clock, I saw a long, moving shadow back of my bait. I jumped up. There was the purple, drifting shape of a swordfish. I felt a slight vibration when he hit the bait with his sword. Then he took the bait. I hooked this swordfish. He leaped eight times before he started out to sea. He took us three miles. In an hour and five minutes I brought him to gaff—a small fish. Captain Dan would take no chances of losing him. He risked much when he grasped the waving sword with his right hand, and with the gaff in his left he hauled the swordfish aboard and let him slide down into the cockpit. For Captain Dan it was no less an overcoming of obstinate difficulty than for me. He was as elated as I, but I forgot the past long, long siege, while he remembered it.

That swordfish certainly looked a tiger of the sea. He had purple fins, long, graceful, sharp; purple stripes on a background of dark, mottled bronze green; mother-of-pearl tint fading into the green; and great opal eyes with dark spots in the center. The colors came out most vividly and exquisitely, the purple blazing, just as the swordfish trembled his last and died. He was nine feet two inches long and weighed one hundred and eighteen pounds.

***

I caught one the next day, one hundred and forty-four pounds. Fought another the next day and he threw the hook after a half-hour. Caught two the following day—one hundred and twenty, and one hundred and sixty-six pounds. And then, Captain Dan foreshadowing my remarkable finish, exclaimed:

"I'm lookin' for busted records now!"

***

One day about noon the sea was calm except up toward the west end, where a wind was whipping the water white. Clemente Island towered with its steep slopes of wild oats and its blue cañons full of haze.

Captain Dan said he had seen a big swordfish jump off to the west, and we put on full speed. He must have been a mile out and just where the breeze ruffled the water. As good luck would have it, we came upon the fish on the surface. I consider this a fine piece of judgment for Captain Dan, to locate him at that distance. He was a monster and fresh run from the outside sea. That is to say, his great fin and tail were violet, almost pink in color. They had not had time to get sunburnt, as those of fish earlier arrived at Clemente.

We made a wide circle round him, to draw the flying-fish bait near him. But before we could get it near he went down. The same old story, I thought, with despair—these floating fish will not bite. We circled over the place where he had gone down, and I watched my bait rising and falling in the low swells.

Suddenly Captain Dan yelled and I saw a great blaze of purple and silver green flashing after my bait. It was the swordfish, and he took the bait on the run. That was a moment for a fisherman! I found it almost impossible to let him have enough line. All that I remember about the hooking of him was a tremendous shock. His first dash was irresistibly powerful, and I had a sensation of the absurdity of trying to stop a fish like that. Then the line began to rise on the surface and to lengthen in my sight, and I tried to control my rapture and fear enough to be able to see him clearly when he leaped. The water split, and up he shot—a huge, glittering, savage, beautiful creature, all purple and opal in the sunlight. He did not get all the way out of the water, but when he dropped back he made the water roar.

Then, tearing off line, he was out of the water in similar leaps—seven times more. Captain Dan had his work cut out for him as well as I had mine. It was utterly impossible to keep a tight line, and when I felt the slacking of weight I grew numb and sick—thinking he was gone. But he suddenly straightened the line with a jerk that lifted me, and he started inshore. He had about four hundred feet of line out, and more slipping out as if the drag was not there. Captain Dan headed the boat after him at full speed. Then followed a most thrilling race. It was over very quickly, but it seemed an age. When he stopped and went down he had pulled thirteen hundred feet off my reel while we were chasing him at full speed. While he sounded I got back half of this line. I wish I could give some impression of the extraordinary strength and speed of this royal purple fish of the sea. He came up again, in two more leaps, one of which showed me his breadth of back, and then again was performed for me the feature of which I had heard so much and which has made the swordfish the most famous of all fish—he rose two-thirds out of the water, I suppose by reason of the enormous power of his tail, though it seemed like magic, and then he began to walk across the sea in a great circle of white foam, wagging his massive head, sword flying, jaws wide, dorsal fin savagely erect, like a lion's mane. He was magnificent. I have never seen fury so expressed or such an unquenchable spirit. Then he dropped back with a sudden splash, and went down and down and down.

All swordfish fight differently, and this one adopted tuna tactics. He sounded and began to plug away and bang the leader with his tail. He would take off three hundred feet of line, and then, as he slowed up, I, by the labor of Hercules, pulled and pumped and wound most of it back on the reel. This kept up for an hour—surely the hardest hour's work of my life.

But a swordfish is changeable. That is the beauty of his gameness. He left off sounding and came up to fight on the surface. In the next hour he pulled us from the Fence to Long Point, a distance of four miles.

Once off the Point, where the tide rip is strong, he began to circle in great, wide circles. Strangely, he did not put out to sea. And here, during the next hour, I had the finest of experiences I think that ever befell a fisherman. I was hooked to a monster fighting swordfish; I was wet with sweat, and salt water that had dripped from my reel, and I was aching in every muscle. The sun was setting in banks of gold and silver fog over the west end, and the sea was opalescent—vast, shimmering, heaving, beautiful. And at this sunset moment, or hour—for time seemed nothing—a school of giant tuna began leaping around us, smashing the water, making the flying-fish rise in clouds, like drifting bees. I saw a whole flock of flying-fish rise into the air with that sunset glow and color in the background, and the exquisite beauty of life and movement was indescribable. Next a bald eagle came soaring down, and, swooping along the surface, he lowered his talons to pick up a crippled flying-fish. And when the hoary-headed bird rose, a golden eagle, larger and more powerful, began to contest with him for the prey.

Then the sky darkened and the moon whitened—and my fight went on. I had taken the precaution to work for two months at rowing to harden my hands for just such a fight as this. Yet my hands suffered greatly. A man who is not in the best of physical trim, with his hands hard, cannot hope to land a big swordfish.

I was all afternoon at this final test, and all in, too, but at last I brought him near enough for Captain Dan to grasp the leader. . . . Then there was something doing around that boat for a spell! I was positive a German torpedo had hit us. But the explosion was only the swordfish's tail and Dan's voice yelling for another gaff. When Captain Dan got the second gaff in him there was another submarine attack, but the boat did not sink.

Next came the job of lassoing the monster's tail. Here I shone, for I had lassoed mountain-lions with Buffalo Jones, and I was efficient and quick. Captain Dan and I were unable to haul the fish on board, and we had to get out the block and tackle and lift the tail on deck, secure that, and then pull up the head from the other side. After that I needed some kind of tackle to hold me up.

We were miles from camp, and I was wet and cold and exhausted, and the pain in my blistered hands was excruciating. But not soon shall I forget that ride down the shore with the sea so rippling and moon-blanched, and the boom of the surf on the rocks, and the peaks of the island standing bold and dark against the white stars.

This swordfish weighed three hundred and sixteen pounds on faulty scales at Clemente. He very likely weighed much more. He was the largest Captain Dan ever saw, up to that time. Al Shade guessed his weight at three hundred and sixty. The market fishermen, who put in at the little harbor the next day, judged him way over three hundred, and these men are accurate. The fish hung head down for a day and night, lost all the water and blood and feed in him, and another day later, when landed at Avalon, he had lost considerable. There were fishermen who discredited Captain Dan and me, who in our enthusiasm claimed a record.

But—that sort of thing is one of the aspects of the sport. I was sorry, for Captain Dan's sake. The rivalries between boatmen are keen and important, and they are fostered by unsportsman-like fishermen. And fishermen live among past associations; they grow to believe their performances unbeatable and they hate to see a new king crowned. This may be human, since we are creatures who want always to excel, but it is irritating to the young fishermen. As for myself, what did I care how much the swordfish weighed? He was huge, magnificent, beautiful, and game to the end of that four-hour battle. Who or what could change that—or the memory of those schools of flying-fish in the sunset glow—or the giant tuna, smashing the water all about me—or the eagles fighting over my head—or the beauty of wild and lonely Clemente under its silver cloud-banks?

***

I went on catching one or two swordfish every day, and Captain Dan averred that the day would come when we would swamp the boat. These days were fruitful of the knowledge of swordfish that I had longed to earn.

They are indeed "queer birds." I learned to recognize the sharp vibration of my line when a swordfish rapped the bait with his sword. No doubt he thought he thus killed his prey. Then the strike would come invariably soon after. No two swordfish acted or fought alike. I hooked one that refused to stand the strain of the line. He followed the boat, and was easily gaffed. I hooked another, a heavy fish, that did not show for two hours. We were sure we had a broadbill, and were correspondingly worried. The broadbill swordfish is a different proposition. He is larger, fiercer, and tireless. He will charge the boat, and nothing but the churning propeller will keep him from ramming the boat. There were eight broadbill swordfish hooked at Avalon during the summer, and not one brought to gaff. This is an old story. Only two have been caught to date. They are so powerful, so resistless, so desperate, and so cunning that it seems impossible to catch them. They will cut bait after bait off your hook as clean as if it had been done with a knife. For that matter, their broad bill is a straight, long, powerful two-edged sword. And the fish perfectly understands its use.

This matter of swordfish charging the boat is apt to be discredited by fishermen. But it certainly is not doubted by the few who know. I have seen two swordfish threaten my boat, and one charge it. Walker, an Avalon boatman, tells of a prodigious battle his angler had with a broadbill giant calculated to weigh five hundred pounds. This fight lasted eight hours. Many times the swordfish charged the boat and lost his nerve. If that propeller had stopped he would have gone through the boat as if it had been paper. After this fish freed himself he was so mad that he charged the boat repeatedly. Boschen fought a big broadbill for eleven hours. And during this fight the swordfish sounded to the bottom forty-eight times, and had to be pumped up; he led the boat almost around Catalina Island—twenty-nine miles; and he had gotten out into the channel, headed for Clemente, when he broke away. This fish did everything. I consider this battle the greatest on record. Only a man of enormous strength and endurance could have lasted so long—not to speak of the skill and wits necessary on the part of both fisherman and boatman. All fishermen fish for the big fish, though it is sport to catch any game fish, irrespective of size. But let any fisherman who has nerve see and feel a big swordfish on his line, and from that moment he is obsessed. Why, a tarpon is child's play compared to holding a fast swordfish.

It is my great ambition now to catch a broadbill. That would completely round out my fishing experience. And I shall try. But I doubt that I will be so fortunate. It takes a long time. Boschen was years catching his fish. Moreover, though it is hard to get a broadbill to bite—and harder to hook him—it is infinitely harder to do anything with him after you do get fast to him.

***

A word about Avalon boatmen. They are a fine body of men. I have heard them maligned. Certainly they have petty rivalries and jealousies, but this is not their fault. They fish all the seasons around and have been there for years. Boatmen at Long Key and other Florida resorts—at Tampico, Aransas Pass—are not in the same class with the Avalon men. They want to please and to excel, and to number you among their patrons for the future. And the boats—nowhere are there such splendid boats. Captain Danielson's boat had utterly spoiled me for fishing out of any other. He had it built, and the ideas of its construction were a product of fifteen years' study. It is thirty-eight feet long, and wide, with roomy, shaded cockpit and cabin, and comfortable revolving chairs to fish from. These chairs have moving sockets into which you can jam the butt of your rod; and the backs can be removed in a flash. Then you can haul at a fish! The boat lies deep, with heavy ballast in the stern. It has a keel all the way, and an enormous rudder. Both are constructed so your line can slip under the boat without fouling. It is equipped with sail and a powerful engine. Danielson can turn this boat, going at full speed, in its own length! Consider the merit of this when a tuna strikes, or a swordfish starts for the open sea. How many tarpon, barracuda, amberjack, and tuna I have lost on the Atlantic seaboard just because the boat could not be turned in time!

***

Clemente Island is a mountain of cliffs and caves. It must be of volcanic origin, and when the lava rose, hot and boiling, great blow-holes formed, and hardened to make the caves. It is an exceedingly beautiful island. The fishing side is on the north, or lee, shore, where the water is very deep right off the rocks. There are kelp-beds along the shore, and the combination of deep water, kelp, and small fish is what holds the swordfish there in August and September. I have seen acres of flying-fish in the air at once, and great swarms of yellowtail, basking on the surface. The color of the water is indigo blue, clear as crystal. Always a fascinating thing for me was to watch the water for new and different fish, strange marine creatures, life of some kind. And the watching was always rewarded. I have been close to schools of devilish blackfish, and I have watched great whales play all around me. What a spectacle to see a whale roll and dip his enormous body and bend and sound, lifting the huge, glistening flukes of his tail, wide as a house! I hate sharks and have caught many, both little and big. When you are watching for swordfish it is no fun to have a big shark break for your bait, throw the water, get your hook, and lift you from your seat. It happened often. But sometimes when I was sure it was a shark it was really a swordfish! I used to love to watch the sunfish leap, they are so round and glistening and awkward. I could tell one two miles away. The blue shark leaps often and he always turns clear over. You cannot mistake it. Nor can you mistake a swordfish when he breaks, even though you only see the splash. He makes two great sheets of water rise and fall. Probably all these fish leap to shake off the remoras. A remora is a parasite, a queer little fish, pale in color, because he probably lives inside the gills of the fish he preys upon, with the suckers on top of his head, arranged in a shield, ribbed like a washboard. This little fish is as mysterious as any creature of the sea. He is as swift as lightning. He can run over the body of a swordfish so quickly you can scarcely follow his movement, and at all times he is fast to the swordfish, holding with that flat sucker head. Mr. Holder wrote years ago that the remora sticks to a fish just to be carried along, as a means of travel, but I do not incline to this belief. We found many remoras inside the gills of swordfish, and their presence there was evidence of their blood-sucking tendencies. I used to search every swordfish for these remoras, and I would keep them in a bucket till we got to our anchorage. A school of tame rock-bass there, and tame yellowtail, and a few great sea-bass were always waiting for us—for our discarded bait or fish of some kind. But when I threw in a live remora, how these hungry fish did dart away! Life in the ocean is strange, complex, ferocious, and wonderful.

Al Shade keeps the only camp at Clemente. It is a clean, comfortable, delightful place. I have found no place where sleep is so easy, so sweet, so deep. Shade lives a lonely life there ten months in the year. And it is no wonder that when a fisherman arrives Al almost kills himself in his good humor and kindness and usefulness. Men who live lonely lives are always glad to see their fellow-men. But he loves Clemente Island. Who would not?

When I think of it many pictures come to mind—evening with the sea rolling high and waves curving shoreward in great dark ripples, that break and spread white and run up the strand. The sky is pale blue above, a green sheen low down, with white stars blinking. The promontories run down into the sea, sheer, black, rugged, bold, mighty. The surf is loud and deep, detonating, and the pebbles scream as the waves draw them down. Strange to realize that surf when on the morrow the sea will be like glass—not a wave nor a ripple under the gray fog! Wild and beautiful Clemente—the island of caves and cañons and cliffs—lilac and cactus and ice-plant and arbor-vitae and ironwood, with the wild goats silhouetted dark against the bold sky-line!

**

There came that day of all days. I never believed Captain Dan, but now I shall never forget. The greatest day that ever befell me! I brought four swordfish to gaff and whipped another, the biggest one of the whole trip, and saw him tear away from the hook just at the last—in all, nine hours of strenuous hanging on to a rod.

I caught the first one before six o'clock, as the sun was rising red-gold, dazzling, glorious. He leaped in the sun eleven times. He weighed one hundred and eighty-seven.

After breakfast we sighted two swordfish on the smooth sea. Both charged the bait. I hooked one of these and he leaped twenty-three times. He weighed one hundred and sixty-eight.

Then off the east end we saw a big swordfish leap five times. We went out toward the open sea. But we never got anywhere near him. I had three strikes, one after another, when we were speeding the boat. Then we shut down and took to slow trolling. I saw another swordfish sail for my bait, and yelled. He shot off with the bait and his dorsal fin stuck out of the water. I hooked him. He leaped thirty-eight times. How the camera did snap during this fight! He weighed two hundred and ten.

I had a fierce strike on the way in. Too fast! We lost him.

"The sea's alive with swordfish!" cried Captain Dan. "It's the day!"

Then I awoke to my opportunity.

Round the east end, close to the great black bluff, where the swells pile up so thunderously, I spied the biggest purple fin I had ever seen. This fellow came to meet us—took my bait. I hooked at him, but did not hurt or scare him. Finally I pulled the hook out of him. While I was reeling in my line suddenly a huge purple shadow hove in sight. It was the swordfish—and certainly one of immense size—the hugest yet.

"He's following the boat!" yelled Captain Dan, in great excitement.

So I saw, but I could not speak or yell. All was intense excitement on that boat. I jumped up on the stern, holding the bait Captain Dan had put on my hook. Then I paused to look. We all looked, spellbound. That was a sight of a lifetime. There he swam, the monster, a few feet under the surface, only a rod back of the boat. I had no calm judgment with which to measure his dimensions. I only saw that he was tremendous and beautiful. His great, yard-wide fins gleamed royal purple. And the purple stripes crossed his silver sides. He glowed in the water, changed color like a chameleon, and drifted, floated after us. I thought of my brother

Reddy—how he would have gloried in that sight! I thought of Dilg, of Bob Davis, of Professor Kellogg—other great fishermen, all in a flash. Indeed, though I gloated over my fortune, I was not selfish.

Then I threw in the flying-fish bait. The swordfish loomed up, while my heart ceased to beat. There, in plain sight, he took the bait, as a trout might have taken a grasshopper. Slowly he sank. The line began to slip off the reel. He ceased to be a bright purple mass—grew dim—then vague—and disappeared.

I sat down, jammed the rod in the socket, and got ready. For the life of me I could not steady my legs.

"What'll he weigh?" I gasped.

"O Lord! he looked twice as big as the big one you got," replied Dan.

"Stand by with the cameras!" I said to my companions, and as they lined up, two on one side and one on the other, I began to strike at that fish with all my might and main. I must have had at least twelve powerful strikes before he began to wake up.

Then!

He came up, throwing the water in angry spouts. If he did not threaten the boat I was crazy. He began an exhibition that dwarfed any other I had seen, and it was so swift that I could scarcely follow him. Yet when I saw the line rise, and then the wonderful, long, shiny body, instinct with fury, shoot into the air, I yelled the number of the leap, and this was the signal for the camera-workers. They held the cameras close, without trying to focus, facing the fish, and they snapped when I yelled. It was all gloriously exciting. I could never describe that exhibition. I only know that he leaped clear forty-six times, and after a swift, hard hour for me he got away. Strangely, I was almost happy that he had shaken loose, for he had given such remarkable opportunities for pictures.

Captain Dan threw the wheel hard over and the boat turned. The swordfish, tired out and unconscious of freedom, was floating near the surface, a drifting blaze of purple. The boat sheered close to him. Captain Dan reached over with a gaff—and all but gaffed that swordfish before he sank too deep. Captain Dan was white with disappointment. That more than anything showed me his earnestness, what it all meant to him.

On the way in, for we had been led out a couple of miles, I saw a blue streak after my bait, and I was ready before the swordfish got to it. He struck viciously and I dared not let him have much line. When I hooked him he started out to sea at a clip that smoked the line off my reel.

Captain Dan got the boat turned before the swordfish began to leap. Then it was almost a straightaway race. This fellow was a greyhound leaper. He did not churn the water, nor dash to and fro on the surface, but kept steadily leaping ahead. He cleared the water thirty-nine times before he gave up leaping. Then he sounded. The line went slack. I thought he was gone. Suddenly he showed again, in a white splash, and he was not half as far away as when he went down. Then I felt the pull on the line. It was heavy, for he had left a great bag in it. I endeavored to recover line, but it came in very slowly. The swordfish then threshed on the surface so that we could hear the water crack. But he did not leap again. He had gone mad with rage. He seemed to have no sense of direction. He went down again, only to rush up, still closer to us. Then it was plain he saw the nature of his foe. Splitting water like a swift motor-boat, he charged us.

I had a cold sensation, but was too excited to be afraid. Almost I forgot to reel in.

"He's after us!" I said, grimly.

Captain Dan started the boat ahead fast. The swordfish got out of line with the boat. But he was close, and he made me think of the charging rhinoceros Dugmore photographed. And then I yelled for the cameras to be snapped. They all clicked—and then, when the swordfish shot close behind us, presenting the most magnificent picture, no one was ready!

As he passed I thought I saw the line round his body. Then he sounded and began to plug. He towed us six miles out to sea. I could not stop him. I had begun to weaken. My hands were sights. My back hurt. But I stayed with him. He felt like a log and I could not recover line. Captain Dan said it was because I was almost all in, but I did not think that. Presently this swordfish turned inshore and towed us back the six miles. By this time it was late and I *was* all in. But the swordfish did not seem nearer the boat. I got mad and found some reserve strength. I simply had to bring him to gaff. I pulled and pumped and wound until I was blind and could scarcely feel. My old blisters opened and bled. My left arm was dead. I seemed to have no more strength than a kitten. I could not lead the fish nor turn him. I had to drag and drag, inch by inch. It was agonizing. But finally I was encouraged by sight of him, a long, fine, game fellow. A hundred times I got the end of the double line near the leader in sight, only to lose it.

Seven o'clock passed. I had fought this swordfish nearly three hours. I could not last much longer. I rested a little, holding hard, and then began a last and desperate effort to bring him to gaff. I was absolutely dripping with sweat, and red flashes passed before my eyes, and queer dots. The last supreme pull—all I had left—brought the end of the leader to Captain Dan's outstretched hand.

The swordfish came in broadside. In the clear water we saw him plainly, beautifully striped tiger that he was! And we all saw that he had not been hooked. He had been lassoed. In some way the leader had looped around him with the hook catching under the wire. No wonder it had nearly killed me to bring him to the boat, and surely I never would have succeeded had it not been for the record Captain Dan coveted. That was the strangest feature in all my wonderful Clemente experience—to see that superb swordfish looped in a noose of my long leader. He was without a scratch. It may serve to give some faint idea of the bewildering possibilities in the pursuit of this royal purple game of the Pacific.

CHAPTER EIGHT

Thoughts in Coltsfoot Time

by Ernest Schwiebert

Ernest Schwiebert was so important in my life that today, years past his pass-
ing in 2005, I still find it hard to accept the fact that he is gone. His friendship
and story contributions to magazines like Sports Afield *and many books I*
have edited form unforgettable parts of my memory. "Thoughts in Coltsfoot
Time" is one of my favorites from Ernie's voluminous works. Here is the way
I introduced it in my book Into the Backing, *in 2001:*

    "It seems hard for me to believe that nearly fifty years have passed since my
colleague, Ernie Schwiebert, emerged as the wunderkind of fly-fishing writers,
with the publication of Matching the Hatch *in 1955, while still an under-*
graduate at Ohio State.

    "Almost twenty books and a lot of fly hatches later, Ernie is still on the
stream every chance he gets, and he still courts the muses of fishing with the skill
and vigor of a young man. As this is being written, he has published magazine
pieces on Saint Petersburg, the New Mexico years of Georgia O'Keeffe, the
great castle hotels of Ireland, and the historic shrines of Ise Shima in Japan. But
he is still reworking and polishing manuscripts on Alaska and its remarkable
ecology, his exploration of little-known Atlantic salmon rivers in old Russia,
a history of the famed Umpqua and its steelhead, and is preparing a definitive
new edition of Matching the Hatch.

    "It has been my good fortune to call him a friend for thirty-odd years, and
to have published many of his stories for the first time, in Sports Afield *and*
Outdoor Life. *I have witnessed his fishing skills firsthand, from the Langa*

in Iceland to the Brodheads in eastern Pennsylvania, and I can assure you that the man does infinitely more than 'talk the talk,' as the younger generation likes to say. Ernie 'walks the walk'"with the best of them.

"As an architect and planner with a doctorate from Princeton, and as an angler and a writer, Ernie has illuminated each of his personal interests with an inquiring mind and a relentless pursuit of understanding. If you are relatively new to fly fishing, perhaps you are not yet familiar with his works, including the definitive Nymphs *and the towering 1,854-page magnum opus called* Trout. *But his collections of stories, like the anthology from which this little tale of Michigan is taken—*Death of a Riverkeeper*—have the overtones of serious fiction and are wonderful reading. Such collections also include* Remembrances of Rivers Past, The Compleat Schwiebert, *and* A River for Christmas and Other Stories. *He also produced a superb travel book called* The Traveling Angler, *which was published by Doubleday in 1991.*

"Arnold Gingrich once observed that Ernie shares a genius for evocative detail. Gingrich is right, and Ernie's stories and books will not only make you a better angler, but they also have about them a sense of place I find irresistible. Sometimes an overpowering sense of nostalgia is found in his best prose.

The story I have elected to include describes his first memories of fishing with his father, on a tiny lake in Michigan, in the middle of the Great Depression. Ernie finally lost his father this year at the age of 104. He had published his last work of history in 1995, on his 100th birthday, and was still fishing for trout at 93. 'Thoughts in Coltsfoot Time' takes us back to southern Michigan, in those boyhood days that were the genesis of everything to come, days when Ernie's father was the one pounding away at the big typewriter, and the young angler was busily watching, learning, filing away potsherds of memory, and beginning to dream."

Although the pretty yellow coltsfoot is not a species entirely native to our shores, its bright palette signals the last of Winter, and its flowering serves as a welcome harbinger of the coming spring.

—THOREAU

IT IS STILL RAINING SOFTLY THIS MORNING, AFTER SEVERAL DAYS OF false spring that started the coltsfoot blooming in the sheltered places. Deer are browsing through the oaks and beeches behind the house, their coats still the somber color of winter leaves, although the snow is finally gone. Grouse are drumming in the overgrown orchard, and it is almost time for fishing.

Coltsfoot is a spare, dandelionlike flower, and as with many other wildflowers, history tells us that coltsfoot is an alien species. It traveled across the Atlantic with our colonial forefathers, since its tiny leaves were dried and burned like incense to treat asthma and colds. Coltsfoot is found on sheltered slopes and in ravines that capture the late winter sun, although only a few blossoms are visible in their carpet of winter leaves. Its flowers signal the weakening of winter, in spite of the bitter April weather, and in my library in these Appalachian foothills, my thoughts are curiously filled with boyhood summers in Michigan.

My first memories of fishing are there, in a simple cedar-shingle cottage among the hardwoods and pines, fifty yards above a lake that shimmered in the August sun.

Lilypads filled its shallows, turning over lazily and drifting in a hot wind that smelled of orchards and cornfields farther south. Red-winged blackbirds called restlessly in the marsh. The lily pads were like the rowboats moored at the rickety dock, shifting and swinging in the wind, until their rubbery stems stretched and pulled them back like anchor lines. The hot wind rose and stirred each morning, offering little relief from the doldrums.

The boats were old and poorly maintained, with peeling paint and rusting oarlocks and eyebolts. Their wrinkled seams desperately needed fresh caulking. Moss-colored water surrounded a half-drowned bailing can in the rowboat that went with the cottage. The other boat was almost filled with water. Its wainscot bottom rested on the mud, in the planking shadows of the pier. Its middle seat sheltered a small colony of tadpoles lurking in the tangles of its weathered anchor cord.

The hot wind finally dropped and died. Locusts began their harshly strident cadenzas in the trees, and the little lake became a tepid mirror at midday, its still surface marred only by the restless foraging of big dragonflies.

My mother was sleeping in the bedroom upstairs, with the window blinds drawn. Our family had rented the cottage for the entire month, and my father planned to complete a textbook he was writing, but fishing held a place in his schedule. The staccato rhythms of his typewriter on the screened porch began after breakfast, and continued after lunch when the work was coming well, and I dozed fitfully in the summer grass, thinking about the ice cream the farmer's wife made across the lake.

One morning when we went for eggs and milk, I watched the farmer's wife working with her tubs and cracked ice and salt in the springhouse. While she stopped to wipe her face, she let me wrestle with the crank of the ice-cream maker.

It was a summer of sweet corn and ripe watermelon and cherries, mixed with fishing for bluegills and yellow perch and bass. My memories are filled with peace and plenty. But it was also a summer of poverty and poor crops and fear, when wheat farmers were driven from family homesteads in the high plains country, and the terrible dust storms soon followed.

During those tragic years, my father and other college teachers were still employed, although their paychecks were thin. There were times when my father was the only man with work in our neighborhood. Small businesses and major corporations and banks were failing too, and factories and mills stood empty in heartbreak and silence. Many families in southern Michigan had lost their orchards and house mortgages and farms, but that boyhood summer beside a small lily-pad lake was strangely filled with riches.

Perhaps the simple rhythms of life sustained us through those Great Depression years, and bass fishing became part of our family rituals that summer.

My father usually awakened just before daylight, in the clamor of his big alarm clock. I could hear him wind it each night, through the thin walls of the cottage. My mother still lay sleeping under the quilts, and I could hear the bedsprings squeak as he reached for the alarm, and dressed in the darkness before descending the narrow backstairs to the kitchen. Cooking smells of scrambled eggs and tiny crumb-batter perch and sausages drifted up through the cottage, and in spite of his efforts to let us sleep, there was always the grating scrape of the skillet on the wood-burning stove, mixed with a muffled clatter of cups and tableware and plates. The rich aroma of coffee lingered long after he was gone.

Late August nights in Michigan are often cool.

Sometimes the tiny lake was shrouded in fog, and I heard him collect the wooden oars and tackle from the porch, before he disappeared into the mist. There was something of alchemy in such liturgies. It was delicious to lie there, partially awake under the patchwork quilting, listening to the familiar sounds of his morning rituals. Planking creaked as he reached the dock, the lures in his tackle box rattled as he placed it in the boat, and its padlock chain rattled as he stripped it through the eyebolt on the bowpiece. Oarlock rhythms marked his slow passage into open water.

His fishing was a mystery that I was still too small to share fully, but he sometimes took me out on short odysseys to explore its secrets, and on such mornings I waited restlessly through breakfast, wracked with delicious shivers of anticipation.

We caught nothing much, as I remember now, but I still savor the flashing handles of his bait casting reel, surrendering line as a lure arched out toward sheltering pockets in the lilies and pickerel weed and elodea. Once there was a wild splash that engulfed his red-and-white plug, but the bass was not hooked, and when the summer ended, it had been our only strike together. It was usually getting hot when we rowed back across the lake, and I sat happily in the boat, trailing my fingers in the cool water.

His textbook manuscript occupied the late mornings, as well as the hours after lunch, and the metallic rattle of his typewriter echoed across the lake. The work progressed well that summer, except for a brief disaster on the screen porch, when a sudden squall scattered his onionskin pages and carbons across the wet floorboards. Late in the afternoons, his interest in history began to wane, and as such academic preoccupations began to ebb, we often heard him start to sort through his fishing tackle.

It was time to clean and lubricate the prized Pflueger reel, and its components lay collected in a saucer on the oilcloth table. Weedless spoons and tiny spinner blades and wobble plates were carefully polished. Hooks on his red-and-white striped spoons were sharpened. Pork frogs and fresh pork-rind strips were cut with his fishing knife on a cheeseboard, much to my mother's dismay, and stored in a pickle jar of briny water to keep them moist.

Supper was always early because of his fishing.

When the shadows of the red maples and oaks and elms began to lengthen across the boat-pier shallows, it was time to return to the lake. My father gathered his equipment and loaded the boat, stroked out through the lily-pad channel, and began to cast toward the weedy shoreline. He always worked clockwise around its periphery, finishing his twilight rituals just after dark. His fishing was a mixture of patient rites, and he seldom returned before nightfall.

I was never permitted to participate in these twilight expeditions, because my mother feared that I might fall overboard in the dark, with less likelihood of rescue. Sometimes it was completely dark when we finally heard his oar strokes, and I usually ran to meet him at the dock, waiting eagerly in the gloom while he fussed with the padlock and chain. Nocturnal returns usually signaled fish. It was always exciting when he reached down to lift a dripping stringer from the black water. There were usually two or three bass, and once we returned in triumph along the path to the cottage, while I proudly held the flashlight on a six-pound largemouth.

It remains a special summer in my mind, rich with memories of learning to dog paddle and fish for pumpkinseeds and perch, and sleeping on the porch, with crickets and katydids and whippoorwills working their magic in the darkness. Their nocturnal chorus seemed as exotic as jungle twilights in the headwaters of the Limpopo or Orinoco. It was a bucolic summer when my parents were both still young, and very much in love, and all the world seemed green. Mixed with such potsherds of memory is a brief encounter that took place during a weekly grocery trip into Baldwin.

Our route into town crossed a pretty trout stream, and my mother stopped the Oldsmobile just beyond the bridge—after a solitary fisherman had caught my eye.

The little river flowed swiftly, tumbling past the timber pilings of the bridge, and there were mayflies dancing in the morning sun. The riffling currents seemed alive over a pea-gravel bottom, where fallen cedar sweepers and deadfalls intercepted their flow, and the river danced and glittered over its bright cobble. The counterpoint of its music filled the moment, its lyric passages as sharply focused as memories of yesterday, after more than sixty years.

The trout stream was utterly unlike the lukewarm shallows of the lake, tumbling crystalline and cold from the springheads in its cedar swamp headwaters. Watercress thrived in the seepage places below the trusswork bridge, where the passage of the river was exposed briefly to the sun. The rest was hidden in its serpentine corridor of trees. Such ephemeral moments of illumination were quickly changing, in a collage of leafy sunlight and shadow. Such patterns seemed to brim with unspoken mysteries and life, collecting its kaleidoscope of foliage and sunlight in swiftly changing prisms, until their music seemed to sing of half-understood secrets.

The most pervasive memory of that summer remains the solitary trout fisherman working patiently upstream, with the swift shallows tumbling between his legs, while his silk fly line worked its amber magic in the brightness of an August morning.

It was the genesis of a lifelong odyssey in search of trout and salmon, a pilgrimage that began in Michigan, and has since carried me to the far-flung corners of the world. There are many happy echoes of those travels, memories embracing rivers and river people, and the richly colored fish themselves. And with a cold rain misting through the skeletal black-trunked trees behind the house, such thoughts of fishing, and the butter-colored coltsfoot in the sheltered places, help to pass this wintry season of discontent.

CHAPTER NINE

A President's Bass Fishing

by Grover Cleveland

President Grover Cleveland (1837–1908) was an avid sportsman, as he showed in his book Fishing and Shooting Sketches *(1903). He was the 22nd and 24th president, the only president to serve two nonconsecutive terms. His bass-fishing experiences led to this fine tribute, written long before bass fishing became the popular pursuit it is today.*

IN SPEAKING OF BLACK BASS I AM NOT DEALING WITH THE large-mouthed variety that are found in both Northern and Southern waters, and which grow in the latter to a very large size, but only with the small-mouthed family inhabiting the streams or lakes and ponds of the North, and which are large when they reach four pounds in weight. I consider these, when found in natural and favorable surroundings, more uncertain, whimsical and wary in biting, and more strong, resolute and resourceful when hooked, than any other fish ordinarily caught in fresh waters. They will in some localities and at certain seasons rise to a fly; but this cannot be relied upon. They can sometimes also be taken by trolling; but this is very often not successful, and is at best a second-class style of fishing. On the whole it is best and most satisfactory to attempt their capture by still fishing with bait.

To those with experience this will not suggest angling of a tame and unruffled sort; and if those without experience have such an estimate of it they are most decidedly reckoning without their host. As teachers of patience in fishing, black bass are at the head of the list. They are so whimsical that the angler never knows whether on a certain day they will take small live fish, worms, frogs, crickets, grasshoppers, crawfish or some other outlandish bait; and he soon learns that in the most favorable conditions of wind and weather they will frequently refuse to touch bait of any kind. In their intercourse with fishermen, especially those in the early stages of proficiency, they are the most aggravating and profanity-provoking animal that swims in fresh water. Whether they will bite or not at any particular time we must freely concede is exclusively their own affair; but having decided this question against the fishermen, nothing but inherent and tantalizing meanness can account for the manner in which a black bass will even then rush for the bait, and after actually mouthing it will turn about and insultingly whack it with his tail. An angler who has seen this performance finds, in his desire to make things even with such unmannerly wretches, a motive in addition to all others for a relentless pursuit of the bass family.

Another and more encouraging stage in bass fishing is reached when biting seems to be the order of the day. It must not be supposed, however, that thereupon the angler's troubles and perplexities are over, or that nothing stands in the way of an easy and satisfying catch. Experience in this kind of fishing never fails to teach that it is one thing to induce these cunning fellows to take the bait, and quite another to accomplish their capture. It is absolutely necessary in this stage of the proceedings that the deliberation and gingerly touch of the fish be matched by the deliberation and care on the part of the fisherman at the butt of the rod; and the strike on his part must not be too much hastened, lest he fail to lodge his hook in a good holding place. Even if he succeeds in well hooking his fish he cannot confidently expect a certain capture. In point of fact the tension and anxiety of the work in hand begins at that very instant.

Ordinarily when a bass is struck with the hook, if he is in surroundings favorable to his activity, he at once enters upon a series of acrobatic performances which, during their continuance, keep the fisherman in a state of acute suspense. While he rushes away from and toward and around and under the boat, and while he is leaping from the water and turning somersaults with ugly shakes of his head, in efforts to dislodge the hook, there is at the other end of the outfit a fisherman, tortured by the fear of infirmity lurking somewhere in his tackle, and wrought to the point of distress by the thought of a light hook hold in the fish's jaw, and its liability to tear out in the struggle. If in the midst of it all a sudden release of pull and a straightening of his rod give the signal that the bass has won the battle, the vanquished angler has, after a short period of bad behavior and language, the questionable satisfaction of attempting to solve a forever unsolvable problem, by studying how his defeat might have been avoided if he had managed differently.

No such perplexing question, however, is presented to the bass fisherman who lands his fish. He complacently regards his triumph as the natural and expected result of steadiness and skill, and excludes from his thoughts all shadow of doubt concerning the complete correctness of his procedure in every detail.

My expressed design to place fishing for black bass with bait in competition with fly-casting for trout will, I hope, be considered a justification for the details I have given of bass fishing. It commends itself in every feature to the sporting instincts of all genuine anglers; and it is because I do not hope to altogether correct the "Affectations and Pretenses of Fishing" that I have felt constrained to rally those who should love angling for bass—to the end that at least a good-natured division may be established within our fraternity between an ornamental and pretense-breeding method and one which cultivates skill, stimulates the best fishing traits, and remains untouched by any form of affectation.

CHAPTER TEN

The Finest Trout in the River

by Harry Plunket Greene

In many ways similar to John Waller Hills's A Summer on the Test, *Harry Plunket Greene's* Where the Bright Waters Meet *is an engaging chronicle of fishing English chalkstreams in the years 1902–12.*

Greene was a classic opera singer who loved flyfishing with a passion. As we mentioned in the introduction to this book, his favorite water was the enchanting little Bourne, and he wrote about his experiences there with a keen eye and great feeling. Greene's title is from a lovely poem by Tom Moore:

There is not in this wide world a valley so sweet
As that vale in whose bosom the bright waters meet.

Where the Bright Waters Meet *was first published in 1924, revised and enlarged in 1936, and was published in the United States by Nick Lyons Books / Winchester Press.*

IT MIGHT NATURALLY BE SUPPOSED THAT IF ONE HAD THE FISHING OF a trout-stream like the Bourne one would not leave an inch of it unexplored, but it was a fact that up to this time none of the rods had ever taken the trouble to investigate the top quarter-mile of the water. Savage and Sharkey had somehow got it into their heads that there was nothing worth troubling about above the "lagoon" immediately beyond the viaduct, and as they lived close to the top of the fishing, all the rest of us, myself included, had tacitly accepted this as a matter of fact. Nowadays the whole of this region is a vast watercress bed, and anyone looking out of the window of the train, when passing over the viaduct, would never realise that there was, or ever had been, a river there at all; but in those days there were two streams above, as well as below, the bridge, meeting a little way up and stretching as one, for a quarter of a mile to the end of the fishing.

We had all of us come on occasions as far as the hatch below this final stretch, but, in the belief that the water above was a blank, had always turned back when we got there.

On August 31st of this year, the last day of the season, I found myself at this hatch at about six o'clock in the evening. I had got four fish averaging 1¼ lbs., but it had been a bad rising day, cold and windy. At six o'clock it suddenly turned warm and calm, and I was sitting on the hatch smoking a pipe before going home, when I thought that, just for fun, I would walk up to the end of the water. I expected nothing, and had half a mind to leave my rod behind and saunter up with my hands in my pockets. I got over the fence and strolled up on to the bank unconcernedly, and, as I did so, from one weed-patch after another there darted off a series of two-pounders racing upstream like motor-boats. I dropped like a stone, but the damage was done. I just sat there cursing the day I was born and myself, not only for having lost the chance of a lifetime—for the iron-blues were beginning to come down thick—but for having left this gold-mine undiscovered and untouched for two years—and to-day was the last day of the season! If there had been any handy way discovered of kicking oneself physically as well as mentally I should have been unrecognisable when I got home. Every fish was under the weeds long ago, and I might just as well pack up my traps and clear out.

There was an old broken-down footbridge about a hundred yards above me, and I thought that I would go up to it and explore the reach beyond, more with a view to the possibilities of next year than with any hope for the present. I got down from the bank and circled round through the meadow till I got to it, and was just picking my way across its rotten planks when under my very feet I saw a small nose appear, followed by a diminutive head and the most enormous shoulder I ever remember to have seen in a chalk stream. I froze stiff where I stood, except that my knees were shaking like aspens, for there right underneath me was gradually emerging the fish of my life. I do not mean to say that I have not caught bigger fish before and since, but this was a veritable star in the dust-heap, a Cinderella stealing out of the kitchen that we had all despised, and the romance of the thing put him (pace Cinderella) on a pedestal of fame from which I have never taken him down.

It was agonising work, for he swam up in the most leisurely way at a rate of about an inch in every five seconds, while I was straddled across two rotten planks, either of which might have given way at any moment, and had to pretend that I was part of the landscape. He was immediately under me when he first showed up and I could easily have touched him with my foot. What fish will see and what they will not see will ever remain a mystery! It was then about half-past six (old time), the time of day when one's visibility is most clear, and yet he took not the smallest notice of me. He just strolled up the middle of the stream contentedly as though he were having a smoke after dinner. I can still feel my joints creaking as I sank slowly to my knees and got my line out. It fell just right and he took no more notice of it than of a water-rat, I tried again and again, lengthening the cast as he moved up, and at last he rose towards it, examined it carefully and, horror of horrors!, swam slowly after it down-stream through the bridge under my feet! It would have been laughable if it had not been so tragic. There was I pulling in the slack like a madman, and leaving it in wisps round my knees, scared lest he should see my hand move; and he passed me by without a word and disappeared into the bowels of the bridge.

I just knelt there and swore, trying to look over my shoulder to see if he had gone down below. There was no sign of him, and the situation was painful in the extreme, for my knees were working through the rotten woodwork, and if I tried to ease myself I should either bring the bridge down with a crash or anyway evict Cinderellum for good and all.

I bore it as long as I could, and was just going to give it up and scram-ble out anyhow, when I saw that nose slide out again beneath me, and my old friend started off on his journey up-stream once more.

I began on him with a shorter line this time, and he took the fly at the very first cast like a lamb. If he was a lamb as he took it he was a lion when he had it. Instead of running up-stream, as I hoped and expected he would do, he gave one swish with his tail and bolted down through the bridge, bending the rod double and dragging the point right under. It was done with such lightning speed I had no time to remonstrate. I threw myself flat on my stomach and got the rod sideways over the bridge, and then the fight began. I was on one side of the bridge, and he was half-way to Southampton on the other. He got farther and farther downstream, going from one patch of weeds to the next, and digging and burrowing his nose into the middle of it, while I just hung on, helpless, waiting for the end. He quieted down after a bit, and finding that he could not rub the annoying thing out of his nose on the south side he determined to explore the north, and he began to swim up towards me. I must have been a ridiculous sight, spread-eagled on the rotting planks with splinters digging into my legs and ants and spiders crawling down my neck, vainly endeavouring to hold the rod over the side with one hand, to wind in the line with the other, and to watch him over my shoulder all at the same time. Fortunately, I must have been invisible from below, but the moment he got under the bridge he saw the rod and tore past me up-stream with the reel screaming. But now we were on even terms and there was a clear stretch of water ahead, and I was able to play him to a finish. I was really proud of that fight, for, in addition to the cramped style which I was compelled to adopt, it took place in a stream ten feet wide, half-choked with weeds, and I got him on a 000 Iron-blue at the end of a 4x point. He weighed 3¾ lbs. when I got him home, and I have always bitterly regretted that I did not get him set up, for, with the exception of an 11¾-pounder in the hall of Longford Castle, caught in the Avon by one of the family on a "local lure" (the name of which neither fork nor spade would dig from me), he was the most beautiful river-trout in shape, colour and proportion I ever saw.

CHAPTER ELEVEN

The Evening Rise

by John Waller Hills

By sheer number of hours of enjoyment, reading and rereading John Waller Hills's classic A Summer on the Test *ranks as my number one choice of English chalkstream literature. As I said in introducing* A Summer on the Test *in another anthology, one reason I enjoy reading the book so much is probably because Hills does not write in an instructional vein, but rather creates a straightforward description of the fishing under varying conditions. When Hills takes to the stream, our spirits fall and rise as his own. The pageant of the seasons, the off-again, on-again nature of the hatches, scroll through* A Summer on the Test *like enchanting but mysterious dramas in which we view our leading player, Mr. Hills, with empathy and hope.*

A Summer on the Test *was first published in a limited edition in 1924 and reprinted in a popular edition with new chapters in 1930. The book was republished by Nick Lyons in 1983.*

In this chapter, John Waller Hills duels with the largest trout he has ever encountered while fishing a dry fly.

SOME TIME AFTER MID-MAY THE EVENING RISE STARTS, AND LASTS till the end of the season. There is a great difference between different rivers. On the Test and Itchen you do not get it before May is well on its way, and the same on the Hertford and Dorset streams: on Driffield Beck not till June. On the Kennet, on the other hand, you get it from earliest times. I have known it in April, and on cold nights, too. But it is nowhere in full swing until June, and one part of it, the sedge rise, till July. It is an unsatisfactory thing, this evening rise. You get fish, certainly, but you seldom get as many as you feel you ought. And the mind is weighted with an unpleasant apprehension of finality. Daylight has a definite end which nothing can prolong. A morning rise, starting at eleven, may last an hour or it may last five. It has the charm of uncertainty and of hope. But an evening rise has a fixed limit. There is no scope for imagination or fortune, and the pleasures of fishing are mental. The trout, too, during an evening rise are always difficult and often exasperating.

But before discussing that, it is necessary to analyse the rise in rather more detail. When the hay has been cut, and wet places are golden with mimulus, and the pomp of high summer is reigning, there are three evening rises. The first begins some time between six and seven (ordinary, not summer time) and lasts till shortly before sunset. This I call the casual rise. The second starts after the last edge of the sun has sunk below the actual horizon and ends when it is too dark to see a small artificial on the water. This is the small fly rise. The third rise then opens and runs for something under half an hour, rarely longer. This is the sedge rise. The casual rise may begin any time after six. Trout move languidly, often taking spinners, but sometimes indecipherable insects. They are difficult, because at no time in the twenty-four hours are they so readily put down. A cast which would pass muster in the stillest noon sends them off like a shot. I suppose this is due to the slanting light. And it is not easy to see what they are taking. Altogether they are a high test of skill. But they can be caught. Try them with the prevailing spinner, or a fancy fly such as the pheasant tail. A blue upright sometimes kills.

The small fly rise has a very different appearance indeed. If it be a good one, trout rise not languidly but eagerly, sometimes madly. And it starts with all the unexpected suddenness of the morning rises of early May. I recollect particularly the 25th July 1918. I was strolling up the bank on a quiet, warm evening. A stile had to be crossed, and I remember stopping a minute or so before crossing it and watching the aquamarine sky and its reflection in the opal water. The stile lay a little back, behind a bushy willow, which shut out the water. Before crossing, not a ring was to be seen: when I had crossed, and cleared the willow, the surface was boiling. The movement had started as though on the stroke of a clock. And often this sudden beginning will come immediately after the last rim of the sun has disappeared.

During the casual rise fish are usually taking spinners, if spinners there be. On warm, still evenings, when the female fly can get back to the river to lay her eggs, there will be spinners. But if it be cold, and particularly if it be windy, the females are driven away, and none of them fall as spinners. Smuts, too, are often on the water at this time, or you may have a hatch of small sedges. If so you will find that trout take the artificial very well. During the small fly rise, trout may want either duns or spinners, or occasionally nymphs. It is often very difficult to see whether they are rising or bulging; or, if they are rising, what they are rising at. During the casual rise, too, the fish, though picksome and hard to please, are not particular about pattern: but during the small fly rise they settle down to one article and refuse everything else. Your fly must be exactly right, or you get nothing till dark. During the casual rise fish are often unapproachable; during the small fly rise they are easy to approach and hard to put down, but hard to catch. You no longer need crawl or kneel, you can stand up. As the dusk deepens, you can get nearer and nearer. Your hook can be a size or two bigger, your gut thicker: though, if you take my advice, you will never, even for mayfly or sedge, use stronger than finest natural, for on that you can kill the biggest trout that swims. But in spite of the advantage of ease of access, larger flies and heavier gut, trout are harder to get: harder than they are in the heat of noon, with 4x points and 000 hooks. They are hard because they take only one kind of food and because they demand a higher standard of imitation. You must copy what they are eating and you must copy it in a way they like.

As I look back over many evening rises, I get the impression of more failures than successes. Not absolute failures, perhaps, but relative; one brings away the sense of not having done as well as one ought. Fish rise so confidently and so often: there are so many: you do not put them down, for they go on rising: but though they are taking winged fly, you they will not take. Rivers differ greatly in the ease with which fish are caught in the evening, and so do different parts of the same river. The Test is easier than the Itchen, and the Kennet a good deal harder than either. But the Test can be difficult enough.

Even if you see what the trout are gulping down, your troubles are not over. A typical summer evening fly is the blue winged olive, and the best artificial is the orange quill. By the bye, never be afraid of a large orange quill, up to No. 1. But sometimes they will not look at the orange quill or at the coot-winged imitation, or at any olive or red or ginger quill that man's wit devised. Then you have an extremely difficult choice to make: are you to go on trying fly after fly, losing precious time in changing, and rattling your nerves, too, or are you to stick to what you think the best pattern? That is to say, are you to change your fly or change your fish?

Before answering that, let me ask you if you are sure that you know what trout are taking. Blue winged olives are floating down, certainly, and fish are breaking the water: but are they feeding on the nymph or the winged fly or the spinner? It is wonderful how hard it is to tell this, in the lessening light. Anyhow, if the winged fly is refused, do not hesitate. Try the hackle blue-wing first, then the sherry spinner, and then the nymph sunk. The pattern of a nymph is given in a later chapter. However, since fishing books should be definite or nothing, I will tell you exactly how I do behave, not how I should. I try first an orange or red quill, according to river, then a hackle blue-wing unoiled and awash, and then probably a sherry spinner. After that, I should think it useless to go on changing, and certainly at some time or other I should go back to the fly I thought best. Whether my final choice were an orange or red quill would depend on the river: at Driffield a red, on the Test, Itchen or Kennet an orange. In streams where you do not get much blue winged olive, such as those of Dorsetshire or Derbyshire, my final selection, if all else failed, would be a ginger quill. I kill more fish nowadays on the ginger than on the red quill, whatever may have been the case twenty years ago.

Hitherto, I have been talking of nights when the blue winged olive alone comes down: but they are rare, for you usually find a mixed mass of pale watery and medium olive as well, and also their spinners, and perhaps that of the iron blue. You can tell if the trout are taking pale watery, for their rise to it is very different from the boil that they make at the blue winged olive, and you can act accordingly. Again, you can sometimes tell when they are taking spinners, but in the dusk you cannot tell which. So you must try the sherry, yellow boy, houghton ruby and Lunn's particular, all of them. But often you are beaten, and then, as I say, at some time of the night, if nothing will induce them to rise, go back to one fly and stick to it. Carry an electric torch, and then you can change your pattern easily on the darkest night.

But here I must interpolate. On some evenings, and indeed some seasons, you get an early hatch of small sedges, and after them come the blue winged olive and sherry spinner. The ordinary procession is reversed. Thus on the 14th and 15th July 1928 there was a hatch of small sedge early and a fall of sherry spinner after dark. On each night I killed on a sedge at about eight o'clock and then on a sherry spinner and 3x gut after eleven o'clock had struck.

But now for the sedge proper. When it gets too dark to see a No. 0 fly on the water, you can try a good sized sedge. It is little use before this, and little use after complete darkness. Do not change to sedge too soon, and if your orange quill is killing well, stick to it. The time during which a sedge is taken rarely exceeds half an hour and is usually only a quarter. Of all fishing the sedge rise is the most uncertain. Not only may you have bad days, but bad years. I am not sure, too, whether success is caused by the presence of sedges themselves. Sometimes they are swarming in the reeds like bees and you cannot get a rise, while at others you may kill fish when there is not a natural fly to be seen: but you do not usually do much with the artificial until the time has come for the natural to hatch out, and it does not hatch in full force until July. A warm, windless night is almost essential. The easiest fish to catch is one lying close under the other bank, provided of course that it is within your reach. Get straight opposite him, and cast two feet above him. Be quite sure that you are reaching him; the tendency in the dusk is to cast short, particularly when you are throwing into the liquid reflection of the reeds. If he does not take, try this: when your fly is about to come over his nose, pull six or eight inches of line sharply through the rings with your spare hand: this has the effect of causing the fly to scutter over the water, and often makes the trout come at you with a glorious smashing rise like a sea trout. Pattern is not important, though size is. In the early part of the season do not go beyond No. 2: in July and August you can get up to No. 4 or 5. Always fish the sedge dry. I myself do not carry more than four patterns: small dark sedge, coachman, large hare's ear sedge, and cinnamon sedge. Of late I have unconsciously dropped the silver sedge, which I used to use greatly: I killed on it the biggest trout I ever got on the dry fly, as will be told later.

Sedge fishing is not scientific, though a good man will always beat a bad one. But fish are often simple-minded, and anyone can catch them, those great cunning creatures which defied the most skilful in daylight. You catch trout by throwing across, or across and down, and either pulling the fly intentionally, or letting the stream cause it to drag. This, though it looks like clumsy fishing, actually reproduces most accurately the path of the natural sedge. But curiously enough it only answers at night, for never have I known shy fish to take a dragging sedge by day. Some fishers despise the sedge: others regard it as the best part of a summer day. I express no opinion one way or another, but only mention three qualities which the sedge rise possesses. First, you may get hold of heavy fish quickly one after another, which is great fun. Second, you can redeem a bad day, and get even with those contemptuous, supercilious trout who have defeated you. Third, you have a chance of getting a real monster. On still summer nights, when not a leaf stirs, and in the pearly shadows you cannot see where the reeds end and their reflection begins, when the ghost moth is rising and falling over the damp meadow, and if you are lucky you may catch a glimpse of the graceful pink elephant hawk moth flying at the yellow iris flowers: when the great red sedge is flopping about in his feeble and aimless flight, and clouds of smaller sedges are flickering tirelessly up and down over the unbroken surface, perchance some dim memory begins to stir in the slow mind of the old trout. All the season through he has fed at the bottom, grubbing on shrimps and caddis and water-snails and minnows and even on his own relatives. But he recalls seasons such as this, far back in former years, when all was quiet and warm and peaceful, when the fat sedges would tumble clumsily on to the water, and in their efforts to escape would make a ripple and commotion spreading far over the placid pool, and he remembers how fresh and fair they were to eat. Then he forsakes his lair under the arched willow roots and rises to the top and takes up his old station in the shadow of the tussock, where he used to lie long ago in his active middle age, when he weighed a bare two pounds. Aye, he weighs more than twice two pounds now, perhaps three times or more, he is the prize of a lifetime—and perhaps as your sedge comes over him you will see a break like that of a big raindrop, a little circle like the palm of a man's hand, and when you strike you will think you have hooked the trunk of a tree. That possibility always gives an excitement to sedge fishing. You are on the edge of the mysterious and the unknown, and you feel as you do when fishing a salmon river in which forty pounders are not an impossibility.

For sedge fishing you must have a warm, still evening, and this is best for the small fly rise, too: but do not be driven home either by mist or cold or rain or wind. If it is cold and wet, spinners will not get on the water, what I call the casual rise will be blank, and you will do nothing till the winged fly hatches; but there is often a good show of this on inclement, tempestuous nights. Do you recollect that typical summer evening, 14th June 1907? It was shiveringly cold, there was a wild wind and pelting showers. When I reached Winchester by the evening train, the weather looked so bad that I only went out because I was too restless to stay in: and yet I got a brace before being driven in to the fireside. Or the 13th June 1922, on the Kennet, a vile day which got viler, until the rain hammered down and the bitter wind blew in your teeth? Yet blue winged olives hatched from eight to half-past nine and I landed ten takeable fish, of which I kept two brace. Or again, that other day in the same year, cold and wild and wet, 15th July 1922? There was a mighty hatch of the same fly just before dark, and I got six fish weighing nine pounds. Or the 23rd May 1924, wintry and wet, with half a gale? There was a splendid evening rise at Mottisfont right up to half-past nine. And perhaps the worst night I ever was out was 9th June 1928, at Stockbridge. So cold and wet was it, that two or three of us sat before the fire in the keeper's house debating whether we should go out. Yet there was a good hatch and we all got fish. I landed one of 3 lb. 7 oz. and broke in another which assuredly was bigger, on the sedge, too. No, never let weather keep you indoors, even on English summer nights. However, warm clear nights are of course the best. Black thunder clouds are very bad, in fact light is of great importance, and fish are often shyer on a cloudy than on a cloudless night. Fog is generally bad, but sometimes, if it is light and silvery, fly will hatch and trout will swallow them.

Many a bad day has the sedge redeemed. My most notable recollections of it, however, relate, not to the Test, but to the Kennet, which is the greatest of all sedge rivers. On 28th June 1914 a friend and I were fishing there. It was clear, summer weather, fair and hot, with an indeterminate breeze varying from south to west. Working hard till dark I got four fish of no great size, none of them on the sedge. Some time between nine and ten at night I reeled up and went in search of my friend. He had caught nothing till the last quarter of an hour; however, in that short space he had beaten my whole day's efforts, for he had taken four fish which weighed a great deal more than mine, all on the coachman. That is no unusual incident. On 26th July in the same year I toiled all day till tea-time for two fish which were only just over the pound limit, and at the small fly I failed to rise fish after fish: but in ten minutes with the coachman I rose all the six fish I tried for and got two brace. Again on 2nd August 1914, the last day's fishing before the war, I laboured unceasingly against a gusty wind for three fish, and once more made an utter mess of a hatch of blue winged olives; whilst in the magic fifteen minutes during which trout take the sedge I landed four out of the six I found rising, and kept three which weighed only a fraction under six pounds. That year, 1914, was a good sedge year, and such years are scarce and should not be missed.

A moon behind your arm, especially a full moon, makes fish nearly impossible to approach. They are put down far more easily than by the brightest sun. You may be rising trout regularly, when suddenly the first cast stops them, because the unnoticed moon has risen. It is an immense advantage to be ambidextrous, and fish underhand with the inshore hand.

Those who fish rivers where mayfly come will agree that, though with it you get a higher average weight, yet actually the biggest fish are killed on the sedge. 1903 on the Kennet was a great mayfly season for heavy fish, and a friend of mine who had the Ramsbury water got the truly remarkable bag of six fish in one day which weighed over nineteen pounds: and yet the two heaviest fish of the year were got on the sedge.

I got the heaviest. It was the 26th July 1903, a cloudy, gusty day, with a downstream wind, and I was on the water from eleven till five without seeing a rise. My friend and I then had tea and walked up the river at a quarter-past six. Olives began to appear and trout to move; and suddenly a really large one started rising. We stood and watched, with growing excitement. He was taking every fly, in solid and determined fashion, and the oftener he appeared the bigger he looked, and the faster beat our hearts. It was settled that I was to try for him. I was nervous and uncomfortable. He was very big: it was a long throw and the wind horrible: I could not reach him, and like a fool I got rattled and pulled off too much line: there was an agonised groan from my friend behind me when a great curl of it was slapped on the water exactly over the trout's nose. We looked at each other without speaking, and he silently walked away up the river, leaving me staring stupidly at the spot where the trout had been rising. Of course he was gone.

The next two hours can be passed over. The small fly rise came and went. I caught a trout on a No. 2 silver sedge and finally, at about a quarter-past eight, found myself gazing gloomily at the place where I had bungled. The wild wind had blown itself out and had swept the sky bare of cloud.

Silence had come, and stillness. The willows, which all through the long summer day had bowed and chattered in the wind, were straightened and motionless, each individual leaf hanging down as though carved in jade: the forest of great sedges, which the gusts had swept into wave after wave of a roaring sea of emerald, was now calm and level, each stalk standing straight and stiff as on a Japanese screen. There had occurred that transition, that transmutation from noise and movement to silence and peace, which would be more wonderful were we not so accustomed to it, when a windy summer day turns over to a moveless summer night: when the swing and clatter and rush of the day is arrested and lifted from the world, and you get the sense that the great hollow of the air is filled with stillness and quiet, as with a tangible presence. They are peaceful things, these summer evenings after wild days, and I remember particularly that this was one of the most peaceful; more so indeed than my thoughts, which were still in a turmoil. I stood watching mechanically, and then, tempting fate to help me, made a cast or two over the spot where the fish had been. How easy it was to reach it now, how lightly my fly settled on the water, how gracefully it swung over the place. All to no purpose, of course, for nothing happened, and I was about to reel up when a fish rose ten yards above, close under my bank. It was one of those small movements, difficult to place. It might be a very large fish or a very small one. A wild thought swept through me that this was my big one: but no, I said to myself, it cannot be. This is not where he was rising. Besides, things do not happen like that, except in books: it is only in books that you make a fearful bungle and go back later and see a small break which you think is a dace, and cast carelessly and hook something the size of an autumn salmon: it is only in books that fate works in such fashion. Why, I know it all so well that I could write it out by heart, every move of it. But this is myself by a river, not reading in a chair. This is the real world, where such things do not happen: that is the rise of a half pound trout.

I cast. I was looking right into the west, and the water was coloured like skim milk by reflection from where the sun had set. My silver sedge was as visible as by day. It floated down, there was a rise, I struck, and something rushed up stream. Then I knew.

Above me was open water for some twenty-five yards, and above that again a solid block of weed, stretching right across. My fish made for this, by short, irresistible runs. To let him get into it would have been folly: he must be stopped: either he is well hooked or lightly, the gut is either sound or rotten: kill or cure, he must be turned, if turned he can be: so I pulled hard, and fortunately got his head round and led him down. He played deep and heavy and I had to handle him roughly, but I brought him down without a smash, and I began to breathe again. But then another terror appeared. At the place we had reached the only clear water was a channel under my bank, and the rest of the river was choked with weed. Should I try to pull him down this channel, about three or four yards wide, to the open water below? No. It was much too dangerous, for the fish was uncontrollable, and if he really wanted to get to weed he would either get there or break me: even with a beaten fish it would be extremely risky, and with an unbeaten one it was unthinkable.

Well, if he would not come down he must go up, and up he went willingly enough, for when I released pressure he made a long rush up to the higher weed bed, whilst I ran up the meadow after him, and with even greater difficulty turned him once more. This time I thought he was really going right through it, so fast and so heavy was his pull, and I think he was making for a hatch hole above: but once more my gallant gut stood the strain and, resisting vigorously, he was led down. This proceeding was repeated either two or three times more, I forget which: either three or four times we fought up and down that twenty-five yards of water. By then he was tiring, and I took up my station in the middle of the stretch, where I hoped to bring him in: my hand was actually on the sling of the net when he suddenly awoke and rushed up. He reached the weed bed at a pace at which he was impossible to stop, shot into it like a torpedo, and I had the sickening certainty that I should lose him after all. To hold him hard now would be to make a smash certain, so I slacked off: when he stopped I tightened again, expecting miserably to feel the dead, lifeless drag of a weeded line. Instead, to my delight, I found I was still in contact with the fish, and he was pulling hard. How he had carried the line through the weeds I do not know. To look at it seemed impossible: and if he had reached them earlier in the fight, when he played deep in the river, before he tired and the pressure brought him near the top, I should have been jammed hopelessly. But the line was clear, and the fish proved it by careering wildly on towards the hatch, making the reel sing. I believe he meant to go through into the carrier, as fish have done before and after, but I turned him. However, we could not stay where we were. The hatch was open at the bottom, there was a strong draw of water through it, and if a heavy, beaten fish got into this, no gut could hold him up. At all risks he must be taken back over the weed into the clear water. I pulled him up to the top and ran him down. Then, for the first time, after so many perils, came the conviction that I should land him. He was obviously big, but how big could not be known, for I had not had a clear sight of him yet. He still pulled with that immovable, quivering solidity only shown by a very heavy fish. But at last even his great strength tired. He gave a wobble or two, yielded, and suddenly he was splashing on the top, looking huge in the dusk. There ensued that agonising time when you have a big fish nearly beat, but he is too heavy to pull in, and nothing you can do gets him up to the net. At last I pulled him over it, but I lifted too soon, the ring caught him in the middle of the body, he wavered a moment in the air and then toppled back into the water with a sickening splash. A judgment, I thought, and for a shattering second I believed he had broken the gut, but he was still on. I was pretty well rattled by then and, in the half light, made two more bad shots, but the end came at last, he was in the net and on the bank.

How big was he? Three pounds? Yes, and more. Four pounds? Yes, and more. Five? He might be, he might. My knees shook and my fingers trembled as I got him on the hook of the steelyard. He weighed a fraction over 4 lb. 8 oz. I walked up to find my friend and asked him to weigh him, too. He made him a fraction under 4 lb. 9 oz. And that is my biggest fish on the floating fly.

CHAPTER TWELVE

The 'Lunge

by Stewart Edward White

In this excerpt from his book The Forest, *Stewart Edward White (1873–1946) shows us the prose skills that produced thirty-nine books, fiction and nonfiction, on outdoor adventures and travel. He was both prolific and popular during his time, turning many of his real episodes of outdoor life into nonfiction accounts of what actually happened. Here he focuses on musky fishing, the famous muskellunge so coveted by North Country anglers.*

For openers, a legal musky today (in Minnesota) must be 40 inches or over. For a wall fish, or a photo to impress your friends, we're talking 55 inches. For a world-record contender, start by revving up to two 60.25-inchers caught by Louis Sprey and Cal Johnson in 1949. Writer John Gierach says the musky caught by Cal Johnson in the 1940s and now residing in the Moccasin Bar in Hayward, Minnesota, looks as big as a canoe. Gierach goes deeper into musky myths by reporting that the common expression "The fish of a thousand casts" is not accurate. Experienced musky addicts up there claim the average works out to be 675 casts. Gierach devotes two chapters on musky fishing in his book Dumb Luck and the Kindness of Strangers *(Simon & Schuster, 2020).*

If that doesn't cheer you up on your musky fishing, perhaps the thought of using rods like telephone poles and lures suggesting that something as big as a squirrel had fallen into the water will do the trick.

Stewart Edward White will show you that in musky fishing, we're talking about a fish with a mouth like Godzilla and teeth to back it up. They can be frightening.

DICK AND I TRAVELLED IN A FIFTEEN-FOOT WOODEN CANOE, WITH grub, duffel, tent, and Deuce, the black-and-white setter dog. As a consequence, we were pretty well down toward the water-line, for we had not realized that a wooden canoe would carry so little weight for its length in comparison with a birch-bark. A good heavy sea we could ride—with proper management and a little baling; but sloppy waves kept us busy.

Deuce did not like it at all. He was a dog old in the wisdom of experience. It had taken him just twenty minutes to learn all about canoes. After a single tentative trial he jumped lightly to the very centre of his place, with the lithe caution of a cat. Then if the water happened to be smooth, he would sit gravely on his haunches, or would rest his chin on the gunwale to contemplate the passing landscape. But in rough weather he crouched directly over the keel, his nose between his paws, and tried not to dodge when the cold water dashed in on him. Deuce was a true woodsman in that respect. Discomfort he always bore with equanimity, and he must often have been very cold and very cramped.

For just over a week we had been travelling in open water, and the elements had not been kind to us at all. We had crept up under rock-cliff points; had weathered the rips of white water to shelter on the other side; had struggled across open spaces where each wave was singly a problem to fail in whose solution meant instant swamping; had baled, and schemed, and figured, and carried, and sworn, and tried again, and succeeded with about two cups to spare, until we as well as Deuce had grown a little tired of it. For the lust of travel was on us.

The lust of travel is a very real disease. It usually takes you when you have made up your mind that there is no hurry. Its predisposing cause is a chart or map, and its main symptom is the feverish delight with which you check off the landmarks of your journey. A fair wind of some force is absolutely fatal. With that at your back, you cannot stop. Good fishing, fine scenery, interesting bays, reputed game, even camps where friends might be visited—all pass swiftly astern. Hardly do you pause for lunch at noon. The mad joy of putting country behind you eats all other interests. You recover only when you have come to your journey's end a week too early, and must then search out new voyages to fill in the time.

All this morning we had been bucking a strong north wind. Fortunately, the shelter of a string of islands had given us smooth water enough, but the heavy gusts sometimes stopped us as effectively as though we had butted solid land. Now about noon we came to the last island, and looked out on a five-mile stretch of tumbling seas. We landed the canoe and mounted a high rock.

"Can't make it like this," said I. "I'll take the outfit over and land it, and come back for you and the dog. Let's see that chart."

We hid behind the rock and spread out the map.

"Four miles," measured Dick. "It's going to be a terror."

We looked at each other vaguely, suddenly tired.

"We can't camp here—at this time of day," objected Dick, to our unspoken thoughts.

And then the map gave him an inspiration. "Here's a little river," ruminated Dick, "that goes to a little lake, and then there's another little river that flows from the lake and comes out about ten miles above here."

"It's a good thirty miles," I objected.

"What of it?" asked Dick calmly.

So the fever-lust of travel broke. We turned to the right behind the last island, searched out the reed-grown opening to the stream, and paddled serenely and philosophically against the current. Deuce sat up and yawned with a mighty satisfaction.

We had been bending our heads to the demon of wind; our ears had been filled with his shoutings, our eyes blinded with tears, our breath caught away from us, our muscles strung to the fiercest endeavour. Suddenly we found ourselves between the ranks of tall forest trees, bathed in a warm sunlight, gliding like a feather from one grassy bend to another of the laziest little stream that ever hesitated as to which way the grasses of its bed should float. As for the wind, it was lost somewhere away up high, where we could hear it muttering to itself about something.

The woods leaned over the fringe of bushes cool and green and silent. Occasionally through tiny openings we caught instant impressions of straight column trunks and transparent shadows. Miniature grass marshes jutted out from the bends of the little river. We idled along as with a homely rustic companion through the aloofness of patrician multitudes.

Every bend offered us charming surprises. Sometimes a muskrat swam hastily in a pointed furrow of ripple; vanishing wings, barely sensed in the flash, left us staring; stealthy withdrawals of creatures, whose presence we realized only in the fact of those withdrawals, snared our eager interest; porcupines rattled and rustled importantly and regally from the water's edge to the woods; herons, ravens, an occasional duck, croaked away at our approach; thrice we surprised eagles, once a tassel-eared Canada lynx. Or, if all else lacked, we still experienced the little thrill of pleased novelty over the disclosure of a group of silvery birches on a knoll; a magnificent white pine towering over the beech and maple forest; the unexpected aisle of a long, straight stretch of the little river.

Deuce approved thoroughly. He stretched himself and yawned and shook off the water, and glanced at me open-mouthed with doggy good-nature, and set himself to acquiring a conscientious olfactory knowledge of both banks of the river. I do not doubt he knew a great deal more about it than we did. Porcupines aroused his special enthusiasm. Incidentally, two days later he returned to camp after an expedition of his own, bristling as to the face with that animal's barbed weapons. Thenceforward his interest waned.

We ascended the charming little river two or three miles. At a sharp bend to the east a huge sheet of rock sloped from a round grass knoll sparsely planted with birches directly down into a pool. Two or three tree trunks jammed directly opposite had formed a sort of half dam under which the water lay dark. A tiny grass meadow forty feet in diameter narrowed the stream to half its width.

We landed. Dick seated himself on the shelving rock. I put my fish-rod together. Deuce disappeared.

Deuce always disappeared whenever we landed. With nose down, hind quarters well tucked under him, ears flying, he quartered the forest at high speed, investigating every nook and cranny of it for the radius of a quarter of a mile. When he has quite satisfied himself that we were safe for the moment, he would return to the fire, where he would lie, six inches of pink tongue vibrating with breathlessness, beautiful in the consciousness of virtue. Dick generally sat on a rock and thought. I generally fished.

After a time Deuce returned. I gave up flies, spoons, phantom minnows, artificial frogs, and crayfish. As Dick continued to sit on the rock and think, we both joined him. The sun was very warm and grateful, and I am sure we both acquired an added respect for Dick's judgment.

Just when it happened neither of us was afterwards able to decide. Perhaps Deuce knew. But suddenly, as often a figure appears in a cinematograph, the diminutive meadow thirty feet away contained two deer. They stood knee-deep in the grass, wagging their little tails in impatience of the flies.

"Look a' there!" stammered Dick aloud.

Deuce sat up on his haunches.

I started for my camera.

The deer did not seem to be in the slightest degree alarmed. They pointed four big ears in our direction, ate a few leisurely mouthfuls of grass, sauntered to the stream for a drink of water, wagged their little tails some more, and quietly faded into the cool shadows of the forest.

An hour later we ran out into reeds, and so to the lake. It was a pretty lake, forest-girt. Across the distance we made out a moving object which shortly resolved itself into a birch canoe. The canoe proved to contain an Indian, an Indian boy of about ten years, a black dog, and a bundle. When within a few rods of each other we ceased paddling, and drifted by with the momentum. The Indian was a fine-looking man of about forty, his hair bound with a red fillet, his feet incased in silk-worked moccasins, but otherwise dressed in white men's garments. He smoked a short pipe, and contemplated us gravely.

"Bo' jou', bo' jou'," we called in the usual double-barrelled North Country salutation.

"Bo' jou', bo' jou," he replied.

"Kée-gons?" we inquired as to the fishing in the lake.

"Áh-hah," he assented.

We drifted by each other without further speech. When the decent distance of etiquette separated us, we resumed our paddles.

I produced a young cable terminated by a tremendous spoon and a solid brass snell as thick as a telegraph wire. We had laid in this formidable implement in hopes of a big muscallunge. It had been trailed for days at a time. We had become used to its vibration, which actually seemed to communicate itself to every fibre of the light canoe. Every once in a while we would stop with a jerk that would nearly snap our heads off. Then we would know we had hooked the American continent. We had become used to that also. It generally happened when we attempted a little burst of speed. So when the canoe brought up so violently that all our tinware rolled on Deuce, Dick was merely disgusted.

"There she goes again," he grumbled. "You've hooked Canada."

Canada held quiescent for about three seconds. Then it started due south.

"Suffering serpents!" shrieked Dick.

"Paddle, you sulphurated idiot!" yelled I.

It was most interesting. All I had to do was to hang on and try to stay in the boat. Dick paddled and fumed and splashed water and got more excited. Canada dragged us bodily backward.

Then Canada changed his mind and started in our direction. I was plenty busy taking in slack, so I did not notice Dick. Dick was absolutely demented. His mind automatically reacted in the direction of paddling. He paddled, blindly, frantically. Canada came surging in, his mouth open, his wicked eyes flaming, a tremendous indistinct body lashing foam. Dick glanced once over his shoulder, and let out a frantic howl.

"You've got the sea-serpent!" he shrieked.

I turned to fumble for the pistol. We were headed directly for a log stranded on shore, and about ten feet from it.

"Dick!" I yelled in warning.

He thrust his paddle out forward just in time. The stout maple bent and cracked. The canoe hit with a bump that threw us forward. I returned to the young cable. It came in limp and slack.

We looked at each other sadly.

"No use," sighed Dick at last. "They've never invented the words, and we'd upset if we kicked the dog."

I had the end of the line in my hands.

"Look here!" I cried. That thick brass wire had been as cleanly bitten through as though it had been cut with clippers. "He must have caught sight of you," said I.

Dick lifted up his voice in lamentation. "You had four feet of him out of water," he wailed, "and there was a lot more."

"If you had kept cool," said I severely, "we shouldn't have lost him. You don't want to get rattled in an emergency; there's no sense in it."

"What were you going to do with that?" asked Dick, pointing to where I had laid the pistol.

"I was going to shoot him in the head," I replied with dignity. "It's the best way to land them."

Dick laughed disagreeably. I looked down. At my side lay our largest iron spoon.

We skirted the left-hand side of the lake in silence. Far out from shore the water was ruffled where the wind swept down, but with us it was as still and calm as the forest trees that looked over into it. After a time we turned short to the left through a very narrow passage between two marshy shores, and so, after a sharp bend of but a few hundred feet, came into the other river.

This was a wide stream, smoothly hurrying, without rapids or tumult. The forest had drawn to either side to let us pass. Here were the wilder reaches after the intimacies of the little river. Across stretches of marsh we could see an occasional great blue heron standing mid-leg deep. Long strings of ducks struggled quacking from invisible pools. The faint marsh odour saluted our nostrils from the point where the lily-pads flashed broadly, ruffling in the wind. We dropped out the smaller spoon and masterfully landed a five-pound pickerel. Even Deuce brightened. He cared nothing for raw fish, but he knew their possibilities. Towards evening we entered the hilly country, and so at the last turned to the left into a sand cove where grew maples and birches in beautiful park order under a hill. There we pitched camp, and, as the flies lacked, built a friendship-fire about which to forgather when the day was done.

Dick, still vocally regretting the muskellunge, told him of my big bear.

One day, late in the summer, I was engaged in packing some supplies along an old fur trail north of Lake Superior. I had accomplished one back-load, and with empty straps was returning to the cache for another. The trail at one point emerged into and crossed an open park some hundreds of feet in diameter, in which the grass grew to the height of the knee. When I was about halfway across, a black bear arose to his hind legs not ten feet from me, and remarked *Woof!* in a loud tone of voice. Now, if a man were to say *woof* to you unexpectedly, even in the formality of an Italian garden or the accustomedness of a city street, you would be somewhat startled. So I went to camp. There I told them about the bear. I tried to be conservative in my description, because I did not wish to be accused of exaggeration. My impression of the animal was that he and a spruce tree that grew near enough for ready comparison were approximately of the same stature. We returned to the grass park. After some difficulty we found a clear footprint. It was a little larger than that made by a good-sized coon.

"So, you see," I admonished didactically, "that lunge probably was not quite so large as you thought."

"It may have been a Chinese bear," said Dick dreamily—"a Chinese lady bear of high degree."

I gave him up.

CHAPTER THIRTEEN

A Bone-Fishing Pioneer

by Zane Grey

Another story from Zane Grey's Tales of Fishes, *this look at the pioneering days of bone-fishing on light tackle reveals a side of Zane Grey's angling adventures almost overlooked amid his nine books on deep-sea fishing. From his boyhood on the Delaware River to his trips to distant destinations where anglers had never been, Zane Grey fished with an inquiring mind and fascination with the habits of game fish and the action they created. (Editor's note: The R. C. referenced in the story is Zane Grey's brother.)*

IN MY EXPERIENCE AS A FISHERMAN THE GREATEST PLEASURE HAS BEEN the certainty of something new to learn, to feel, to anticipate, to thrill over. An old proverb tells us that if you wish to bring back the wealth of the Indias you must go out with its equivalent. Surely the longer a man fishes the wealthier he becomes in experience, in reminiscence, in love of nature, if he goes out with the harvest of a quiet eye, free from the plague of himself.

As a boy, fishing was a passion with me, but no more for the conquest of golden sunfish and speckled chubs and horny catfish than for the haunting sound of the waterfall and the color and loneliness of the cliffs. As a man, and a writer who is forever learning, fishing is still a passion, stronger with all the years, but tempered by an understanding of the nature of primitive man, hidden in all of us, and by a keen reluctance to deal pain to any creature. The sea and the river and the mountain have almost taught me not to kill except for the urgent needs of life; and the time will come when I shall have grown up to that. When I read a naturalist or a biologist I am always ashamed of what I have called a sport. Yet one of the truths of evolution is that not to practise strife, not to use violence, not to fish or hunt—that is to say, not to fight—is to retrograde as a natural man. Spiritual and intellectual growth is attained at the expense of the physical.

Always, then, when I am fishing I feel that the fish are incidental, and that the reward of effort and endurance, the incalculable and intangible knowledge emanate from the swelling and infinite sea or from the shaded and murmuring stream. Thus I assuage my conscience and justify the fun, the joy, the excitement, and the violence.

Five years ago I had never heard of a bonefish. The first man who ever spoke to me about this species said to me, very quietly with serious intentness: "Have you had any experience with bonefish?" I said no, and asked him what kind that was. His reply was enigmatical. "Well, don't go after bonefish unless you can give up all other fishing." I remember I laughed. But I never forgot that remark, and now it comes back to me clear in its significance. That fisherman read me as well as I misunderstood him.

Later that season I listened to talk of inexperienced bonefishermen telling what they had done and heard. To me it was absurd. So much fishing talk seems ridiculous, anyway. And the expert fishermen, wherever they were, received the expressive titles: "Bonefish Bugs and Bonefish Nuts!" Again I heard arguments about tackle rigged for these mysterious fish and these arguments fixed my vague impression. By and by some bonefishermen came to Long Key, and the first sight of a bonefish made me curious. I think it weighed five pounds—a fair-sized specimen. Even to my prejudiced eye that fish showed class. So I began to question the bonefishermen.

At once I found this type of angler to be remarkably reticent as to experience and method. Moreover, the tackle used was amazing to me. Stiff rods and heavy lines for little fish! I gathered another impression, and it was that bonefish were related to dynamite and chain lightning. Everybody who would listen to my questions had different things to say.

No two men agreed on tackle or bait or ground or anything. I enlisted the interest of my brother R.C., and we decided, just to satisfy curiosity, to go out and catch some bonefish. The complacent, smug conceit of fishermen! I can see now how funny ours was. Fortunately it is now past tense. If I am ever conceited again I hope no one will read my stories.

My brother and I could not bring ourselves to try for bonefish with heavy tackle. It was preposterous. Three—four—five-pound fish! We had seen no larger. Bass tackle was certainly heavy enough for us. So in the innocence of our hearts and the assurance of our vanity we sallied forth to catch bonefish.

That was four years ago. Did we have good luck? No! Luck has nothing to do with bonefishing. What happened? For one solid month each winter of those four years we had devoted ourselves to bonefishing with light tackle. We stuck to our colors. The space of this whole volume would not be half enough to tell our experience—the amaze, the difficulty, the perseverance, the defeat, the wonder, and at last the achievement. The season of 1918 we hooked about fifty bonefish on three-six tackles—that is, three-ounce tips and six-thread lines—and we landed fourteen of them. I caught nine and R.C. caught five. R.C.'s eight-pound fish justified our contention and crowned our efforts.

To date, in all my experience, I consider this bonefish achievement the most thrilling, fascinating, difficult, and instructive. That is a broad statement and I hope I can prove it. I am prepared to state that I feel almost certain, if I spent another month bonefishing, I would become obsessed and perhaps lose my enthusiasm for other kinds of fish.

Why?

There is a multiplicity of reasons. My reasons range from the exceedingly graceful beauty of a bonefish to the fact that he is the best food fish I ever ate. That is a wide range. He is the wisest, shyest, wariest, strangest fish I ever studied; and I am not excepting the great *Xiphias gladius*—the broadbill swordfish. As for the speed of a bonefish, I claim no salmon, no barracuda, no other fish celebrated for swiftness of motion, is in his class. A bonefish is so incredibly fast that it was a long time before I could believe the evidence of my own eyes. You see him; he is there perfectly still in the clear, shallow water, a creature of fish shape, pale green and silver, but crystal-like, a phantom shape, staring at you with strange black eyes; then he is gone. Vanished! Absolutely without your seeing a movement, even a faint streak! By peering keenly you may discern a little swirl in the water. As for the strength of a bonefish, I actually hesitate to give my impressions. No one will ever believe how powerful a bonefish is until he has tried to stop the rush and heard the line snap. As for his cunning, it is utterly baffling. As for his biting, it is almost imperceptible. As for his tactics, they are beyond conjecture.

I want to append here a few passages from my note-books, in the hope that a bare, bald statement of fact will help my argument.

***

This wide area of coral mud was dry at low tide. When we arrived the tide was rising. Water scarcely a foot deep, very clear. Bottom white, with patches of brown grass. We saw bonefish everywhere and expected great sport. But no matter where we stopped we could not get any bites. Schools of bonefish swam up to the boat, only to dart away. Everywhere we saw thin white tails sticking out, as they swam along, feeding with noses in the mud. When we drew in our baits we invariably found them half gone, and it was our assumption that the blue crabs did this.

At sunset the wind quieted. It grew very still and beautiful. The water was rosy. Here and there we saw swirls and tails standing out, and we heard heavy thumps of plunging fish. But we could not get any bites.

When we returned to camp we were told that the half of our soldier-crab baits had been sucked off by bonefish. Did not believe that.

Tide bothered us again this morning. It seems exceedingly difficult to tell one night before what the tide is going to do the next morning. At ten o'clock we walked to the same place we were yesterday. It was a bright, warm day, with just enough breeze to ruffle the water and make fishing pleasant, and we certainly expected to have good luck. But we fished for about three hours without any sign of a fish. This was discouraging and we could not account for it.

So we moved. About half a mile down the beach I thought I caught a glimpse of a bonefish. It was a likely-looking contrast to the white marl all around. Here I made a long cast and sat down to wait. My brother lagged behind. Presently I spied two bonefish nosing along not ten feet from the shore. They saw me, so I made no attempt to drag the bait near them, but I called to my brother and told him to try to get a bait ahead of them. This was a little after flood-tide. It struck me then that these singular fish feed up the beach with one tide and down with another.

Just when my brother reached me I got a nibble. I called to him and then stood up, ready to strike. I caught a glimpse of the fish. He looked big and dark. He had his nose down, fooling with my bait. When I struck him he felt heavy. I put on the click of the reel, and when the bonefish started off he pulled the rod down hard, taking the line fast. He made one swirl on the surface and then started up-shore. He seemed exceedingly swift. I ran along the beach until presently the line slackened and I felt that the hook had torn out. This was disappointment. I could not figure that I had done anything wrong, but I decided in the future to use a smaller and sharper hook. We went on down the beach, seeing several bonefish on the way, and finally we ran into a big school of them. They were right alongshore, but when they saw us we could not induce them to bite.

***

Every day we learn something. It is necessary to keep out of sight of these fish. After they bite, everything depends upon the skilful hooking of the fish. Probably it will require a good deal of skill to land them after you have hooked them, but we have had little experience at that so far. When these fish are along the shore they certainly are feeding, and presumably they are feeding on crabs of some sort. Bonefish appear to be game worthy of any fisherman's best efforts.

It was a still, hot day, without any clouds. We went up the beach to a point opposite an old construction camp. To-day when we expected the tide to be doing one thing it was doing another. Ebb and flow and flood-tide have become as difficult as Sanskrit synonyms for me. My brother took an easy and comfortable chair and sat up the beach, and I, like an ambitious fisherman, laboriously and adventurously waded out one hundred and fifty feet to an old platform that had been erected there. I climbed upon this, and found it a very precarious place to sit. Come to think about it, there is something very remarkable about the places a fisherman will pick out to sit down on. This place was a two-by-four plank full of nails, and I cheerfully availed myself of it and, casting my bait out as far as I could, I calmly sat down to wait for a bonefish. It has become a settled conviction in my mind that you have to wait for bonefish. But all at once I got a hard bite. It quite excited me. I jerked and pulled the bait away from the fish and he followed it and took it again. I saw this fish and several others in the white patch of ground where there were not any weeds. But in my excitement I did not have out a long enough line, and when I jerked the fish turned over and got away. This was all right, but the next two hours sitting in the sun on that seat with a nail sticking into me were not altogether pleasurable. When I thought I had endured it as long as I could I saw a flock of seven bonefish swimming past me, and one of them was a whopper. The sight revived me. I hardly breathed while that bunch of fish swam right for my bait, and for all I could see they did not know it was there. I waited another long time. The sun was hot—there was no breeze—the heat was reflected from the water. I could have stood all this well enough, but I could not stand the nails. So I climbed down off my perch, having forgotten that all this time the tide had been rising. And as I could not climb back I had to get wet, to the infinite amusement of my brother. After that I fished from the shore.

Presently my brother shouted and I looked up to see him pulling on a fish. There was a big splash in the water and then I saw his line running out. The fish was heading straight for the framework on which I had been seated and I knew if he ever did get there he would break the line. All of a sudden I saw the fish he had hooked. And he reached the framework all right!

I had one more strike this day, but did not hook the fish. It seems this bonefishing takes infinite patience. For all we can tell, these fish come swimming along with the rising tide close in to shore and they are exceedingly shy and wary. My brother now has caught two small bonefish and each of them gave a good strong bite, at once starting off with the bait. We had been under the impression that it was almost impossible to feel the bonefish bite. It will take work to learn this game.

***

Yesterday we went up on the north side of the island to the place near the mangroves where we had seen some bonefish. Arriving there, we found the tide almost flood, with the water perfectly smooth and very clear and about a foot deep up at the mangrove roots. Here and there at a little distance we could see splashes. We separated, and I took the outside, while R.C. took the inside close to the mangroves. We waded along. Before I had time to make a cast I saw a three-pound bonefish come sneaking along, and when he saw me he darted away like an arrow. I made a long cast and composed myself to wait. Presently a yell from R.C. electrified me with the hope that he had hooked a fish. But it turned out that he had only seen one. He moved forward very cautiously in the water and presently made a cast. He then said that a big bonefish was right near his hook, and during the next few minutes this fish circled his bait twice, crossing his line. Then he counted out loud: one, two, three, four, five bonefish right in front of him, one of which was a whopper. I stood up myself and saw one over to my right, of about five pounds, sneaking along with his nose to the bottom. When I made a cast over in his direction he disappeared as suddenly as if he had dissolved in the water. Looking out to my left, I saw half a dozen bonefish swimming toward me, and they came quite close. When I moved they vanished. Then I made a cast over in this direction. The bonefish came back and swam all around my bait, apparently not noticing it. They were on the feed, and the reason they did not take our bait must have been that they saw us. We fished there for an hour without having a sign of a bite, and then we gave it up.

To-day about flood-tide I had a little strike. I jerked hard, but failed to see the fish, and then when I reeled in I found he still had hold of it. Then I struck him, and in one little jerk he broke the leader.

***

I just had a talk with a fellow who claims to know a good deal about bonefishing. He said he had caught a good many ranging up to eight pounds. His claim was that soldier crabs were the best bait. He said he had fished with professional boatmen who knew the game thoroughly. They would pole the skiff alongshore and keep a sharp lookout for what he called bonefish mud. And I assume that he meant muddy places in the water that had been stirred up by bonefish. Of course, any place where these little swirls could be seen was very likely to be a bonefish bank. He claimed that it was necessary to hold the line near the reel between the forefingers, and to feel for the very slightest vibration. Bonefish have a sucker-like mouth. They draw the bait in, and smash it. Sometimes, of course, they move away, drawing out the line, but that kind of a bite is exceptional. It is imperative to strike the fish when this vibration is felt. Not one in five bonefish is hooked.

We have had two northers and the water grew so cold that it drove the fish out. The last two or three days have been warm and to-day it was hot. However, I did not expect the bonefish in yet, and when we went in bathing at flood-tide I was very glad to see two fish. I hurried out and got my rod and began to try. Presently I had a little strike. I waited and it was repeated; then I jerked and felt the fish. He made a wave and that was the last I knew of him.

Reeling in, I looked at my bait, to find that it had been pretty badly chewed, but I fastened it on again and made another cast. I set down the rod. Then I went back after the bucket for the rest of the bait. Upon my return I saw the line jerking and I ran to the rod. I saw a little splash, and a big white tail of a bonefish stick out of the water. I put my thumb on the reel and jerked hard. Instantly I felt the fish, heavy and powerful. He made a surge and then ran straight out. The line burned my thumb so I could not hold it. I put on the click and the fish made a swifter, harder run for at least a hundred yards, and he tore the hook out.

This makes a number of fish that have gotten away from me in this manner. It is exasperating and difficult to explain. I have to use a pretty heavy sinker in order to cast the bait out. I have arranged this sinker, which has a hole through it, so that the line will run freely. This seems to work all right on the bite, but I am afraid it does not work after the fish is hooked. That sinker drags on the bottom. This is the best rigging that I can plan at the present stage of the game. I have an idea now that a bonefish should be hooked hard and then very carefully handled.

I fished off the beach awhile in front of the cabin. We used both kinds of crabs, soldier and hermit. I fished two hours and a half, from the late rising tide to the first of the ebb, without a sign or sight of a fish. R.C.

finally got tired and set his rod and went in bathing. Then it happened. I heard his reel singing and saw his rod nodding; then I made a dash for it. The fish was running straight out, heavy and fast, and he broke the line.

This may have been caused by the heavy sinker catching in the weeds. We must do more planning to get a suitable rig for these bonefish.

***

Day before yesterday R.C. and I went up to the Long Key point, and rowed in on the mangrove shoal where once before I saw so many bone-fish. The tide was about one-quarter in, and there was a foot of water all over the flats. We anchored at the outer edge and began to fish. We had made elaborate preparations in the way of tackle, bait, canoe, etc., and it really would have been remarkable if we had had any luck. After a little while I distinctly felt something at my hook, and upon jerking I had one splendid surge out of a good, heavy bonefish. That was all that happened in that place.

It was near flood-tide when we went back. I stood up and kept a keen watch for little muddy places in the water, also bonefish. At last I saw several fish, and there we anchored. I fished on one side of the boat, and R.C. on the other. On two different occasions, feeling a nibble on his line, he jerked, all to no avail. The third time he yelled as he struck, and I turned in time to see the white thresh of a bonefish. He made a quick dash off to the side and then came in close to the boat, swimming around with short runs two or three times, and then, apparently tired, he came close. I made ready to lift him into the boat, when, lo and behold! he made a wonderful run of fully three hundred feet before R.C. could stop him. Finally he was led to the boat, and turned out to be a fish of three and a half pounds. It simply made R.C. and me gasp to speak of what a really large bonefish might be able to do. There is something irresistible about the pursuit of these fish, and perhaps this is it. We changed places, and as a last try anchored in deeper water, fishing as before. This time I had a distinct tug at my line and I hooked a fish. He wiggled and jerked and threshed around so that I told R.C. that it was not a bonefish, but R.C. contended it was. Anyway, he came toward the boat rather easily until we saw him and he saw us, and then he made a dash similar to that of R.C.'s fish and he tore out the hook. This was the extent of our adventure that day, and we were very much pleased.

Next morning we started out with a high northeast trade-wind blowing. Nothing could dampen our ardor.

It was blowing so hard up at No. 2 viaduct that we decided to stay inside. There is a big flat there cut up by channels, and it is said to be a fine ground for bonefish. The tide was right and the water was clear, but even in the lee of the bank the wind blew pretty hard. We anchored in about three feet of water and began to fish.

After a while we moved. The water was about a foot deep, and the bottom clean white marl, with little patches of vegetation. Crabs and crab-holes were numerous. I saw a small shark and a couple of rays. When we got to the middle of a big flat I saw the big, white, glistening tails of bonefish sticking out of the water. We dropped anchor and, much excited, were about to make casts, when R.C. lost his hat. He swore. We had to pull up anchor and go get the hat. Unfortunately this scared the fish. Also it presaged a rather hard-luck afternoon. In fishing, as in many other things, if the beginning is tragedy all will be tragedy, growing worse all the time. We moved around up above where I had seen these bonefish, and there we dropped anchor. No sooner had we gotten our baits overboard than we began to see bonefish tails off at quite some distance. The thing to do, of course, was to sit right there and be patient, but this was almost impossible for us. We moved again and again, but we did not get any nearer to the fish. Finally I determined that we would stick in one place. This we did, and the bonefish began to come around. When they would swim close to the boat and see us they would give a tremendous surge and disappear, as if by magic. But they always left a muddy place in the water. The speed of these fish is beyond belief. I could not cast where I wanted to; I tried again and again. When I did get my bait off at a reasonable distance, I could feel crabs nibbling at it. These pests robbed us of many a good bait. One of them cut my line right in two. They seemed to be very plentiful, and that must be why the bonefish were plentiful, too. R.C. kept losing bait after bait, which he claimed was the work of crabs, but I rather believed it to be the work of bonefish. It was too windy for us to tell anything about the pressure of the line. It had to be quite a strong tug to be felt at all. Presently I felt one, and instead of striking at once I waited to see what would happen. After a while I reeled in to find my bait gone. Then I was consoled by the proof that a bonefish had taken the bait off for me. Another time three bonefish came along for my bait and stuck their tails up out of the water, and were evidently nosing around it, but I felt absolutely nothing on the line. When I reeled in the bait was gone.

We kept up this sort of thing for two hours. I knew that we were doing it wrong. R.C. said bad conditions, but I claimed that these were only partly responsible for our failure. I knew that we moved about too much, that we did not cast far enough and wait long enough, and that by all means we should not have cracked bait on the bottom of the boat, and particularly we did not know when we had a bite! But it is one thing to be sure of a fact and another to be able to practise it. At last we gave up in despair, and upon paddling back toward the launch we saw a school of bonefish with their tails in the air. We followed them around for a while, apparently very much to their amusement. At sunset we got back to the launch and started for camp.

This was a long, hard afternoon's work for nothing. However, it is my idea that experience is never too dearly bought. I will never do some things again, and the harder these fish are to catch, the more time and effort it takes—the more intelligence and cunning—all the more will I appreciate success if it ever does come. It is in the attainment of difficult tasks that we earn our reward. There are several old bonefish experts here in camp, and they laughed when I related some of our experiences. Bonefishermen are loath to tell anything about their methods. This must be a growth of the difficult game. I had an expert bonefisherman tell me that when he was surprised while fishing on one of the shoals, he always dropped his rod and pretended to be digging for shells. And it is a fact that the bonefish guides at Metacumbe did not let any one get a line on their methods. They will avoid a bonefishing-ground while others are there, and if they are surprised there ahead of others, they will pull up anchor and go away. May I be preserved from any such personal selfishness and reticence as this! One of these bonefish experts at the camp told me that in all his years of experience he had never gotten a bonefish bite. If you feel a tug, it is when the bonefish is ejecting the hook. Then it is too late. The bonefish noses around the bait and sucks it in without any apparent movement of the line. And that can be detected first by a little sagging of the line or by a little strain upon it. That is the time to strike. He also said that he always broke his soldier crabs on a piece of lead to prevent the jar from frightening the fish.

Doctor B. tells a couple of interesting experiences with bonefish. On one occasion he was fishing near another boat in which was a friend. The water was very clear and still, and he could see his friend's bait lying upon the sand. An enormous bonefish swam up and took the bait, and Doctor B. was so thrilled and excited that he could not yell. When the man hooked the fish it shot off in a straightaway rush, raising a ridge upon the water. It ran the length of the line and freed itself. Later Doctor B.'s friend showed the hook, that had been straightened out. They measured the line and found it to be five hundred and fifty-five feet. The bonefish had gone the length of this in one run, and they estimated that he would have weighed not less than fifteen pounds.

On another occasion Doctor B. saw a heavy bonefish hooked. It ran straight off shore, and turning, ran in with such speed that it came shooting out upon dry land and was easily captured. These two instances are cases in point of the incredible speed and strength of this strange fish.

R.C. had a splendid fight with a bonefish to-day. The wind was blowing hard and the canoe was not easy to fish out of. We had great difficulty in telling when we did have a bite. I had one that I know of. When R.C. hooked his fish it sheered off between the canoe and the beach and ran up-shore quite a long way. Then it headed out to sea and made a long run, and then circled. It made short, quick surges, each time jerking R.C.'s rod down and pulling the reel handle out of his fingers. He had to put on a glove. We were both excited and thrilled with the gameness of this fish. It circled the canoe three times, and tired out very slowly. When he got it close the very thing happened that I feared. It darted under the anchor rope and we lost it. This battle lasted about fifteen minutes, and afforded us an actual instance of the wonderful qualities of this fish.

Yesterday R.C. hooked a bonefish that made a tremendous rush straight offshore, and never stopped until he had pulled out the hook. This must have been a very heavy and powerful fish.

I had my taste of the same dose to-day. I felt a tiny little tug upon my line that electrified me and I jerked as hard as I dared. I realized that I had hooked some kind of fish, but, as it was wiggling and did not feel heavy, I concluded that I had hooked one of those pesky blowfish. But all of a sudden my line cut through the water and fairly whistled. I wound in the slack and then felt a heavy fish. He made a short plunge and then a longer one, straight out, making my reel scream. I was afraid to thumb the line, so I let him go. With these jerky plunges he ran about three hundred feet. Then I felt my line get fast, and, handing my rod to R.C., I slipped off my shoes and went overboard. I waded out, winding as I went, to find that the bonefish had fouled the line on a sponge on the bottom, and he had broken free just above the hook.

**

Yesterday the fag end of the northeast gale still held on, but we decided to try for bonefish. Low tide at two o'clock.

I waded up-shore with the canoe, and R.C. walked. It was a hard job to face the wind and waves and pull the canoe. It made me tired and wet.

When we got above the old camp the tide had started in. We saw bonefish tails standing up out of the water. Hurriedly baiting our hooks, we waded to get ahead of them. But we could not catch them wading, so went back to the canoe and paddled swiftly ahead, anchored, and got out to wade once more.

R.C. was above me. We saw the big tail of one bonefish and both of us waded to get ahead of him. At last I made a cast, but did not see him any more. The wind was across my line, making a big curve in it, and I was afraid I could not tell a bite if I had one. Was about to reel in when I felt the faint tug. I swept my rod up and back, hard as I dared. The line came tight, I felt a heavy weight; a quiver, and then my rod was pulled down. I had hooked him. The thrill was remarkable. He took a short dash, then turned. I thought I had lost him. But he was running in. Frantically I wound the reel, but could not get in the slack. I saw my line coming, heard it hiss in the water, then made out the dark shape of a bonefish. He ran right at me—almost hit my feet. When he saw me he darted off with incredible speed, making my reel scream. I feared the strain on the line, and I plunged through the water as fast as I could after him. He ran four hundred feet in that dash, and I ran fifty. Not often have I of late years tingled and thrilled and panted with such excitement. It was great. It brought back the days of boyhood. When he stopped that run I was tired and thoroughly wet. He sheered off as I waded and wound in. I got him back near me. He shot off in a shoal place of white mud where I saw him plainly, and he scared a school of bonefish that split and ran every way. My fish took to making short circles; I could not keep a tight line. Lost! I wound in fast, felt him again, then absolutely lost feel of him or sight of him. Lost again! My sensations were remarkable, considering it was only a fish of arm's-length at the end of the line. But these bonefish rouse an angler as no other fish can. All at once I felt the line come tight. He was still on, now running inshore.

The water was about a foot deep. I saw the bulge, or narrow wave, he made. He ran out a hundred feet, and had me dashing after him again. I could not trust that light line at the speed he swam, so I ran to release the strain. He led me inshore, then up-shore, and out toward sea again, all the time fighting with a couple of hundred feet of line out. Occasionally he would make a solid, thumping splash. He worked offshore some two hundred yards, where be led me in water half to my hips. I had to try to stop him here, and with fear and trepidation I thumbed the reel. The first pressure brought a savage rush, but it was short. He turned, and I wound him back and waded inshore.

From that moment I had him beaten, although I was afraid of his short thumps as he headed away and tugged. Finally I had him within twenty feet circling around me, tired and loggy, yet still strong enough to require careful handling.

He looked short and heavy, pale checked green and silver; and his staring black eye, set forward in his pointed white nose, could be plainly seen. This fish made a rare picture for an angler.

So I led him to the canoe and, ascertaining that I had him well hooked, I lifted him in.

Never have I seen so beautiful a fish. A golden trout, a white sea-bass, a dolphin, all are beautiful, but not so exquisite as this bonefish. He seemed all bars of dazzling silver. His tail had a blue margin and streaks of lilac. His lower (anal) fins were blazing with opal fire, and the pectoral fins were crystal white. His eye was a dead, piercing black, staring and deep. We estimated his weight. I held for six pounds, but R.C. shook his head. He did not believe that. But we agreed on the magnificent fight he had made.

Then we waded up-shore farther and began to fish. In just five minutes I had the same kind of strike, slight, almost imperceptible, vibrating, and I hooked a fish exactly as I had the first one. He was light of weight, but swift as a flash. I played him from where I stood. This time I essayed with all skill to keep a taut line. It was impossible. Now I felt his weight and again only a slack line. This fish, too, ran right to my feet, then in a boiling splash sheered away. But he could not go far. I reeled him back and led him to the canoe. He was small, and the smallness of him was such a surprise in contrast to what his fight had led me to imagine he was.

R.C. had one strike and broke his line on the jerk. We had to give up on account of sunset at hand.

***

There was another hard thunder-storm last night. The last few days have begun the vernal equinox. It rained torrents all night and stopped at dawn. The wind was northeast and cool. Cloudy overhead, with purple horizon all around—a forbidding day. But we decided to go fishing, anyhow. We had new, delicate three-six tackles to try. About seven the wind died away. There was a dead calm, and the sun tried to show. Then another breeze came out of the east.

We went up on the inside after bait, and had the luck to find some. Crossing the island, we came out at the old construction camp where we had left the canoe. By this time a stiff breeze was blowing and the tide was rising fast. We had our troubles paddling and poling up to the grove of cocoanuts. Opposite this we anchored and began to fish.

Conditions were not favorable. The water was choppy and roily, the canoe bobbed a good deal, the anchors dragged, and we did not see any fish. All the same, we persevered. At length I had a bite, but pulled too late. We tried again for a while, only to be disappointed. Then we moved.

We had to put the stern anchor down first and let it drag till it held and the canoe drifted around away from the wind, then we dropped the bow anchor. After a time I had a faint feeling at the end of my line—an indescribable feeling. I jerked and hooked a bonefish. He did not feel heavy. He ran off, and the wind bagged my line and the waves also helped to pull out the hook.

Following that we changed places several times, in one of which R.C. had a strike, but failed to hook the fish. Just opposite the old wreck on the shore I had another fish take hold, and, upon hooking him, had precisely the same thing happen as in the first instance. I think the bag of my line, which I could not avoid, allowed the lead to sag down and drag upon the bottom. Of course when it caught the bonefish pulled free.

In some places we found the water clearer than in others. Flood-tide had long come when we anchored opposite the old camp. R.C. cast out upon a brown patch of weeds where we have caught some fine fish, and I cast below. Perhaps in five minutes or less R.C. swept up his rod. I saw it bend forward, down toward the water. He had hooked a heavy fish. The line hissed away to the right, and almost at once picked up a good-sized piece of seaweed.

"It's a big fish!" I exclaimed, excitedly. "Look at him go! . . . That seaweed will make you lose him. Let me wade out and pull it off?"

"No! Let's take a chance. . . . Too late, anyhow! Gee! He's going! . . . He's got two hundred yards out!"

Two-thirds of the line was off the reel, and the piece of seaweed seemed to be a drag on the fish. He slowed up. The line was tight, the rod bent. Suddenly the tip sprang back. We had seen that often before.

"Gone!" said R.C., dejectedly.

But I was not so sure of that, although I was hopeless. R.C. wound in, finding the line came slowly, as if weighted. I watched closely. We thought that was on account of the seaweed. But suddenly the reel began to screech.

"I've got him yet!" yelled R.C., with joy.

I was overjoyed, too, but I contained myself, for I expected dire results from that run.

Zee! Zee! Zee! went the reel, and the rod nodded in time.

"We must get rid of that seaweed or lose him. . . . Pull up your anchor with one hand. . . . Careful now."

He did so, and quickly I got mine up. What ticklish business!

"Keep a tight line!" I cautioned, as I backed the canoe hard with all my power. It was not easy to go backward and keep head on to the wind. The waves broke over the end of the canoe, splashing me in the face so I could taste and smell the salt. I made half a dozen shoves with the paddle. Then, nearing the piece of seaweed, I dropped my anchor.

In a flash I got that dangerous piece of seaweed off R.C.'s line.

"Good work! . . . Say, but that helps. . . . We'd never have gotten him," said R.C., beaming. I saw him look then as he used to in our sunfish, bent-pin days.

"We've not got him yet," I replied, grimly. "Handle him as easily as you can."

Then began a fight. The bonefish changed his swift, long runs, and took to slow sweeps to and fro, and whenever he was drawn a few yards closer he would give a solid jerk and get that much line back. There was much danger from other pieces of floating weed. R.C. maneuvered his line to miss them. All the time the bonefish was pulling doggedly. I had little hope we might capture him. At the end of fifteen minutes he was still a hundred yards from the canoe and neither of us had seen him. Our excitement grew tenser every moment. The fish sheered to and fro, and would not come into shallower water. He would not budge. He took one long run straight up the shore, in line with us, and then circled out. This alarmed me, but he did not increase his lead. He came slowly around, yard by yard. R.C. reeled carefully, not hard enough to antagonize him, and after what seemed a long time got him within a hundred feet, and I had a glimpse of green and silver. Then off he ran again. How unbelievably swift! He had been close—then almost the same instant he was far off.

"I saw him! On a wave!" yelled R.C. "That's no bonefish! What can he be, anyhow? I believe I've got a barracuda!"

I looked and looked, but I could not see him.

"No matter what you think you saw, that fish is a bonefish," I declared, positively. "The runs he made! I saw silver and green! Careful now. I *know* he's a bonefish. And he must be big."

"Maybe it's only the wind and waves that make him feel so strong," replied R.C.

"No! You can't fool me! Play him for a big one. He's been on twenty-three minutes now. Stand up—I'll steady the canoe—and watch for that sudden rush when he sees the canoe. The finish is in sight."

It was an indication of a tiring fish that he made his first circle of the canoe, but too far out for us to see him. This circling a boat is a remarkable feature, and I think it comes from the habit of a bonefish of pulling broadside. I cautioned R.C. to avoid the seaweed and to lead him a little more, but to be infinitely careful not to apply too much strain. He circled us again, a few yards closer. The third circle he did not gain a foot. Then he was on his fourth lap around the canoe, drawing closer. On his fifth lap clear round us he came near as fifty feet. I could not resist standing up to see. I got a glimpse of him and he looked long. But I did not say anything to R.C. We had both hooked too many big bonefish that got away immediately. This was another affair.

He circled us the sixth time. Six times! Then he came rather close. On this occasion he saw the canoe. He surged and sped out so swiftly that I was simply paralyzed. R.C. yelled something that had a note of admiration of sheer glory in the spirit of that fish.

"Here's where he leaves us!" I echoed.

But, as luck would have it, he stopped that run short of two hundred yards; and turned broadside to circle slowly back, allowing R.C. to get in line. He swam slower this time, and did not make the heavy tugs. He came easily, weaving to and fro. R.C. got him to within twenty-five feet of the boat, yet still could not see him. It was my job to think quick and sit still with ready hands on the anchor rope. He began to plunge, taking a little line each time. Then suddenly I saw R.C.'s line coming toward us. I knew that would happen.

"Now! Look out! Reel in fast!" I cried, tensely.

As I leaned over to heave up the anchor, I saw the bonefish flashing nearer. At that instant of thrilling excitement and suspense I could not trust my eyesight. There he was, swimming heavily, and he looked three feet long, thick and dark and heavy. I got the anchor up just as he passed under the canoe. Maybe I did not revel in pride of my quickness of thought and action!

"Oh! He's gone under the rope!" gasped R.C.

"No!" I yelled, sharply. "Let your line run out! Put your tip down! We'll drift over your line."

R.C. was determined to do so, and presently the canoe drifted over where the line was stretched. That second ticklish moment passed. It had scared me. But I could not refrain from one sally.

"I got the anchor up. What did you think I'd do?"

R.C. passed by my remark. This was serious business for him. He looked quite earnest and pale.

"Say! did you see him?" he ejaculated, looking at me.

"Wish I hadn't," I replied.

We were drifting inshore, which was well, provided we did not drift too hard to suit the bonefish. He swam along in plain sight, and he seemed so big that I would not have gazed any longer if I could have helped it.

I kept the canoe headed in, and we were not long coming to shallow water. Here the bonefish made a final dash for freedom, but it was short and feeble, compared with his first runs. He got about twenty feet away, then sheered, showing his broad, silver side. R.C. wound him in close, and an instant later the bow of the canoe grated on shore.

"Now what?" asked R.C. as I stepped out into the water. "Won't it be risky to lift him into the canoe?"

"Lift nothing! I have this all figured out. Lead him along."

R.C. stepped out upon the beach while I was in the water. The bonefish lay on his side, a blaze of silver. I took hold of the line very gently and led the fish a little closer in. The water was about six inches deep. There were waves beating in—a miniature surf. And I calculated on the receding of a wave. Then with one quick pull I slid our beautiful quarry up on the coral sand. The instant he was out of the water the leader snapped. I was ready for this, too. But at that it was an awful instant! As the wave came back, almost deep enough to float the bonefish, I scooped him up.

"He's ours!" I said, consulting my watch. "Thirty-three minutes! I give you my word that fight was comparable to ones I've had with a Pacific swordfish."

"Look at him!" R.C. burst out. "Look at him! When the leader broke I thought he was lost. I'm sick yet. Didn't you almost bungle that?"

"Not a chance, R.C.," I replied. "Had that all figured. I never put any strain on your line until the wave went back. Then I slid him out, the leader broke, and I scooped him up."

R.C. stood gazing down at the glistening, opal-spotted fish. What a contrast he presented to any other kind of a fish! How many beautiful species have we seen lying on sand or moss or ferns, just come out of the water! But I could remember no other so rare as this bonefish. The exceeding difficulty of the capture of this, our first really large bonefish, had a great deal to do with our admiration and pride. For the hard work of any achievement is what makes it worth while. But this had nothing to do with the exquisite, indescribable beauty of the bonefish. He was long, thick, heavy, and round, with speed and power in every line; a sharp white nose and huge black eyes. The body of him was live, quivering silver, molten silver in the sunlight, crossed and barred with blazing stripes. The opal hues came out upon the anal fin, and the broad tail curled up, showing lavender tints on a background of brilliant blue. He weighed eight pounds. Symbolic of the mysterious life and beauty in the ocean! Wonderful and prolific as nature is on land, she is infinitely more so in the sea. By the sun and the sea we live; and I shall never tire of seeking and studying the manifold life of the deep.

CHAPTER FOURTEEN

A Leaf of Spearmint: Recollections of a Boy and a Rod

by Henry van Dyke

I must confess to never tiring of reading Henry van Dyke. This wonderful story is from Little Rivers *(1895).*

> "It puzzles me now, that I remember all these young impressions so, because I took no heed of them at the time whatever; and yet they come upon me bright, when nothing else is evident in the gray fog of experience."
> —B. D. BLACKMORE: *LORNA DOONE*

OF ALL THE FACULTIES OF THE HUMAN MIND, MEMORY IS THE ONE that is most easily "led by the nose." There is a secret power in the sense of smell which draws the mind backward into the pleasant land of old times.

If you could paint a picture of Memory, in the symbolical manner of Quarles's Emblems, it should represent a man travelling the highway with a dusty pack upon his shoulders, and stooping to draw in a long, sweet breath from the small, deep-red, golden-hearted flowers of an old-fashioned rose-tree straggling through the fence of a neglected garden. Or perhaps, for a choice of emblems, you would better take a yet more homely and familiar scent: the cool fragrance of lilacs drifting

145

through the June morning from the old bush that stands between the kitchen door and the well; the warm layer of pungent, aromatic air that floats over the tansy-bed in a still July noon; the drowsy dew of odour that falls from the big balm-of-Gilead tree by the roadside as you are driving homeward through the twilight of August; or, best of all, the clean, spicy, unexpected, unmistakable smell of a bed of spearmint—that is the bed whereon Memory loves to lie and dream!

Why not choose mint as the symbol of remembrance? It is the true spice-tree of our Northern clime, the myrrh and frankincense of the land of lingering snow. When its perfume rises, the shrines of the past are unveiled, and the magical rites of reminiscence begin.

I

You are fishing down the Swiftwater in the early Spring. In a shallow pool, which the drought of summer will soon change into dry land, you see the pale-green shoots of a little plant thrusting themselves up between the pebbles, and just beginning to overtop the falling water. You pluck a leaf of it as you turn out of the stream to find a comfortable place for lunch, and, rolling it between your fingers to see whether it smells like a good salad for your bread and cheese, you discover suddenly that it is new mint. For the rest of that day you are bewitched; you follow a stream that runs through the country of "Auld Lang Syne," and fill your creel with the recollections of a boy and a rod.

And yet, strangely enough, you cannot recall the boy himself at all distinctly. There is only the faintest image of him on the endless roll of films that has been wound through your mental camera: and in the very spots where his small figure should appear, it seems as if the pictures were always light-struck. Just a blur, and the dim outline of a new cap, or a well-beloved jacket with extra pockets, or a much-hated pair of copper-toed shoes—that is all you can see.

But the people that the boy saw, the companions who helped or hindered him in his adventures, the sublime and marvellous scenes among the Catskills and the Adirondacks and the Green Mountains, in the midst of which he lived and moved and had his summer holidays—all these stand out sharp and clear, as the "Bab Ballads" say,

Photographically lined
On the tablets of your mind.

And most vivid do these scenes and people become when the vague and irrecoverable boy who walks among them carries a rod over his shoulder, and you detect the soft bulginess of wet fish about his clothing, and perhaps the tail of a big one emerging from his pocket. Then it seems almost as if these were things that had really happened, and of which you yourself were a great part.

The rod was a reward, yet not exactly of merit. It was an instrument of education in the hand of a father less indiscriminate than Solomon, who chose to interpret the text in a new way, and preferred to educate his child by encouraging him in pursuits which were harmless and wholesome, rather than by chastising him for practices which would likely enough never have been thought of, if they had not been forbidden. The boy enjoyed this kind of father at the time, and later he came to understand, with a grateful heart, that there is no richer inheritance in all the treasury of unearned blessings. For, after all, the love, the patience, the kindly wisdom of a grown man who can enter into the perplexities and turbulent impulses of a boy's heart, and give him cheerful companionship, and lead him on by free and joyful ways to know and choose the things that are pure and lovely and of good report, make as fair an image as we can find of that loving, patient Wisdom which must be above us all if any good is to come out of our childish race.

Now this was the way in which the boy came into possession of his undreaded rod. He was by nature and heredity one of those predestined anglers whom Izaak Walton tersely describes as "born so." His earliest passion was fishing. His favourite passage in Holy Writ was that place where Simon Peter throws a line into the sea and pulls out a great fish at the first cast.

But hitherto his passion had been indulged under difficulties—with improvised apparatus of cut poles, and flabby pieces of string, and bent pins, which always failed to hold the biggest fish; or perhaps with borrowed tackle, dangling a fat worm in vain before the noses of the staring, supercilious sunfish that poised themselves in the clear water around the

Lake house dock at Lake George; or, at best, on picnic parties across the lake, marred by the humiliating presence of nurses, and disturbed by the obstinate refusal of old Horace, the boatman, to believe that the boy could bait his own hook, but sometimes crowned with the delight of bringing home a whole basketful of yellow perch and goggle-eyes. Of nobler sport with game fish, like the vaulting salmon and the merry, pugnacious trout, as yet the boy had only dreamed. But he had heard that there were such fish in the streams that flowed down from the mountains around Lake George, and he was at the happy age when he could believe anything—if it was sufficiently interesting.

There was one little river, and only one, within his knowledge and the reach of his short legs. It was a tiny, lively rivulet that came out of the woods about half a mile away from the hotel, and ran down cater-cornered through a sloping meadow, crossing the road under a flat bridge of boards, just beyond the root-beer shop at the lower end of the village. It seemed large enough to the boy, and he had long had his eye upon it as a fitting theatre for the beginning of a real angler's life. Those rapids, those falls, those deep, whirling pools with beautiful foam on them like soft, white custard, were they not such places as the trout loved to hide in?

You can see the long hotel piazza, with the gossipy groups of wooden chairs standing vacant in the early afternoon; for the grown-up people are dallying with the ultimate nuts and raisins of their mid-day dinner. A villainous clatter of innumerable little vegetable-dishes comes from the open windows of the pantry as the boy steals past the kitchen end of the house, with Horace's lightest bamboo pole over his shoulder, and a little brother in skirts and short white stockings tagging along behind him.

When they come to the five-rail fence where the brook runs out of the field, the question is, Over or under? The lowlier method seems safer for the little brother, as well as less conspicuous for persons who desire to avoid publicity until their enterprise has achieved success. So they crawl beneath a bend in the lowest rail,—only tearing one tiny three-cornered hole in a jacket, and making some juicy green stains on the white stock- ings—and emerge with suppressed excitement in the field of the cloth of buttercups and daisies.

What an afternoon—how endless and yet how swift! What perilous efforts to leap across the foaming stream at its narrowest points; what escapes from quagmires and possible quicksands; what stealthy creeping through the grass to the edge of a likely pool, and cautious dropping of the line into an unseen depth, and patient waiting for a bite, until the restless little brother, prowling about below, discovers that the hook is not in the water at all, but lying on top of a dry stone—thereby proving that patience is not the only virtue—or, at least, that it does a better business when it has a small vice of impatience in partnership with it!

How tired the adventurers grow as the day wears away; and as yet they have taken nothing! But their strength and courage return as if by magic when there comes a surprising twitch at the line in a shallow, unpromising rapid, and with a jerk of the pole a small, wiggling fish is whirled through the air and landed thirty feet back in the meadow.

"For pity's sake, don't lose him! There he is among the roots of the blue flag."

"I've got him! How cold he is—how slippery—how pretty! Just like a piece of rainbow!"

"Do you see the red spots? Did you notice how gamy he was, little brother; how he played? It is a trout, for sure; a real trout, almost as long as your hand."

So the two lads tramp along up the stream, chattering as if there were no rubric of silence in the angler's code. Presently another simple-minded troutling falls a victim to their unpremeditated art; and they begin already, being human, to wish for something larger. In the very last pool that they dare attempt—a dark hole under a steep bank, where the brook issues from the woods—the boy drags out the hoped-for prize, a splendid trout, longer than a new lead-pencil. But he feels sure that there must be another, even larger, in the same place. He swings his line out carefully over the water, and just as he is about to drop it in, the little brother, perched on the sloping brink, slips on the smooth pine-needles, and goes sliddering down into the pool up to his waist. How he weeps with dismay, and how funnily his dress sticks to him as he crawls out! But his grief is soon assuaged by the privilege of carrying the trout strung on an alder twig; and it is a happy, muddy, proud pair of urchins that climb over the fence out of the field of triumph at the close of the day.

II

The arrival of the rod, in four joints, with an extra tip, a brass reel, and the other luxuries for which a true angler would willingly exchange the necessaries of life, marked a new epoch in the boy's career. At the uplifting of that wand, as if it had been in the hand of another Moses, the waters of infancy rolled back, and the way was opened into the promised land, whither the tyrant nurses, with all their proud array of baby-chariots, could not follow. The way was open, but not by any means dry. One of the first events in the dispensation of the rod was the purchase of a pair of high rubber boots. Inserted in this armour of modern infantry, and transfigured with delight, the boy clumped through all the little rivers within a circuit of ten miles from Caldwell, and began to learn by parental example the yet unmastered art of complete angling.

But because some of the streams were deep and strong, and his legs were short and slender, and his ambition was even taller than his boots, the father would sometimes take him up pickaback, and wade along carefully through the perilous places—which are often, in this world, the very places one longs to fish in. So, in your remembrance, you can see the little rubber boots sticking out under the father's arms, and the rod projecting over his head, and the bait dangling down unsteadily into the deep holes, and the delighted boy hooking and playing and basketing his trout high in the air. How many of our best catches in life are made from some one else's shoulders!

From this summer the whole earth became to the boy, as Tennyson describes the lotus country, "a land of streams." In school-days and in town he acknowledged the sway of those mysterious and irresistible forces which produce tops at one season, and marbles at another, and kites at another, and bind all boyish hearts to play mumble-the-peg at the due time more certainly than the stars are bound to their orbits. But when vacation came, with its annual exodus from the city, there was only one sign in the zodiac, and that was Pisces.

No country seemed to him tolerable without trout, and no landscape beautiful unless enlivened by a young river. Among what delectable mountains did those watery guides lead his vagrant steps, and with what curious, mixed, and sometimes profitable company did they make him familiar!

There was one exquisite stream among the Alleghanies, called Lycoming Creek, beside which the family spent a summer in a decadent inn, kept by a tremulous landlord who was always sitting on the steps of the porch, and whose most memorable remark was that he had "a misery in his stomach." This form of speech amused the boy, but he did not in the least comprehend it. It was the description of an unimaginable experience in a region which was as yet known to him only as the seat of pleasure. He did not understand how any one could be miserable when he could catch trout from his own dooryard.

The big creek, with its sharp turns from side to side of the valley, its hemlock-shaded falls in the gorge, and its long, still reaches in the "sugar-bottom," where the maple-trees grew as if in an orchard, and the superfluity of grasshoppers made the trout fat and dainty, was too wide to fit the boy. But nature keeps all sizes in her stock, and a smaller stream, called Rocky Run, came tumbling down opposite the inn, as if made to order for juvenile use.

How well you can follow it, through the old pasture overgrown with alders, and up past the broken-down mill-dam and the crumbling sluice, into the mountain-cleft from which it leaps laughing! The water, except just after a rain-storm, is as transparent as glass—old-fashioned window-glass, I mean, in small panes, with just a tinge of green in it, like the air in a grove of young birches. Twelve feet down in the narrow chasm below the falls, where the water is full of tiny bubbles, like Apollinaris, you can see the trout poised, with their heads up-stream, motionless, but quivering a little, as if they were strung on wires.

The bed of the stream has been scooped out of the solid rock. Here and there banks of sand have been deposited, and accumulations of loose stone disguise the real nature of the channel. Great boulders have been rolled down the alleyway and left where they chanced to stick; the stream must get around them or under them as best it can. But there are other places where everything has been swept clean; nothing remains but the primitive strata, and the flowing water merrily tickles the bare ribs of mother earth. Whirling stones, in the spring floods, have cut well-holes in the rock, as round and even as if they had been made with a drill, and sometimes you can see the very stone that sunk the well lying at the bottom. There are long, straight, sloping troughs through which the water runs like a mill-race. There are huge basins into which the water rumbles over a ledge, as if some one were pouring it very steadily out of a pitcher, and from which it glides away without a ripple, flowing over a smooth pavement of rock which shelves down from the shallow foot to the deep head of the pool.

The boy wonders how far he dare wade out along that slippery floor. The water is within an inch of his boot-tops now. But the slope seems very even, and just beyond his reach a good fish is rising. Only one step more, and then, like the wicked man in the psalm, his feet begin to slide. Slowly, and standing bolt upright, with the rod held high above his head, as if it must on no account get wet, he glides forward up to his neck in the ice-cold bath, gasping with amazement. There have been other and more serious situations in life into which, unless I am mistaken, you have made an equally unwilling and embarrassed entrance, and in which you have been surprised to find yourself not only up to your neck, but over—and you are a lucky man if you have had the presence of mind to stand still for a moment, before wading out, and make sure at least of the fish that tempted you into your predicament.

But Rocky Run, they say, exists no longer. It has been blasted by miners out of all resemblance to itself, and bewitched into a dingy water-power to turn wheels for the ugly giant, Trade. It is only in the valley of remembrance that its current still flows like liquid air; and only in that country that you can still see the famous men who came and went along the banks of the Lyocoming when the boy was there.

There was Collins, who was a wondrous adept at "daping, dapping, or dibbling" with a grasshopper, and who once brought in a string of trout which he laid out head to tail on the grass before the house in a line of beauty forty-seven feet long. A mighty bass voice had this Collins also, and could sing, "Larboard Watch, Ahoy!" "Down in a Coal-Mine," and other profound ditties in a way to make all the glasses on the table jingle; but withal, as you now suspect, rather a fishy character, and undeserving of the unqualified respect which the boy had for him. And there was Dr. Romsen, lean, satirical, kindly, a skilful though reluctant physician, who regarded it as a personal injury if any one in the party fell sick in summer time; and a passionately unsuccessful hunter, who would sit all night in the crotch of a tree beside an alleged deer-lick, and come home perfectly satisfied if he had heard a hedgehog grunt. It was he who called attention to the discrepancy between the boy's appetite and his size by saying loudly at a picnic, "I wouldn't grudge you what you eat, my boy, if I could only see that it did you any good,"—which remark was not forgiven until the doctor redeemed his reputation by pronouncing a serious medical opinion, before a council of mothers, to the effect that it did not really hurt a boy to get his feet wet. That was worthy of Galen in his most inspired moment. And there was hearty, genial Paul Merit, whose mere company was an education in good manners, and who could eat eight hard-boiled eggs for supper without ruffling his equanimity; and the tall, thin, grinning Major, whom an angry Irishwoman once described as "like a comb, all back and teeth;" and many more were the comrades of the boy's father, all of whom he admired (and followed when they would let him), but none so much as the father himself, because he was the wisest, kindest, and merriest of all that merry crew, now dispersed to the uttermost parts of the earth and beyond.

Other streams played a part in the education of that happy boy: the Kaaterskill, where there had been nothing but the ghosts of trout for the last thirty years, but where the absence of fish was almost forgotten in the joy of a first introduction to Dickens, one very showery day, when dear old Ned Mason built a smoky fire in a cave below Haines's Falls, and, pulling The Old Curiosity Shop out of his pocket, read aloud about Little Nell until the tears ran down the cheeks of reader and listener—the smoke was so thick, you know: and the Neversink, which flows through John Burroughs's country, and past one house in particular, perched on a high bluff, where a very dreadful old woman come out and throws stones at "city fellers fishin' through her land" (as if any one wanted to touch her land! It was the water that ran over it, you see, that carried the fish with it, and they were not hers at all): and the stream at Healing Springs, in the Virginia mountains, where the medicinal waters flow down into a lovely wild brook without injuring the health of the trout in the least, and where the only drawback to the angler's happiness is the abundance of rattlesnakes—but a boy does not mind such things as that; he feels as if he were immortal. Over all these streams memory skips lightly, and strikes a trail through the woods to the Adirondacks, where the boy made his first acquaintance with navigable rivers—that is to say, rivers which are traversed by canoes and hunting-skiffs, but not yet defiled by steamboats—and slept, or rather lay awake, for the first time on a bed of balsam-boughs in a tent.

III

The promotion from all-day picnics to a two weeks' camping-trip is like going from school to college. By this time a natural process of evolution has raised the first rod to something lighter and more flexible—a fly-rod, so to speak, but not a bigoted one—just a serviceable, unprejudiced article, not above using any kind of bait that may be necessary to catch the fish. The father has received the new title of "governor," indicating not less, but more authority, and has called in new instructors to carry on the boy's education: real Adirondack guides—old Sam Dunning and one-eyed Enos, the last and laziest of the Saranac Indians. Better men will be discovered for later trips, but none more amusing, and none whose woodcraft seems more wonderful than that of this queerly matched team, as they make the first camp in a pelting rain-storm on the shore of Big Clear Pond. The pitching of the tents is a lesson in architecture, the building of the camp-fire a victory over damp nature, and the supper of potatoes and bacon and fried trout a veritable triumph of culinary art.

At midnight the rain is pattering persistently on the canvas; the fronts flaps are closed and tied together; the lingering fire shines through them, and sends vague shadows wavering up and down: the governor is rolled up in his blankets, sound asleep. It is a very long night for the boy.

What is that rustling noise outside the tent? Probably some small creature, a squirrel or a rabbit. Rabbit stew would be good for breakfast. But it sounds louder now, almost loud enough to be a fox—there are no wolves left in the Adirondacks, or at least only a very few. That is certainly quite a heavy footstep prowling around the provision-box. Could it be a panther—they step very softly for their size—or a bear perhaps? Sam Dunning told about catching one in a trap just below here. (Ah, my boy, you will soon learn that there is no spot in all the forests created by a bountiful Providence so poor as to be without its bear story.) Where was the rifle put? There it is, at the foot of the tent-pole. Wonder if it is loaded?

"Waugh-ho! Waugh-ho-o-o-o!"

The boy springs from his blankets like a cat, and peeps out between the tent-flaps. There sits Enos, in the shelter of a leaning tree by the fire, with his head thrown back and a bottle poised at his mouth. His lonely eye is cocked up at a great horned owl on the branch above him. Again the sudden voice breaks out:

"Whoo! whoo! whoo cooks for you all?" [Editor's note: Such a call is not that of the great horned owl as referenced by the author, but is the barred owl.]

Enos puts the bottle down, with a grunt, and creeps off to his tent.

"De debbil in dat owl," he mutters. "How he know I cook for dis camp? How he know 'bout dat bottle? Ugh!"

There are hundreds of pictures that flash into light as the boy goes on his course, year after year, through the woods. There is the luxurious camp on Tupper's Lake, with its log cabins in the spruce-grove, and its regiment of hungry men who ate almost a deer a day; and there is the little bark shelter on the side of Mount Marcy, where the governor and the boy, with baskets full of trout from the Opalescent River, are spending the night, with nothing but a fire to keep them warm. There is the North Bay at Moosehead, with Joe La Croix (one more Frenchman who thinks he looks like Napoleon) posing on the rocks beside his canoe, and only reconciled by his vanity to the wasteful pastime of taking photographs while the big fish are rising gloriously out at the end of the point. There is the small spring-hole beside the Saranac River, where Pliny Robbins and the boy caught twenty-three noble trout, weighing from one to three pounds apiece, in the middle of a hot August afternoon, and hid themselves in the bushes when ever they heard a party coming down the river, because they did not care to attract company; and there are the Middle Falls, where the governor stood on a long spruce log, taking two-pound fish with the fly, and stepping out at every cast a little nearer to the end of the log, until it slowly tipped with him, and he settled down into the river.

Among such scenes as these the boy pursued his education, learning many things that are not taught in colleges; learning to take the weather as it comes, wet or dry, and fortune as it falls, good or bad; learning that a meal which is scanty fare for one becomes a banquet for two—provided the other is the right person; learning that there is some skill in everything, even in digging bait, and that what is called luck consists chiefly in having your tackle in good order; learning that a man can be just as happy in a log shanty as in a brownstone mansion, and that the very best pleasures are those that do not leave a bad taste in the mouth. And in all this the governor was his best teacher and his closest comrade.

Dear governor, you have gone out of the wilderness now, and your steps will be no more beside these remembered little rivers—no more, forever and forever. You will not come in sight around any bend of this clear Swiftwater stream where you made your last cast; your cheery voice will never again ring out through the deepening twilight where you are lingering for your disciple to catch up with you; he will never again hear you call: "Hallo, my boy! What luck? Time to go home!" But there is a river in the country where you have gone, is there not?—a river with trees growing all along it—evergreen trees; and somewhere by those shady banks, within sound of clear running waters, I think you will be dreaming and waiting for your boy, if he follows the trail that you have shown him even to the end.

CHAPTER FIFTEEN

The Night of the Gytefisk

by Ernest Schwiebert

The occasions when I had the opportunity to fish with my friend the late Ernie Schwiebert were far fewer than I would have liked, but they qualify as memorable experiences in every way. In Iceland, on the storied Brodheads in Pennsylvania, I watched Ernie dissect salmon and trout water with the skilled cuts of a master surgeon. Ernie didn't merely fish a stream: He stripped it bare, from the outer layers of skin to the marrow of the bones. No secrets could remain hidden long from his detailed analysis. It's all very simple, really. Ernest Schwiebert found where the fish were, figured out why they were there and what they were doing, then proceeded to catch them. Or maybe I've got it backwards. Perhaps he figured out what they were doing first, then found them. In any case, as likely as not when you looked his way on the stream you'd see the bowed, straining hoop of his rod.

Ernie's literary output was nothing short of prodigious. He wrote magazine pieces on the New Mexico years of the artist Georgia O'Keeffe, Russia's Saint Petersburg, the great castle hotels of Ireland, and the historic shrines of Ise Shima in Japan. He published books about Alaska, its fishing, and amazing ecology; the legendary Umpqua and its steelhead; and the salmon rivers of Russia. He also prepared updated editions of his classic Matching the Hatch *and* Nymphs *for publication by Lyons Press.*

"The Night of the Gytefisk" is from Ernie's collection of stories A River for Christmas and Other Stories, *published by The Stephen Greene Press, Inc., of Viking Penguin, Inc., in 1988. In this tale we'll be journeying as close as*

most of us will ever get to Norway's legendary Alta, home of record-breaking Atlantic salmon and the Aberdeen Proving Ground where reel drags, backing, and fish-playing skills are tested to their limits.

Skree-jah! THE TERNS SCREAMED. *Skree-jah!*

The midnight sun hung low on the northern horizon, strangely bright at two o'clock in the morning. The ghillies decided to stop for lunch. No one fished except in the twelve-hour twilight that passed for night. The boatmen skillfully worked our slender Karasjok riverboat ashore, and its graceful Viking-shaped prow grated on the gravelly shingle. Such boats have been used by river Lapps for centuries and are perfectly suited for salmon fishing.

It was quite cool for July, and a brisk wind riffled the great pool at Steinfossnakken. The ghillies built a fire on the beach, and I studied the midnight sun on the waterfalls that spill like Yosemite from the escarpment at Sautso, their plumes a thousand feet above the river. Cooking smells of bouillon and hot coffee eddied on the wind, and we sat on the mossy boulders, listening to the muted thunder of the Gabofoss Rapids a mile upstream.

Skree-jah! the terns cried.

The graceful birds were catching Metretopis flies that were hatching from the river, and I watched their hovering and fluttering before they dropped like ospreys to seize the mayflies with a rapier-swift strike of their beaks. Grayling worked softly to the hatching flies. The grayling ran between two and three pounds, but we were after bigger game. Three salmon lay gleaming in the boat, wedged crosswise to ballast its slender lapstrake hull. The best had been taken at Mostajokka, bright with sea-lice and thirty-three pounds. The smallest went twenty-one, less than average for the river. When it had cartwheeled awkwardly on its first eighty-yard run, the ghillies had laughed contemptuously and called it a grilse.

The thick sandwiches and hot soup warmed our bodies, and we sipped coffee laced with cognac, watching the river. Two wiry Lapps went past in the mail boat, bound for the Sautso camp at Sirpinakken. The Lapps waved and we waved back. We were in no hurry, with three fine salmon in the boat, although we would fish another two hours before reaching the middle camp at Sandia.

It was my second night at Sandia, and in the morning, the mail boat was scheduled to ferry me upriver to Sautso. The Sandia camp had been built for the Duke of Roxburgh in 1873, its simple log frame almost unchanged in more than a century. There are two bedrooms with private baths. Its sitting room has a fireplace, and four trophy fish between forty and fifty pounds. The trophies were taken by the Duke and Duchess of Roxburgh, and the room has become something of a shrine. The fishing house at Sandia sits high above the river, with a grassy clearing that reaches down from its porch to the boat landing.

The river itself begins in the treeless snowmelt plateaus and escarpments of the Finnmarksvidda, two hundred miles above the polar circle in Norway. It lies eight hundred miles north of Oslo, at the latitude of Point Barrow in Alaska. The valley floor is thickly forested, while the Finnmarksvidda is a granite highland that bears the lakes and grinding scars of the Pleistocene glaciers that shaped most of northern Europe. These arctic barrens are a world of scattered taiga and immense tundra moors, pockmarked and scoured with dark peat-stained tarns. The river gathers in the lichens and pothole seepages below Kautokeino, the settlement that is considered the capital of Lapland. The district shelters a number of Lapp encampments, with their pyramidal log roofs and storehouses on stilts and turf cabins. The settlements are permanent sites where the Lapp herdsmen winter with their reindeer. They migrate with their herds each spring, carrying their skin-covered pole shelters on the treks. The Lapps are patient and hardy. There is both wry humor and sadness in their coppery faces, deeply wrinkled by the weather at such latitudes—it is a swiftly vanishing tribal way of life.

The river rises slowly in its lacework of glacial ponds and burns, mixing and gathering until it finally spills into a series of deeply scoured gorges, fifty miles north of Kautokeino. Its first twenty miles are lost in steep-walled faults and chasms, filled with the spilling of countless waterfalls. Salmon are thought to spawn in these headwaters, using the labyrinths of impassable cliffs and rapids. Below the little gorge at Sautso, the river changes completely.

Between Sautso and its estuary, the river is a symphony in three movements. Below the first tumbling chutes at Svartfossnakken and Bolvero, its moods are almost pastoral, sliding into the two-mile mirror of smooth water below the fishing-camp at Sirpinakken. Such pianissimo passages change swiftly at the Velliniva Narrows, eddying into the deep half-mile lake that ends in the Gabofoss Rapids. The river plunges wildly through truck-sized boulders there, dropping almost eighty feet in less than a quarter mile.

Downstream from the Gabofoss portage, the river gathers itself again. It spills into the swirling amphitheater at Steinfossnakken, and its famous Sandia beats begin. The Sandia beats are a stairsteps of boulder pockets and brief holding-lies, rather than salmon pools in the classic sense. These reaches of river spill into brief, connecting rapids before swelling and spreading into another pool. Sandia ends in the moss-walled gorge above Battagorski, where the river fights its way through cottage-sized boulders. The river has claimed many lives here, its angry music filled with brass and kettledrums and cymbals.

The forests become dense at Battagorski, thriving on the sheltered valley floor. There is a magnificent salmon pool there, deep and smooth flowing above the great boulders that hide in its Stygian currents. It is a favorite midnight-lunch pool. Twenty-five summers ago, I watched Sampson Field hook a heavy salmon at Battagorski. It took a Silver Durham with a strike that wrenched his two-handed rod into a tight circle. The fight began as a stubborn tug of war. The ghillies worked hard to hold the boat against the strong current, and Field leaned back into the fish. It was sullen and strong. It did not jump and it steadily forced the boat downstream. The oarsman was sculling hard, his face tightening into a grimace of pain, watching the mossy boulders slip past. The current hissed past their longboat, its stern trailing a thickly eddying line of foam, and it drifted inexorably toward the rapids.

The big salmon was winning. It forced the boat into the swiftly gathering currents and bulled off into the chutes downstream. We still had not seen the fish and scrambled to follow in a second boat. The salmon was still taking line. It was exciting to follow down the rapids, watching the boatmen fight to stay alive and stay with the fish, and changing priorities in the wild chutes. The war lasted almost a mile, until it ended in a rocky backwater and the ghillie waited like a heron with the gaff.

Field pumped the fish close. The ghillie stared into the dark tea-colored currents and spume. Suddenly his shoulders tightened and he struck, swinging the great fish aboard. It was dispatched with a priest while Field rummaged through his tackle bag for the scale.

Twenty kilos! he said excitedly.

Forty-four pounds, I said and shook hands with him. Congratulations!

It was some fight, Field nodded.

Battagorski is a huge pool, its eddying depths brooding and mysterious, tracing fingerprints of foam. Its salmon lies mark the beginning of the classic Jøraholmen beats. These lower pools include such famous water as Gargia and Bradstraumen, where I watched the Duchess of Roxburgh boat a forty-six pound cockfish in 1963. Bradstraumen is also the pool that surrendered a forty-nine pound salmon to Charles Ritz in 1954, fishing as a guest of Herbert Pulitzer, and Ritz wrote knowledgeably about the river in his book *A Flyfisher's Life*. Ritz fished two seasons at Jøraholmen and its sweeping salmon pools, where the river finally winds through a valley of farmsteads and forests to the villages at its mouth. The estuary itself is unimpressive. Its shallows spread across a series of gravelly channels a hundred miles south of Hammarfest and its North Cape. Bossekop is the village at its mouth, its cheerful houses a brightly painted collage of color scattered along its hillsides. The fjord itself is more sprawling than scenic. It was not always so peaceful, because its sheltered moorings held German pocket battleships forty-five years ago, during the bitter convoy campaigns between Reykjavik and Murmansk. The river is the finest salmon fishery in the world.

It is the storied Alta.

The Alta has been fished since the Duke of Roxburgh first sailed his yacht into its fjord in 1862 and discovered that the river teemed with big salmon. Roxburgh shared its sport for many years with the Duke of Westminster, who was famous for both salmon fishing and his liaisons with the French couturier, Coco Chanel. Roxburgh built the Sandia and Sautso camps in Victorian times, but in earlier seasons his parties fished from steam yachts moored off Bossekop. The beats were fished in rotation, splitting the rods into four groups. Each party was patiently ferried and poled to Sautso, where they camped and floated back to their luxurious quarters on the yachts. When the first party reached the middle beats at Sandia, the second was ferried past them to the upper river, and the third group soon followed. These parties poled and portaged along the river throughout July, fishing back from Sautso to the comfort and cuisine of the yachts, stopping at rough camps along the river.

It was a time of great wealth and privilege.

Alta has been fished in our century by a parade of celebrated anglers. The Duke of Windsor and his equerry, the Earl of Dudley, were regulars on the river more than a half century ago. The Duke and Duchess of Westminster fished it steadily until his death in 1953, except during the Second World War, when German forces occupied Norway.

The Roxburgh family fished the river for more than a century, except for the war years, and the late Duke of Roxburgh had fished it every summer since childhood. The family seat was the Floors Castle at Kelso-on-Tweed, which commands the great salmon pool where the Teviot joins the Tweed. Roxburgh fished its spring runs from early childhood, sailed to fish the Alta for an entire month each summer, returned to shoot grouse in the highlands, and fished the autumn salmon run on the Tweed in Roxburghshire.

It's been wonderful, Roxburgh admitted over supper at Jøraholmen on the Alta. It's been a life spent rather well, I think.

Death duties and other changes in British life eventually ended British control of the river at midcentury. Anglers like Admiral Edward MacDonald, Herbert Pulitzer, Charles Ritz, Tony Pulitzer, Seward Johnson, Carter Nicholas, Anderson Fowler, Edward Litchfield, Robert Pabst, Ted Benzinger, Ralph Strauss, Roger Gaillard, R. R. Donnelly, Sampson Field, Peter Pleydell-Bouverie, Peter Kriendler, Robert Graham, Thomas Lenk, James Graham, Ogden Goelet, Cornelius Ryan, Robert Goelet, George Coe, Lee Wulff, General Lawrence Kuter, Charles Vaughan, General Thomas White, Walton Ferguson, Warrington Gillett, Sir Thomas Sopwith, Nathaniel Pryor Reed, Sir James Pearman, Earl Worsham, Philip Kingsland Crowe, and Admiral William Read—who successfully flew an NC-4 flying boat across the Atlantic before Lindbergh—became pilgrims to the Alta fishery over the past thirty-odd years.

Its fishing is unique. Twice in the past century, the river surrendered more than thirty fish to a solitary angler in a single night's sport. The Duke of Roxburgh took thirty-nine in 1860, and James Harewood killed twenty-six 16 years later. Major Courtney Trotter caught twenty-nine weighing 615 pounds in 1925. The following season, the Duke of Westminster boated thirty-three salmon weighing 792 pounds in twelve hours. Such catches averaged approximately twenty-three pounds. Sampson Field holds the modern record, with seventeen fish from the storied Gargia in a single night—all taken with flies and averaging just under thirty pounds, and the Alta surrendered eleven salmon weighing better than forty pounds that season.

Charles Ritz has written about such sport in *A Flyfisher's Life*, and I have heard him sing its praises from the little bar just off the rue Cambon, in his famous hotel at the Place Vendôme in Paris. It is simply unique! Ritz insisted excitedly with Gallic gestures and staccato speech. There are no mountains except the Himalayas, no oceans to equal the Pacific, no fish like the Atlantic salmon—and there is only a single Alta!

Ritz was right. Like a rock climber who has not tested his skills against Dhaulagiri or Annapurna in Nepal, and like the hunter who has not seen the Serengeti, the salmon fisherman dreams of fishing the Alta. Although I had boated a half-dozen fish over twenty pounds on three brief visits to Jøraholmen, I had been awestruck by a brace of cockfish weighed at its ghillie's hut that weighed over forty pounds in 1963. Those trophies had been taken by the Duchess of Roxburgh and Peter Pleydell-Bouverie, who had served with the British Western Desert Force, elite commando troops that gathered intelligence behind German lines in Africa. The Alta has the smell of history.

Valhalla! Ritz insisted over lunch with Robert Pabst and Ralph Strauss at the River Club in Manhattan. It's the Valhalla of salmon fishing—and once you have tasted it, nothing in your life is the same!

My first night at Sandia was something of an accident. I had been fishing the Reisa, and it had been so poor that we decided to leave three days early. When I arrived at Bossekop, there was a message telling me to come immediately to Sandia. Its party was a rod short, since one of the fishermen had become ill, and I had been asked to fish out his last day. It was not so much a day of fishing I had been offered, since the salmon I might catch belonged to the river owners and were worth considerable money. The night's fishing proved wonderful. Although I felt a little like a Danish trawler, I took ten salmon averaging twenty-three pounds with a ten-foot Garrison that had belonged to the late Paul Hyde Bonner.

The boatmen arrived after lunch to ferry me farther up the river to Sautso, and we motored upstream through famous pools like Ronga and Mostajokka to the foot of the boulder-strewn portage at Steinfossnakken. We changed boats there. The ghillies carried my duffle and baggage between them on a heavy pole, past the wild torrent of the Gabofoss rapids to the lip of the Gabofoss waterfall itself. I carried the tackle and a small duffle of fly-tying gear. Gabofoss thundered past in its chill explosions of spray, its roar blotting out all thought and other sounds, filling the morning with its icy breath. The rocky trail was traversed slowly, and finally we reached the Sautso stillwater.

We spooked a great fish lying off the upper boat mooring, and its wake disturbed the rocky shallows. The old boatman stood looking at the towering cliffs, squinting into a surprising midday sun.

Sautso is a paradise, he said.

Several terns circled and screamed, capturing salmon fry in the shallows. We rested before loading my baggage into the second Karasjok longboat and started upstream toward the Sautso camp, crossing the smooth flowage that lies between Sirpinakken and the Gabofoss Rapids.

The Sautso camp stands astride the small tributary at Sirpinakken, under the thousand-foot escarpments across the river. Its fishing house is simple and rough. It was also built by the Duke of Roxburgh just after our Civil War. There is a sitting room with log walls sheathed in wainscoting, two bedrooms with rudimentary baths, a small kitchen, and quarters for a cook and serving girl. The ghillies sleep in a Lapp turf cabin near the river. The sitting room wall had a pale pencil-tracing of the fifty-nine pound salmon caught by Admiral William Read at Steinfossnakken in 1962. It had been taken with a 3/0 hairwing Abbey dressed for the admiral at William Mills & Son. The salmon tracing was primitive and faint, in great danger of fading away. I reverently retraced its muscular outlines on the wainscoting with black fly-head lacquer, like the delicate brushwork in Japanese calligraphy.

The afternoon was still bright when the cook informed me that supper was scheduled for seven o'clock. Fishing would start at eight. Black curtains kept the light from the sleeping quarters, but I slept only fitfully, dreaming of giant salmon. Sleep proved difficult all week with the day's clock turned upside down. Supper is actually breakfast, since the fishing starts at eight and lasts until midnight, when the ghillies break to eat lunch, drink coffee, and plan tactics for the rest of the night. The midnight break is welcome. Depending on the night's sport, the fishing can last until five o'clock. Whisky is also welcome after an entire night on the river, and a wonderful cold buffet is always waiting too. Breakfast is transformed into an early-morning supper, and the anglers sleep through the morning until the late afternoon. Clocks are set for three o'clock, leaving a leisurely time to prepare tackle and dress flies. Cocktails come again at six, with dinner at seven o'clock, while the ghillies prepare their Karasjok longboats for another night's fishing.

The dice cup was brought out over coffee. We rolled dice, and my boat was awarded the upper river from Toppen, where the river finally escapes its impenetrable gorges, to the pretty pool called Dormenin. It is among the few wadable pools on the entire twenty-seven miles of river. We carried my tackle to the boat after supper, and I clambered eagerly aboard, trying hard to conceal a wildly swelling sense of excitement.

The motor caught quickly and we circled out. We traveled upstream swiftly, hand-lining the longboat around the Svartfossen Rapids and past the rocky chutes called Bolvero and Jagorski. Toppen lay still farther, flowing smooth and almost still between low cliffs that rise straight from the river. The ghillies put me ashore on the rocks and lined the boat farther upstream to the last mooring. They secured it there. The boatmen built a fire, brewed a pot of fresh coffee, and filled their pipes.

We pulled the boat over the fish, they explained in Norwegian. We must give the salmon time to forget us.

The coffee tastes good, I nodded.

Finally we doused the fire and started fishing. We clambered down through the boulders and pushed off, rowing furtively upstream. We waited quietly and I checked my tackle again. Leader knots are critical on fish averaging between twenty and thirty pounds. The pool seems quite deep, its secrets hidden in tea-colored depths. The ghillies had selected a big Orange Blossom, a silver-bodied hairwing dressed on a 3/0 double. Alta is a big-fly river. The current was swift and smooth against the opposite wall of rocks. It was a roll-casting place with another cliff of rhyolite behind us, and I had to loop the big fly only thirty-five feet to cover the fish. Their lie was tight against the cliffs. The boatman at the bow rowed patiently, measuring the current's speed and letting our boat drop about two feet downstream between each successive cast. It was obvious that he used outcroppings and other benchmarks to calibrate his work. It required great strength and discipline, mixed with intimate knowledge of the river. His skills were remarkable.

The fish were holding in a classic lie. I worked through ten casts against the cliffs, locking the line under my index finger with the rod-tip held low, pointing toward the fly as I patiently followed its swing. Our salmon tactics were basic.

But the Alta boatmen have evolved some footnotes over the century. The ghillie seated at the stern works a single scull to sweep the boat's stern with the fly-swing. The fisherman stands at the middle of the boat, bracing his legs against a cross-thwart shaped to cup his knees.

When the fly-swing came around toward the stern, I lifted the rod over the ghillie to extend its teasing half-circle, letting it work well behind the boat. The boat's stern followed smoothly, controlled perfectly by the ghillies, and deftly came back into line. My pickup was roughly parallel to the boat, and I false-cast once, changing direction into the final cast itself. It was beautiful fishing teamwork, rhythmic and metronome smooth, and I have not seen its equal elsewhere.

Before picking up each cast at the end of its fly-swing, I let it hang there swimming in the current a few seconds. Several six-inch pulls followed in a retrieve of about ten feet. Sometimes a fish following a swinging fly will take it when the fly-swing stops. Sometimes a fish will follow through its entire swing, circling under the fly when it stops, and take when its final retrieve is started back toward the boat. The ghillies believe the big Alta fish follow a fly surprising distances, and experience on the river confirms their judgment.

Salmon fishing is discipline and patience. Anglers must cover half-mile riffles with hundreds of patient, concentric fly-swings. The mind drifts and daydreams with the steady drumbeats of muffled oar-locks and casting, and I had started to think of other things when there was a big swirl.

Laks! said the ghillie softly.

The fish had rolled at the fly without taking, and the boatman stroked hard to hold our position, helping me repeat the cast.

He comes again! the ghillie hissed.

The entire current had bulged when my fly worked past, and there was literally a bow-wave showing, but there was still no weight. The fish had still not touched the big Orange Blossom.

Did you feel anything? he asked. Did you feel him?

No, I said.

Cast back to him again, he whispered.

Sometimes a fish can be teased into taking by changing the fly-swing. It was possible that my fly was swimming through too fast, perhaps faster than it seemed. The third cast dropped and settled into its swing, and I slowed the teasing rod-tip, stripping about six inches of line into its bellying quarter-cycle. It slowed the fly just as it reached the salmon's lie, until it seemed to hang momentarily, and the fish was hooked.

There had been no warning, no bulging swirl when the fish rolled to follow. Its weight was surprising. The rod had simply snapped down as the bellying line sliced back against the current, and there was a tail splash when the fish bored deep and sounded.

Good fish! I thought wildly.

Several times it threatened to leave Toppen, working deep under the boat and bolting back into the shallows at its tail. Each time we patiently worked it back into the pool. It was almost thirty minutes before we finally controlled its strength. The boatman worked us back against the cliffs, between some sheltering rocks, and I pumped the salmon close. The ghillie in the stern reached with his gaff, deftly wrestling a thirty-pound henfish over the gunwale, and dispatched it. He washed the priest and laid our prize across the boat.

Det var findt! he grinned.

We rested the pool again, holding the longboat among the rocks while the boatmen smoked their pipes, and I ate a little Toblerone chocolate. We took a second twenty-pound fish farther down the pool, landing it easily after its first run threatened to reach the rapids.

Below the broken quarter-mile at Toppen lies the Jagotku Pool, the swift boulder-filled chute where the late Joe Brooks took a forty-pound cockfish, sharing a rod with his host, Warrington Gillett. The boatman walked our craft down the shallows while I waded and fished through Jagotku. It did not seem a likely holding-lie. But when the fly worked past a giant boulder, almost skittering across the choppy spume, a third salmon slashed out to seize it. The fish fought well but did not try to reach the chutes farther downstream, and it surrendered almost meekly. It weighed twenty-two pounds, and the boatmen came running to help just before I tailed the fish myself.

We laid the fish crosswise in the boat and decided to stop fishing. It was almost midnight, and it was getting overcast and cold, although it was still surprisingly bright. The fire on the rocky bar felt good. The boatman gathered more firewood while the ghillie laid out the midnight supper, making fresh coffee and heating a thick cauliflower soup. There were smoked reindeer and sausages and dill-cured salmon, and we finished with thick rose-hip jelly and cookies. It was quite cold when we doused the fire and launched the boat again.

Svartfossnakken was next, a sprawling rough-water pool where the river turned sharply toward the west, gathering itself to plunge into the Svartfossen Rapids. Their currents looked fierce, tumbling through a long sickle-shaped curve at the base of the mountain. Huge boulders and scour lines high above the river bore witness to the volume of its spring spates. The rapids are almost frightening downstream. The boatman held us expertly above the chute, back-rowing with seemingly effortless skill, while I covered the pool. We hooked another salmon after changing flies, and the boatman fought to hold our position, while I tried to force the fish. It proved foolish and the fly pulled out.

The ghillies quickly saw that I was not unhappy, and we laughed together, deciding to rest the pool. It was already almost two o'clock. We had three fish in the boat, and that was considered par on the Sautso water.

We hooked a second fish at Svartfossen almost immediately. It was a smaller fish, perhaps twelve pounds, and I suspect it was a stray from the Eiby tributary on the lower river. It fought well, but unlike the others, it lacked the weight to use the river and beat us. The fish was quickly boated.

Grilse, the ghillie teased wryly.

The boatmen lined their way down through the Svartfossen Rapids while I walked downstream through the boulders to Dormenin. It was our last salmon pool that night. Dormenin is the only real greased-line pool on the entire Sautso water, and I changed reels while the ghillies brought the boat downstream. Fishing from the shore, I moved a fish twice from a shallow lie where I once saw Ralph Strauss lose an immense salmon when the knot failed at the fly. I tried the fish for thirty minutes, but it did not show itself again. Another fish rolled farther downstream. The boatmen arrived, and I got aboard to fish the place it had porpoised, where the pool slides into Ovre Harstrommen. It was cold and starting to rain, and we fished through without moving another salmon. Dormenin was the bottom pool of our first night's beat.

It had been a good night, and we were ahead of the three-fish average at Sautso, although the Eiby stray was small. The boatmen were pleased with our night's work. It was four o'clock and still dark and overcast. When we reached the camp at the Jotkajavrre tributary, the ghillies were studying the sky. The smooth expanse of the Sautso was lost in misting rain.

Russian weather, the boatman said.

It will be stormy, the ghillie agreed, but tomorrow we have Gabo and Velliniva to fish.

Good pools? I asked.

Excellent pools, the ghillie said. Velliniva is our favorite.

It was raining hard before we finished eating and went to bed, and we fell asleep to its steady kettledrum pounding on the roof. I had stayed up long enough to dress several big Orange Blossoms. With the black curtains drawn tight, I fell asleep gratefully, listening to the rain.

It was late afternoon when the serving girl awakened us, but it was still gloomy and dark. The overcast had settled between the ragged escarpments until it hung like a shroud, a hundred feet above the river. Our breakfast omelets and goat cheese and brislings were ready, and the ghillies sat unhappily in the kitchen, staring at the barometer.

Russian weather, they muttered.

It did not feel like a fishing night. The barometer dropped right through the glass last night, I said. It's really low.

Ja, they agreed sourly.

It was raw and cold when we loaded the boats. We traveled slowly upstream to the gravel-bar island at Dormenin, rigged our tackle in the rain, and started at Ovre Harstrommen. The boatmen looked dour and sat staring at the current. The night grew more gloomy, its overcast settling until great scraps of mist drifted through the trees. It was raining harder now. We shouldered into our ponchos and slickers, watching the tea-colored river. It was rising slightly and looked murky. The ghillie had pointed happily to a freshly tied Orange Blossom, the pattern that had killed well the night before, and insisted on knotting it to the nylon himself. Since the ghillies share in the salmon which are sold, they seldom trust knots tied by others. The boatman worked us patiently into position, his leather oar pads squeaking in the rain, while we fished the sixty-yard pool.

Nothing! I said quietly when we had fished it out. Too gloomy for fishing.

Perhaps it's a gytefisk night.

What's a gytefisk?

It's a really big cockfish, the ghillie explained. Some nights we catch nothing, even on the Alta—but when we finally catch something on such nights, it is often a big gytefisk!

And nothing else? I asked.

Ja, he nodded. We get the gytefisk when others will not take the fly.

Pray for a gytefisk night! I laughed.

Ja, they smiled.

We worked back to the top of the pool. The currents seemed like strong tea but were still clear enough for fishing. It seemed wise to change flies, selecting something like a bright yellow-hackled Torrish. It was obviously visible in the tea-colored shallows beside the boat, with its canary-bright throat and silvery body. The Torrish was dressed on a 2/0 double, and it had been given to me by Clare de Bergh over lunch with Charles Woodman in Oslo.

They had been fishing the Jøraholmen beats with Seward Johnson, Anderson Fowler, and Carter Nicholas two weeks before, and Clare de Bergh had outfished them all. She had boated thirty-seven salmon weighing 987 pounds, including a superb Alta cockfish of fifty-seven.

Every bloody one took the Torrish, she laughed and handed me the fly. You take the last one and try it.

I'll try to dress copies, I said.

The dressing was a pale hairwing version of the Torrish that some anglers call the Scalscraggie. It had looked enticing in the Wheatley box, set among a covey of somber patterns like the Ackroyd and Black Doctor and Black Dose. The ghillie seemed lukewarm about my choice, but he took the fly and clinched it to the leader, preening its feathers and wing. We fished it carefully through Ovre Harstrommen without moving a fish. It was raining harder when we reached Nedri Harstrommen. It is a strong hundred-yard reach of water named for its heavy flow. The ghillies worked us expertly into position, and I stripped off line to cover the pool.

Good place? I asked in Norwegian.

Ja, they shook their heads. We do not hook many salmon at Harstrommen—but the fish we hook are usually big.

Gytefisk pool, I suggested.

Perhaps, they said.

It was almost prophetic. The line worked out into the darkness and rain, dropping the pale Torrish sixty-five feet across the currents in the throat of the pool. I lowered the rod and let the fly settle deep before it worked into its bellying swing. There was a heavy pull and the line came sullenly taut.

Fouled on something, I said.

It's not possible, the ghillie shook his head. There's nothing out there.

Gytefisk? I suggested.

The ghillies said nothing and looked grim. The boatman worked steadily to hold our position, and we stared at the throbbing line. It still felt snagged. The rod strained into a sullen circle. Both men seemed unusually concerned at the tenor of the fight, and suddenly I understood. The stalemate ended when an immense sow-sized fish cartwheeled awkwardly in the rain, landing with a gargantuan splash.

My God! I gasped.

The reel surrendered line in a wild series of ratchety jerks. The boatmen seemed almost stunned. The fish burst halfway out again in a huge gout of spray, broaching like a whale just off our boat, and fell heavily again.

Thirty kilos! the ghillie hissed.

The boatman nodded, pulling hard at his oars. Both men began chattering excitedly, more agitated than I had seen them with fish between twenty and thirty pounds, and we settled into the grim business of fighting such a fish in heavy water with a single-handed rod. The salmon shook its head angrily, turned almost majestically downstream, and gathered speed. The current was a powerful flood. The fish was strong too, ignoring any rod pressure we could apply, and it took a full hundred yards of backing with almost ridiculous ease. Its run was a little frightening, and I sighed with relief when it finally stopped. The fish still seemed like a snag. The boatmen used the time to maneuver into better position, and we crossed the middle of Nedri Harstrommen into the quiet shallows, a little below the fish. I worried about changing our angle so radically but dismissed those doubts when the fish began head-shaking. It moved upstream and shook itself angrily again.

The fish finally stopped, and I had just started to pump-and-reel like a tarpon fisherman when it turned and slowly left the pool. Its strength was still awesome. There was nothing we could do except follow, and it had simply shouldered us aside, floundering into the rapids downstream.

How big did you think he was? I asked.

Thirty kilos, they said.

But thirty kilos is over sixty-five pounds! I calculated its metric weight wildly. Sixty-five pounds!

Storlaks, the ghillie agreed.

The backing was dwindling too fast. Both ghillies worked desperately to follow, rowing and poling to keep the line free of the rocks. It was a wild half-mile trip with little control over the salmon. It escaped the pool downstream too, forcing us through the pools called Battanielo and Banas, until it finally stopped in the throat of Sirpinakken.

More swift water lay below, but it was tumbling and broken, and we came chuting through with the fish still hooked. The fight went better in the lake-sized shallows above our camp. The fish had started to porpoise, circling the backwater stubbornly, fifty yards out. It had finally seemed to weaken. The steady rod pressure forced it closer and closer, muting its weakening runs. I forced it into the Jotkajavrre backwater until there was line on the reel again, its dark green covering the pale backing. The fish circled closer still, until the leader knot was visible just under the surface. It foundered weakly and we gasped.

Thirty kilos, the ghillies were awestruck.

The fish bolted again weakly and stopped. It stripped off fifty feet and faltered, and I turned it back toward the boat. The boatman stroked patiently to hold our position. The ghillie slipped his gaff free, moved soundlessly into position, and sat waiting. The fish bulged to the surface, rolling and working its gills. It was floundering and beaten. The giant salmon was almost in reach of the gaff when it worked its jaws yawning until the fly came free.

Damn! I groaned.

The fish drifted just beyond our reach and the ghillie threw his gaff angrily. The boatman slumped exhausted at his oars, like a beaten sculler at Henley, and stared helplessly as the fish gathered its strength. It shuddered and turned back into the river, pushing a giant bow-wave like a half-submerged submarine. Alta ghillies are used to huge salmon and are usually so taciturn and laconic that their anger startled me.

The big cockfish was gone.

Our riverkeeper explained later that the biggest salmon killed on the Alta was a sixty-pound cockfish, and the boatmen were convinced that our fish was bigger, perhaps a new record for the river. The existing record-fish was caught by the Earl of Dudley, who came to the river while serving as Royal Equerry to the late Duke of Windsor.

Lord Dudley became one of the wealthiest peers in the United Kingdom before his death in 1969. He died in Paris and had lived abroad for many years, dividing his time between country houses in France and the Bahamas. The family seat was in Worcestershire at Dudley Castle, and its original title dates back to 1604. Dudley held extensive lands, but his family's great wealth lay primarily with its holdings of iron and coal, and the ancestor who developed a coal-fired iron smelter in the late seventeenth century. The earl was brusque and unpopular with the Alta ghillies, so intensely disliked that he is the only fisherman who was ever tipped into the river, belly flopping over the gunwale of his Karasjok boat at Kirkaplassen. The ghillies only smile when asked about Dudley's baptism, executed with a deft shift of balance.

The Earl of Dudley was a difficult man, the riverkeeper explained. We have fished with dukes and kings and princes all our lives—and we know that equerries are little more than ghillies in the world of palaces.

The great fish had easily won. It had carried the fight through several pools, down more than two miles of river, and it had fought an hour and forty minutes. My boatmen had wanted to share a new record fish and displace the Earl of Dudley. We sat quietly in the boat, trying to gather ourselves, knowing we had lost the salmon of a lifetime. It was starting to rain again, with mist hanging only fifty feet above the river. The night held little promise.

Let's quit, I suggested.

Nei, the ghillie shook his head stubbornly. We hooked a gytefisk!

Let's try another pool, I agreed unhappily.

Goddanieni lies just below the fishing camp, where a foamy current-tongue works two hundred yards along the rocky talus slopes under the Steinfjeldet escarpment. Its eddies slide past a boulder fall into a similar holding-lie called Goddanielo. We worked patiently through both pools, because they had been quite productive a few days earlier, but the only fish was a two-pound breakfast grayling. The Sautso flowage is filled with such fish, but even its flotillas of grayling were not dimpling to the swarming Anisomera midges that night. It was even more discouraging to find the grayling dour.

It's dead, I shook my head unhappily. It's so dead the grayling are still sleeping too.

We must fish the Velliniva, they said.

It's your favorite pool?

That's right, the ghillie smiled. It's the best pool at Sautso—and we must fish it on such a gytefisk night.

Let's go, I agreed.

Velliniva is not really a pool, but a beautiful hourglass narrows in the Sautso flowage. Ancient rock slides have pinched off the river, leaving immense puzzles of boulders in its bed. It was quite still and strangely quiet. The Gabofoss waterfall was clearly audible downstream. The mist was clearing swiftly at midnight, and we built a cook fire in the trees. The river boils and slides past the truck-sized boulders at the throat of Velliniva, and there are broken ledges that stairstep across the current, forming its tail-shallows. It is the last taking-lie before the Gabofoss, at the bottom of the Sautso beats. Gabofoss is a place I have never liked. When a salmon is hooked there, the boatman cannot hold the boat by rowing, and the ghillie starts the outboard to tow the fish upstream. It seems foolhardy to row steadily only a single cast away from a chute that spells certain death.

Both ghillies often row simultaneously at Gabofoss, watching the chute warily to judge their remaining margin of safety. We finished our midnight supper among the trees above Velliniva, and the night grew almost soft and mild. It seemed better for fishing. But we fished both Velliniva and Gabofoss without moving a salmon and returned to rebuild our fire. We talked about giving up, sharing the last of our chocolate and coffee. The weather was getting better.

Let's fish through again, I said.

We always fish through Velliniva again, the ghillie smiled.

It was already two o'clock. The pool was a polished mirror, and it grew strangely warm. The overcast grew bright orange and gold, with a morning sky that seemed robin's-egg blue. Flies were hatching and the arctic terns were back. The pool had come to life swiftly.

Let's fish, they suggested.

Our fatigue was forgotten, and we drifted stealthily into position, dropping a quartering cast eighty feet across the current. The ghillie smiled and nodded, and I lifted the fly into another cast, mending line as it settled across the flow. The bellying fly-swing stopped on the third cast, and a huge swirl erupted just before I felt the salmon. There was a second bulge as the line tightened across the current, a swelling that carried swiftly down the pool, with a huge coppery flash in its depths.

It's not like the fish we lost, I babbled excitedly, but it's big!

Twenty kilos, they guessed.

The fight went well. Twice I felt the line rake huge boulders that had calved off from the cliffs into the narrows. The boatman rowed hard to work us away from the principal holding-lie in the throat of the pool, and the fish came slowly. It seemed well hooked. It jumped twice, and I thought I could see my fly firmly seated in its jaw. It came stubbornly when I pumped it away from the main currents, and it did not jump again. It spent its remaining strength running upstream against the line belly. The ghillie gaffed it cleanly in twenty minutes.

Twenty kilos, we confirmed.

It was a fine cockfish, just beginning to lose its polished sea armor to the first bronzish cast of spawning. It was sleek and hard-muscled and strong. It weighed just under twenty kilos, pulling my Chatillon scale to the forty-three pound mark. The ghillie bled the fish and laid it across the thwarts. It seemed like a perfect climax to the night's fishing, but the ghillies stopped me when I started to strip down my tackle.

We have our gytefisk, I said.

Nei, they insisted. We have hooked two gytefisker tonight—they are taking well, and we still have two hours left to fish!

Fine, I laughed. We'll fish.

Fifty yards below the lie where the first salmon had taken the fly, the currents had quickened perceptibly above the sunken boulders. The boatman pulled hard at his oars and changed his rhythm to hold us against the flow. Both men watched the pool intently. It was obviously the primary taking-lie, and I began to drop my casts closer together. Terns were busily working the shallows. The morning grew brighter until the cliffs were visible through the mist, strangely pink and violet, and it was getting almost warm. The overcast was gone, and the mist was burning off quickly.

Norwegian weather, I thought.

We were six casts into the pool before I dropped the Torrish well across the current, rolling a big mend before the line could settle and sink. I pointed the rod at the fly and held its tip low, teasing it with a subtle rhythm. The currents bulged behind the fly, welling up until a fifteen-foot circle drifted and died in the current, but I felt no weight until the fish flashed full length in the throat of the pool. It rolled powerfully, well hooked and strong, showing its guillotine-sized tail. It flashed again in the depths of the pool, bolting suddenly upstream until the line ripped through the water. When it jumped, writhing almost six feet from the river and falling straight back on its tail, I was almost certain that I had seen the bright-canary hackles of the Torrish.

My God! I shouted. It's huge!

It was another big cockfish, cartwheeling full length across the pool, until it fell with a heavy splash. The terns screamed in protest. The big fish jumped again, porpoising and splashing belly-down like a giant marlin. It held briefly in the heaviest current, shook its head sullenly, and bolted a hundred yards upstream into the Sautso stillwater. We followed it grudgingly to recover line and control our playing angles on the fish. The backing was almost entirely on the reel, when the big salmon turned back with sudden, explosive power and bulldogged angrily past the boat. The big Saint Andrews rattled and growled and shrieked, surrendering line as the fish gathered speed, and the pale backing blurred out through the guides.

We turned desperately to follow. The fish was still running wildly, and I was worried that it might foul the line in the boulders and ledges deep in the belly of the pool. It threshed powerfully through the ledge-rock shallows, riding their chutes into the stillwater below Velliniva. The fish had traveled a rough chute so filled with broken ledges that we did not follow and circled farther out to use a quiet channel. We negotiated it safely, lucky the fish had not stopped to sound among the worst rocks, and our luck still held. The fish had circled back while we were coming through with the boat, and the slack line had settled deep, fouling in a shoal of rocks. But the fish had largely spent its strength before it fouled the line. It lay resting in quiet water, too tired to break off. The boatman rowed furtively toward the stones while the ghillie probed and freed my line with his boat pole.

It took several minutes to work the line completely free, but the fish was still hooked and held quietly on the bottom. With the line untangled from the stones, it stirred itself to make a few strong runs that stopped. It was possible to turn the fish now. It flashed and writhed. I pumped it back until it rolled weakly at the surface, and I worked it close, holding my breath.

The big gaff sliced home. The great fish came wrestling in over the gunwale, and when the priest had stilled its struggling, we saw that it was bigger than our first salmon at Velliniva. It weighed more than forty-six pounds, and I stood beside the boat when we came ashore, staring in disbelief.

Gytefisk natt, the ghillies teased.

Kanskje, I agreed happily. Men dette gytefisk natt var stor findt—tusen takk for alt!

Ingen årsak! they said.

But our night at Velliniva was still not over. The ghillies brewed the last of the coffee, and we shared the cookies and Toblerone chocolate and last pieces of sausage. It was almost an anticlimax when we hooked another fish in the throat of Velliniva, and it steeplechased wildly toward Gabofoss. Its fight was explosive and berserk, too wild to last, and the fish spent itself quickly. Its last run lasted less than forty yards, circling almost blindly behind a shoal of rocks. It fouled the line weakly too, but it failed to break off, and the ghillie easily worked it loose with the boat hook. It tried to bolt again, but I snubbed and forced it back, until it floundered and circled our boat.

It's a pretty good fish too, I said.

Changing rod angles, I fought the fish in quickly. It seemed smaller and I forced it. The fish was still surprisingly strong, but it drifted weakly to the surface and the ghillie gaffed it. It twisted and writhed angrily. The ghillie deftly parried its struggles and killed it with a single blow. It weighed just over thirty-nine pounds. The ghillie laid it beside the brace of cockfish in the boat, and we sat quietly.

The ghillie scissored the Torrish from my leader and studied it. It had lost both junglecock feathers. Its hairwing was ragged and thin, showing the scarlet and bright blue and yellow hairs still left. The bucktail fibers were brittle and bent, and the canary hackles were matted with slime. Its dark ostrich butt was missing. Two long spirals of loose tinsel wound free of its body, and the working thread was worn thin, showing the hook. The fly had done its work, although I had never made copies, and I stood looking at the big cockfish in the boat.

Gytefisk night! I thought happily.

The ghillie climbed high on a mossy boulder, held the withered, brightly hackled Torrish above his head, and threw it out across the pool. It belongs to the river now, he said.

CHAPTER SIXTEEN

A Wedding Gift

by John Taintor Foote

During his tenure as editor of Field & Stream magazine in the thirties and forties of the last century, Ray P. Holland called John Taintor Foote "The greatest writer of sporting fiction this country has ever produced." Tall as those words are, Holland knew they could be backed up by Foote's stories in magazines and books that grabbed readers and held onto them. Foote was a frequent companion of Holland in the field, but their friendship was not the reason Ray P. liked Taintor Foote stories so much. Foote's storytelling abilities made his prose special and lasting.

GEORGE BALDWIN POTTER IS A PURIST. THAT IS TO SAY, HE EITHER takes trout on a dry fly or he does not take them at all. He belongs to a number of fishing clubs, any member of which might acquire his neighbor's wife, beat his children, or poison a dog and still cast a fly, in all serenity, upon club waters; but should he impale on a hook a lowly though succulent worm and immerse the creature in those same waters it would be better that he send in his resignation at once, sooner than face the shaken committee that would presently wait upon him.

George had become fixed in my mind as a bachelor. This, of course, was a mistake. I am continually forgetting that purists rush into marriage when approaching or having just passed the age of forty. The psychology of this is clear.

For twenty years, let us say, a purist's life is completely filled by his efforts to convert all reasonable men to his own particular method of taking trout. He thinks, for example, that a man should not concern himself with more than a dozen types of standard flies. The manner of presenting them is the main consideration. Take any one of these flies, then, and place it, by means of an eight-foot rod, a light, tapered line, and a mist-colored leader of reasonable length, on fast water—if you want trout. Of course, if you want to listen to the birds and look at the scenery, fish the pools with a long line and an eight-foot leader. Why, it stands to reason that—

The years go by as he explains these vital facts patiently, again and again, to Smith and Brown and Jones. One wet, cold spring, after fighting a muddy stream all day, he reexplains for the better part of an evening and takes himself, somewhat wearily upstairs. The damp and chill of the room at whatever club he may be fishing is positively tomblike. He can hear the rain drumming on the roof and swishing against the windows. The water will be higher than ever tomorrow, he reflects, as he puts out the lights and slides between the icy sheets. Steeped to the soul in cheerless dark, he recalls numbly that when he first met Smith and Brown and Jones they were fishing the pools with a long line. That was, let's see—fifteen—eighteen—twenty years ago. Then he must be forty. It isn't possible! Yes, it is a fact that Smith and Brown and Jones are still fishing the pools with a long line.

In the first faint light of dawn he falls into an uneasy, muttering slumber. The dark hours between have been devoted to intense thought and a variety of wiggles which have not succeeded in keeping the bedclothes against his shoulder blades.

Some time within the next six months you will remember that you have forgotten to send him a wedding present.

George, therefore, having arrived at his fortieth birthday, announced his engagement shortly thereafter. Quite by chance I ran across his bride-to-be and himself a few days before the ceremony, and joined them at lunch. She was a blonde in the early twenties, with wide blue eyes and a typical rose-and-white complexion. A rushing, almost breathless account of herself, which she began the moment we were seated, was curious, I thought. It was as though she feared an interruption at any moment. I learned that she was an only child, born and reared in Greater New York; that her family had recently moved to New Rochelle; that she had been shopping madly for the past two weeks; that she was nearly dead, but that she had some adorable things.

At this point George informed me that they would spend their honeymoon at a certain fishing club in Maine. He then proceeded to describe the streams and lakes in that section at some length—during the rest of the luncheon, as a matter of fact. His fiancée, who had fallen into a wordless abstraction, only broke her silence with a vague murmur as we parted.

Owing to this meeting I did not forget to send a wedding present. I determined that my choice should please both George and his wife through the happy years to come.

If I had had George only to consider, I could have settled the business in two minutes at a sporting-goods store. Barred from these for obvious reasons, I spent a long day in a thoroughly exhausting search. Late in the afternoon I decided to abandon my hopeless task. I had made a tremendous effort and failed. I would simply buy a silver doodad and let it go at that.

As I staggered into a store with the above purpose in view, I passed a show case devoted to fine china, and halted as my eyes fell on a row of fish plates backed by artfully rumpled blue velvet. The plates proved to be hand painted. On each plate was one of the different varieties of trout, curving up through green depths to an artificial fly just dropping on the surface of the water.

In an automatic fashion I indicated the plates to a clerk, paid for them, gave him my card and the address, and fled from the store. Some time during the next twenty-four hours it came to me that George Potter was not among my nearest and dearest. Yet the unbelievable sum I had left with that clerk in exchange for those fish plates could be justified in no other way.

I thought this fact accounted for the sort of frenzy with which George flung himself upon me when next we met, some two months later. I had been week-ending in the country and encountered him in the Grand Central Station as I emerged from the lower level. For a long moment he wrung my hand in silence, gazing almost feverishly into my face. At last he spoke:

"Have you got an hour to spare?"

It occurred to me that it would take George an hour at least to describe his amazed delight at the splendor of my gift. The clock above Information showed that it was 12:45. I therefore suggested that we lunch together.

He, too, glanced at the clock, verified its correctness by his watch, and seized me by the arm.

"All right," he agreed, and was urging me toward the well-filled and somewhat noisy station café before I grasped his intention and tried to suggest that we go elsewhere. His hand only tightened on my arm.

"It's all right," he said; "good food, quick service—you'll like it."

He all but dragged me into the café and steered me to a table in the corner. I lifted my voice above an earnest clatter of gastronomical utensils and made a last effort.

"The Biltmore's just across the street."

George pressed me into my chair, shoved a menu card at me and addressed the waiter.

"Take his order." Here he jerked out his watch and consulted it again. "We have forty-eight minutes. Service for one. I shan't eat anything; or, no—bring me some coffee—large cup—black."

Having ordered mechanically, I frankly stared at George. He was dressed, I now observed, with unusual care. He wore a rather dashing gray suit. His tie, which was an exquisite shade of gray-blue, was embellished by a handsome pearl. The handkerchief, appearing above his breast pocket, was of the same delicate gray-blue shade as the tie. His face had been recently and closely shaven, also powdered; but above that smooth whiteness of jowl was a pair of curiously glittering eyes and a damp, a beaded brow. This he now mopped with his napkin.

"Good God," said I, "what is it, George?"

His reply was to extract a letter from his inside coat pocket and pass it across the table, his haunted eyes on mine. I took in its few lines at a glance:

Father has persuaded me to listen to what you call your explanation. I arrive Grand Central 2:45, daylight saving, Monday.

Isabelle

Poor old George, I thought; some bachelor indiscretion; and now, with his honeymoon scarcely over, blackmail, a lawsuit, heaven only knew what.

"Who," I asked, returning the letter, "is Isabelle?"

To my distress, George again resorted to his napkin. Then, "My wife," he said.

"Your wife!"

George nodded.

"Been living with her people for the last month. Wish he'd bring that coffee. You don't happen to have a flask with you?"

"Yes, I have a flask." George brightened. "But it's empty. Do you want to tell me about your trouble? Is that why you brought me here?"

"Well, yes," George admitted. "But the point is—will you stand by me? That's the main thing. She gets in"—here he consulted his watch—"in forty-five minutes, if the train's on time." A sudden panic seemed to seize him. His hand shot across the table and grasped my wrist. "You've got to stand by me, old man—until the ice is broken. That's all I ask. Just stick until the train gets in. Then act as if you knew nothing. Say you ran into me here and stayed to meet her. I'll tell you what—say I didn't seem to want you to stay. Kid me about wanting her all to myself, or something like that. Get the point? It'll give me a chance to sort of—well, you understand."

"I see what you mean, of course," I admitted. "Here's your coffee. Suppose you have some and then tell me what this is all about—if you care to, that is."

"No sugar, no cream," said George to the waiter; "just pour it. Don't stand there waving it about—pour it, pour it!" He attempted to swallow a mouthful of steaming coffee, gurgled frightfully and grabbed his water glass. "Great jumping Jehoshaphat!" he gasped, when he could speak, and glared at the waiter, who promptly moved out into the sea of diners and disappeared among a dozen of his kind.

"Steady, George," I advised as I transferred a small lump of ice from my glass to his coffee cup.

George watched the ice dissolve, murmured "Idiot" several times, and presently swallowed the contents of the cup in two gulps.

"I had told her," he said suddenly, "exactly where we were going. She mentioned Narragansett several times—I'll admit that. Imagine—Narragansett! Of course I bought her fishing things myself. I didn't buy knickers or woolens or flannel shirts—naturally. You don't go around buying a girl breeches and underwear before you're married. It wouldn't be—well, it isn't done, that's all. I got her the sweetest three-ounce rod you ever held in your hand. I'll bet I could put out sixty feet of line with it against the wind. I got her a pair of English waders that didn't weigh a pound. They cost me forty-five dollars. The rest of the outfit was just as good. Why, her fly box was a Truxton. I could have bought an American imitation for eight dollars. I know a lot of men who'll buy leaders for themselves at two dollars apiece and let their wives fish with any kind of tackle. I'll give you my word I'd have used anything I got for her myself. I sent it all out to be packed with her things. I wanted her to feel that it was her own—not mine. I know a lot of men who give their wives a high-class reel or an imported reel and then fish with it themselves. What time is it?"

"Clock right up there," I said. But George consulted his watch and used his napkin distressingly again.

"Where was I?"

"You were telling me why you sent her fishing things out to her."

"Oh, yes! That's all of that. I simply wanted to show you that from the first I did all any man could do. Ever been in the Cuddiwink district?"

I said that I had not.

"You go in from Buck's Landing. A lumber tug takes you up to the head of Lake Owonga. Club guides meet you there and put you through in one day—twenty miles by canoe and portage up the west branch of the Penobscot; then nine miles by trail to Lost Pond. The club's on Lost Pond. Separate cabins, with a main dining and loafing camp, and the best squaretail fishing on earth—both lake and stream. Of course, I don't fish the lakes. A dry fly belongs on a stream and nowhere else. Let me make it perfectly clear."

George's manner suddenly changed. He hunched himself closer to the table, dropped an elbow upon it and lifted an expository finger.

"The dry fly," he stated, with a new almost combative ring in his voice, "is designed primarily to simulate not only the appearance of the natural insect but its action as well. This action is arrived at through the flow of the current. The moment you move a fly by means of a leader you destroy the—"

I saw that an interruption was imperative.

"Yes, of course," I said; but your wife will be here in—"

It was pitiful to observe George. His new-found assurance did not flee—flee suggests a withdrawal, however swift—it was immediately and totally annihilated. He attempted to pour himself some coffee, take out his watch, look at the clock, and mop his brow with his napkin at one and the same instant.

"You were telling me how to get to Lost Pond," I suggested.

"Yes, to be sure," said George. "Naturally you go in light. The things you absolutely have to have—rods, tackle, waders, wading shoes, and so forth, are about all a guide can manage at the portages in addition to the canoe. You pack in extras yourself—change of underclothes, a couple of pairs of socks, and a few toilet articles. You leave a bag or trunk at Buck's Landing. I explained this to her. I explained it carefully. I told her either a week-end bag or one small trunk. Herb Trescott was my best man. I left everything to him. He saw us on the train and handed me tickets and reservations just before we pulled out. I didn't notice in the excitement of getting away that he'd given me three trunk checks all stamped 'Excess.' I didn't notice it till the conductor showed up, as a matter of fact. Then I said, 'Darling, what in heaven's name have you brought three trunks for?' She said—I can remember her exact words—'Then you're not going to Narragansett?'

"I simply looked at her. I was too dumbfounded to speak. At last I pulled myself together and told her in three days we'd be whipping the best squaretail water in the world. I took her hand, I remember, and said, 'You and I together, sweetheart,' or something like that."

George sighed and lapsed into a silence which remained unbroken until his eye happened to encounter the face of the clock. He started and went on:

"We got to Buck's Landing, by way of Bangor, at six in the evening of the following day. Buck's Landing is a railroad station with grass growing between the ties, a general store and hotel combined, and a lumber wharf. The store keeps canned peas, pink-and-white-candy, and felt boots. The hotel part is—well, it doesn't matter except that I don't think I ever saw so many deer heads; a few stuffed trout, but mostly deer heads. After supper the proprietor and I got the three trunks up to the largest room: We just got them in and that was all. The tug left for the head of the lake at seven next morning. I explained this to Isabelle. I said we'd leave the trunks there until we came out, and offered to help her unpack the one her fishing things were in. She said, 'Please go away!' So I went. I got out a rod and went down to the wharf. No trout there, I knew; but I thought I'd limber up my wrist. I put on a Cahill Number Fourteen—or was it Sixteen—"

George knitted his brows and stared intently but unseeingly at me for some little time.

"Call it a Sixteen," I suggested.

George shook his head impatiently and remained concentrated in thought.

"I'm inclined to think it was a Fourteen," he said at last. "But let it go; it'll come to me later. At any rate, the place was alive with big chub—a foot long, some of 'em. I'll bet I took fifty—threw 'em back, of course. They kept on rising after it got dark. I'd tell myself I'd go after one more cast. Each time I'd hook a big chub, and—well, you know how the time slips away.

"When I got back to the hotel all the lights were out. I lit matches until I got upstairs and found the door to the room. I'll never forget what I saw when I opened that door—never! Do you happen to know how many of the kind of things they wear a woman can get into one trunk? Well, she had three and she'd unpacked them all. She had used the bed for the gowns alone. It was piled with them—literally piled; but that wasn't a starter. Everywhere you looked was a stack of things with ribbons in 'em. There were enough shoes and stockings for a girls' school; silk stockings, mind you, and high-heeled shoes and slippers." Here George consulted clock and watch. "I wonder if that train's on time," he wanted to know.

"You have thirty-five minutes, even if it is," I told him; "go right ahead."

"Well, I could see something was wrong from her face. I didn't know what, but I started right in to cheer her up. I told her all about the chub fishing I'd been having. At last she burst into tears. I won't go into the scene that followed. I'd ask her what was the matter and she'd say, 'Nothing,' and cry frightfully. I know a lot of men who would have lost their tempers under the circumstances, but I didn't; I give you my word. I simply said, 'There, there,' until she quieted down. And that isn't all. After a while she began to show me her gowns. Imagine—at eleven o'clock at night, at Buck's Landing! She'd hold up a dress and look over the top of it at me and ask me how I liked it, and I'd say it was all right. I know a lot of men who wouldn't have sat there two minutes.

"At last I said, 'They're all right, darling,' and yawned. She was hold-ing up a pink dress covered with shiny dingle-dangles, and she threw the dress on the bed and all but had hysterics. It was terrible. In trying to think of some way to quiet her it occurred to me that I'd put her rod together and let her feel the balance of it with the reel I'd bought her—a genuine Fleetwood, mind you—attached. I looked around for her fishing things and couldn't find them. I'll tell you why I couldn't find them." George paused for an impressive instant to give his next words the full significance due them. "They weren't there!"

"No?" I murmured weakly.

"No," said George. "And what do you suppose she said when I ques-tioned her? I can give you her exact words—I'll never forget them. She said, 'There wasn't any room for them.'" Again George paused. "I ask you," he inquired at last, "I ask you as man to man; what do you think of that?"

I found no adequate reply to this question and George, now thor-oughly warmed up, rushed on.

"You'd swear I lost my temper then, wouldn't you? Well, I didn't. I did say something to her later, but I'll let you be the judge when we come to that. I'll ask you to consider the circumstances. I'll ask you to get Old Faithful in your mind's eye."

"Old Faithful?" I repeated. "Then you went to the Yellowstone later?"

"Yellowstone! Of course not! Haven't I told you we were already at the best trout water in America? Old Faithful was a squaretail. He'd been in the pool below Horseshoe Falls for twenty years, as a matter of record. We'll come to that presently. How are we off for time?"

"Thirty-one minutes," I told him. "I'm watching the clock—go ahead."

"Well, there she was, on a fishing trip with nothing to fish with. There was only one answer to that—she couldn't fish. But I went over everything she'd brought in three trunks and I'll give you my word she didn't have a garment of any sort you couldn't see through.

"Something had to be done and done quick, that was sure. I fitted her out from my own things with a sweater, a flannel shirt, and a pair of knickerbockers. Then I got the proprietor up and explained the situation. He got me some heavy underwear and two pairs of woolen stockings that belonged to his wife. When it came to shoes it looked hopeless, but the proprietor's wife, who had got up, too, by this time, thought of a pair of boy's moccasins that were in the store and they turned out to be about the right size. I made arrangements to rent the room we had until we came out again to keep her stuff in, and took another room for the night— what was left of it after she'd repacked what could stay in the trunks and arranged what couldn't so it wouldn't be wrinkled.

"I got up early, dressed, and took my duffle down to the landing. I wakened her when I left the room. When breakfast was ready I went to see why she hadn't come down. She was all dressed, sitting on the edge of the bed. I said, 'Breakfast is ready, darling,' but I saw by her face that something was wrong again. It turned out to be my knickers. They fitted her perfectly—a little tight in spots—except in the waist. They would simply have fallen off if she hadn't held them up.

"Well, I was going in so light that I only had one belt. The proprietor didn't have any—he used suspenders. Neither did his wife—she used—well, whatever they use. He got me a piece of clothesline and I knotted it at each end and ran it through the what-you-may-call-'ems of the knickers and tied it in front. The knickers sort of puckered all the way round, but they couldn't come down—that was the main thing. I said, 'There you are, darling.' She walked over and tilted the mirror of the bureau so that she could see herself from head to foot. She said, 'Who are going to be at this place where we are going?' I said, 'Some of the very best dry-fly men in the country.' She said, 'I don't mean them; I mean the women. Will there be any women there?'

"I told her, certainly there would be women. I asked her if she thought I would take her into a camp with nothing but men. I named some of the women: Mrs. Fred Beal and Mrs. Brooks Carter and Talcott Ranning's sister and several more.

"She turned around slowly in front of the mirror, staring into it for a minute. Then she said, 'Please go out and close the door.' I said, 'All right, darling; but come right down. The tug will be here in fifteen minutes.'

"I went downstairs and waited ten minutes, then I heard the tug whistle for the landing and ran upstairs again. I knocked at the door. When she didn't answer I went in. Where do you suppose she was?"

I gave it up.

"In bed!" said George in an awe-struck voice. "In bed with her face turned to the wall; and listen, I didn't lose my temper as God is my judge. I rushed down to the wharf and told the tug captain I'd give him twenty-five dollars extra if he'd hold the boat till we came. He said all right and I went back to the room.

"The breeches had done it. She simply wouldn't wear them. I told her that at a fishing camp in Maine clothes were never thought of. I said, 'No one thinks of anything but trout, darling.' She said, 'I wouldn't let a fish see me looking like that.'" George's brow beaded suddenly. His hands dived searchingly into various pockets. "Got a cigarette? I left my case in my other suit."

He took a cigarette from me, lighted it with shaking fingers and inhaled deeply.

"It went on like that for thirty minutes. She was crying all the time, of course. I had started down to tell the tug captain it was all off, and I saw a woman's raincoat hanging in the hall. It belonged to some one up in one of the camps, the proprietor told me. I gave him seventy-five dollars to give to whoever owned it when he came out, and took it upstairs. In about ten minutes I persuaded her to wear it over the rest of her outfit until we got to camp. I told her one of the women would be able to fix her up all right when we got there. I didn't believe it, of course. The women at camp were all old-timers; they'd gone in as light as the men; but I had to say something.

"We had quite a trip going in. The guides were at the head of the lake all right—Indian Joe and a new man I'd never seen, called Charlie. I told Joe to take Isabelle—he's one of the best canoemen I ever saw. I was going to paddle bow for my man, but I'd have bet a cooky Indian Joe could stay with us on any kind of water. We had to beat it right through to make camp by night. It's a good stiff trip, but it can be done. I looked back at the other canoe now and then until we struck about a mile of white water that took all I had. When we were through the other canoe wasn't in sight. The river made a bend there, and I thought it was just behind and would show up any minute.

"Well, it didn't show up and I began to wonder. We hit our first portage about ten o'clock and landed. I watched downstream for twenty minutes, expecting to sight the other canoe every instant. Then Charlie, who hadn't opened his head, said, 'Better go back,' and put the canoe in again. We paddled downstream for all that was in it. I was stiff with fright. We saw 'em coming about three miles lower down and back-paddled till they came up. Isabelle was more cheerful-looking than she'd been since we left New York, but Joe had that stony face an Indian gets when he's sore.

"I said, 'Anything wrong?' Joe just grunted and drove the canoe past us. Then I saw it was filled with wild flowers. Isabelle said she'd been picking them right off the banks all the way long. She said she'd only had to get out of the boat once, for the blue ones. Now, you can't beat that—not in a thousand years. I leave it to you if you can. Twenty miles of stiff current, with five portages ahead of us and a nine-mile hike at the end of that. I gave that Indian the devil for letting her do such a thing, and tipped the flowers into the Penobscot when we unloaded for the first portage. She didn't speak to me on the portage, and she got into her canoe without a word.

"Nothing more happened going in, except this flower business had lost us two hours, and it was so dark when we struck the swamp at Loon Lake that we couldn't follow the trail well and kept stumbling over down timber and stepping into bog holes. She was about fagged out by then, and the mosquitoes were pretty thick through there. Without any warning she sat down in the trail. She did it so suddenly I nearly fell over her. I asked her what was the matter and she said, 'This is the end'—just like that—'this is the end!' I said, 'The end of what, darling. Just think, to-morrow we'll be on the best trout water in the world!' With that she said, 'I want my mother, my darling mother,' and bowed her head in her hands. Think it over, please; and remember, I didn't lose my temper. You're sure there's nothing left in your flask?"

"Not a drop, George," I assured him. "Go ahead; we've only twenty-five minutes."

George looked wildly at the clock, then at his watch.

"A man never has it when he wants it most. Have you noticed that? Where was I?"

"You were in the swamp."

"Oh, yes! Well, she didn't speak after that, and nothing I could say would budge her. The mosquitoes had got wind of us when we stopped and were coming in swarms. We'd be eaten alive in another ten minutes. So I told Joe to give his pack to Charlie and help me pick her up and carry her. Joe said, 'No, by damn!' and folded his arms. When an Indian gets sore he stays sore, and when he's sore he's stubborn. The mosquitoes were working on him good and plenty, though, and at last he said, 'Me carry packs. Charlie help carry—that.' He flipped his hand over in the direction of Isabelle and took the pack from Charlie.

"It was black as your hat by now, and the trail through there was only about a foot wide with swamp on each side. It was going to be some job getting her out of there. I thought Charlie and I would make a chair of our arms and stumble along with her some way; but when I started to lift her up she said, 'Don't touch me!' and got up and went on. A blessing if there ever was one. We got to camp at ten that night.

"She was stiff and sore next morning—you expect it after a trip like that—besides, she'd caught a little cold. I asked her how she felt, and she said she was going to die and asked me to send for a doctor and her mother. The nearest doctor was at Bangor and her mother was in New Rochelle. I carried her breakfast over from the dining camp to our cabin. She said she couldn't eat any breakfast, but she did drink a cup of coffee, telling me between sips how awful it was to die alone in a place like that.

"After she'd had the coffee she seemed to feel better. I went to the camp library and got *The Dry Fly on American Waters*, by Charles Darty. I consider him the soundest man in the country. He's better than Pell or Fawcett. My chief criticism of him is that in his chapter on Streams East of the Alleghenies—east of the Alleghenies, mind you—he recommends the Royal Coachman. I consider the Lead-Wing Coachman a serviceable fly on clear, hard-fished water; but the Royal—never! I wouldn't give it a shade over the Professor or the Montreal. Just consider the body alone of the Royal Coachman—never mind the wings and hackle—the body of the Royal is—"

"Yes, I know, George," I said; "but—"

I glanced significantly at the clock. George started, sighed, and resumed his narrative.

"I went back to the cabin and said, 'Darling, here is one of the most intensely interesting books ever written. I'm going to read it aloud to you. I think I can finish it to-day. Would you like to sit up in bed while I read?' She said she hadn't strength enough to sit up in bed, so I sat down beside her and started reading. I had read about an hour, I suppose, when she did sit up in bed quite suddenly. I saw she was staring at me in a queer, wild way that was really startling. I said, 'What is it, darling?' She said, 'I'm going to get up. I'm going to get up this instant.'

"Well, I was delighted, naturally. I thought the book would get her by the time I'd read it through. But there she was, as keen as mustard before I'd got well into it. I'll tell you what I made up my mind to do, right there. I made up my mind to let her use my rod that day. Yes, sir—my three-ounce Spinoza, and what's more, I did it."

George looked at me triumphantly, then lapsed into reflection for a moment.

"If ever a man did everything possible to—well, let it go. The main thing is, I have nothing to reproach myself with—nothing. Except—but we'll come to that presently. Of course, she wasn't ready for dry flies yet. I borrowed some wet flies from the club steward, got some cushions for the canoe and put my rod together. She had no waders, so a stream was out of the question. The lake was better, anyway, that first day; she'd have all the room she wanted for her back cast.

"I stood on the landing with her before we got into the canoe and showed her just how to put out a fly and recover it. Then she tried it." A sort of horror came into George's face. "You wouldn't believe any one could handle a rod like that," he said huskily. "You couldn't believe it unless you'd seen it. Gimme a cigarette.

"I worked with her a half hour or so and saw no improvement—none whatever. At last she said, 'The string is too long. I can't do anything with such a long string on the pole.' I told her gently—gently, mind you—that the string was an eighteen-dollar double-tapered Hurdman line, attached to a Gebhardt reel on a three-ounce Spinoza rod. I said, 'We'll go out on the lake now. If you can manage to get a rise, perhaps it will come to you instinctively.'

"I paddled her out on the lake and she went at it. She'd spat the flies down and yank them up and spat them down again. She hooked me several times with her back cast and got tangled up in the line herself again and again. All this time I was speaking quietly to her, telling her what to do. I give you my word I never raised my voice—not once—and I thought she'd break the tip every moment.

"Finally she said her arm was tired and lowered the rod. She'd got everything messed up with her last cast and the flies were trailing just over the side of the canoe. I said, 'Recover your cast and reel in, darling.' Instead of using her rod, she took hold of the leader close to the flies and started to pull them into the canoe. At that instant a little trout—couldn't have been over six inches—took the tail fly. I don't know exactly what happened, it was all over so quickly. I think she just screamed and let go of everything. At any rate, I saw my Spinoza bounce off the gunwale of the canoe and disappear. There was fifty feet of water just there. And now listen carefully: not one word did I utter—not one. I simply turned the canoe and paddled to the landing in absolute silence. No reproaches of any sort. Think that over!"

I did. My thoughts left me speechless. George proceeded:

"I took out a guide and tried dragging for the rod with a gang hook and heavy sinker all the rest of the day. But the gangs would only foul on the bottom. I gave up at dusk and paddled in. I said to the guide—it was Charlie—I said, 'Well, it's all over, Charlie.' Charlie said, 'I brought Mr. Carter in and he had an extra rod. Maybe you could borrow it. It's a four-ounce Meecham.' I smiled. I actually smiled. I turned and looked at the lake. 'Charlie,' I said, 'somewhere out there in that dark water, where the eye of man will never behold it again, is a three-ounce Spinoza—and you speak of a Meecham.' Charlie said, 'Well, I just thought I'd tell you.' I said, 'That's all right, Charlie. That's all right.' I went to the main camp, saw Jean, the head guide, and made arrangements to leave the next day. Then I went to our cabin and sat down before the fire. I heard Isabelle say something about being sorry. I said, 'I'd rather not talk about it, darling. If you don't mind, we'll never mention it again.' We sat there in silence, then, until dinner.

"As we got up from dinner, Nate Griswold and his wife asked us to play bridge with them that evening. I'd told no one what had happened, and Nate didn't know, of course. I simply thanked him and said we were tired, and we went back to our cabin. I sat down before the fire again. Isabelle seemed restless. At last she said, 'George.' I said, 'What is it, darling?' She said, 'Would you like to read to me from that book?' I said, 'I'm sorry, darling; if you don't mind I'll just sit here quietly by the fire.'

"Somebody knocked at the door after a while. I said, 'Come in.' It was Charlie. I said, 'What is it, Charlie?' Then he told me that Bob Frazer had been called back to New York and was going out next morning. I said, 'Well, what of it?' Charlie said, 'I just thought you could maybe borrow his rod.' I said, 'I thought you understood about that, Charlie.' Charlie said, 'Well, that's it. Mr. Frazer's rod is a three-ounce Spinoza.'

"I got up and shook hands with Charlie and gave him five dollars. But when he'd gone I began to realize what was before me. I'd brought in a pint flask of prewar Scotch. Prewar—get that! I put this in my pocket and went over to Bob's cabin. Just as I was going to knock I lost my nerve.

I sneaked away from the door and went down to the lake and sat on the steps of the canoe landing. I sat there for quite a while and took several nips. At last I thought I'd just go and tell Bob of my loss and see what he said. I went back to his cabin and this time I knocked. Bob was putting a few odds and ends in a shoulder pack. His rod was in its case, standing against the wall.

"I said, 'I hear you're going out in the morning.' He said, 'Yes, curse it, my wife's mother has to have some sort of a damned operation or other.' I said, 'How would a little drink strike you, Bob?' He said, 'Strike me! Wait a minute! What kind of a drink?' I took out the flask and handed it to him. He unscrewed the cap and held the flask to his nose. He said, 'Great heavens above, it smells like—' I said, 'It is.' He said, 'It can't be!' I said, 'Yes, it is.' He said, 'There's a trick in it somewhere.' I said, 'No, there isn't—I give you my word.' He tasted what was in the flask carefully. Then he said, 'I call this very nice of you, George,' and took a good stiff snort. When he was handing back the flask he said, 'I'll do as much for you some day, if I ever get the chance.' I took a snifter myself.

"Then I said, 'Bob, something awful has happened to me. I came here to tell you about it.' He said, 'Is that so? Sit down.' I sat down and told him. He said, 'What kind of a rod was it?' I said, 'A three-ounce Spinoza.' He came over and gripped my hand without a word. I said, 'Of course, I can't use anything else.' He nodded, and I saw his eyes flicker toward the corner of the room where his own rod was standing. I said, 'Have another drink, Bob.' But he just sat down and stared at me. I took a good stiff drink myself. Then I said, 'Under ordinary circumstances, nothing on earth could hire me to ask a man to—' I stopped right there.

"Bob got up suddenly and began to walk up and down the room. I said, 'Bob, I'm not considering myself—not for a minute. If it was last season, I'd simply have gone back to-morrow without a word. But I'm not alone any more. I've got the little girl to consider. She's never seen a trout taken in her life—think of it, Bob! And here she is, on her honeymoon, at the best water I know of. On her honeymoon, Bob!' I waited for him to say something, but he went to the window and stared out, with his back to me. I got up and said good-night and started for the door. Just as I reached it he turned from the window and rushed over and picked up his rod. He said, 'Here, take it,' and put the rod case in my hands. I started to try to thank him, but he said, 'Just go ahead with it,' and pushed me out the door."

The waiter was suddenly hovering above us with his eyes on the dishes.

"Now what do you want?" said George.

"Never mind clearing here," I said. "Just bring me the check. Go ahead, George."

"Well, of course, I can't any more than skim what happened finally, but you'll understand. It turned out that Ernie Payton's wife had an extra pair of knickers and she loaned them to Isabelle. I was waiting outside the cabin while she dressed next morning, and she called out to me. 'Oh, George, they fit!' Then I heard her begin to sing. She was a different girl when she came out to go to breakfast. She was almost smiling. She'd done nothing but slink about the day before. Isn't it extraordinary what will seem important to a woman? Gimme a cigarette."

"Fifteen minutes, George," I said as I supplied him.

"Yes, yes, I know. I fished the Cuddiwink that day. Grand stream, grand. I used a Pink Lady—first day on a stream with Isabelle—little touch of sentiment—and it's a darn good fly. I fished it steadily all day. Or did I try a Seth Green about noon? It seems to me I did, now that I recall it. It seems to me that where the Katahdin brook comes in I—"

"It doesn't really matter, does it, George?" I ventured.

"Of course, it matters!" said George decisively. "A man wants to be exact about such things. The precise details of what happens in a day's work on a stream are of real value to yourself and others. Except in the case of a record fish, it isn't important that you took a trout; it's exactly how you took him that's important."

"But the time, George," I protested.

He glanced at the clock, swore softly, mopped his brow—this time with the blue-gray handkerchief—and proceeded.

"Isabelle couldn't get into the stream without waders, so I told her to work along the bank a little behind me. It was pretty thick along there, second growth and vines mostly; but I was putting that Pink Lady on every foot of good water and she kept up with me easily enough. She didn't see me take many trout, though. I'd look for her, after landing one, to see what she thought of the way I'd handled the fish, and almost invariably she was picking ferns or blueberries, or getting herself untangled from something. Curious things, women. Like children, when you stop to think of it."

George stared at me unseeingly for a moment.

"And you never heard of Old Faithful?" he asked suddenly. "Evidently not, from what you said a while ago. Well, a lot of people have, believe me. Men have gone to the Cuddiwink district just to see him. As I've already told you, he lay beside a ledge in the pool below Horseshoe Falls. Almost nothing else in the pool. He kept it cleaned out. Worst sort of cannibal, of course—all big trout are. That was the trouble—he wanted something that would stick to his ribs. No flies for him. Did his feeding at night.

"You could see him dimly if you crawled out on a rock that jutted above the pool and looked over. He lay in about ten feet of water, right by his ledge. If he saw you he'd back under the ledge, slowly, like a submarine going into dock. Think of the biggest thing you've ever seen, and that's the way Old Faithful looked, just lying there as still as the ledge. He never seemed to move anything, not even his gills. When he backed in out of sight he seemed to be drawn under the ledge by some invisible force.

"Ridgway—R. Campbell Ridgway—you may have read his stuff, Brethren of the Wild, that sort of thing—claimed to have seen him move. He told me about it one night. He said he was lying with just his eyes over the edge of the rock, watching the trout. Said he'd been there an hour, when down over the falls came a young red squirrel. It had fallen in above and been carried over. The squirrel was half drowned, but struck out feebly for shore. Well, so Ridgway said—Old Faithful came up and took Mister Squirrel into camp. No hurry; just came drifting up, sort of inhaled the squirrel and sank down to the ledge again. Never made a ripple, Ridgway said; just business.

"I'm telling you all this because it's necessary that you get an idea of that trout in your mind. You'll see why in a minute. No one ever had hold of him. But it was customary, if you fished the Cuddiwink, to make a few casts over him before you left the stream. Not that you ever expected him to rise. It was just a sort of gesture. Everybody did it.

"Knowing that Isabelle had never seen trout taken before, I made a day of it—naturally. The trail to camp leaves the stream just at the falls. It was pretty late when we got to it. Isabelle had her arms full of—heaven knows what—flowers and grass and ferns and fir branches and colored leaves. She'd lugged the stuff for hours. I remember once that day I was fighting a fourteen-inch fish in swift water and she came to the bank and wanted me to look at a ripe blackberry—I think it was—she'd found. How does that strike you? And listen! I said, 'It's a beauty, darling.' That's what I said—or something like that . . . Here, don't you pay that check! Bring it here, waiter!"

"Go on, George!" I said. "We haven't time to argue about the check. You'd come to the trail for camp at the falls."

"I told Isabelle to wait at the trail for a few minutes, while I went below the falls and did the customary thing for the edification of Old Faithful. I only intended to make three or four casts with the Number Twelve Fly and the hair-fine leader I had on, but in getting down to the pool I hooked the fly in a bush. In trying to loosen it I stumbled over something and fell. I snapped the leader like a thread, and since I had to put on another, I tied on a fairly heavy one as a matter of form.

"I had reached for my box for a regulation fly of some sort when I remembered a fool thing that Billy Roach had given me up on the Beaverkill the season before. It was fully two inches long; I forget what he called it. He said you fished it dry for bass or large trout. He said you worked the tip of your rod and made it wiggle like a dying minnow. I didn't want the contraption, but he'd borrowed some fly oil from me and insisted on my taking it. I'd stuck it in the breast pocket of my fishing jacket and forgotten it until then.

"Well, I felt in the pocket and there it was. I tied it on and went down to the pool. Now let me show you the exact situation." George seized a fork. "This is the pool." The fork traced an oblong figure on the tablecloth. "Here is Old Faithful's ledge." The fork deeply marked this impressive spot. "Here are the falls, with white water running to here. You can only wade to this point here, and then you have an abrupt six-foot depth. 'But you can put a fly from here to here with a long line,' you say. No, you can't. You've forgotten to allow for your back cast. Notice this bend here?

That tells the story. You're not more than twenty feet from a lot of birch and whatnot, when you can no longer wade. 'Well, then, it's impossible to put a decent fly on the water above the sunken ledge,' you say. It looks like it, but this is how it's done: right here is a narrow point running to here, where it dwindles off to a single flat rock. If you work out on the point you can jump across to this rock—situated right there—and there you are, with about a thirty-foot cast to the sunken ledge. Deep water all around you, of course, and the rock is slippery; but—there you are. Now notice this small cove, right there. The water from the falls rushes past it in a froth, but in the cove it forms a deep eddy, with the current moving round and round, like this." George made a slow circular motion with the fork. "You know what I mean?"

I nodded.

"I got out on the point and jumped to the rock; got myself balanced, worked out the right amount of line and cast the dingaree Bill had forced on me, just above the sunken ledge. I didn't take the water lightly and I cast again, but I couldn't put it down decently. It would just flop in—too much weight and too many feathers. I suppose I cast it a dozen times, trying to make it settle like a fly. I wasn't thinking of trout—there would be nothing in there except Old Faithful—I was just monkeying with this doodle-bug thing, now that I had it on.

"I gave up at last and let it lie out where I had cast it. I was standing there looking at the falls roaring down, when I remembered Isabelle, waiting up on the trail. I raised my rod preparatory to reeling in and the what-you-may-call-'em made a kind of a dive and wiggle out there on the surface. I reached for my reel handle. Then I realized that the thingamajig wasn't on the water. I didn't see it disappear, exactly; I was just looking at it, and then it wasn't there. 'That's funny,' I thought, and struck instinctively. Well, I was fast—so it seemed—and no snags in there. I gave it the butt three or four times, but the rod only bowed and nothing budged. I tried to figure it out. I thought perhaps a water-logged timber had come diving over the falls and upended right there. Then I noticed the rod take more of a bend and the line began to move through the water. It moved out slowly, very slowly, into the middle of the pool. It was exactly as though I was hooked on to a freight train just getting under way.

"I knew what I had hold of then, and yet I didn't believe it. I couldn't believe it. I kept thinking it was a dream. I remember. Of course, he could have gone away with everything I had any minute if he'd wanted to, but he didn't. He just kept moving slowly, round and round the pool. I gave him what pressure the tackle would stand, but he never noticed a little thing like that; just kept moving around the pool for hours, it seemed to me. I'd forgotten Isabelle; I admit that. I'd forgotten everything on earth. There didn't seem to be anything else on earth, as a matter of fact, except the falls and the pool and Old Faithful and me. At last Isabelle showed up on the bank above me, still lugging her ferns and whatnot. She called down to me above the noise of the falls. She asked me how long I expected her to wait alone in the woods, with night coming on.

"I hadn't had the faintest idea how I was going to try to land the fish until then. The water was boiling past the rock I was standing on, and I couldn't jump back to the point without giving him slack and perhaps falling in. I began to look around and figure. Isabelle, said, 'What on earth are you doing?' I took off my landing net and tossed it to the bank. I yelled, 'Drop that junk quick and pick up that net!' She said, 'What for, George?' I said, 'Do as I tell you and don't ask questions!' She laid down what she had and picked up the net and I told her to go to the cove and stand ready.

"She said, 'Ready for what?' I said, 'You'll see what presently. Just stand there.' I'll admit I wasn't talking quietly. There was the noise of the falls to begin with, and—well, naturally I wasn't.

"I went to work on the fish again. I began to educate him to lead. I thought if I could lead him into the cove he would swing right past Isabelle and she could net him. It was slow work—a three-ounce rod— imagine! Isabelle called, 'Do you know what time it is?' I told her to keep still and stand where she was. She didn't say anything more after that.

"At last the fish began to come. He wasn't tired—he'd never done any fighting, as a matter of fact—but he'd take a suggestion as to where to go from the rod. I kept swinging him nearer and nearer the cove each time he came around. When I saw he was about ready to come I yelled to Isabelle. I said, 'I'm going to bring him right past you, close to the top. All you have to do is to net him.'

"When the fish came round again I steered him into the cove. Just as he was swinging past Isabelle the stuff she'd been lugging began to roll down the bank. She dropped the landing net on top of the fish and made a dive for those leaves and grasses and things. Fortunately the net handle lodged against the bank, and after she'd put her stuff in a nice safe place she came back and picked up the net again. I never uttered a syllable. I deserve no credit for that. The trout had made a surge and shot out into the pool and I was too busy just then to give her any idea of what I thought.

"I had a harder job getting him to swing in again. He was a little leery of the cove, but at last he came. I steered him toward Isabelle and lifted him all I dared. He came up nicely, clear to the top. I yelled, 'Here he comes! For God's sake, don't miss him!' I put everything on the tackle it would stand and managed to check the fish for an instant right in front of Isabelle.

"And this is what she did: it doesn't seem credible—it doesn't seem humanly possible; but it's a fact that you'll have to take my word for. She lifted the landing net above her head with both hands and brought it down on top of the fish with all her might!"

George ceased speaking. Despite its coating of talcum powder, I was able to detect an additional pallor in his countenance.

"Will I ever forget it as long as I live?" he inquired at last.

"No, George," I said, "but we've just exactly eleven minutes left."

George made a noticeable effort and went on:

"By some miracle the fish stayed on the hook; but I got a faint idea of what would have happened if he'd taken a real notion to fight. He went around the pool so fast it must have made him dizzy. I heard Isabelle say, 'I didn't miss him, George'; and then—well, I didn't lose my temper; you wouldn't call it that exactly. I hardly knew what I said. I'll admit I shouldn't have said it. But I did say it; no doubt of that; no doubt of that whatever."

"What was it you said?" I asked.

George looked at me uneasily.

"Oh, the sort of thing a man would say impulsively—under the circumstances."

"Was it something disparaging about her?" I inquired.

"Oh, no," said George, "nothing about her. I simply intimated—in a somewhat brutal way, I suppose—that she'd better get away from the pool—er—not bother me any more is what I meant to imply."

For the first time since George had chosen me for a confidant I felt a lack of frankness on his part.

"Just what did you say, George?" I insisted.

"Well, it wasn't altogether my words," he evaded. "It was the tone I used, as much as anything. Of course, the circumstances would excuse— Still, I regret it. I admit that. I've told you so plainly."

There was no time in which to press him further.

"Well, what happened then?" I asked.

"Isabelle just disappeared. She went up the bank, of course, but I didn't see her go. Old Faithful was still nervous and I had to keep my eye on the line. He quieted down in a little while and continued to promenade slowly around the pool. I suppose this kept up for half an hour more. Then I made up my mind that something had to be done. I turned very carefully on the rock, lowered the tip until it was on a line with the fish, turned the rod under my arm until it was pointing behind me and jumped.

"Of course, I had to give him slack; but I kept my balance on the point by the skin of my teeth, and when I raised the rod he was still on. I worked to the bank, giving out line, and crawled under some bushes and things and got around to the cove at last. Then I started to work again to swing him into the cove, but absolutely nothing doing. I could lead him anywhere except into the cove. He'd had enough of that; I didn't blame him, either.

"To make a long story short, I stayed with him for two hours. For a while it was pretty dark; but there was a good-sized moon that night, and when it rose it shone right down on the pool through a gap in the trees fortunately. My wrist was gone completely, but I managed to keep some pressure on him all the time, and at last he forgot about what had happened to him in the cove. I swung him in and the current brought him past me. He was on his side by now. I don't think he was tired even then—just discouraged. I let him drift over the net, heaved him out on the bank and sank down beside him, absolutely all in. I couldn't have got to my feet on a bet. I just sat there in a sort of daze and looked at Old Faithful, gleaming in the moonlight.

"After a half-hour's rest I was able to get up and go to camp. I planned what I was going to do on the way. There was always a crowd in the main camp living room after dinner. I simply walked into the living room without a word and laid Old Faithful on the center table.

"Well, you can imagine faintly what happened. I never got any dinner—couldn't have eaten any, as a matter of fact. I didn't even get a chance to take off my waders. By the time I'd told just how I'd done it to one crowd, more would come in and look at Old Faithful; and then stand and look at me for a while; and then make me tell it all over again. At last everybody began to dig up anything they had with a kick in it. Almost every one had a bottle he'd been hoarding. There was Scotch and gin and brandy and rye and a lot of experimental stuff. Art Bascom got a tin dish pan from the kitchen and put it on the table beside Old Faithful. He said, 'Pour your contributions right in here, men.' So each man dumped whatever he had into the dish pan and everybody helped himself.

"It was great, of course. The biggest night of my life, but I hope I'll never be so dog-tired again. I felt as though I'd taken a beating. After they'd weighed Old Faithful—nine pounds five and a half ounces; and he'd been out of water two hours—I said I had to go to bed, and went.

"Isabelle wasn't in the cabin. I thought, in a hazy way, that she was with some of the women, somewhere. Don't get the idea I was stewed. But I hadn't had anything to eat, and the mixture in that dish pan was plain TNT.

"I fell asleep as soon as I hit the bed; slept like a log till daylight. Then I half woke up, feeling that something terrific had happened. For a minute I didn't know what; then I remembered what it was. I had landed Old Faithful on a three-ounce rod!

"I lay there and went over the whole thing from the beginning, until I came to Isabelle with the landing net. That made me look at where her head should have been on the pillow. It wasn't there. She wasn't in the cabin. I thought perhaps she'd got up early and gone out to look at the lake or the sunrise or something. But I got up in a hurry and dressed.

"Well, I could see no signs of Isabelle about camp. I ran into Jean just coming from the head guide's cabin and he said, 'Too bad about your wife's mother.' I said, 'What's that?' He repeated what he'd said, and added, 'She must be an awful sick woman.' Well, I got out of him finally that Isabelle had come straight up from the stream the evening before, taken two guides and started for Buck's Landing. Jean had urged her to wait until morning, naturally; but she'd told him she must get to her mother at once, and took on so, as Jean put it, that he had to let her go.

"I said, 'Let me have Indian Joe, stern, and a good man, bow. Have 'em ready in ten minutes.' I rushed to the kitchen, drank two cups of coffee and started for Buck's Landing. We made the trip down in seven hours, but Isabelle had left with her trunks on the 10:40 train.

"I haven't seen her since. Went to her home once. She wouldn't see me; neither would her mother. Her father advised not forcing things— just waiting. He said he'd do what he could. Well, he's done it—you read the letter. Now you know the whole business. You'll stick, of course, and see me through just the first of it, old man. Of course, you'll do that, won't you? We'd better get down to the train now. Track Nineteen."

George rose from the table. I followed him from the café, across the blue-domed rotunda to a restraining rope stretched before the gloomy entrance to Track Nineteen.

"George," I said, "one thing more: just what did you say to her when she—"

"Oh, I don't know," George began vaguely.

"George," I interrupted, "no more beating about the bush. What did you say?"

I saw his face grow even more haggard, if possible. Then it mottled into a shade resembling the brick on an old colonial mansion.

"I told her—" he began in a low voice.

"Yes?" I encouraged.

"I told her to get the hell out of there."

And now a vision was presented to my mind's eye; a vision of twelve fish plates, each depicting a trout curving up through green waters to an artificial fly. The vision extended on through the years. I saw Mrs. George

Baldwin Potter ever gazing upon those rising trout and recalling the name on the card which had accompanied them to her door.

I turned and made rapidly for the main entrance of the Grand Central Station. In doing so I passed the clock above Information and saw that I still had two minutes in which to be conveyed by a taxicab far, far from the entrance to Track Nineteen.

I remember hearing the word "quitter" hurled after me by a hoarse, despairing voice.

CHAPTER SEVENTEEN

Just Fishing

by Tom Hennessey

The late Tom Hennessey was a dear friend whose engaging prose helped launch this book in Chapter Four. Here he's back, with another excerpt from his book Feathers 'n Fins. *Tom was a Maine outdoorsman who knew, from experience, how to handle any challenge the outdoor life could throw his way.*

This article makes me cast my mind into the backyard of my memory and recall an old fishing bromide: "Take a boy fishing, and you'll never have to go hunting for him."

Tom takes that old idea to new depths in this story. I have a friend who followed that advice but managed to mess things up. He was an avid trout angler, and he started his son with wading gear, plus wading vest with a half-zillion flies. He took him to a river and set about teaching him leader strengths and knots, dry fly presentations, and hours of looking into a stream to pick out the shapes of trout. It didn't work. No, his son did not end up being a delinquent or anything like that, but he ignored the angling life. His dad had taken the fun out of fishing: catching fish, regardless of size, and plenty of them.

ONE OF THE CARDINAL RULES FOR TRAINING HUNTING DOGS IS: "END every training session on a pleasant note." Make sense? You bet it does. A dog's hunting instincts will develop quickly if it receives praise and encouragement while afield. Now wouldn't it make sense to keep that simple guideline in mind when introducing a kid to hunting or fishing? Think about it.

Let's say, for instance, that you have a young son who, in less time than it takes to unsnarl a backlash, reaches boyhood. Like most boys, he is fascinated by rods, reels, lures, and the fish you bring home. Soon, you notice that you can no longer pick up your tacklebox without being asked, "Can I go?"

Here is where you should do a little backtracking. Remember when you were asking that question? It didn't make any difference where your father, grandfather, or uncle took you fishing—all that mattered was that they took you. Right? You must admit, though, that you probably had more fun worm fishing for white perch out at the Red Bridge than you did trolling smelts for salmon on Moosehead Lake. The reason being, of course, that the perch were more cooperative. Keep in mind, kids are kids. Names of far-flung fishing grounds don't impress them. Neither do top-of-the-line rods and reels, or boats that cost as much as the first house you bought. What impresses them most is just being with you and catching a fish or two.

To ensure that your boy's first fishing experience will be an enjoyable one, it's important that you do some preparation of your own. Forget about Atlantic salmon, landlocked salmon, squaretails, and togue. Forget about sewing on smelts or bumping with a Dave Davis spoon. In short, fishing and, for one day—his day—think about guiding.

As you know, a guide's worth is judged on his ability to find fish. Accordingly, take your "sport" fishing in a place where you know his rigging will tighten up frequently. Do that and you'll never again have to scare up a fishing partner. Warm-water ponds are, of course, most likely to produce fast and furious action. Their weed-choked shorelines and stump-studded coves are battlegrounds where perch, bass, and pickerel are always willing to start a war.

You'll need as much patience to teach your boy to fish as you will to make a setter pup staunch on point. It's important that a pup be allowed to chase a few birds over the horizon just to whet its appetite for hunting. Likewise, your pupil should be granted his privileges of youthful careless-ness, awkwardness and impulsiveness.

Resign yourself to the fact that you'll spend a good part of the day undoing the boat, the landing net, rocks, and yourself from ambitiously but errantly tossed flies and lures. So what? I'm sure you can remember—against advice offered from the stern seat of the canoe—trying to drop a bass plug right at the edge of a raft of dead snags. Paddling in to pry the plug loose, the Old Man would shake his head patiently and say, "Those snags fight hard, but they don't jump much, do they?"

It's not the end of the world if your boy tips the bait bucket over, or drops your tackle box. You know he'll step on the flyline, sit on the knapsack containing the sandwiches, lose his paddle in the swiftest part of the stream, and leave the insect repellent on a rock back where you put in. And you can bet your best reel that sometime during the day he'll go in over his boots—but won't dump them out until he's back in the canoe. Years later, you'll laugh at all that. Why not laugh at it then? It'll mean more.

A boy's curiosity and competitive nature make him an eager student. You'll be surprised at how quickly he'll learn knots, the names of flies and lures, and how to rig tackle. If he were half as attentive in school, he'd be on the honor roll. The courses offered in the classroom of the great outdoors are, however, infinitely more interesting and challenging, and the teachers far less demanding.

Don't be in such a hurry that you neglect to point out the shells of freshwater clams on the muskrat's feed bed—which contradicts the furbearer's herbivorous classification. Call attention to the hatch of mayflies—all flying upstream so that when the females dip to the surface, the current facilitates the release of eggs from their legs and bodies. Your pupil will ask more questions than an IRS auditor, but you'll begin feeling a little pleased with yourself for being able to answer them.

When you go ashore for lunch, build a fire. The world turns slowly when you sit by a fire, and a sandwich seems like a full-course meal. Better yet, bring along a frying pan and watch a kid who turns his nose up at haddock or halibut fill up on fillets of bass sprinkled with wood ash.

Most of all, don't let catching fish take precedence over the little things that, to a boy, make "goin' fishin'" so much fun. Show him how to whittle a whistle from a piece of willow, see who can skip rocks the farthest, catch frogs, and maybe a turtle to take home and keep in a washtub. Teach him to row or paddle. What difference does it make if you go around in circles for a few minutes? You've been doing that all your life. Ask him what pattern of fly he thinks you should use. Let him net a fish for you, and although you've stressed the importance of "catch-and-release," let him take a couple home. Aside from making him feel like a man and you feel like a boy, I'll guarantee that next time you pick up your tackle box he'll ask, "Can I go?"

Chapter Eighteen

Little Rivers

by Henry van Dyke

*We introduced this wonderful writer back in Chapter Fourteen, with another
of his trout essays from his book* Little Rivers *(1895). This is the title piece of
that book, which he called, "A book of essays in profitable idleness."*

A RIVER IS THE MOST HUMAN AND COMPANIONABLE OF ALL INANIMATE
things. It has a life, a character, a voice of its own, and is as full of good
fellowship as a sugar-maple is of sap. It can talk in various tones, loud or
low, and of many subjects, grave and gay. Under favourable circumstances
it will even make a shift to sing, not in a fashion that can be reduced to
notes and set down in black and white on a sheet of paper, but in a vague,
refreshing manner, and to a wandering air that goes
"Over the hills and far away."

For real company and friendship, there is nothing outside of the
animal kingdom that is comparable to a river.

I will admit that a very good case can be made out in favour of some
other objects of natural affection. For example, a fair apology has been
offered by those ambitious persons who have fallen in love with the sea.
But, after all, that is a formless and disquieting passion. It lacks solid
comfort and mutual confidence. The sea is too big for loving, and too
uncertain. It will not fit into our thoughts. It has no personality because
it has so many. It is a salt abstraction. You might as well think of loving

a glittering generality like "the American woman." One would be more to the purpose.

Mountains are more satisfying because they are more individual. It is possible to feel a very strong attachment for a certain range whose outline has grown familiar to our eyes, or a clear peak that has looked down, day after day, upon our joys and sorrows, moderating our passions with its calm aspect. We come back from our travels, and the sight of such a well-known mountain is like meeting an old friend unchanged. But it is a one-sided affection. The mountain is voiceless and imperturbable; and its very loftiness and serenity sometimes make us the more lonely.

Trees seem to come closer to our life. They are often rooted in our richest feelings, and our sweetest memories, like birds, build nests in their branches. I remember, the last time that I saw James Russell Lowell, (only a few weeks before his musical voice was hushed,) he walked out with me into the quiet garden at Elmwood to say good-bye. There was a great horse-chestnut tree beside the house, towering above the gable, and covered with blossoms from base to summit,—a pyramid of green supporting a thousand smaller pyramids of white. The poet looked up at it with his gray, pain-furrowed face, and laid his trembling hand upon the trunk. "I planted the nut," said he, "from which this tree grew. And my father was with me and showed me how to plant it."

Yes, there is a good deal to be said in behalf of tree-worship; and when I recline with my friend Tityrus beneath the shade of his favourite oak, I consent in his devotions. But when I invite him with me to share my orisons, or wander alone to indulge the luxury of grateful, unlaborious thought, my feet turn not to a tree, but to the bank of a river, for there the musings of solitude find a friendly accompaniment, and human intercourse is purified and sweetened by the flowing, murmuring water. It is by a river that I would choose to make love, and to revive old friendships, and to play with the children, and to confess my faults, and to escape from vain, selfish desires, and to cleanse my mind from all the false and foolish things that mar the joy and peace of living. Like David's hart, I pant for the water-brooks. There is wisdom in the advice of Seneca, who says, "Where a spring rises, or a river flows, there should we build altars and offer sacrifices."

The personality of a river is not to be found in its water, nor in its bed, nor in its shore. Either of these elements, by itself, would be nothing. Confine the fluid contents of the noblest stream in a walled channel of stone, and it ceases to be a stream; it becomes what Charles Lamb calls "a mockery of a river—a liquid artifice—a wretched conduit." But take away the water from the most beautiful river-banks, and what is left? An ugly road with none to travel it; a long, ghastly scar on the bosom of the earth.

The life of a river, like that of a human being, consists in the union of soul and body, the water and the banks. They belong together. They act and react upon each other. The stream moulds and makes the shore; hollowing out a bay here, and building a long point there; alluring the little bushes close to its side, and bending the tall slim trees over its current; sweeping a rocky ledge clean of everything but moss, and sending a still lagoon full of white arrow-heads and rosy knot-weed far back into the meadow. The shore guides and controls the stream; now detaining and now advancing it; now bending it in a hundred sinuous curves, and now speeding it straight as a wild-bee on its homeward flight; here hiding the water in a deep cleft overhung with green branches, and there spreading it out, like a mirror framed in daisies, to reflect the sky and the clouds; sometimes breaking it with sudden turns and unexpected falls into a foam of musical laughter, sometimes soothing it into a sleepy motion like the flow of a dream.

***

Go out to the Beaver-kill "In the tassel-time of spring," and follow its brimming waters through the budding forests, to that corner which we call the Painter's Camp. See how the banks are all enamelled with the pale hepatica, the painted trillium, and the delicate pink-veined spring beauty. A little later in the year, when the ferns are uncurling their long fronds, the troops of blue and white violets will come dancing down to the edge of the stream, and creep venturously out to the very end of that long, moss-covered log in the water. Before these have vanished, the yellow crow-foot and the cinquefoil will appear, followed by the star-grass and the loose-strife and the golden St. John's-wort. Then the unseen painter begins to mix the royal colour on his palette, and the red of the bee-balm catches your eye. If you are lucky, you may find, in midsummer, a slender fragrant spike of the purple-fringed orchis, and you cannot help finding the universal self-heal. Yellow returns in the drooping flowers of the jewel-weed, and blue repeats itself in the trembling hare-bells, and scarlet is glorified in the flaming robe of the cardinal-flower. Later still, the summer closes in a splendour of bloom, with gentians and asters and goldenrod.

You never get so close to the birds as when you are wading quietly down a little river, casting your fly deftly under the branches for the wary trout, but ever on the lookout for all the various pleasant things that nature has to bestow upon you. Here you shall come upon the cat-bird at her morning bath, and hear her sing, in a clump of pussy-willows, that low, tender, confidential song which she keeps for the hours of domestic intimacy. The spotted sandpiper will run along the stones before you, crying, "wet-feet, wet-feet!" and bowing and teetering in the friendliest manner, as if to show you the way to the best pools. In the thick branches of the hemlocks that stretch across the stream, the tiny warblers, dressed in a hundred colours, chirp and twitter confidingly above your head; and the Maryland yellow-throat, flitting through the bushes like a little gleam of sunlight, calls "witchery, witchery, witchery!" That plaintive, forsaken, persistent note, never ceasing, even in the noonday silence, comes from the wood-pewee, drooping upon the bough of some high tree, and complaining, like Mariana in the moated grange, "weary, weary, weary!"

When the stream runs out into the old clearing, or down through the pasture, you find other and livelier birds,—the robins, with his sharp, saucy call and breathless, merry warble; the bluebird, with his notes of pure gladness, and the oriole, with his wild, flexible whistle; the chewink, bustling about in the thicket, talking to his sweetheart in French, "cherie, cherie!" and the song-sparrow, perched on his favourite limb of a young maple, close beside the water, and singing happily, through sunshine and through rain. This is the true bird of the brook, after all: the winged spirit of cheerfulness and contentment, the patron saint of little rivers, the fisherman's friend. He seems to enter into your sport with his good wishes, and for an hour at a time, while you are trying every fly in your book, from a black gnat to a white miller, to entice the crafty old trout at the foot of the meadow-pool, the song-sparrow, close above you, will be chanting patience and encouragement. And when at last success crowns your endeavour, and the parti-coloured prize is glittering in your net, the bird on the bough breaks out in an ecstasy of congratulation: "catch 'im, catch 'im, catch 'im; oh, what a pretty fellow! sweet!"

There are other birds that seem to have a very different temper. The blue-jay sits high up in the withered-pine tree, bobbing up and down, and calling to his mate in a tone of affected sweetness, "salute-her, salute-her," but when you come in sight he flies away with a harsh cry of "thief, thief, thief!" The kingfisher, ruffling his crest in solitary pride on the end of a dead branch, darts down the stream at your approach, winding up his red angrily as if he despised you for interrupting his fishing. And the cat-bird, that sang so charmingly while she thought herself unobserved, now tries to scare you away by screaming "snake, snake!"

As evening draws near, and the light beneath the trees grows yellower, and the air is full of filmy insects out for their last dance, the voice of the little river becomes louder and more distinct. The true poets have often noticed this apparent increase in the sound of flowing waters at nightfall. Gray, in one of his letters, speaks of "hearing the murmur of many waters not audible in the daytime." Wordsworth repeats the same thought almost in the same words:

"A soft and lulling sound is heard
Of streams inaudible by day."

And Tennyson, in the valley of Cauteretz, tells of the river

"Deepening his voice with deepening of the night."

It is in this mystical hour that you will hear the most celestial and entrancing of all bird-notes, the songs of the thrushes,—the hermit, and the wood-thrush, and the veery. Sometimes, but not often, you will see the singers. I remember once, at the close of a beautiful day's fishing on the Swiftwater, I came out, just after sunset, into a little open space in an elbow of the stream. It was still early spring, and the leaves were tiny. On the top of a small sumac, not thirty feet away from me, sat a veery. I could see the pointed spots upon his breast, the swelling of his white throat, and the sparkle of his eyes, as he poured his whole heart into a long liquid chant, the clear notes rising and falling, echoing and interlacing in endless curves of sound,

"Orb within orb, intricate, wonderful."

Other bird-songs can be translated into words, but not this. There is no interpretation. It is music,—as Sidney Lanier defines it,—

"Love in search of a word."

But it is not only to the real life of birds and flowers that the little rivers introduce you. They lead you often into familiarity with human nature in undress, rejoicing in the liberty of old clothes, or of none at all. People do not mince along the banks of streams in patent-leather shoes or crepitating silks. Corduroy and home-spun and flannel are the stuffs that suit this region; and the frequenters of these paths go their natural gaits, in calf-skin or rubber boots, or bare-footed. The girdle of conventionality is laid aside, and the skirts rise with the spirits.

A stream that flows through a country of upland farms will show you many a pretty bit of genre painting. Here is the laundry-pool at the foot of the kitchen garden, and the tubs are set upon a few planks close to the water, and the farmer's daughters, with bare arms and gowns tucked up, are wringing out the clothes. Do you remember what happened to Ralph Peden in *The Lilac Sunbonnet* when he came on a scene like this? He tumbled at once into love with Winsome Charteris—and far over his head.

And what a pleasant thing it is to see a little country lad riding one of the plough-horses to water, thumping his naked heels against the ribs of his stolid steed, and pulling hard on the halter as if it were the bridle of Bucephalus! Or perhaps it is a riotous company of boys that have come down to the old swimming-hole, and are now splashing and gambolling through the water like a drove of white seals very much sun-burned. You had hoped to catch a goodly trout in that hole, but what of that? The sight of a harmless hour of mirth is better than a fish, any day.

Possibly you will overtake another fisherman on the stream. It may be one of those fabulous countrymen, with long cedar poles and bed-cord lines, who are commonly reported to catch such enormous strings of fish, but who rarely, so far as my observation goes, do anything more than fill their pockets with fingerlings. The trained angler, who uses the finest tackle, and drops his fly on the water as accurately as Henry James places a word in a story, is the man who takes the most and the largest fish in the long run. Perhaps the fisherman ahead of you is such an one,—a man whom you have known in town as a lawyer or a doctor, a merchant or a preacher, going about his business in the hideous respectability of a high silk hat and a long black coat. How good it is to see him now in the freedom of a flannel shirt and a broad-brimmed gray felt with flies stuck around the band.

In Professor John Wilson's *Essays Critical and Imaginative*, there is a brilliant description of a bishop fishing, which I am sure is drawn from the life:

> *Thus a bishop, sans wig and petticoat, in a hairy cap, black jacket, corduroy breeches and leathern leggins, creel on back and rod in hand, sallying from his palace, impatient to reach a famous salmon-cast ere the sun leave his cloud, . . . appears not only a pillar of his church, but of his kind, and in such a costume is manifestly on the high road to Canterbury and the Kingdom-Come.*

I have had the good luck to see quite a number of bishops, parochial and diocesan, in that style, and the vision has always dissolved my doubts in regard to the validity of their claim to the true apostolic succession.

Men's "little ways" are usually more interesting, and often more instructive than their grand manners. When they are off guard, they frequently show to better advantage than when they are on parade. I get more pleasure out of Boswell's Johnson than I do out of Rasselas or The Rambler. The Little Flowers of St. Francis appear to me far more precious than the most learned German and French analyses of his character. There is a passage in Jonathan Edwards' *Personal Narrative*, about a certain walk that he took in the fields near his father's house, and the blossoming of the flowers in the spring, which I would not exchange for the whole of his dissertation "On the Freedom of the Will." And the very best thing of Charles Darwin's that I know is a bit from a letter to his wife: "At last I fell asleep," says he, "on the grass, and awoke with a chorus of birds singing around me, and squirrels running up the tree, and some woodpeckers laughing; and it was as pleasant and rural a scene as ever I saw; and I did not care one penny how any of the birds or beasts had been formed."

Little rivers have small responsibilities. They are not expected to bear huge navies on their breast or supply a hundred-thousand horse-power to the factories of a monstrous town. Neither do you come to them hoping to draw out Leviathan with a hook. It is enough if they run a harmless, amiable course, and keep the groves and fields green and fresh along their banks, and offer a happy alternation of nimble rapids and quiet pools,

"With here and there a lusty trout,
And here and there a grayling."

When you set out to explore one of these minor streams in your canoe, you have no intention of epoch-making discoveries, or thrilling and world-famous adventures. You float placidly down the long stillwaters, and make your way patiently through the tangle of fallen trees that block the stream, and run the smaller falls, and carry your boat around the larger ones, with no loftier ambition than to reach a good camp-ground before dark and to pass the intervening hours pleasantly, "without offence to God or man." It is an agreeable and advantageous frame of mind for one who has done his fair share of work in the world, and is not inclined to grumble at his wages. There are few moods in which we are more susceptible of gentle instruction; and I suspect there are many tempers and attitudes, often called virtuous, in which the human spirit appears to less advantage in the sight of Heaven.

It is not required of every man and woman to be, or to do, something great; most of us must content ourselves with taking small parts in the chorus. Shall we have no little lyrics because Homer and Dante have written epics? And because we have heard the great organ at Freiburg, shall the sound of Kathi's zither in the alpine hut please us no more? Even those who have greatness thrust upon them will do well to lay the burden down now and then, and congratulate themselves that they are not altogether answerable for the conduct of the universe, or at least not all the time. "I reckon," said a cowboy to me one day, as we were riding through the Bad Lands of Dakota, "there's some one bigger than me, running this outfit. He can 'tend to it well enough, while I smoke my pipe after the round-up."

There is such a thing as taking ourselves and the world too seriously, or at any rate too anxiously. Half of the secular unrest and dismal, profane sadness of modern society comes from the vain idea that every man is bound to be a critic of life, and to let no day pass without finding some fault with the general order of things, or projecting some plan for its improvement. And the other half comes from the greedy notion that a man's life does consist, after all, in the abundance of the things that he possesses, and that it is somehow or other more respectable and pious to be always at work making a larger living, than it is to lie on your back in the green pastures and beside the still waters, and thank God that you are alive.

Come, then, my gentle reader (for by this time you have discovered that this chapter is only a preface in disguise,—a declaration of principles or the want of them, an apology or a defence, as you choose to take it,) and if we are agreed, let us walk together; but if not, let us part here with out ill-will.

You shall not be deceived in this book. It is nothing but a handful of rustic variations on the old tune of "Rest and be thankful," a record of unconventional travel, a pilgrim's scrip with a few bits of blue-sky philosophy in it. There is, so far as I know, very little useful information and absolutely no criticism of the universe to be found in this volume. So if you are what Izaak Walton calls "a severe, sour-complexioned man," you would better carry it back to the bookseller, and get your money again, if he will give it to you, and go your way rejoicing after your own melancholy fashion.

But if you care for plain pleasures, and informal company, and friendly observations on men and things, (and a few true fish-stories,) then perhaps you may find something here not unworthy your perusal. And so I wish that your winter fire may burn clear and bright while you read these pages; and that the summer days may be fair, and the fish may rise merrily to your fly, whenever you follow one of these little rivers.

1895.

CHAPTER NINETEEN

Thread of the River

by Odell Shepard

The classic book Thy Rod and Thy Creel *by Odell Shepard was first published in 1930 and had long been out of print when Nick Lyons republished it in 1984. With an introduction by Paul Schullery, the new edition was immediately embraced by new generations of readers, eager to enjoy Shepard's insightful and illuminating reflections.* Legendary Esquire *editor and publisher Arnold Gingrich said, "I can think of nobody who has written about angling more beautifully than Odell Shepard, at least since Walton."*

WHAT SEEMS TO ME THE PRIMARY AND MOST ENDURING SOURCE OF THE angler's happiness has already been mentioned. This, in a word, is wild nature—a very ancient word which has been grossly sentimentalized of late, and is soiled with all ignoble use, but which must still serve our turn. Every good angler will have his notion of what I mean by it—a notion that will certainly over-lap my own without being exactly coincident with it—and I believe that if he could analyze all the many elements of his pleasure in fishing he would find that this one predominates. As a rule, and quite properly, he does not analyze them, being too much occupied with what seem for the time more important considerations. His impressions come to him, as William James says the first experiences of life come to an infant, in a vast humming and buzzing confusion. Nevertheless, for nine good anglers out of ten, although nearly the same number would probably deny it, the sights and sounds and odors that surround the fisherman are more than the fishing. Set one of them to angling in an indoor swimming pool well stocked with three-pounders, and the most dubious will admit the truth of what I say.

Angling is of course by no means the only sport of which this may be said, let any grown American who enjoyed a normal boyhood think back far enough through the years and he will find that all his recollections of his early out-door games are entangled with faint or vivid memories of weather and of seasons. Peg-tops and top-spinning are associated with the end of winter, marbles with earliest spring, kite-flying with June and July, baseball with the blazing days of August, and the thought of football comes mingled with colors of flying leaves and smoke of autumnal bonfires. Skating, tobogganing, snowshoeing, skiing, bring other associations not less vivid, and the still earlier games of childhood such as prisoner's base, pull-away, and hide-and-go-seek are even more heavily charged with memories of nature. There must be a million Americans living today who can recall the time when nutting was a festival that took us every October into the enchanted woods. We did not come back from those excursions in farm-carts and buckboards quite the same boys and girls that we were when we set out. Certain things were decided for us once and for all by influences of which we were scarcely aware—by the odors of decaying foliage, by the patterns of gold against the blue, by the twirling fall of a leaf. We may think that we have forgotten all these things, but the sight of a single flaming maple or even some vaguely related strain of music brings them back, and it would require half of an eternity to wear away the gold of those high hickories from our thoughts. All day long we were climbing trees, throwing sticks, gathering fallen nuts, and the closest observation would not have discovered that we paid a moment's attention to the banners of autumn about us, and yet today we discover this fine deposit in the cells of memory—whisper of ferns, scents, blue of the asters that withered three decades ago, gold of the leaves that have gone back into sod and climbed again into trees and flowers.

What can all this mean, if not that some part, apparently a large one, of our enjoyment in those old games and excursions was derived, although we did not know it, from natural influences? We must have seen those immense cities of cloud, splendidly domed and turreted, that loomed above the baseball diamond, and seen them with strange intensity, while we thought we were wholly occupied with watching the ball, else they would not come so vividly back to us now. The chill of evening and approaching winter, cold airs and odors of burning leaves and of wood-smoke, that used to creep or flow across the field during the last minutes of a football game, must have been felt most keenly at the time in the midst of all our rough-and-tumble, or else they would not now lie waiting for us in the darkened rooms of memory whenever we turn the keys in those old wards. No doubt it was the "subliminal mind" that snatched up and stored these treasures while all the conscious attention was earnestly trained upon the game, but that does not lessen their potency or dim their present charm. The game itself, even the mighty effort to win or to excel in that game, occupied the center of attention, but quite other things, having no apparent relation to the game, were seen, so to speak, with the more sensitive outer fringes of the retina and recorded indelibly.

Now there is no reason to suppose that this faculty of gathering impressions from fields outside the focus of attention is peculiar to childhood. We know that it is not. Considered all together, these impressions are more important to feeling than sport itself; they compose the nimbus or aureole through which the sportsman sees his game, whatever it may be, and only by reference to them can we explain how it happens that thousands of intelligent men derive from sport somewhat the same satisfactions that others do from art and religion.

What is the difference in attitude toward the game of golf between an ignorant and unimaginative spectator and an expert player? To the former it consists entirely in knocking a little hard ball here and there over the grass until it rolls finally into a hole, after which it is extracted and knocked some more—a sufficiently dull and childish pastime. To the skillful player it is ten thousand other things, such as a delight and a despair, schooling in accuracy of mind and body and in self-control, opportunity for self-conquest. He sees it not baldly and barely but as a multiple thing; he thinks of it in connection with all its rich connotations and in terms of a million memories stored away in nerves and muscles and brain. The most useful of these memories for practical purposes are those that preserve successful stances and strokes, bodily motions and balances, but the most important to his pleasure in the game are those that seem secondary or even unrelated to the sport. Say the word "golf" to him and he is as likely as not to smell the dewy grass just warmed by the sun of early morning, to feel the firm soft sod of the green under foot, to see a spot of brightness edged by shadow lifting against a summer cloud, or to hear the drone of friendly voices chaffing in the locker-room. He cares no more for merely knocking a small white ball about than any other sensible man, but he loves the game of golf—loves it in its entirety, somewhat as one loves a woman, not solely or chiefly because she has blue eyes.

Something like this may be said of all out-door sports, but of none more emphatically than of angling. There are people in the world who see nothing in the angler's occupation but tedium, laziness, cruelty, and lies—or, as some wiseacre has phrased it, "a fly at one end of a line and a fool at the other." Peace be to all such, and a better way—if they can find it—of spending their leisure time, more human, more humane, more fit for an honest man. Say "fishing" to the angler, however, or mention any one of the tools of his sport, and you call up more memories than could be named in a year—memories of sunny days and foul, of virgin dawns and serene nightfalls, of bending rods, leaping gold and crimson, rippling green, of camp fires far and near, of talk and of silence and of friends. Into his mental pictures of angling he has painted the sky, the trees, the ferns and moss, most of all, the water, and the colors run. Probably there is no other sport that carries one so far toward the secret heart of nature as angling does. This is to say that the memories of nature laid away by the angler are richer, more vivid and more various, than those acquired in other sports.—If one were disposed to follow this line of argument a little further he might succeed in proving what every angler knows, that fishing is the finest sport in the world. But anglers are seldom argumentative. They prefer to make their assertions and have done. Furthermore, they are never eager for converts, at any rate in our time, feeling more than satisfied with the number of fishermen they find on the stream at dawn of opening day. Therefore they may sometimes say that angling is the best of sports, but they seldom attempt to prove it.

Wild nature, as I have said, is the most important, as it is also the most enduring source of the angler's pleasure, and the phase of nature with which he is most concerned is the most beautiful, mysterious, and fascinating of all—wild water. Any one who has once seen and felt the amazing loveliness of swiftly running water, whether in the meadow brook or the mountain torrent, whether lustrous under leaves or flashing to the open sky, can understand without elaborate explanation the charm that lures and holds the angler. He has fallen under a spell that has been known in all ages and has been symbolized in many a legend of Sirens, Loreleis, Undines, and other water-witches. He is bemused by the babble of water, by the fragrance and song of it, by its broken and reflected and piercing and shimmering lights, by its constant change on the surface of its deep changelessness, and most of all by its motion. To his ears the stream sings in a hundred voices low and high, intermittent or continuous, and he can separate these voices and hear what each is saying as a conductor unravels the total harmony of his orchestra and finds the throbbing of a single string. To his eyes the stream brings glitter, ever-changing hues, curves of inimitable and never-failing grace, and the magical effect of motion in the midst of a stable landscape—the leaping white jet of life. And this beauty, moreover, is always mysterious to him, meaning something beyond what it shows and says; and after he has studied it for a life time it is not less mysterious but more so, more strange and so more alluring. It is this mystery and challenging strangeness that the angler sets his will and wit to explore. Standing in one element, he invades another, striving to search it thoroughly. With a fifty-foot finger of bamboo and silk and gut he probes the deeps and the shallows, feels along the riffles, glides slowly out into bays of glitter, striving toward and almost attaining a sixth sense, trying to surprise the water's innermost secret law.—But this, of course, he will never do. In other arts and crafts, and even in a few sports, we can distinguish the three stages of apprentice, journeyman, and master; but in angling few ever pass beyond apprenticeship, and masters there are none.

Wild water—how it draws us back to itself from our boyhood to our oldest age, and lures us on and on, down and down, as though just beyond each bend lay the answers to all our questionings and the goal of all our hopes. It draws and lures us by an infinite variety. No two stretches of any living brook are the same or similar to a seeing eye, and no square foot of it is the same for two moments together. Depth, color, bottom, angle of light from above and from below, rapidity of current, speed and size of ripples, vagaries of breeze and calm, time of day, season of the year—all of these and a thousand other factors and influences playing together and into one another make any wayside brook more bewilderingly various than anything short of a lifelong study can teach one to realize. In streams well supplied with rocks and boulders standing up from the surface there is, in addition all the grade of water-curves never-ending, looping long and far, shaping streams within the stream, edged and flecked with foam. Where trees grow near there is added the dappling of light and shade, slumbrous when the breeze is still and dancing when the boughs are set aswing.

But the brook is not for the eye alone; it is the string of a mighty violin, stretched between the mountains and the sea. And it has a great gamut, from the broad rumbling bass of the main current rounding a granite boulder to the tiny trebles of little ripples sparkling pizzicato in the shallows. Where the stream flows wide over gravel beds there are numberless singers blending their tones like so many leaves in a tree, but where it narrows and bores between rocky walls the voices crowd together in one vague shout. Comes a fall, and the shout deepens to a roar, overlaid by faint screams and splashings and by tones that sound in desolate places like those of the human voice calling from far away. Below the fall there is heard, underneath the sound of steady onrush, a half-drowned subaqueous grumbling from the under-tow as of some giant tossing there, and a clamor of somersaulting currents that boil upward and break outward into the day. Every bubble of the thousands bursting here adds its particle to the tumult, and the long sigh of the current slipping past reeds at the stream's edge is added also. One hundred feet farther down the water quiets into a pool. All the uproar becomes an echo, then a memory. There is only the faint ruffling of the breeze on the backs of the ripples. But at the sill of the pool a stickle begins; this grows to a water-slide; then comes a fallen tree through whose branches the stream washes and gurgles in muted tones. After that, once more there is the broad deep rumbling of the main current and all the repertoire is played over again, though never in the same order or with exact repetition of any part. Usually, too, more than one variety of stream-song is heard at the same moment. The string is double-stopped.

Thomas Hardy somewhere says that an English peasant who has been brought up among trees can tell where he is in a familiar country-side on the darkest night, merely by the sound of the wind among the leaves, which varies widely from one species to another. However this may be, it is certain that an experienced trout-fisher can guide himself fairly well in night-fishing by the sound of the water alone; and in the daytime he has always some idea of the stretches ahead of him before he rounds a bend. Instinctively, he estimates the depth of a pool and the strength of a current almost as much by the ear as by the eye, and the sounds of the water suggest to him many devices, warn him that rocks will roll or that the trout are lying against the farther bank. He hears and analyzes a hundred signals in the hurl of the water of which he is never consciously aware.

What can a man desire more when standing knee-deep in a moun-tain river, rod in hand, with trout on the rise? Here he has earth and air and sky before him, strangely interfused and woven into one element. The brook runs over the bones of the planet and carries the sky on its back, so that it is a complete world, and one who gazes into this crystal long and steadily will find there not food and drink only but work and play, patience and excitement, knowledge and wisdom, fact and dream. Here indeed is one of the forms of nature that pass into our moods with tran-quil restoration. Either the stream teaches or else it recalls to mind some of the deeper truths that are seldom thought of but are good to know. Consider, for example, the almost universal belief—universal, at any rate, in the western world—that every one desires to live forever, preserving his own individuality forever intact. What has the stream to say about that matter? Well, we see that it is moving steadily, as swiftly as possible and by the shortest possible course, toward the sea and the merging of its tiny self into a vastly greater. What sort of water is it that "lives forever" and preserves its identity intact? The stagnant pool, mantled with obscene scum and foul with all forms of death.—Deeper teachings than this the stream has for us—as, how to mingle freedom with restraint and law with liberty. It keeps pace with us, or rather it runs on before. In its slender source far up the mountain there was already a sure and glad foreknowledge of the end. One who could understand wild water—as no man ever will—would be far on the road to understanding all things, so full it is of symbols and correspondencies with our lives; and it may be a dim realization of this that brings us back to the stream's side whenever we can get there, that keeps us bending for hour after hour over bridges, that makes the heart leap when we see from a passing train the white feather of a brook on a distant hillside, and that holds us awake in the night listening to the voice of a river rushing through darkness. That river is the metaphor of time to us, and we are children of Time. It rushes toward the sea of oblivion, as we do. It would linger if it could in this pool, in that eddy, under such a bending elm, but a stronger need and wish draws it down, forever down, toward its swaying and softly breathing rest.

Down and down, forever down. Imagination faints in the effort to realize how long it has been falling. The angler comes to a gorge worn hundreds of feet deep in solid rock by nothing but the everlasting trample of tiny water-drops. He casts his flies over huge circular pools of granite scooped by the slow gyration of pebbles and sand during years hardly to be expressed by arithmetic. Numberless pools such as these are to be seen in the Rocky Mountains, fifty feet deep and as many in diameter, where the great trout swim in a liquid emerald. "Earth has not anything to show more fair." Neither is there anything to be seen on this side of the Pearly Gates more lovely than the grottoes and caverns carved by flowing water in a mountain's flank, banked with moss and overhung by ferns. The boulders strewn up and down such rivers have a more savage grandeur than boulders to be seen elsewhere, as though they had learned nobility from the song of the water round them. The fisherman comes to a huge fallen crag rising thirty feet or more above the stream and commanding a long vista of checkered shade and shine, leaping foam and trembling sun-dazzle, and the sun may go down upon him while he sits there, his tackle at his feet. Or he finds small crevices in the rocky bed where the water is a flowing topaz that checks the swing of his wrist almost in mid-cast by its beauty, and many a pool that must contain good trout he walks round without throwing a line, because it seems too perfect for him to profane even by the fluttering of a tuft of feathers. He need not be superstitious, or even much of a scholar, to feel that such places are sanctified by some tutelary spirit or local goddess such as Milton's youths invoked:

> Sabrina fair,
> Listen where thou art sitting
> Under the glassy, cool, translucent wave,
> In twisted braids of lilies knitting
> The loose train of thine amber-dropping hair.

Wild water left to itself can never fail to be beautiful, and it will not endure the slightest ugliness about it. This is true not only of the mountain river but of the meadow brook as well, flowing almost mute among reeds and grasses and under willow trees. There are stretches of the upper Thames, where it winds among the level lands that William Morris loved and flows twenty miles to make five of headway, that are as beautiful in their July coloring as anything to be seen in high Switzerland. The little Musketaquid also, that steals through Concord with so slow a tread that Hawthorne was for three weeks in doubt which way it flows, has nothing to learn in the lore of rivers. Indeed, almost any nameless rivulet creeping from root to tussock in a New England pasture reveals all the range of loveliness to be seen in the Amazon from source to mouth, if only one has the patience and skill to find it.

CHAPTER TWENTY

The Beginning of the Season
by John Waller Hills

Among the several classic chronicles of English chalkstream fishing, the one I find myself returning to most often for sheer enjoyable reading is John Waller Hills's Summer on the Test. *One reason might be that Hills's book is not written in an "instructional" vein, but rather as a straightforward description of the fishing under varying conditions. When Hills takes us to the stream, our spirits fall and rise as his own. The river gives for a while, then it takes away, as hatches disappear and trout sulk. The pageant of the seasons, the off-again, on-again nature of the hatches, scroll through* Summer on the Test *like enchanting but mysterious dramas in which we view our leading player, Mr. Hills, with empathy and hope.*

Summer on the Test was first published in a limited edition in 1924 and reprinted in a popular edition with new chapters in 1930. The book endures today as a classic of the first rank.

The Seasons, surely in these northern climes,
Laugh at their image drawn by modern Rhimes.
For spring oft shivers in the British Isle,
But warms, in British song, with Maia's smile.

The Anglers.
By Dr. Thomas Scott.
1758.

THE SPRING OF 1924 WAS BLACK AND COLD. BY THE BEGINNING OF April few flowers and leaves had succeeded in the hard struggle, and indeed I have known the north of Scotland more forward than was the Test valley. Through the first half of the month we had bitter north winds, frequent hail and occasional snow. A miraculous change came just before Easter, and for four or five days from the 18th the conditions were like June. Then the fine weather broke, and there followed a series of gales, lasting till nearly the end of the month, culminating in a regular hurricane on the 27th. Now, it so happens that these conditions combine all the elements adverse to fly fishing. Extreme cold in early spring may bring up fly, but makes trout lethargic. Very hot weather means a poor hatch, and so do gales. Thus our three types of weather were all unpropitious; but of the three, the cold spell at the beginning was best, for at any rate there was fly, and without fly you are defeated, since even the accommodating trout of the Test cannot rise at nothing. Still, there were many occasions when fly was abundant but hardly a trout moved, and on the best days you did not have the chance of many fish, often only two or three; and you had to be lucky if you landed a brace of these, and they turned out to be over the limit of a pound and a half. In the hot weather the surroundings were delightful, but fly very scarce. And the days of gale were the worst of all.

I fished at Mottisfont on eight or nine days in April, somewhat unsuccessfully it is true, though I got some good trout. An exceptional number of bungles were made, and some very heavy fish were lost, one, which I shall always regret because he cannot have been less than three pounds, defeated me after a long fight in a manner which I cannot bear to recall. However, though rewards were small, the days were interesting. The rise was usually concentrated and short, the trout were particular about pattern, and fine gut had to be used. 26th April was a day typical of many. There was a wild wind from the south-east, heavy rain until one o'clock, and it was cold. But, when I started out, even under these unpromising conditions, I did not despair. At any rate, I said, the day was better than the one before. Then the wind had blown from the south-west, masses of inky black, rain-soaked clouds had scurried in succession across the sky, and there was that uncomfortable heavy feeling in the air beloved of our forefathers but which is the worst in the world for the floating fly. The present day was much better, for the air was nimble, and if it had a bite in it, why the large dark olive of spring is a lover of cold. Sure enough, at half-past twelve, summer time, the first olives appeared, and they were large and smoky grey, flickering delicately in the gale, tempting food for winter-starved stomachs. But, as usual, the fish paid no notice at first: so when it grew too cold to sit still any longer I walked up, eyes roaming over the water.

At last there was a movement under my bank; it might be a rat, but let us try my dark olive quill; its size was 0, and my gut 3x. The first cast was swept wide by the wind, but at the second there was a confident rise and a good fish careered down stream. The river was fairly clear of weed, the current ran full and strong, and after a merry fight I netted a fat fish, not two pounds in weight it is true, but well over the pound and a half limit. I walked up, and suddenly, without preparation, unexpected and wonderful as it always is, however often you see it, the real hatch started. Olives were coming down thick, in little bands of half a dozen or so, blown together by the wind, and trout were rising quietly and quickly and continuously, all up the river, three or four of them within reach, and good fish too. There is a quality of magic about these early spring rises. The river looks dead and lifeless, and this impression is heightened by the bare meadows and the leafless trees. The stream runs with a dull lead-like surface, which nothing disturbs and apparently nothing ever will disturb. You expect a rise and it does not come, and then suddenly, when you have given up expecting, trout start moving simultaneously as though the signal had been passed round. At one moment you see fly after fly sailing down untaken, and you think nothing will ever break the unbroken surface: at the next the river is alive with rings of rising fish. It has come to life, and the sturdy vital trout, which a moment ago were hidden so completely that you doubted their existence, have mysteriously reappeared. I crawled to the bank, knelt down and watched. There were five fish within reach, and I looked eagerly to see which was the best. This period of expectation, when fish are well on the feed, is one of unmixed happiness. When action begins, when you have to cast, you may put the trout down, or you may break, or make some other dreadful bungle: but in the stage of exciting anticipation, when you see that great trout are to be caught if you can catch them, any extravagant success is possible and your pleasure is unalloyed. However, I did not spend as long as it takes to write this in deciding, for near me, and above, a big fish was swallowing olive after olive, almost in perpetual motion. I was rather too close to him, but the wild wind ruffled the water, and concealed my presence: I put my dark olive over him three or four times: I made certain he would take, but he did not, though he went on steadily eating natural fly. What is the meaning of that? Another fish was rising, opposite me, smaller but takeable, as was a third, higher up in the middle, and I could reach each without putting line over the first. I was not sure about the size of either, but I must know if my pattern is right. They both disregarded it. When it was certain that all had seen and neglected it (and as usual I kept it on too long) I reeled up and knotted on a medium, not dark, olive quill, a size smaller. The effect was immediate. I floated it over the first fish, he rose, but I think I struck too quickly. Anyway, I did not hook him, alas, for he was heavy. Next I tried the one under the opposite bank. He took at the first cast, and I pulled him downstream, out of the way, and netted him out. He also was not two pounds, but he was some ounces bigger than the first I had killed. Then I crawled back to my position: two or three fish were still rising, not perhaps so madly as at first, and I was perfectly certain they would not go on long. Quickly I picked out the best and, after considerable trouble with the wind, managed to get a fly to him. He took, made a gallant, hard run, but then came off: the wind was so strong and wild that it was impossible to keep the line taut, and I lost him, the best fish of the morning, without a doubt. Then all was over. The rise, the concentrated part of it, had lasted barely half an hour. I ended up with two trout, no great bag, but a brace that weigh not far from four pounds is something.

This indeed is the peculiarity of early spring rises, that they start and end suddenly. You are lucky to get a fish before they begin: when they end, you can go home. Whilst they are on, fish are not difficult, provided there is not too much fly: but you very rarely do well when your artificial has to be a member of a drove of naturals, for the competition is too severe. But, in these short April rises, you have no time for bungles or disasters or changes of fly: if you are to do well, your fly must be right to begin with. And this is not so simple as it sounds.

Hampshire was backward in April 1924. Not a kingcup was out, not a sign of white appeared on the dark twigs of the blackthorn, not a glint of green on the willows. And this is not favourable for sport, for my experience is that the earlier the season the better you do. If you were back from France in 1918, and keep a diary, turn up the month of April, and you will see that that spring was a full month earlier than the spring of 1924. It was a very good April. I got fish from the beginning, and I well remember two days towards the end, days which are symbolic of the conditions required for spring fishing. The 29th April was a hot, summer-like day, cloudless, with a light variable breeze. There was a bad hatch of olives, and a poor rise. With difficulty I got a brace of fish. The following day was the greatest contrast imaginable. There was a savage north-east wind, a heavy shower in the morning, the sky was overcast, and the air freezingly cold. I was on the Kennet, and went out at half-past ten, but nothing stirred till mid-day. Then I got three, one after another, in rapid succession: there were a few olives out, and fish took a blue quill, size 0. I had by then reached the top of the water, a broad, deep weir pool, with a rushing stream through the middle, and whirling eddies and backwaters at its head. In one of these, in a small, slow whirlpool, a big fish was lying low down, busy feeding on nymphs. I put on a greenwell's glory, wetted it, and after several casts managed to get it over him; he took, and rushed straight down to the tail of the pool. When I got down to him he rushed up, and I rather weakly allowed him to get into a patch of weed; but the water was shallow, I waded out, cleared my line, and the fish bolted into a second patch and from there into a third. I could wade out to that, and could see the fish lying in the weeds. Then I did a silly thing: instead of clearing the line or hand-lining him out, I tried to net him in the weeds. The result was that I missed him, he dashed out, and the hook came away. He was a fish between two and three pounds.

Chastened and pensive, I walked down to a sheltered spot to eat my sandwiches. As I had been playing the big fish, I had noticed more olives coming down, but now suddenly they appeared in droves, one of the larg-est hatches I have ever seen. A few fish rose, but only tentatively: I kept on my blue quill, and after considerable casting, for the trout were not taking one natural fly in twenty, I managed to kill two fish and returned an undersized one. After that not a fish moved, so I sat down to my sandwiches, watching the water. The weather was as inclement as ever, a raging north-east wind, and bitterly cold, but still olives sailed down in fleet after fleet. Caught by the northerly wind they were driven in packs into the southern bank, where they lay in all the little bays and curves of the shore, hardly floating with the current, and indeed often driven upstream by a more furious gust than usual. I expected every minute to see a quiet rise in one of these bays and a trout cruising about, picking the motionless fly off the water, but nothing happened. Three o'clock came, the wind grew colder and the fly thicker, but not a trout broke the surface and reluctantly I felt that it was hopeless, and there was nothing for it but to go home. Walking slowly back, watching the water intently, at last I saw what I had so long expected, a quiet rise and a good trout swimming around, swallowing fly after fly. He was on the lee shore, in the glass edge, in quite smooth water, cruising in an area of three or four square yards, making no more break than a minnow. Such fish are difficult, for you cannot always see where they are and make sure that your fly goes over them, and you are very likely to put the line across them, and then all is up. That particular fish I put down, but there was another small rise above. At the first cast I got hung up and lost my blue quill, which was a good thing, for it was too big, and I knotted on a Lock's fancy, size 00. No use, so I reeled up and tied on a hackle olive, 00, and this after many casts he took and I killed him. Then I rose and missed two more (you have to strike very slowly with these gentlemen), killed two, and rose and missed another. All this meant a lot of careful casting, and it was then six o'clock and the rise over. So I finished up with eight fish: a good day.

Now these two days were the opposite of each other; the first, fine and hot, produced hardly any fly and two fish, and the second, bitterly cold, showed an immense hatch and four brace of fine trout. Never, never believe that cold weather hinders fly. You will hear it, always and every-where; but it is not only untrue but the reverse of truth. Except at the very beginning of April, you get more fly on a cold day than on a warm.

A good many Aprils have been spent after salmon, or after trout in northern waters, far from the Test. The great lesson which April trout fishing in these streams teaches you is never to despair. Fortune may suddenly change, and you never know what your bag will be till you have reeled up: and indeed I have actually done this and started for home, tired and dispirited, when I have been tempted back to the water, with the result that the basket which was light at five o'clock has been so full and heavy at six that my shoulder has ached agreeably under the weight. You get this on chalk streams, too, but not so often. You may get a fall of spinner as late as six o'clock or even seven. But on most days you are dependent on the hatch of duns, and this hardly ever starts later than three o'clock: in fact rarely as late, for from eleven to one is the usual time for it to begin. If I had to choose an hour in April, it would be between twelve and one. But though I have often wandered afar from Hampshire, I have many recollections of April in the south country as well as in the north. It is not one of the best of fishing months, but the Test valley shows then an individual beauty which is missed by those who do not start till May. Not many flowers are out, it is true, and the forest trees are still leafless: but there is a wash of green on the willows, the banks are tufted with primroses, and the kingcup makes broad patches of liquid gold over the meadows. This flower is a great favourite of mine, with its bowls of clear yellow and its dark glossy leaves. It has a bold, vigorous growth, typical of spring. It is at its best when it first flowers, for later on it gets ragged and straggly. Every day, also, the summer birds are arriving and one by one you can greet them all again. But the chief joys of April are anticipation and the sense that you are getting something for nothing. All the best of the year is in front of you, and you have not used it up yet. However bad your luck, nothing is wasted. The real season has not begun. And so, if you do get a good day, it is something additional and unexpected, something that was not in the programme, a pure gain, unlooked for and welcome: and if you get a bad one, there is no loss. It is this, and the delicious beginning of flower and leaf, which make April so enjoyable.

The Angler's Year may be divided into three stages. The first runs from the opening down to about the middle of May. It is marked by rises which begin and end suddenly: those of April are often quite short, but they lengthen gradually as May is reached. In the earlier part you depend chiefly on the daily hatch of duns, first of olives, later of iron blues as well, and later still of pale watery duns also. But do not neglect either spinners or nymphs. Always keep looking at the water to see if spinners are coming down. Try bulging fish with a rough olive, or your favourite nymph, or, what is best of all, an orange partridge. Look out for smuts, also, for they appear even on cold days. Above all, waste no time. You do not, either in April or in early May, find those casual risers which move at something all through the long June days. As the afternoons grow lighter, trout begin to eat spinners more and more, and there are signs of the evening rise starting, whereupon the first stage of the Angler's Year ends. Then on the lower Test comes the mayfly interlude: after that the second stage, with the typical long drawn out hatches of duns, beginning and ending in more indeterminate fashion than those of the first stage, the falls of spinners, the evening rise, smuts, and sedge fishing. This lasts till some date in mid-August, and after that comes the third stage of the Angler's Year, running until the end of the season.

Now, it will be obvious that both the fisherman's day and the flies he uses will be governed by these considerations. In early April most is done during the hatch, and since that hatch is short the one essential thing is that the angler should be at the right place at the right time and with the right fly. There is no room for the leisured experiments of June. But, as April runs towards May, and more especially during May itself, after the iron blue has appeared, you will do as much with the spinner as with the dun. The female iron blue spinner is a mighty favourite with trout. In fact in some years fish do not get really on to spinners until they have had a good meal off the spent iron blue. And, of course, nymphs will be taken right through the period. That great Test fly, the caperer, only appears at about its end, but you must always be on the watch for it. It is a marvellous good fly.

I consider the best early spring fly to be a blue upright, ribbed with gold wire, and you can use as a big a hook as No. 0 on a wild April day. The dark olive quill, the gold ribbed hare's ear, or greenwell's glory all kill well. The variant, also an imitation of the dark olive, does not to my fancy do well till later. And you must never think that, though it is early April and blowing or raining or both, trout are not particular about pattern, for often they are. More and more, as years go on, do I use hackle flies. I have killed numberless trout on the hackle dark olive quill, but of late the blue upright has superseded it.

As May draws nearer, duns get smaller and lighter in colour, and your hook can be No. 00, or, if that is refused, 000. Your blue upright can be dressed without gold wire. If this is refused, my first change would be to a dressing which has a brown or ginger hackle, such as a ginger quill. Had I to choose one fly for the whole year, it would be a ginger quill. A tup will often be successful, especially on a hot, still day. And, for those who like it, the alder appears, but it is not a fly I often use. On the other hand, I use the welshman's button (the caperer of the Test) increasingly. It appears at the beginning of May, and both the winged and hackle dressings are very useful.

Imitations of spinners are exceeding hard to find, for most of those sold in the shops are worthless, whilst Halford's dressings, fairly good for olives and pale wateries, utterly fail to reproduce the glowing flame of the sherry spinner or the burning red of the female iron blue. However, this is to anticipate. No spinner, early in the season or late, equals Lunn's particular. In fact, I believe it to be the best fly in the world. It imitates admirably the spinner of the olive. And as soon as the iron blue has appeared, use the houghton ruby. It is a magnificent imitation of the female spinner. Mr. Skues, too, should be consulted, and so should a new book by Mr. Dunne, *Sunshine and the Dry Fly*.

In April and early May, you find the best fish in quick, rather deep, water of the main river. Not many are on the shallows as yet, or in still deeps, or in eddies, or in carriers. But as the weather grows warmer, they move into the thinner water. The first hatches of dark olives often bring up large and wary trout, and you may hook something unexpectedly heavy.

CHAPTER TWENTY-ONE

Mid-Stream Crisis

by Lamar Underwood

This story first appeared in Sports Afield *in February 1983. When I wrote it, I was doing a lot of thinking about the ups and downs of fishing. Sometimes I even found myself wondering if less demanding hobbies might be right for me. Such thoughts were immediately extinguished by more fishing and more writing.*

AS THE YEAR BEGAN, I DECIDED TO EMBRACE THE ADVICE OF MY FRIEND Sparse Grey Hackle, who told me: "Let the wolf out!" He was dead right. It was the only way to go. No more Mister Nice Guy!

My New Year's resolution was a notice served on all creatures, great and small, that in the open seasons ahead I was going to fill my hand. I was fed up with two-trout days, three-bass weekends, and no-deer vacations. I'd had it with calling to bird dogs that wouldn't stand still and turkeys that would (two ridges away!). I didn't want to see another pheasant getting up 200 yards away down a com row or another bay full of ducks and geese rafted up and preening their feathers under skies that had flown in from Palm Springs.

Government wags told me that in the previous season, some 2.5 million hunters had shot 12 million ducks. The calculator that lives beside my checkbook told me that works out to five or six ducks per hunter. I didn't get any five ducks! Who the hell shot my ducks?

All around, the previous year had not just been bad; it had been a disaster. I zigged when they zagged. The northeasters and I booked into the same places at the same times. I frightened the spots off brown trout while bass slept through my offerings. The deer left the mountain country I hunt, but those from the woods alongside my house found my tulips and peas in the spring, then shredded two young pines during rub-time in the fall. Plenty of geese crossed the pit blinds I hunkered in all season, but they were so high they were a menace to aviation—and they held express tickets.

My dismal performances afield forced me to face what the late John Foster Dulles called "an agonizing reappraisal." Clearly, my tactics were lousy; my timing stank; my equipment belonged in a museum.

I knew better than to seek some all-embracing formula as my game plan. Each subject would have to be tackled separately, tactics and gear made precise. The geese, I felt, would be the problem to deal with. I began squirreling away the bucks to purchase a 10-gauge magnum automatic, with which I intended to wreak havoc on the Eastern Shore. My more immediate problem—and infinitely more complex—was what to do about those trout.

Since the Romans knew nothing about split-cane rods and matching the hatch, they invented a calendar that starts the new year off from the pit of winter. For me and millions of other fishermen, the real new year begins on the opening day of trout season. My usual opening-day scenario looked like this:

An already-pudgy figure, bulked further by enough clothes to outfit the Klondike gold rush, stands hip-deep in a flow of black water torn into sudsy rips by protruding rocks and bearing of the countryside what the winter snows have been holding in storage: sticks, leaves, tires, a bloated cat, the occasional beer can. Overhead the sky is a glowering mass of putty, against which the bare branches of the trees snap and creak with iron-hard stiffness as blasts of wind arrive from Siberia. For hours our man alternates making casts, peering intently at the jaunty little flies that ride the current like miniature galleons, and fumbling stiff fingers through his fly box in search of new offerings. To find a greater fool, you would have to look inside an ice fishing shanty.

The bottom of a trout stream is its food factory, and on this day it will not be violated by anything except the soles of *el piscator's* waders. Although he will soon abandon his dry flies (how quickly the credo fades: "I'd rather catch one on top than five down deep"), our man will make only tentative probes into the depths. His wet flies, streamers, and nymphs will sweep harmlessly over the heads of the stone-hugging trout. Troutless by three o'clock, he will seek the solace of the ledge where fire, firewater, and kindred snake-bit companions will be waiting with tales of woe and livers in various stages of distress.

Long before opening day dawned last season, I was determined to never again be a part of this demented tableau.

For weeks I hit the books with an intensity seldom mounted in my professional life. Schwiebert, Whitlock, Marinaro, Swisher-Richards— the great masters of flyfishing for trout were devoured. Their instruction manifested itself in a barrage of catalogs and small packages of flies arriving daily from every corner of troutdom. My wading vest bulged with trinkets. Latin names of bugs came trippingly off the tongue.

Opening day, I stood thigh-deep at the head of a pool of black water, frigid and swollen with runoff. Coming to the stream, I had received the usual assortment of reports that the fish were in a coma. The voice on the car radio had said something about snow. None of these things intimidated me at all. This year I was ready.

To meet this early and elemental trouting condition, I pried open a box of nymphs. These were not ordinary nymphs, but masterpieces of illusion—caterpillar-like, hairy-leggy-juicy-looking. Each was weighted with enough piano wire to outfit a Steinway. Never mind that they would hit the water with the finesse of a slam dunk. They would go down, my friend, down, down to the very noses of these frozen wisenheimers. I would fish these creations with a leader hacked to three feet. (Long leaders, I had learned, rise in the pushing and swelling of the current.) The whole outfit would ride down with high-density sinking line topped by a fluorescent strike indicator to tell me when I had a customer.

You don't cast such a rig. What you do is sort of heave the whole mess out and to one side, paying close attention that a hook in the ear is not the immediate result of the effort.

I watched the curls of line and leader straighten downstream toward a boulder that slashed the smooth flow. I tried to form a mental image of what the nymph was doing—sinking, tumbling, ticking over rocks. The line straightened past the boulder. I paid out three more long pulls from the reel, watching the strike indicator bob on downstream. Suddenly I thought I saw it dart forward. I came back with rod and line and felt the weight of a trout. As the brown—a lovely 15-incher—darted and splashed on the way to the net, my elation soared. My patience and virtue and hard study were to be rewarded. The masters of the game were indeed wise and learned men.

After that, you can imagine my heart-hammering excitement when the next 30 minutes yielded two more fish, about the same size as the first.

Then the devil sent his disciples to descend upon me like a plague of locusts. First one, then two, then three other anglers were crowding into my stretch of water. Not one asked what I was using. They simply assumed I had found "The Place." Never mind, I told myself. You can afford to be generous. I waded from the stream and pointed up toward uninhabited water. In a few minutes I was sloshing, much too fast, through a bouldery run of pocket water when I felt my right foot sliding down an eel-slick ledge. I lurched hard to the left, but that leg would not bear the burden. I went down into the water on my back with a teeth-jarring crash. Totally submerged for a second, I stood up and cursed my luck and the worn felt soles of my waders. I was drenched, achingly cold, and clearly out of action for the rest of the day.

As I waded to the edge of the stream, I discovered another result of my accident with dramatic suddenness. As I made a little sideways move with my left leg to step around a rock, I felt a nauseating wave of pain. I did not want to feel such a shock again, ever, so now I picked my way gingerly along, trying to protect the knee.

Yuk! Yuk! See the man all soaking wet and limping toward his car. Fat-ass must've fallen in. Yuk! Yuk!

A prominent physician whom I trust sentenced the knee to six weeks of healing. Because I could not wade the stream, I could not fish for trout. The great fly hatches of early spring for which I had prepared myself so diligently came and went: the Blue Quills, the Hendricksons, the Grannom caddis, the March Browns.

My mood was foul and depressed. Without my jogging program, with which I had successfully been losing weight, I quickly regained ten pounds. Going to work in New York on the train one day, I was struck by a thought as morbid as any I've ever had. The obituary page of the *New York Times* named very few males in their 90s. No, the ages of the boys getting their names in the paper were in the 70s and 80s. At age 45 I had the startling realization that in all likelihood, I was more than halfway to the barn. Life begins at 80? Give me a break!

Okay, my somber mood told me, so you've lost some of your good moves and speed. You can't hit a 60-yard mallard or sink a three-foot putt. On the tennis court, children who can't get into an R-rated film have you gasping like a beached whale. The guide can show you a tarpon at 60 feet, and you may or may not be able to get the fly to it (probably not, given any kind of wind). But relax, buster. For the years have given you wisdom. Look at what you did with those opening-day trout!

I was still clinging to this slightly uplifting notion when I finally got back to the river in late May. One of the year's best hatches remained. According to the grapevine, the Sulphurs had arrived in tentative numbers two days earlier, and all signs pointed to their major emergence late that evening.

The hatch of *Ephemerella dorothea* Sulphurs which goes on with diminishing consistency for about six weeks on good eastern streams, ranks as a favorite because it stirs smart, self-respecting trout into an unusual orgy of gluttony. Unlike some mayfly hatches, which deliver more sizzle than steak, the appearance of the No. 16 yellow-and-dun flies in the last hour before darkness produces fishing so fast and exciting that it is the stuff for cool hands and stout hearts.

My favorite slick-water was flat empty that evening. My recent misfortune was all forgotten as I waded into position and made a few desultory casts while waiting for the hatch to begin. The air was heavy with humidity, and low clouds on the ridges promised that darkness would come early and perhaps a thunderstorm with it.

The time that passed seemed interminable. Nothing came off the darkening water, not even caddis. A kingfisher flew upstream, scolding my presence. I heard a great horned owl up on the mountain and an answering cry from nearby. Then I saw the first delicate yellow mayfly climbing steeply toward the trees. In a few moments there was another, then another, then another, and then I actually saw one in the instant it left the water—and beyond it the swirl of a trout.

My line arched through the growing dusk. I saw my artificial Sulphur begin its jaunty ride down the feeding lane where the trout had swirled. It floated on downstream, unharmed. There were other rises all over the pool now—not splashy water-throwing slaps, but subtle bulges and swirls.

I really started worrying when my bogus Sulphur made three more rides through the melee without interesting a trout. What was wrong? The fly? The leader? My thoughts screamed as I watched the hatch and rises go on: You've been out of action so long you don't know what you're doing.

In the middle of this burst of self-condemnation I saw something—flashes of darting trout just beneath the surface. That was it! The trout were not taking the surface duns! They were nymphing, gulping the insects as they rose to the surface and in the film as they emerged into winged shape.

I was prepared for this, but my hands trembled as I opened the fly box and got out a floating nymph. The light was going fast, but I managed to tie on the fly without digging out my night light. In my excitement, however, I dropped my reading halfglasses into the stream. Klutz! Fool! I should have had them on a cord around my neck.

No matter. I had the right ammo now, and the fish were still going strong as I roll-cast the nymph to the top of the pool. Instantly a trout was on, and I felt a flush of ultimate satisfaction. The fish was a strong pulsating weight as it struggled upstream for a few seconds. Then the line went slack as the trout bolted downstream almost past my legs, a momentary shadow that caused me to gasp: I was into my largest trout ever.

The reel screamed appropriately as the fish bolted downstream. He reached the lip of the falls that terminated the pool and turned to face the current. The steady pressure on the 5X felt unbelievable. I had the feeling of the fish backing up, backing to the edge of the tumbling water. He was going to be washed over the lip! I had to do something! I palmed the flange of the reel, increasing the drag, and thereby succeeded in instantly breaking off the trout as surely as though I'd been trying to.

I reeled in the sickeningly slack line and looked at the 5X tippet. So many trout were still taking the Sulphur nymphs all over the pool that the excitement smothered the loss of the big fish. I quickly had another floating nymph out, ready to tie on. I felt my shirt pocket for my reading glasses and remembered where they had gone. I held the fly at arm's length against the gloom of the darkening sky. No way. I could not thread the eye of the hook in that dimness.

No problem. My night light had a magnifying glass that fit over the top of the light. No sweat, just stay cool.

I was deeply aware of the rises continuing all over the pool as I pulled the light out and draped its cord around my neck. I felt deeper into the pocket for the magnifying glass. It wasn't there! I flipped the switch on the light. Nothing! *Click, click. Click, click.* Still nothing! Okay, the batteries are dead. You're on your own. Now just hold the fly very still against what is left of the sky and tie it on.

My panic rose as I tried unsuccessfully to tie on the No. 16 Sulphur. I tried a No. 14. It would not go. In a final burst of madness and inspiration, I dug out a No. 10 Blonde Wulff, the biggest fly in my vest. Maybe it would work on these feeding fish.

Perhaps it would have. I don't know. I never got the Wulff tied on. My vision is 20-20, but at age 45 I could not see close-up well enough to tie on a fly and resume fishing a hatch that I had waited for all winter.

I reeled in slowly, felt the end of the leader reach the reel, then broke down my rod. The splashes of feeding trout popped out from the darkness. I could not see the rises now, but they were distinctive above the murmur the current made as it tailed from the pool downstream.

Slowly the disappointment drained away. The easy moves, the good speed. Going, going with the years. Yet it was true. You were wiser, vastly richer in the things you knew. Such as realizing right now that what made fishing so great was that on any given outing, things could happen that you would remember all of your days. Few other times in life could offer that.

That is the easy part of change—the knowing, the feeling. The other side is that you have left something precious behind—something you had used up and would have to go on without.

Flashes of lightning came across the ridgetop, then the roll of advancing thunder. The feeding grew quieter, then died out completely. The bursts of lightning helped me find my way up the hillside to the lane that led back to the car.

I did not know if I had reached the end of something or the beginning.

The wind blew on the high ridges, gusting along the slopes, coming down to the river.

CHAPTER TWENTY-TWO

The Angler

by Washington Irving

The author of the unforgettable classics "Rip Van Winkle" and "The Legend of Sleepy Hollow," Washington Irving (1783–1859) grew up in New York City. As a young man fascinated by the outdoor life, he began spending as much time as possible in New York's Catskill Mountain region. He was a wonderful short story writer, and his talent shines through in this tale of his passion for trout fishing.

IT IS SAID THAT MANY AN UNLUCKY URCHIN IS INDUCED TO RUN AWAY from his family and betake himself to a seafaring life, from reading the history of Robinson Crusoe; and I suspect that, in like manner, many of those worthy gentlemen who are given to haunt the sides of pastoral streams with angle rods in hand, may trace the origin of their passion to the seductive pages of honest Izaak Walton. I recollect studying his *Compleat Angler* several years since, in company with a knot of friends in America, and moreover that we were all completely bitten with the angling mania. It was early in the year; but as soon as the weather was auspicious, and that the spring began to melt into the verge of summer, we took rod in hand and sallied into the country, as stark mad as was ever Don Quixote from reading books of chivalry.

One of our party had equalled the Don in the fullness of his equipments; being attired *cap-à-pie* for the enterprise. He wore a broad-skirted fustian coat, perplexed with half a hundred pockets; a pair of stout shoes and leathern gaiters; a basket slung on one side for fish; a patent rod, a landing-net, and a score of other inconveniences, only to be found in the true angler's armoury. Thus harnessed for the field, he was as great a matter of stare and wonderment among the country folk, who had never seen a regular angler, as was the steel-clad hero of La Mancha among the goatherds of the Sierra Morena.

Our first essay was along a mountain brook, among the highlands of the Hudson; a most unfortunate place for the execution of those piscatory tactics which had been invented along the velvet margins of quiet English rivulets. It was one of those wild streams that lavish, among our romantic solitudes, unheeded beauties, enough to fill the sketch book of a hunter of the picturesque. Sometimes it would leap down rocky shelves, making small cascades, over which the trees threw their broad balancing sprays, and long nameless weeds hung in fringes from the impending banks, dripping with diamond drops. Sometimes it would brawl and fret along a ravine in the matted shade of a forest, filling it with murmurs; and, after this termagant career, would steal forth into open day with the most placid demure face imaginable; as I have seen some pestilent shrew of a housewife, after filling her home with uproar and ill-humour, come dimpling out of doors, swimming and courtseying, and smiling upon all the world.

How smoothly would this vagrant brook glide, at such times, through some bosom of green meadow-land among the mountains; where the quiet was only interrupted by the occasional tinkling of a bell from the lazy cattle among the clover, or the sound of a woodcutter's axe from the neighbouring forest.

For my part, I was always a bungler at all kinds of sport that required either patience or adroitness, and had not angled above half an hour before I had completely "satisfied the sentiment," and convinced myself of the truth of Izaak Walton's opinion, that angling is something like poetry—a man must be born to it. I hooked myself instead of the fish; tangled my line in every tree; lost my bait; broke my rod; until I gave up the attempt in despair, and passed the day under the trees, reading old Izaak; satisfied that it was his fascinating vein of honest simplicity and rural feeling that had bewitched me, and not the passion for angling. My companions, however, were more persevering in their delusion. I have them at this moment before my eyes, stealing along the border of the brook, where it lay open to the day, or was merely fringed by shrubs and bushes. I see the bittern rising with hollow scream as they break in upon his rarely invaded haunt; the kingfisher watching them suspiciously from his dry tree that overhangs the deep black millpond, in the gorge of the hills; the tortoise letting himself slip sideways from off the stone or log on which he is sunning himself; and the panic-struck frog plumping in headlong as they approach, and spreading an alarm throughout the watery world around.

I recollect also, that, after toiling and watching and creeping about for the greater part of a day, with scarcely any success, in spite of all our admirable apparatus, a lubberly country urchin came down from the hills with a rod made from a branch of a tree, a few yards of twine, and, as Heaven shall help me! I believe a crooked pin for a hook, baited with a vile earthworm—and in half an hour caught more fish than we had nibbles throughout the day!

But, above all, I recollect the "good, honest, wholesome, hungry" repast, which we made under a beech-tree, just by a spring of pure sweet water that stole out of the side of a hill; and how, when it was over, one of the party read old Izaak Walton's scene with the milkmaid, while I lay on the grass and built castles in a bright pile of clouds, until I fell asleep. All this may appear like mere egotism; yet I cannot refrain from uttering these recollections, which are passing like a strain of music over my mind, and have been called up by an agreeable scene which I witnessed not long since.

In a morning stroll along the banks of Alun, a beautiful little stream which flows down from the Welsh hills, and throws itself into the Dee, my attention was attracted to a group seated on the margin. On approaching, I found it to consist of a veteran angler and two rustic disciples. The former was an old fellow with a wooden leg, with clothes very much but very carefully patched, betokening poverty, honestly come by, and decently maintained. His face bore the marks of former storms, but present fair weather; its furrows had been worn into an habitual smile; his iron-gray locks hung about his ears, and he had altogether the good-humoured air of a constitutional philosopher who was disposed to take the world as it went. One of his companions was a ragged wight, with the skulking look of an arrant poacher, and I'll warrant could find his way to any gentleman's fish-pond in the neighbourhood in the darkest night. The other was a tall, awkward, country lad, with a lounging gait, and apparently somewhat of a rustic beau. The old man was busy in examining the maw of a trout which he had just killed, to discover by its contents what insects were seasonable for bait; and was lecturing on the subject to his companions, who appeared to listen with infinite deference. I have a kind feeling towards all "brothers of the angle," ever since I read Izaak Walton. They are men, he affirms, of a "mild, sweet, and peaceable spirit"; and my esteem for them has been increased since I met with an old *Tretyse of fishing with the Angle*, in which are set forth many of the maxims of their inoffensive fraternity. "Take good hede," sayeth this honest little tretyse, "that in going about your disportes ye open no man's gates, but that ye shet them again. Also ye shall not use this forsayd crafti disport for no covetousness to the encreasing and sparing of your money only, but principally for your solace, and to cause the helth of your body and specyally of your soule."

I thought that I could perceive in the veteran angler before me an exemplification of what I had read; and there was a cheerful contentedness in his looks that quite drew me towards him. I could not but remark the gallant manner in which he stumped from one part of the brook to another; waving his rod in the air, to keep the line from dragging on the ground, or catching among the bushes; and the adroitness with which he would throw his fly to any particular place; sometimes skimming it lightly along a little rapid; sometimes casting it into one of those dark holes made by a twisted root or overhanging bank, in which the large trout are apt to lurk. In the meanwhile he was giving instructions to his two disciples; showing them the manner in which they should handle their rods, fix their flies, and play them along the surface of the stream. The scene brought to my mind the instruction of the sage Piscator to his scholar. The country around was of that pastoral kind which Walton is fond of describing. It was a part of the great plain of Cheshire, close by the beautiful vale of Gessford, and just where the inferior Welsh hills begin to swell up from among fresh-smelling meadows. The day, too, like that recorded in his work, was mild and sunshiny, with now and then a soft-dropping shower, that sowed the whole earth with diamonds.

I soon fell into conversation with the old angler, and was so much entertained, that, under pretext of receiving instructions in his art, I kept company with him almost the whole day; wandering along the banks of the stream, and listening to his talk. He was very communicative, having all the easy garrulity of cheerful old age; and I fancy was a little flattered by having an opportunity of displaying his piscatory lore; for who does not like now and then to play the sage?

He had been much of a rambler in his day, and had passed some years of his youth in America, particularly in Savannah, where he had entered into trade and had been ruined by the indiscretion of a partner. He had afterwards experienced many ups and downs in life, until he got into the navy, where his leg was carried away by a cannon-ball, at the battle of Camperdown. This was the only stroke of real good fortune he had ever experienced, for it got him a pension, which, together with some small paternal property brought him in a revenue of nearly forty pounds. On this he retired to his native village where he lived quietly and independently; and devoted the remainder of his life to the "noble art of angling."

I found that he had read Izaak Walton attentively, and he seemed to have imbibed all his simple frankness and prevalent good humour. Though he had been sorely buffeted about the world, he was satisfied that the world, in itself, was good and beautiful. Though he had been as roughly used in different countries as a poor sheep that is fleeced by every hedge and thicket, yet he spoke of every nation with candour and kindness, appearing to look only on the good side of things; and, above all, he was almost the only man I had ever met with who had been an unfortunate adventurer in America and had honesty and magnanimity enough to take the fault to his own door, and not to curse the country. The lad that was receiving his instructions, I learnt, was the son and heir apparent of a fat old widow who kept the village inn, and of course a youth of some expectation, and much courted by the idle gentleman-like personages of the place. In taking him under his care, therefore, the old man had probably an eye to a privileged corner in the taproom, and an occasional cup of cheerful ale free of expense.

There is certainly something in angling, if we could forget, which anglers are apt to do, the cruelties and tortures inflicted on worms and insects, that tends to produce a gentleness of spirit, and a pure serenity of mind. As the English are methodical, even in their recreations, and are the most scientific of sportsmen, it has been reduced among them to perfect rule and system. Indeed, it is an amusement peculiarly adapted to the mild and highly cultivated scenery of England, where every roughness has been softened away from the landscape. It is delightful to saunter along those limpid streams which wander, like veins of silver, through the bosom of this beautiful country; leading one through a diversity of small home scenery; sometimes winding through ornamented grounds; sometimes brimming along through rich pasturage, where the fresh green is mingled with sweet-smelling flowers; sometimes venturing in sight of villages and hamlets, and then running capriciously away into shady retirements. The sweetness and serenity of nature, and the quiet watchfulness of the sport, gradually bring on pleasant fits of musing, which are now and then agreeably interrupted by the song of a bird, the distant whistle of the peasant, or perhaps the vagary of some fish, leaping out of the still water, and skimming transiently about its glassy surface. "When I would beget content," says Izaak Walton, "and increase confidence in the power and wisdom and providence of Almighty God, I will walk the meadows by some gliding stream, and there contemplate the lilies that take no care, and those very many other little living creatures that are not only created, but feed (man knows not how) by the goodness of the God of nature, and therefore trust in him."

I cannot forbear to give another quotation from one of those ancient champions of angling, which breathes the same innocent and happy spirit:

> *Let me live harmlessly, and near the brink*
> *Of Trent or Avon have a dwelling-place,*
> *Where I may see my quill, or cork, down sink,*
> *With eager bite of pike, or bleak, or dace;*

And on the world and my Creator think:
Whilst some men strive ill-gotten goods t' embrace;
And others spend their time in base excess
Of wine, or worse, in war, or wantonness.
Let them that will, these pastimes still pursue,
And on such pleasing fancies feed their fill;
So I the fields and meadows green may view,
And daily by fresh rivers walk at will,
Among the daisies and the violets blue,
Red hyacinth and yellow daffodil.

On parting with the old angler, I inquired after his place of abode, and happening to be in the neighbourhood of the village a few evenings afterwards, I had the curiosity to seek him out. I found him living in a small cottage, containing only one room, but a perfect curiosity in its method and arrangement. It was on the skirts of the village, on a green bank, a little back from the road, with a small garden in front, stocked with kitchen herbs, and adorned with a few flowers. The whole front of the cottage was overrun with a honeysuckle. On the top was a ship for a weathercock. The interior was fitted up in a truly nautical style, his ideas of comfort and convenience having been acquired on the berth-deck of a man-of-war. A hammock was slung from the ceiling, which, in the day-time, was lashed up so as to take but little room. From the centre of the chamber hung a model of a ship, of his own workmanship. Two or three chairs, a table, and a large sea-chest, formed the principal moveables. About the wall were stuck up naval ballads, such as "Admiral Hosier's Ghost," "All in the Downs," and "Tom Bowling," intermingled with pictures of sea-fights, among which the battle of Camperdown held a distinguished place. The mantelpiece was decorated with sea-shells, over which hung a quadrant, flanked by two wood-cuts of most bitter-looking naval commanders. His implements for angling were carefully disposed on nails and hooks about the room. On a shelf was arranged his library, containing a work on angling, much worn, a Bible covered with canvas, an odd volume or two of voyages, a nautical almanack, and a book of songs.

His family consisted of a large black cat with one eye, and a parrot which he had caught and tamed, and educated himself, in the course of one of his voyages; and which uttered a variety of sea phrases with the hoarse brattling tone of a veteran boatswain. The establishment reminded me of that of the renowned Robinson Crusoe; it was kept in neat order, everything being "stowed away" with the regularity of a ship of war; and he informed me that he "scoured the deck every morning, and swept it between meals."

I found him seated on a bench before the door, smoking his pipe in the soft evening sunshine. His cat was purring soberly on the threshold, and his parrot describing some strange evolutions in an iron ring that swung in the centre of his cage. He had been angling all day, and gave me a history of his sport with as much minuteness as a general would talk over a campaign; being particularly animated in relating the manner in which he had taken a large trout, which had completely tasked all his skill and wariness, and which he had sent as a trophy to mine hostess of the inn.

How comforting it is to see a cheerful and contented old age; and to behold a poor fellow, like this, after being tempest-tost through life, safely moored in a snug and quiet harbour in the evening of his days! His happiness, however, sprung from within himself, and was independent of external circumstances; for he had that inexhaustible good nature, which is the most precious gift of Heaven; spreading itself like oil over the troubled sea of thought, and keeping the mind smooth and equable in the roughest weather.

On inquiring further about him, I learnt that he was a universal favourite in the village, and the oracle of the tap-room; where he delighted the rustics with his songs, and, like Sinbad, astonished them with his stories of strange lands, and shipwrecks, and sea-fights. He was much noticed, too, by gentlemen sportsmen of the neighbourhood; had taught several of them the art of angling; and was a privileged visitor to their kitchens. The whole tenor of his life was quiet, and inoffensive, being principally passed about the neighbouring streams, when the weather and season were favourable; and at other times he employed himself at home, preparing his fishing tackle for the next campaign, or manufacturing rods, nets, and flies, for his patrons and pupils among the gentry.

He was a regular attendant at church on Sundays, though he generally fell asleep during the sermon. He had made it his particular request that when he died he should be buried in a green spot, which he could see from his seat in church, and which he had marked out ever since he was a boy, and had thought of when far from home on the raging sea, in danger of being food for the fishes—it was the spot where his father and mother had been buried.

I have done, for I fear that my reader is growing weary; but I could not refrain from drawing the picture of this worthy "brother of the angle"; who has made me more than ever in love with the theory, though I fear I shall never be adroit in the practice, of his art; and I will conclude this rambling sketch in the words of honest Izaak Walton, by craving the blessing of St. Peter's master upon my reader, "and upon all that are true lovers of virtue; and dare trust in his providence; and be quiet; and go a angling."

CHAPTER TWENTY-THREE

A Fatal Success

by Henry van Dyke

We introduced Henry van Dyke back in two previous chapters. He returns to our pages here in his most popular story, from his book Fisherman's Luck, *1899.*

> "What surprises me in her behaviour," said he, "is its thoroughness. Woman seldom does things by halves, but often by doubles."
>
> —SOLOMON SINGLEWITZ: THE LIFE OF ADAM.

BEEKMAN DE PEYSTER WAS PROBABLY THE MOST PASSIONATE AND TRIumphant fisherman in the Petrine Club. He angled with the same dash and confidence that he threw into his operations in the stock-market. He was sure to be the first man to get his flies on the water at the opening of the season. And when we came together for our fall meeting, to compare notes of our wanderings on various streams and make up the fish-stories for the year, Beekman was almost always "high hook." We expected, as a matter of course, to hear that he had taken the most and the largest fish.

It was so with everything that he undertook. He was a masterful man. If there was an unusually large trout in a river, Beekman knew about it before any one else, and got there first, and came home with the fish. It did not make him unduly proud, because there was nothing uncommon about it. It was his habit to succeed, and all the rest of us were hardened to it.

When he married Cornelia Cochrane, we were consoled for our partial loss by the apparent fitness and brilliancy of the match. If Beekman was a masterful man, Cornelia was certainly what you might call a mistressful woman. She had been the head of her house since she was eighteen years old. She carried her good looks like the family plate; and when she came into the breakfast-room and said good-morning, it was with an air as if she presented every one with a check for a thousand dollars. Her tastes were accepted as judgments, and her preferences had the force of laws. Wherever she wanted to go in the summertime, there the finger of household destiny pointed. At Newport, at Bar Harbor, at Lenox, at Southampton, she made a record. When she was joined in holy wedlock to Beekman De Peyster, her father and mother heaved a sigh of satisfaction, and settled down for a quiet vacation in Cherry Valley.

It was in the second summer after the wedding that Beekman admitted to a few of his ancient Petrine cronies, in moments of confidence (unjustifiable, but natural), that his wife had one fault.

"It is not exactly a fault," he said, "not a positive fault, you know. It is just a kind of a defect, due to her education, of course. In everything else she's magnificent. But she doesn't care for fishing. She says it's stupid—can't see why any one should like the woods—calling camping out the lunatic's diversion. It's rather awkward for a man with my habits to have his wife take such a view. But it can be changed by training. I intend to educate her and convert her. I shall make an angler of her yet."

And so he did.

The new education was begun in the Adirondacks, and the first lesson was given at Paul Smith's. It was a complete failure.

Beekman persuaded her to come out with him for a day on Meacham River, and promised to convince her of the charm of angling. She wore a new gown, fawn-colour and violet, with a picture-hat, very taking. But the Meacham River trout was shy that day; not even Beekman could induce him to rise to the fly. What the trout lacked in confidence the mosquitoes more than made up. Mrs. De Peyster came home much sunburned, and expressed a highly unfavorable opinion of fishing as an amusement and of Meacham River as a resort.

"The nice people don't come to the Adirondacks to fish," said she; "they come to talk about the fishing twenty years ago. Besides, what do you want to catch that trout for? If you do, the other men will say you bought it, and the hotel will have to put in another for the rest of the season."

The following year Beekman tried Moosehead Lake. Here he found an atmosphere more favourable to his plan of education. There were a good many people who really fished, and short expeditions in the woods were quite fashionable. Cornelia had a camping-costume of the most approved style made by Dewlap on Fifth Avenue—pearl-gray with linings of rose-silk—and consented to go with her husband on a trip up Moose River. They pitched their tent the first evening at the mouth of Misery Stream, and a storm came on. The rain sifted through the canvas in a fine spray, and Mrs. De Peyster sat up all night in a waterproof cloak, holding an umbrella. The next day they were back at the hotel in time for lunch.

"It was horrid," she told her most intimate friend, "perfectly horrid. The idea of sleeping in a shower-bath, and eating your breakfast from a tin plate, just for sake of catching a few silly fish! Why not send your guides out to get them for you?"

But, in spite of this profession of obstinate heresy, Beekman observed with secret joy that there were signs, before the end of the season, that Cornelia was drifting a little, a very little but still perceptibly, in the direction of a change of heart. She began to take an interest, as the big trout came along in September, in the reports of the catches made by the different anglers. She would saunter out with the other people to the corner of the porch to see the fish weighed and spread out on the grass. Several times she went with Beekman in the canoe to Hardscrabble Point, and showed distinct evidences of pleasure when he caught large trout. The last day of the season, when he returned from a successful expedition to Roach River and Lily Bay, she inquired with some particularity about the results of his sport; and in the evening, as the company sat before the great open fire in the hall of the hotel, she was heard to use this information with considerable skill in putting down Mrs. Minot Peabody of Boston, who was recounting the details of her husband's catch at Spencer Pond. Cornelia was not a person to be contented with the back seat, even in fish-stories.

When Beekman observed these indications he was much encouraged, and resolved to push his educational experiment briskly forward to his customary goal of success.

"Some things can be done, as well as others," he said in his masterful way, as three of us were walking home together after the autumnal dinner of the Petrine Club, which he always attended as a graduate member. "A real fisherman never gives up. I told you I'd make an angler out of my wife; and so I will. It has been rather difficult. She is 'dour' in rising. But she's beginning to take notice of the fly now. Give me another season, and I'll have her landed."

Good old Beekman! Little did he think—But I must not interrupt the story with moral reflections.

The preparations that he made for his final effort at conversion were thorough and prudent. He had a private interview with Dewlap in regard to the construction of a practical fishing-costume for a lady, which resulted in something more reasonable and workmanlike than had ever been turned out by that famous artist. He ordered from Hook & Catchett a lady's angling-outfit of the most enticing description—a split-bamboo rod, light as a girl's wish and strong as a matron's will; an oxidized silver reel, with a monogram on one side, and a sapphire set in the handle for good luck; a book of flies, of all sizes and colours, with the correct names inscribed in gilt letters on each page. He surrounded his favorite sort with an aureole of elegance and beauty. And then he took Cornelia in September to the Upper Dam at Rangeley.

She went reluctant. She arrived disgusted. She stayed incredulous. She returned—Wait a bit, and you shall hear how she returned.

The Upper Dam at Rangeley is the place, of all others in the world, where the lunacy of angling may be seen in its incurable stage. There is a cosy little inn, called a camp, at the foot of a big lake. In front of the inn is a huge dam of gray stone, over which the river plunges into a great oval pool, where the trout assemble in the early fall to perpetuate their race.

From the tenth of September to the thirtieth, there is not an hour of the day or night when there are no boats floating on that pool, and no anglers trailing the fly across its waters. Before the late fishermen are ready to come in at midnight, the early fishermen may be seen creeping down to the shore with lanterns in order to begin before cock-crow. The number of fish taken is not large—perhaps five or six for the whole company on an average day—but the size is sometimes enormous—nothing under three pounds is counted—and they pervade thought and conversation at the Upper Dam to the exclusion of every other subject. There is no driving, no dancing, no golf, no tennis. There is nothing to do but fish or die.

At first, Cornelia thought she would choose the latter alternative. But a remark of that skilful and morose old angler, McTurk, which she overheard on the verandah after supper, changed her mind.

"Women have no sporting instinct," said he. "They only fish because they see men doing it. They are imitative animals."

That same night she told Beekman, in the subdued tone which the architectural construction of the house imposes upon all confidential communications in the bedrooms, but with resolution in every accent, that she proposed to go fishing with him on the morrow.

"But not on that pool, right in front of the house, you understand. There must be some other place, out on the lake, where we can fish for three or four days, until I get the trick of this wobbly rod. Then I'll show that old bear, McTurk, what kind of an animal woman is."

Beekman was simply delighted. Five days of diligent practice at the mouth of Mill Brook brought his pupil to the point where he pronounced her safe.

"Of course," he said patronizingly, "you haven't learned all about it yet. That will take years. But you can get your fly out thirty feet, and you can keep the tip of your rod up. If you do that, the trout will hook himself, in rapid water, eight times out of ten. For playing him, if you follow my directions, you'll be all right. We will try the pool tonight, and hope for a medium-sized fish."

Cornelia said nothing, but smiled and nodded. She had her own thoughts.

At about nine o'clock Saturday night, they anchored their boat on the edge of the shoal where the big eddy swings around, put out the lantern and began to fish. Beekman sat in the bow of the boat, with his rod over the left side; Cornelia in the stern, with her rod over the right side. The night was cloudy and very black. Each of them had put on the largest possible fly, one a "Bee-Pond" and the other a "Dragon"; but even these were invisible. They measured out the right length of line, and let the flies drift back until they hung over the shoal, in the curly water where the two currents meet.

There were three other boats to the left of them. McTurk was their only neighbour in the darkness on the right. Once they heard him swearing softly to himself, and knew that he had hooked and lost a fish.

Away down at the tail of the pool, dimly visible through the gloom, the furtive fisherman, Parsons, had anchored his boat. No noise ever came from that craft. If he wished to change his position, he did not pull up the anchor and let it down again with a bump. He simply lengthened or shortened his anchor rope. There was no click of the reel when he played a fish. He drew in and paid out the line through the rings by hand, without a sound. What he thought when a fish got away, no one knew, for he never said it. He concealed his angling as if it had been a conspiracy. Twice that night they heard a faint splash in the water near his boat, and twice they saw him put his arm over the side in the darkness and bring it back again very quietly.

"That's the second fish for Parsons," whispered Beekman, "what a secretive old Fortunatus he is! He knows more about fishing than any man on the pool, and talks less."

Cornelia did not answer. Her thoughts were all on the tip of her own rod. About eleven o'clock a fine, drizzling rain set in. The fishing was very slack. All the other boats gave it up in despair; but Cornelia said she wanted to stay out a little longer, they might as well finish up the week.

At precisely fifty minutes past eleven, Beekman reeled up his line, and remarked with firmness that the holy Sabbath day was almost at hand and they ought to go in.

"Not till I've landed this trout," said Cornelia.

"What? A trout! Have you got one?"

"Certainly; I've had him on for at least fifteen minutes. I'm playing him Mr. Parsons' way. You might as well light the lantern and get the net ready; he's coming in towards the boat now."

Beekman broke three matches before he made the lantern burn; and when he held it up over the gunwale, there was the trout sure enough, gleaming ghostly pale in the dark water, close to the boat, and quite tired out. He slipped the net over the fish and drew it in—a monster.

"I'll carry that trout, if you please," said Cornelia, as they stepped out of the boat; and she walked into the camp, on the last stroke of midnight, with the fish in her hand, and quietly asked for the steelyard.

Eight pounds and fourteen ounces—that was the weight. Everybody was amazed. It was the "best fish" of the year. Cornelia showed no sign of exultation, until just as John was carrying the trout to the icehouse. Then she flashed out: "Quite a fair imitation, Mr. McTurk—isn't it?"

Now McTurk's best record for the last fifteen years was seven pounds and twelve ounces.

So far as McTurk is concerned, this is the end of the story. But not for the De Peysters. I wish it were. Beekman went to sleep that night with a contended spirit. He felt that his experiment in education had been a success. He had made his wife an angler.

He had indeed, and to an extent which he little suspected. That Upper Dam trout was to her like the first taste of blood to the tiger. It seemed to change, at once, not so much her character as the direction of her vital energy. She yielded to the lunacy of angling, not by slow degrees (as first a transient delusion, then a fixed idea, then a chronic infirmity, finally a mild insanity), but by a sudden plunge into the most violent mania. So far from being ready to die at Upper Dam, her desire now was to live there—and to live solely for the sake of fishing—as long as the season was open.

There were two hundred and forty hours left to midnight on the thirtieth of September. At least two hundred of these she spent on the pool; and when Beekman was too exhausted to manage the boat and the net and the lantern for her, she engaged a trustworthy guide to take Beekman's place while he slept. At the end of the last day her score was twenty-three, with an average of five pounds and a quarter. His score was nine, with an average of four pounds. He had succeeded far beyond his wildest hopes.

The next year his success became even more astonishing. They went to the Titan Club in Canada. The ugliest and most inaccessible sheet of water in that territory is Lake Pharaoh. But it is famous for the extraordinary fishing at a certain spot near the outlet, where there is just room enough for one canoe. They camped on Lake Pharaoh for six weeks, by Mrs. De Peyster's command; and her canoe was always the first to reach the fishing-ground in the morning, and the last to leave it in the evening.

Someone asked him, when he returned to the city, whether he had good luck.

"Quite fair," he tossed off in a careless way; "we took over three hundred pounds."

"To your own rod?" asked the inquirer, in admiration.

"No-o-o," said Beekman, "there were two of us."

There were two of them, also, the following year, when they joined the Natasheebo Salmon Club and fished that celebrated river in Labrador. The custom of drawing lots every night for the water that each member was to angle over the next day, seemed to be especially designed to fit the situation. Mrs. De Peyster could fish her own pool and her husband's too. The result of that year's fishing was something phenomenal. She had a score that made a paragraph in the newspapers and called out editorial comment. One editor was so inadequate to the situation as to entitle the article in which he described her triumph "The Equivalence of Woman." It was well-meant, but she was not at all pleased with it.

She was now not merely an angler, but a "record" angler of the most virulent type. Wherever they went, she wanted, and she got, the pick of the water. She seemed to be equally at home on all kinds of streams, large and small. She would pursue the little mountain-brook trout in the early spring, and the Labrador salmon in July, and the huge speckled trout of the northern lakes in September, with the same avidity and resolution. All that she cared for was to get the best and the most of the fishing at each place where she angled. This she always did.

And Beekman—well, for him there were no more long separations from the partner of his life while he went off to fish some favourite stream. There were no more home-comings after a good day's sport to find her clad in cool and dainty raiment on the verandah, ready to welcome him with friendly badinage. There was not even any casting of the fly around Hardscrabble Point while she sat in the canoe reading a novel, looking up with mild and pleasant interest when he caught a larger fish than usual, as an older and wiser person looks at a child playing some innocent game. Those days of a divided interest between man and wife were gone. She was now fully converted, and more. Beekman and Cornelia were one; and she was the one.

The last time I saw the De Peysters he was following her along the Beaverkill, carrying a landing-net and a basket, but no rod. She paused for a moment to exchange greetings, and then strode on down the stream. He lingered for a few minutes longer to light a pipe.

"Well, old man," I said, "you certainly have succeeded in making an angler of Mrs. De Peyster."

"Yes, indeed," he answered—"haven't I?" Then he continued, after a few thoughtful puffs of smoke. "Do you know, I'm not quite so sure as I used to be that fishing is the best of all sports. I sometimes think of giving it up and going in for croquet."

Chapter Twenty-Four

The River God

by Roland Pertwee

A ten-year-old boy and his best friend, age 70, experience angling passion lived to the ultimate in this tale from the English playwright and film writer Roland Pertwee (1865–1963). The story originally appeared in the Saturday Evening Post *magazine, July 7, 1928. It was reprinted in private editions. Nick Lyons included it in his wonderful anthology* Hook, Line, and Sinker: Classic Fishing Stories *(2014).*

WHEN I WAS A LITTLE BOY I HAD A FRIEND WHO WAS A COLONEL. He was not the kind of colonel you meet nowadays, who manages a motor showroom in the West End of London and wears crocodile shoes and a small mustache and who calls you "old man" and slaps your back, independent of the fact that you may have been no more than a private in the war. My colonel was of the older order that takes a third of a century and a lot of Indian sun and Madras curry in the making. A veteran of the Mutiny he was, and wore side whiskers to prove it. Once he came upon a number of Sepoys conspiring mischief in a byre with a barrel of gunpowder. So he put the butt of his cheroot into the barrel and presently they all went to hell. That was the kind of man he was in the way of business.

In the way of pleasure he was very different. In the way of pleasure he wore an old Norfolk coat that smelt of heather and brine, and which had no elbows to speak of. And he wore a Sherlock Holmesy kind of cap with a swarm of salmon flies upon it, that to my boyish fancy was more splendid than a crown. I cannot remember his legs, because they were nearly always under water, hidden in great canvas waders. But once he sent me a photograph of himself riding on a tricycle, so I expect he had some knickerbockers, too, which would have been that tight kind, with box cloth under the knees. Boys don't take much stock of clothes. His head occupied my imagination. A big, brave, white-haired head with cherry-red rugose cheeks and honest, laughing, puckered eyes, with gunpowder marks in their corners.

People at the little Welsh fishing inn where we met said he was a bore; but I knew him to be a god and shall prove it.

I was ten years old and his best friend.

He was seventy something and my hero.

Properly I should not have mentioned my hero so soon in this narrative. He belongs to a later epoch, but sometimes it is forgivable to start with a boast, and now that I have committed myself I lack the courage to call upon my colonel to fall back two paces to the rear, quick march, and wait until he is wanted.

The real beginning takes place, as I remember, somewhere in Hampshire on the Grayshott Road, among sandy banks, sentinel firs and plum-colored wastes of heather. Summer-holiday time it was, and I was among folks whose names have since vanished like lizards under the stones of forgetfulness. Perhaps it was a picnic walk; perhaps I carried a basket and was told not to swing it for fear of bursting its cargo of ginger beer. In those days ginger beer had big bulgy corks held down with a string. In a hot sun or under stress of too much agitation the string would break and the corks fly. Then there would be a merry foaming fountain and someone would get reproached.

One of our company had a fishing rod. He was a young man who, one day, was to be an uncle of mine. But that didn't concern me. What concerned me was the fishing rod and presently—perhaps because he felt he must keep in with the family—he let me carry it. To the fisherman born there is nothing so provoking of curiosity as a fishing rod in a case.

Surreptitiously I opened the flap, which contained a small grass spear in a wee pocket, and, pulling down the case a little, I admired the beauties of the cork butt, with its gun-metal ferrule and reel rings and the exquisite frail slenderness of the two top joints.

"It's got two top joints—two!" I exclaimed ecstatically.

"Of course," said he. "All good trout rods have two."

I marveled in silence at what seemed to me then a combination of extravagance and excellent precaution.

There must have been something inherently understanding and noble about that young man who would one day be my uncle, for, taking me by the arm, he sat me down on a tuft of heather and took the pieces of rod from the case and fitted them together. The rest of the company moved on and left me in Paradise.

It is thirty-five years ago since that moment and not one detail of it is forgotten. There sounds in my ears today as clearly as then, the faint, clear pop made by the little cork stoppers with their boxwood tops as they were withdrawn. I remember how, before fitting the pieces together, he rubbed the ferrules against the side of his nose to prevent them sticking. I remember looking up the length of it through a tunnel of sneck rings to the eyelet at the end. Not until he had fixed a reel and passed a line through the rings did he put the lovely thing into my hand. So light it was, so firm, so persuasive; such a thing alive—a scepter. I could do no more than say "Oo!" and again, "Oo!"

"A thrill, ain't it?" said he.

I had no need to answer that. In my new-found rapture was only one sorrow—the knowledge that such happiness would not endure and that, all too soon, a blank and rodless future awaited me.

"They must be awfully—awfully 'spensive," I said.

"Couple of guineas," he replied offhandedly.

A couple of guineas! And we were poor folk and the future was more rodless than ever.

"Then I shall save and save and save," I said.

And my imagination started to add up twopence a week into guineas. Two hundred and forty pennies to the pound, multiplied by two—four hundred and eighty—and then another twenty-four pennies—five hundred and four. Why, it would take a lifetime, and no sweets, no elastic for catapults, no penny novelty boxes or air-gun bullets or ices or anything.

Tragedy must have been writ large upon my face, for he said suddenly, "When's your birthday?"

I was almost ashamed to tell him how soon it was. Perhaps he, too, was a little taken aback by its proximity, for that future uncle of mine was not so rich as uncles should be.

"We must see about it."

"But it wouldn't—it couldn't be one like that," I said.

I must have touched his pride, for he answered loftily, "Certainly it will."

In the fortnight that followed I walked on air and told everybody I had as good as got a couple-of-guineas rod.

No one can deceive a child, save the child himself, and when my birthday came and with it a long brown paper parcel, I knew, even before I had removed the wrappers, that this two-guinea rod was not worth the money. There was a brown linen case, it is true, but it was not a case with a neat compartment for each joint, nor was there a spear in the flap. There was only one top instead of two, and there were no popping little stoppers to protect the ferrules from dust and injury. The lower joint boasted no elegant cork hand piece, but was a tapered affair coarsely made and rudely varnished. When I fitted the pieces together, what I balanced in my hand was tough and stodgy, rather than limber. The reel, which had come in a different parcel, was of wood. It had neither check nor brake, the line overran and backwound itself with distressing frequency.

I had not read and reread Gamages' price list without knowing something of rods, and I did not need to look long at this rod before realizing that it was no match to the one I had handled on the Grayshott Road.

I believe at first a great sadness possessed me, but very presently imagination came to the rescue. For I told myself that I had only to think that this was the rod of all other rods that I desired most and it would be so. And it was so.

Furthermore, I told myself that, in this great wide ignorant world, but few people existed with such expert knowledge of rods as I possessed. That I had but to say, "here is the final word in good rods," and they would accept it as such.

Very confidently I tried the experiment on my mother, with inevitable success. From the depths of her affection and her ignorance on all such matters, she produced:

"It's a magnificent rod."

I went my way, knowing full well that she knew not what she said, but that she was kind.

With rather less confidence I approached my father, saying, "Look, father! It cost two guineas. It's absolutely the best sort you can get."

And he, after waggling it a few moments in silence, quoted cryptically:

"There is nothing either good or bad but thinking makes it so."

Young as I was, I had some curiosity about words, and on any other occasion I would have called on him to explain. But this I did not do, but left hurriedly, for fear that he should explain.

In the two years that followed I fished every day in the slip of a back garden of our tiny London house. And, having regard to the fact that this rod was never fashioned to throw a fly, I acquired a pretty knack in the fullness of time and performed some glib casting at the nasturtiums and marigolds that flourished by the back wall.

My parents' fortunes must have been in the ascendant, I suppose, for I call to mind an unforgettable breakfast when my mother told me that father had decided we should spend our summer holiday at a Welsh hotel on the river Lledr. The place was called Pont-y-pant, and she showed me a picture of the hotel with a great knock-me-down river creaming past the front of it.

Although in my dreams I had heard fast water often enough, I had never seen it, and the knowledge that in a month's time I should wake with the music of a cataract in my ears was almost more than patience could endure.

In that exquisite, intolerable period of suspense I suffered as only childish longing and enthusiasm can suffer. Even the hank of gut that I bought and bent into innumerable casts failed to alleviate that suffering. I would walk for miles for a moment's delight captured in gluing my nose to the windows of tackleists' shops in the West End. I learned from my grandmother—a wise and calm old lady—how to make nets and, having mastered the art, I made myself a landing net. This I set up on a frame fashioned from a penny schoolmaster's cane bound to an old walking stick. It would be pleasant to record that this was a good and serviceable net, but it was not. It flopped over in a very distressing fashion when called upon to lift the lightest weight. I had to confess to myself that I had more enthusiasm than skill in the manufacture of such articles.

At school there was a boy who had a fishing creel, which he swapped with me for a Swedish knife, a copy of *Rogues of the Fiery Cross*, and an Easter egg which I had kept on account of its rare beauty. He had forced a hard bargain and was sure he had the best of it, but I knew otherwise.

At last the great day dawned, and after infinite travel by train we reached our destination as the glow of sunset was graying into dark. The river was in spate, and as we crossed a tall stone bridge on our way to the hotel I heard it below me, barking and grumbling among great rocks. I was pretty far gone in tiredness, for I remember little else that night but a rod rack in the hall—a dozen rods of different sorts and sizes, with gaudy salmon flies, some nets, a gaff and an oak coffer upon which lay a freshly caught salmon on a blue ashet. Then supper by candlelight, bed, a glitter of stars through the open window, and the ceaseless drumming of water.

By six o'clock next morning I was on the river bank, fitting my rod together and watching in awe the great brown ribbon of water go fleetly by.

Among my most treasured possessions were half a dozen flies, and two of these I attached to the cast with exquisite care. While so engaged, a shadow fell on the grass beside me and, looking up, I beheld a lank, shabby individual with a walrus mustache and an unhealthy face who, the night before, had helped with our luggage at the station.

"Water's too heavy for flies," said he, with an uptilting inflection. "This evening, yes; now, no—none whateffer. Better try with a worrum in the burrun."

He pointed at a busy little brook which tumbled down the steep hillside and joined the main stream at the garden end.

"C-couldn't I fish with a fly in the—the burrun?" I asked, for although I wanted to catch a fish very badly, for honor's sake I would fain take it on a fly.

"Indeed, no," he replied, slanting the tone of his voice skyward. "You cootn't. Neffer. And that isn't a fly rod whateffer."

"It is," I replied hotly. "Yes, it is."

But he only shook his head and repeated, "No," and took the rod from my hand and illustrated its awkwardness and handed it back with a wretched laugh.

If he had pitched me into the river I should have been happier.

"It is a fly rod and it cost two guineas," I said, and my lower lip trembled.

"Neffer," he repeated. "Five shillings would be too much."

Even a small boy is entitled to some dignity.

Picking up my basket, I turned without another word and made for the hotel. Perhaps my eyes were blinded with tears, for I was about to plunge into the dark hall when a great, rough, kindly voice arrested me with:

"Easy does it."

At the thick end of an immense salmon rod there strode out into the sunlight the noblest figure I had ever seen.

There is no real need to describe my colonel again—I have done so already—but the temptation is too great. Standing in the doorway, the sixteen-foot rod in hand, the deer-stalker hat, besprent with flies, crowning his shaggy head, the waders, like seven-league boots, braced up to his armpits, the creel across his shoulder, a gaff across his back, he looked what he was—a god. His eyes met mine with that kind of smile one good man keeps for another.

"An early start," he said. "Any luck, old fellar?"

I told him I hadn't started—not yet.

"Wise chap," said he. "Water's a bit heavy for trouting. It'll soon run down, though. Let's vet those flies of yours."

He took my rod and whipped it expertly.

"A nice piece—new, eh?"

"N-not quite," I stammered; "but I haven't used it yet, sir, in water."

That god read men's minds.

"I know—garden practice; capital; nothing like it."

Releasing my cast, he frowned critically over the flies—a Blue Dun and a March Brown.

"Think so?" he queried. "You don't think it's a shade late in the season for these fancies?" I said I thought perhaps it was. "Yes, I think you're right," said he. "I believe in this big water you'd do better with a livelier pattern. Teal and Red, Cock-y-bundy, Greenwell's Glory."

I said nothing, but nodded gravely at these brave names.

Once more he read my thoughts and saw through the wicker sides of my creel a great emptiness.

"I expect you've fished most in southern rivers. These Welsh trout have a fancy for a spot of color."

He rummaged in the pocket of his Norfolk jacket and produced a round tin which once had held saddle soap.

"Collar on to that," said he; "there's a proper pickle of flies and casts in that tin that, as a keen fisherman, you won't mind sorting out. Still, they may come in useful."

"But, I say, you don't mean—" I began.

"Yes, go in; stick to it. All fishermen are members of the same club and I'm giving the trout a rest for a bit." His eyes ranged the hills and trees opposite. "I must be getting on with it before the sun's too high."

Waving his free hand, he strode away and presently was lost to view at a bend in the road.

I think my mother was a little piqued by my abstraction during breakfast. My eyes never, for an instant, deserted the round tin box which lay open beside my plate. Within it were a paradise and a hundred miracles all tangled together in the pleasantest disorder. My mother said something about a lovely walk over the hills, but I had other plans, which included a very glorious hour which should be spent untangling and wrapping up in neat squares of paper my new treasures.

"I suppose he knows best what he wants to do," she said.

So it came about that I was left alone and betook myself to a sheltered spot behind a rock where all the delicious disorder was remedied and I could take stock of what was mine.

I am sure there were at least six casts all set up with flies, and ever so many loose flies and one great stout, tapered cast, with a salmon fly upon it, that was so rich in splendor that I doubted if my benefactor could really have known that it was there.

I felt almost guilty at owning so much, and not until I had done full justice to everything did I fasten a new cast to my line and go a-fishing.

There is a lot said and written about beginners' luck, but none of it came my way. Indeed, I spent most of the morning extricating my line from the most fearsome tangles. I had no skill in throwing a cast with two droppers upon it and I found it was an art not to be learned in a minute. Then, from overeagerness, I was too snappy with my back cast, whereby, before many minutes had gone, I heard that warning crack behind me that betokens the loss of a tail fly. I must have spent half an hour searching the meadow for that lost fly and finding it not. Which is not strange, for I wonder has any fisherman ever found that lost fly. The reeds, the buttercups, and the little people with many legs who run in the wet grass conspire together to keep the secret of its hiding place. I gave up at last, and with a feeling of shame that was only proper, I invested a new fly on the point of my cast and set to work again, but more warily.

In that hard racing water a good strain was put upon my rod, and before the morning was out it was creaking at the joints in a way that kept my heart continually in my mouth. It is the duty of a rod to work with a single smooth action and by no means to divide its performance into three sections of activity. It is a hard task for any angler to persuade his line austerely if his rod behaves thus.

When, at last, my father strolled up the river bank, walking, to his shame, much nearer the water than a good fisherman should, my nerves were jumpy from apprehension.

"Come along. Food's ready. Done any good?" said he.

Again it was to his discredit that he put food before sport, but I told him I had had a wonderful morning, and he was glad.

"What do you want to do this afternoon, old man?" he asked.

"Fish," I said.

"But you can't always fish," he said.

I told him I could, and I was right and have proved it for thirty years and more.

"Well, well," he said, "please yourself, but isn't it dull not catching anything?"

And I said, as I've said a thousand times since, "As if it could be."

So that afternoon I went downstream instead of up, and found myself in difficult country where the river boiled between the narrows of two hills. Stunted oaks overhung the water and great boulders opposed its flow. Presently I came to a sort of natural flight of steps—a pool and a cascade three times repeated—and there, watching the maniac fury of the waters in awe and wonderment, I saw the most stirring sight in my young life. I saw a silver salmon leap superbly from the caldron below into the pool above. And I saw another and another salmon do likewise. And I wonder the eyes of me did not fall out of my head.

I cannot say how long I stayed watching that gallant pageant of leaping fish—in ecstasy there is no measurement of time—but at last it came upon me that all the salmon in the sea were careering past me and that if I were to realize my soul's desire I must hasten to the pool below before the last of them had gone by.

It was a mad adventure, for until I had discovered that stout cast, with the gaudy fly attached in the tin box, I had given no thought to such noble quarry. My recent possessions had put ideas into my head above my station and beyond my powers. Failure, however, means little to the young and, walking fast, yet gingerly, for fear of breaking my rod top against a tree, I followed the path downstream until I came to a great basin of water into which, through a narrow throat the river thundered like a storm.

At the head of the pool was a plate of rock scored by the nails of fishermen's boots, and here I sat me down to wait while the salmon cast, removed from its wrapper, was allowed to soak and soften in a puddle left by the rain.

And while I waited a salmon rolled not ten yards from where I sat. Head and tail, up and down he went, a great monster of a fish, sporting and deriding me.

With that performance so near at hand, I have often wondered how I was able to control my fingers well enough to tie a figure-eight knot between the line and the cast. But I did, and I'm proud to be able to

record it. Your true-born angler does not go blindly to work until he has
first satisfied his conscience. There is a pride, in knots, of which the laity
knows nothing, and if, through neglect to tie them rightly, failure and
loss should result, pride may not be restored nor conscience salved by the
plea of eagerness. With my trembling fingers I bent the knot and, with a
pummeling heart, launched the line into the broken water at the throat
of the pool.

At first the mere tug of the water against that large fly was so thrilling to me that it was hard to believe that I had not hooked a whale. The
trembling line swung round in a wide arc into a calm eddy below where
I stood. Before casting afresh I shot a glance over my shoulder to assure
myself there was no limb of a tree behind me to foul the fly. And this was
a gallant cast, true and straight, with a couple of yards more length than
its predecessor, and a wider radius. Instinctively I knew, as if the surface
had been marked with an X where the salmon had risen, that my fly must
pass right over the spot. As it swung by, my nerves were strained like
piano wires. I think I knew something tremendous, impossible, terrifying,
was going to happen. The sense, the certitude was so strong in me that I
half opened my mouth to shout a warning to the monster, not to.

I must have felt very, very young in that moment. I, who that same
day had been talked to as a man by a man among men. The years were
stripped from me and I was what I was—ten years old and appalled. And
then, with the suddenness of a rocket, it happened. The water was cut into
a swath. I remember a silver loop bearing downward—a bright, shining,
vanishing thing like the bobbin of my mother's sewing machine—and a
tug. I shall never forget the viciousness of that tug. I had my fingers tight
upon the line, so I got the full force of it. To counteract a tendency to go
headfirst into the spinning water below, I threw myself backward and sat
down on the hard rock with a jar that shut my teeth on my tongue—like
the jaws of a trap.

Luckily I had let the rod go out straight with the line, else it must
have snapped in the first frenzy of the downstream rush. Little ass that I
was, I tried to check the speeding line with my forefinger, with the result
that it cut and burnt me to the bone. There wasn't above twenty yards of
line in the reel, and the wretched contrivance was trying to be rid of the

line even faster than the fish was wrenching it out. Heaven knows why it didn't snarl, for great loops and whorls were whirling, like Catherine wheels, under my wrist. An instant's glance revealed the terrifying fact that there was not more than half a dozen yards left on the reel and the fish showed no sign of abating his rush. With the realization of impending and inevitable catastrophe upon me, I launched a yell for help, which, rising above the roar of the waters, went echoing down the gorge.

And then, to add to my terrors, the salmon leaped—a winging leap like a silver arch appearing and instantly disappearing upon the broken surface. So mighty, so all-powerful he seemed in that sublime moment that I lost all sense of reason and raised the rod, with a sudden jerk, above my head.

I have often wondered, had the rod actually been the two-guinea rod my imagination claimed for it, whether it could have withstood the strain thus violently and unreasonably imposed upon it. The wretched thing that I held so grimly never even put up a fight. It snapped at the ferrule of the lower joint and plunged like a toboggan down the slanting line, to vanish into the black depths of the water.

My horror at this calamity was so profound that I was lost even to the consciousness that the last of my line had run out. A couple of vicious tugs advised me of this awful truth. Then, snap! The line parted at the reel, flickered out through the rings and was gone. I was left with nothing but the butt of a broken rod in my hand and an agony of mind that even now I cannot recall without emotion.

I am not ashamed to confess that I cried. I lay down on the rock, with my cheek in the puddle where I had soaked the cast, and plenished it with my tears. For what had the future left for me but a cut and burning finger, a badly bumped behind, the single joint of a broken rod and no faith in uncles? How long I lay there weeping I do not know. Ages, perhaps, or minutes, or seconds.

I was roused by a rough hand on my shoulder and a kindly voice demanding, "Hurt yourself, Ike Walton?"

Blinking away my tears, I pointed at my broken rod with a bleeding forefinger.

"Come! This is bad luck," said my colonel, his face grave as a stone. "How did it happen?"

"I c-caught a s-salmon."

"You what?" said he.

"I d-did," I said.

He looked at me long and earnestly; then, taking my injured hand, he looked at that and nodded.

"The poor groundlings who can find no better use for a river than something to put a bridge over think all fishermen are liars," said he. "But we know better, eh? By the bumps and breaks and cuts I'd say you made a plucky fight against heavy odds. Let's hear all about it."

So, with his arm round my shoulders and his great shaggy head near to mine, I told him all about it.

At the end he gave me a mighty and comforting squeeze, and he said, "The loss of one's first big fish is the heaviest loss I know. One feels, whatever happens, one'll never—" He stopped and pointed dramatically. "There is goes—see! Down there at the tail of the pool!"

In the broken water where the pool emptied itself into the shallows beyond, I saw the top joints of my rod dancing on the surface.

"Come on!" he shouted, and gripping my hand, jerked me to my feet. "Scatter your legs! There's just a chance!"

Dragging me after him, we raced along by the river path to the end of the pool, where, on a narrow promontory of grass, his enormous salmon rod was lying.

"Now," he said, picking it up and making the line whistle to and fro in the air with sublime authority, "keep your eyes skinned on those shallows for another glimpse of it."

A second later I was shouting, "There! There!"

He must have seen the rod point at the same moment, for his line flowed out and the big fly hit the water with a plop not a couple of feet from the spot.

He let it ride on the current, playing it with a sensitive touch like the brushwork of an artist.

"Half a jiffy!" he exclaimed at last. "Wait! Yes, I think so. Cut down to that rock and see if I haven't fished up the line."

I needed no second invitation, and presently was yelling, "Yes—yes, you have!"

"Stretch yourself out then and collar hold of it."

With the most exquisite care he navigated the line to where I lay stretched upon the rock. Then:

"Right you are! Good lad! I'm coming down."

Considering his age, he leaped the rocks like a chamois.

"Now," he said, and took the wet line delicately between his forefinger and thumb. One end trailed limply downstream, but the other end seemed anchored in the big pool where I had my unequal and disastrous contest.

Looking into his face, I saw a sudden light of excitement dancing in his eyes.

"Odd," he muttered, "but not impossible."

"What isn't?" I asked breathlessly.

"Well, it looks to me as if the joints of that rod of yours have gone downstream."

Gingerly he pulled up the line, and presently an end with a broken knot appeared.

"The reel knot, eh?" I nodded gloomily. "Then we lose the rod," said he. That wasn't very heartening news. "On the other hand, it's just possible the fish is still on—sulking."

"Oo!" I exclaimed.

"Now, steady does it," he warned, "and give me my rod."

Taking a pair of clippers from his pocket, he cut his own line just above the cast.

"Can you tie a knot?" he asked.

"Yes," I nodded.

"Come on, then; bend your line onto mine. Quick as lightning."

Under his critical eye, I joined the two lines with a blood knot. "I guessed you were a fisherman," he said, nodded approvingly and clipped off the ends. "And now to know the best or the worst."

I shall never forget the music of that check reel or the suspense with which I watched as, with the butt of the rod bearing against the hollow of his thigh, he steadily wound up the wet slack line. Every instant I expected it to come drifting downstream, but it didn't. Presently it rose in a tight slant from the pool above.

"Snagged, I'm afraid," he said, and worked the rod with an easy straining motion to and fro. "Yes, I'm afraid—no, by Lord Bobs, he's on!"

I think it was only right and proper that I should have launched a yell of triumph as, with the spoken word, the point at which the line cut the water shifted magically from the left side of the pool to the right.

"And a fish too," said he.

In the fifteen minutes that followed, I must have experienced every known form of terror and delight.

"Youngster," said he, "you should be doing this, by rights, but I'm afraid the rod's a bit above your weight."

"Oh, go on and catch him," I pleaded.

"And so I will," he promised; "unship the gaff, young un, and stand by to use it, and if you break the cast we'll never speak to each other again, and that's a bet."

But I didn't break the cast. The noble, courageous, indomitable example of my river god had lent me skill and precision beyond my years. When at long last a weary, beaten, silver monster rolled within reach of my arm into a shallow eddy, the steel gaff shot out fair and true, and sank home.

And then I was lying on the grass, with my arms round a salmon that weighed twenty-two pounds on the scale and contained every sort of happiness known to a boy.

And best of all, my river god shook hands with me and called me "partner."

That evening the salmon was placed upon the blue ashet in the hall, bearing a little card with its weight and my name upon it.

And I am afraid I sat on a chair facing it, for ever so long, so that I could hear what the other anglers had to say as they passed by. I was sitting there when my colonel put his head out of his private sitting room and beckoned me to come in.

"A true fisherman lives in the future, not the past, old man," said he; "though, for this once, it 'ud be a shame to reproach you."

I suppose I colored guilty—at any rate, I hope so.

"We got the fish," said he, "but we lost the rod, and a future without a rod doesn't bear thinking of. Now"—and he pointed at a long wooden box on the floor, that overflowed with rods of different sorts and sizes—"rummage among those. Take your time and see if you can find anything to suit you."

"But do you mean—can I—"

"We're partners, aren't we? And p'r'aps as such you'd rather we went through our stock together."

"Oo, sir," I said.

"Here, quit that," he ordered gruffly. "By Lord Bobs, if a show like this afternoon's don't deserve a medal, what does? Now, here's a handy piece by Hardy—a light and useful tool—or if you fancy greenheart in preference to split bamboo—"

I have the rod to this day, and I count it among my dearest treasures. And to this day I have a flick of the wrist that was his legacy. I have, too, some small skill in dressing flies, the elements of which were learned in his company by candlelight after the day's work was over. And I have countless memories of that month-long, month-short friendship—the closest and most perfect friendship, perhaps, of all my life.

He came to the station and saw me off. How vividly I remember his shaggy head at the window, with the whiskered cheeks and the gunpowder marks at the corners of his eyes! I didn't cry, although I wanted to awfully. We were partners and shook hands. I never saw him again, although on my birthdays I would have colored cards from him, with Irish, Scotch, Norwegian postmarks. Very brief they were: "Water very low." "Took a good fish last Thursday." "Been prawning, but don't like it."

Sometimes at Christmas I had gifts—a reel, a tapered line, a fly book. But I never saw him again.

Came at last no more cards or gifts, but in the *Fishing Gazette,* of which I was a religious reader, was an obituary telling how one of the last of the Mutiny veterans had joined the great majority. It seems he had been fishing half an hour before he died. He had taken his rod down and passed out. They had buried him at Totnes, overlooking the River Dart.

So he was no more—my river god—and what was left of him they had put into a box and buried it in the earth.

But that isn't true; nor is it true that I never saw him again. For I seldom go a-fishing but that I meet him on the river banks.

The banks of a river are frequented by a strange company and are full of mysterious and murmurous sounds—the cluck and laughter of water, the piping of birds, the hum of insects, and the whispering of wind in the willows. What should prevent a man in such a place having a word and speech with another who is not there? So much of fishing lies in imagination, and mine needs little stretching to give my river god a living form.

"With this ripple," says he, "you should do well."

"And what's it to be," say I—"Blue Upright, Red Spinner? What's your fancy, sir?"

Spirits never grow old. He has begun to take an interest in dry-fly methods—that river god of mine, with his seven-league boots, his shaggy head, and the gaff across his back.

CHAPTER TWENTY-FIVE

Crocker's Hole

by R. D. Blackmore

This angling classic has been a reader favorite since it was first published in 1895.

I

The Culm, which rises in Somersetshire, and hastening into a fairer land (as the border waters wisely do) falls into the Exe near Killerton, formerly was a lovely trout stream, such as perverts the Devonshire angler from due respect toward Father Thames and the other canals round London. In the Devonshire valleys it is sweet to see how soon a spring becomes a rill, and a rill runs on into a rivulet, and a rivulet swells into a brook; and before one has time to say, "What are you at?"—before the first tree it ever spoke to is a dummy, or the first hill it ever ran down has turned blue, here we have all the airs and graces, demands and assertions of a full-grown river.

But what is the test of a river? Who shall say? "The power to drown a man," replies the river darkly. But rudeness is not argument. Rather shall we say that the power to work a good undershot wheel, without being dammed up all night in a pond, and leaving a tidy back stream to spare at the bottom of the orchard, is a fair certificate of riverhood. If so, many Devonshire streams attain that rank within five miles of their spring; aye, and rapidly add to it. At every turn they gather aid, from ash-clad dingle and aldered meadow, mossy rock and ferny wall, hedge-trough-roofed with bramble netting, where the baby water lurks, and lanes that coming down to ford bring suicidal tribute. Arrogant, all-engrossing river, now it has claimed a great valley of its own; and whatever falls within the hill scoop sooner or later belongs to itself. Even the crystal "shutt" that crosses the farmyard by the woodrick, and glides down an aqueduct of last year's bark for Mary to fill the kettle from; and even the tricklets that have no organs for telling or knowing their business, but only get into unwary oozings in and among the water grass, and there make moss and forget themselves among it—one and all, they come to the same thing at last, and that is the river.

The Culm used to be a good river at Culmstock, tormented already by a factory, but not strangled as yet by a railroad. How is it now the present writer does not know, and is afraid to ask, having heard of a vile "Culm Valley Line." But Culmstock bridge was a very pretty place to stand and contemplate the ways of trout; which is easier work than to catch them. When I was just big enough to peep above the rim, or to lie upon it with one leg inside for fear of tumbling over, what a mighty river it used to seem, for it takes a treat there and spreads itself. Above the bridge the factory stream falls in again, having done its business, and washing its hands in the innocent half that has strayed down the mead-ows. Then under the arches they both rejoice and come to a slide of about two feet, and make a short, wide pool below, and indulge themselves in perhaps two islands, through which a little river always magnifies itself and maintains a mysterious middle. But after that, all of it used to come together, and make off in one body for the meadows, intent upon nurtur-ing trout with rapid stickles, and buttercuppy corners where fat flies may tumble in. And here you may find in the very first meadow, or at any rate you might have found, forty years ago, the celebrated "Crocker's Hole."

The story of Crocker is unknown to me, and interesting as it doubt-less was, I do not deal with him, but with his Hole. Tradition said that he was a baker's boy who, during his basket rounds, fell in love with a maiden who received the cottage loaf, or perhaps good "Households," for her master's use. No doubt she was charming, as a girl should be, but whether she encouraged the youthful baker and then betrayed him with false role, or whether she "consisted" throughout—as our cousins across the water express it—is known to their *manes* only. Enough that she would not have the floury lad; and that he, after giving in his books and money, sought an untimely grave among the trout. And this was the first pool below the bread walk deep enough to drown a five-foot baker boy. Sad it was; but such things must be, and bread must still be delivered daily.

A truce to such reflections—as our foremost writers always say, when they do not see how to go on with them—but it is a serious thing to know what Crocker's Hole was like; because at a time when (if he had only persevered, and married the maid, and succeeded to the oven, and reared a large family of short-weight bakers) he might have been leaning on his crutch beside the pool, and teaching his grandson to swim by precept (that beautiful proxy for practice)—at such a time, I say, there lived a remarkable fine trout in that hole. Anglers are notoriously truthful, especially as to what they catch, or even more frequently have not caught. Though I may have written fiction, among many other sins—as a nice old lady told me once—now I have to deal with facts; and foul scorn would I count it ever to make believe that I caught that fish. My length at that time was not more than the butt of a four-jointed rod, and all I could catch was a minnow with a pin, which our cook Lydia would not cook, but used to say, "Oh, what a shame, Master Richard! They would have been trout in the summer, please God! if you would only a' let 'em grow on." She is living now and will bear me out in this.

But upon every great occasion there arises a great man; or to put it more accurately, in the present instance, a mighty and distinguished boy. My father, being the parson of the parish, and getting, need it be said, small pay, took sundry pupils, very pleasant fellows, about to adorn the universities. Among them was the original "Bude Light," as he was satirically called at Cambridge, for he came from Bude, and there was no light in him. Among them also was John Pike, a born Zebedee if ever there was one.

John Pike was a thickset younker, with a large and bushy head, keen blue eyes that could see through water, and the proper slouch of shoulder into which great anglers ripen; but greater still are born with it; and of these was Master John. It mattered little what the weather was, and scarcely more as to the time of year, John Pike must have his fishing every day, and on Sundays he read about it, and made flies. All the rest of the time he was thinking about it.

My father was coaching him in the fourth book of *The Aeneid* and all those wonderful species of Dido, where passion disdains construction; but the only line Pike cared for was of horsehair. "I fear, Mr. Pike, that you are not giving me your entire attention," my father used to say in his mild dry way; and once when Pike was more than usually abroad, his tutor begged to share his meditations. "Well, sir," said Pike, who was very truthful, "I can see a green drake by the strawberry tree, the first of the season, and your derivation of 'barbarous' put me in mind of my barberry dye." In those days it was a very nice point to get the right tint for the mallard's feather.

No sooner was lesson done than Pike, whose rod was ready upon the lawn, dashed away always for the river, rushing headlong down the hill, and away to the left through a private yard, where "No Thoroughfare" was put up and a big dog stationed to enforce it. But Cerberus himself could not have stopped John Pike; his conscience backed him up in trespass the most sinful when his heart was inditing of a trout upon the rise.

All this, however, is preliminary, as the boy said when he put his father's coat upon his grandfather's tenterhooks, with felonious intent upon his grandmother's apples; the main point to be understood in this, that nothing—neither brazen tower, hundred-eyed Argus, nor Cretan Minotaur—could stop John Pike from getting at a good stickle. But, even as the world knows nothing of its greatest men, its greatest men know nothing of the world beneath their very nose, till fortune sneezes dexter. For two years John Pike must have been whipping the water as hard as Xerxes, without having ever once dreamed of the glorious trout that lived in Crocker's Hole. But why, when he ought to have been at least on bowing terms with every fish as long as his middle finger, why had he failed to know this champion? The answer is simple—because of his short cuts. Flying as he did like an arrow from a bow, Pike used to hit his beloved river at an elbow, some furlong below Crocker's Hole, where a sweet little stickle sailed away downstream, whereas for the length of a meadow upward the water lay smooth, clear, and shallow; therefore the youth, with so little time to spare, rushed into the downward joy.

And here it may be noted that the leading maxim of the present period, that man can discharge his duty only by going counter to the stream, was scarcely mooted in those days. My grandfather (who was a wonderful man, if he was accustomed to fill a cart in two days of fly fishing on the Barle) regularly fished downstream; and what more than a cartload need anyone put into his basket?

And surely it is more genial and pleasant to behold our friend the river growing and thriving as we go on, strengthening its voice and enlarging its bosom, and sparkling through each successive meadow with richer plenitude of silver, than to trace it against its own grain and good will toward weakness, and littleness, and immature conceptions.

However, you will say that if John Pike had fished upstream, he would have found this trout much sooner. And that is true; but still, as it was, the trout had more time to grow into such a prize. And the way in which John found him out was this. For some days he had been tormented with a very painful tooth, which even poisoned all the joys of fishing. Therefore he resolved to have it out and sturdily entered the shop of John Sweetland, the village blacksmith, and there paid his sixpence. Sweetland extracted the teeth of the village, whenever they required it, in the simplest and most effectual way. A piece of fine wire was fastened round the tooth, and the other end round the anvil's nose, then the sturdy blacksmith shut the lower half of his shop door, which was about breast-high, with the patient outside and the anvil within; a strong push of the foot upset the anvil, and the tooth flew out like a well-thrown fly.

When John Pike had suffered this very bravely, "Ah, Master Pike," said the blacksmith, with a grin, "I reckon you won't pull out thic there big vish"—the smithy commanded a view of the river—"clever as you be, quite so peart as thiccy."

"What big fish?" asked the boy, with deepest interest, though his mouth was bleeding fearfully.

"Why, that girt mortial of a vish as hath his hover in Crocker's Hole. Zum on 'em saith as a' must be a zammon."

Off went Pike with his handkerchief to his mouth, and after him ran Alec Bolt, one of his fellow pupils, who had come to the shop to enjoy the extraction.

"Oh, my!" was all that Pike could utter, when by craftily posting himself he had obtained a good view of this grand fish.

"I'll lay you a crown you don't catch him!" cried Bolt, an impatient youth, who scorned angling.

"How long will you give me?" asked the wary Pike, who never made rash wagers.

"Oh! till the holidays if you like; or, if that won't do, till Michaelmas."

Now the midsummer holidays were six weeks off—boys used not to talk of "vacations" then, still less of "recesses."

"I think I'll bet you," said Pike, in his slow way, bending forward carefully, with his keen eyes on this monster; "but it would not be fair to take till Michaelmas. I'll bet you a crown that I catch him before the holidays—at least, unless some other fellow does."

II

The day of that most momentous interview must have been the 14th day of May. Of the year I will not be so sure; for children take more note of days than of years, for which the latter have their full revenge thereafter. It must have been the 14th, because the morrow was our holiday, given upon the 15th of May, in honor of a birthday.

Now, John Pike was beyond his years wary as well as enterprising, calm as well as ardent, quite as rich in patience as in promptitude and vigor. But Alec Bolt was a headlong youth, volatile, hot, and hasty, fit only to fish the Maelstrom, or a torrent of new lava. And the moment he had laid that wager he expected his crown piece; though time, as the lawyers phrase it, was "expressly of the essence of the contract." And now he demanded that Pike should spend the holiday in trying to catch that trout.

"I shall not go near him," that lad replied, "until I have got a new collar." No piece of personal adornment was it, without which he would not act, but rather that which now is called the fly cast, or the gut cast, or the trace, or what it may be. "And another thing," continued Pike; "the bet is off if you go near him, either now or at any other time, without asking my leave first, and then only going as I tell you."

"What do I want with the great slimy beggar?" the arrogant Bolt made answer. "A good rat is worth fifty of him. No fear of my going near him, Pike. You shan't get out of it that way."

Pike showed his remarkable qualities that day, by fishing exactly as he would have fished without having heard of the great Crockerite. He was upon and away upon the millstream before breakfast; and the forenoon he devoted to his favorite course—first down the Craddock stream, a very pretty confluent of the Culm, and from its junction, down the pleasant hams, where the river winds toward Uffculme. It was my privilege to accompany this hero, as his humble Sancho; while Bolt and the faster race went up the river ratting. We were back in time to have Pike's trout (which ranged between two ounces and one half pound) fried for the early dinner; and here it may be lawful to remark that the trout of the Culm are of the very purest excellence, by reason of the flinty bottom, at any rate in these the upper regions. For the valley is the western outlet of the Black Down range, with the Beacon hill upon the north, and the Hackpen long ridge to the south; and beyond that again the Whetstone hill, upon whose western end dark portholes scarped with white grit mark the pits. But flint is the staple of the broad Culm Valley, under good, well-pastured loam; and here are chalcedonies and agate stones.

At dinner everybody had a brace of trout—large for the larger folk, little for the little ones, with coughing and some patting on the back for bones. What of equal purport could the fierce rat hunter show? Pike explained many points in the history of each fish, seeming to know them none the worse, and love them all the better, for being fried. We banqueted, neither a whit did soul get stinted of banquet impartial. Then the wielder of the magic rod very modestly sought leave of absence at the teatime.

"Fishing again, Mr. Pike, I suppose," my father answered pleasantly; "I used to be fond of it at your age; but never so entirely wrapped up in it as you are."

"No, sir; I am not going fishing again. I want to walk to Wellington, to get some things at Cherry's."

"Books, Mr. Pike? Ah! I am very glad of that. But I fear it can only be fly books."

"I want a little Horace for eighteenpence—the Cambridge one just published, to carry in my pocket—and a new hank of gut."

"Which of the two is more important? Put that into Latin, and answer it."

"*Utrum pluris facio? Flaccum flocci. Viscera magni.*" With this vast effort Pike turned as red as any trout spot.

"After that who could refuse you?" said my father. "You always tell the truth, my boy, in Latin or in English."

Although it was a long walk, some fourteen miles to Wellington and back, I got permission to go with Pike; and as we crossed the bridge and saw the tree that overhung Crocker's Hole, I begged him to show me that mighty fish.

"Not a bit of it," he replied. "It would bring the blackguards. If the blackguards once find him out, it is all over with him."

"The blackguards are all in factory now, and I am sure they cannot see us from the windows. They won't be out till five o'clock."

With the true liberality of young England, which abides even now as large and glorious as ever, we always called the free and enlightened operatives of the period by the courteous name above set down, and it must be acknowledged that some of them deserved it, although perhaps they poached with less of science than their sons. But the cowardly murder of fish by liming the water was already prevalent.

Yielding to my request and perhaps his own desire—manfully kept in check that morning—Pike very carefully approached that pool, commanding me to sit down while he reconnoitered from the meadow upon the right bank of the stream. And the place which had so sadly quenched the fire of the poor baker's love filled my childish heart with dread and deep wonder at the cruelty of women. But as for John Pike, all he thought of was the fish and the best way to get at him.

Very likely that hole is "holed out" now, as the Yankees well express it, or at any rate changed out of knowledge. Even in my time a very heavy flood entirely altered its character; but to the eager eye of Pike it seemed pretty much as follows, and possibly it may have come to such a form again:

The river, after passing through a hurdle fence at the head of the meadow, takes a little turn or two of bright and shallow indifference, then gathers itself into a good strong slide, as if going down a slope instead of steps. The right bank is high and beetles over with yellow loam and grassy fringe; but the other side is of flinty shingle, low and bare and washed by floods. At the end of this rapid, the stream turns sharply under an ancient alder tree into a large, deep, calm repose, cool, unruffled, and sheltered from the sun by branch and leaf—and that is the hole of poor Crocker.

At the head of the pool (where the hasty current rushes in so eagerly, with noisy excitement and much ado) the quieter waters from below, having rested and enlarged themselves, come lapping up round either curve, with some recollection of their past career, the hoary experience of foam. And sidling toward the new arrival of the impulsive column, where they meet it, things go on which no man can describe without his mouth being full of water. A V is formed, a fancy letter V, beyond any designer's tracery, and even beyond his imagination, a perpetually fluctuating limpid wedge, perpetually creneled and rippled into by little ups and downs that try to make an impress but can only glide away upon either side or sink in dimples under it. And here a gray bough of the ancient alder stretches across, like a thirsty giant's arm, and makes it a very ticklish place to throw a fly. Yet this was the very spot our John Pike must put his fly into, or lose his crown.

Because the great tenant of Crocker's Hole, who allowed no other fish to wag a fin there, and from strict monopoly had grown so fat, kept his victualing yard—if so low an expression can be used concerning him—without above a square yard of this spot. He had a sweet hover, both for rest and recreation, under the bank, in a placid antre, where the water made no noise, but tickled his belly in digestive ease. The loftier the character is of any being, the slower and more dignified his movements are. No true psychologist could have believed—as Sweetland the blacksmith did, and Mr. Pook the tinman—that this trout could ever be the embodiment of Crocker. For this was the last trout in the universal world to drown himself for love; if truly any trout has done so.

"You may come now, and try to look along my back," John Pike, with a reverential whisper, said to me. "Now, don't be in a hurry, young stupid; kneel down. He is not to be disturbed at his dinner, mind. You keep behind me, and look along my back; I never clapped eyes on such a whopper."

I had to kneel down in a tender reminiscence of pastureland and gaze carefully; and not having eyes like those of our Zebedee (who offered his spine for a camera, as he crawled on all fours in front of me), it took me a long time to descry an object most distinct to all who have that special gift of piercing with their eyes the water. See what is said upon this subject in that delicious book, *The Gamekeeper at Home.*

"You are no better than a muff," said Pike, and it was not in my power to deny it.

"If the sun would only leave off," I said. But the sun, who was having a very pleasant play with the sparkle of the water and the twinkle of the leaves, had no inclination to leave off yet, but kept the rippling crystal in a dance of flashing facets, and the quivering verdure in a steady flush of gold.

But suddenly a May fly, a luscious gray drake, richer and more delicate than canvasback or woodcock, with a dart and a leap and a merry zigzag, began to enjoy a little game above the stream. Rising and falling like a gnat, thrilling her gauzy wings, and arching her elegant pellucid frame, every now and then she almost dipped her three long tapering whisks into the dimples of the water.

"He sees her! He'll have her as sure as a gun!" cried Pike, with a gulp, as if he himself were "rising." "Now can you see him, stupid?"

"Crikey, crokums!" I exclaimed, with classic elegance; "I have seen that long thing for five minutes; but I took it for a tree."

"You little"—animal quite early in the alphabet—"now don't you stir a peg, or I'll dig my elbow into you."

The great trout was stationary almost as a stone, in the middle of the V above described. He was gently fanning with his large clear fins, but holding his own against the current mainly by the wagging of his broad-fluked tail. As soon as my slow eyes had once defined him, he grew upon them mightily, molding himself in the matrix of the water, as a thing put into jelly does. And I doubt whether even John Pike saw him more accurately than I did. His size was such, or seemed to be such, that I fear to say a word about it; not because language does not contain the word, but from dread of exaggeration. But his shape and color may be reasonably told without wounding the feeling of an age whose incredulity springs from self-knowledge.

His head was truly small, his shoulders vast; the spring of his back was like a rainbow when the sun is southing; the generous sweep of his deep elastic belly, nobly pulped out with rich nurture, showed what the power of his brain must be, and seemed to undulate, time for time, with the vibrant vigilance of his large wise eyes. His latter end was consistent also. An elegant taper run of counter, coming almost to a cylinder, as a mackerel does, boldly developed with a hugeous spread to a glorious amplitude of swallowtail. His color was all that can well be desired, but ill described by any poor word palette. Enough that he seemed to tone away from olive and umber, with carmine stars, to glowing gold and soft pure silver, mantled with a subtle flush of rose and fawn and opal.

Swoop came a swallow, as we gazed, and was gone with a flick, having missed the May fly. But the wind of his passage, or the stir of wing, struck the merry dancer down, so that he fluttered for one instant on the wave, and that instant was enough. Swift as the swallow, and more true of aim, the great trout made one dart, and a sound, deeper than a tinkle, but as silvery as a bell, rang the poor ephemerid's knell. The rapid water scarcely showed a break; but a bubble sailed down the pool, and the dark hollow echoed with the music of a rise.

"He knows how to take a fly," said Pike; "he has had too many to be tricked with mine. Have him I must; but how ever shall I do it?"

All the way to Wellington he uttered not a word, but shambled along with a mind full of care. When I ventured to look up now and then, to surmise what was going on beneath his hat, deeply set eyes and a wrinkled forehead, relieved at long intervals by a solid shake, proved that there are meditations deeper than those of philosopher or statesman.

III

Surely no trout could have been misled by the artificial May fly of that time, unless he were either a very young fish, quite new to entomology, or else one afflicted with a combination of myopy and bulimy. Even now there is room for plenty of improvement in our counterfeit presentment; but in those days the body was made with yellow mohair, ribbed with red silk and gold twist and as thick as a fertile bumblebee. John Pike perceived that to offer such a thing to Crocker's trout would probably consign him—even if his great stamina should over-get the horror—to an uneatable death, through just and natural indignation. On the other hand, while the May fly lasted, a trout so cultured, so highly refined, so full of light and sweetness, would never demean himself to low bait, or any coarse son of a maggot.

Meanwhile, Alec Bolt allowed poor Pike no peaceful thought, no calm absorption of high mind into the world of flies, no placid period of cobbler's wax, floss silk, turned hackles, and dubbing. For in making of flies John Pike had his special moments of inspiration, times of clearer insight into the everlasting verities, times of brighter conception and more subtle execution, tails of more elastic grace and heads of a neater and nattier expression. As a poet labors at one immortal line, compressing worlds of wisdom into the music of ten syllables, so toiled the patient Pike about the fabric of a fly comprising all the excellence that ever sprang from maggot. Yet Bolt rejoiced to jerk his elbow at the moment of sublimest art. And a swarm of flies was blighted thus.

Peaceful, therefore, and long-suffering, and full of resignation as he was, John Pike came slowly to the sad perception that arts avail not without arms. The elbow, so often jerked, at last took a voluntary jerk from the shoulder, and Alec Bolt lay prostrate, with his right eye full of cobbler's wax. This put a desirable check upon his energies for a week or more, and by that time Pike had flown his fly.

When the honeymoon of spring and summer (which they are now too fashionable to celebrate in this country), the hey-day of the whole year marked by the budding of the wild rose, the start of the wheat ear from its sheath, the feathering of the lesser plantain, and flowering of the meadowsweet, and, foremost for the angler's joy, the caracole of May flies—when these things are to be seen and felt (which has not happened at all this year), then rivers should be mild and bright, skies blue and white with fleecy cloud, the west wind blowing softly, and the trout in charming appetite.

On such a day came Pike to the bank of Culm, with a loudly beating heart. A fly there is, not ignominious, or of cowdab origin, neither gross and heavy-bodied, from cradlehood of slimy stones, nor yet of menacing aspect and suggesting deeds of poison, but elegant, bland, and of sunny nature, and obviously good to eat. Him or her—why quest we which?— the shepherd of the dale, contemptuous of gender, except in his own species, has called, and as long as they two coexist will call, the Yellow Sally. A fly that does not waste the day in giddy dances and the fervid waltz, but undergoes family incidents with decorum and discretion. He or she, as the case may be—for the natural history of the riverbank is a book to come hereafter, and of fifty men who make flies not one knows the name of the fly he is making—in the early morning of June, or else in the second quarter of the afternoon, this Yellow Sally fares abroad, with a nice well-ordered flutter.

Despairing of the May fly, as it still may be despaired of, Pike came down to the river with his masterpiece of portraiture. The artificial Yellow Sally is generally always—as they say in Cheshire—a mile or more too yellow. On the other hand, the Yellow Dun conveys no idea of any Sally. But Pike had made a very decent Sally, not perfect (for he was young as well as wise), but far above any counterfeit to be had in fishing-tackle shops. How he made it, he told nobody. But if he lives now, as I hope he does, any of my readers may ask him through the G. P. O. and hope to get an answer.

It fluttered beautifully on the breeze, and in such living form that a brother or sister Sally came up to see it, and went away sadder and wiser. Then Pike said: "Get away, you young wretch," to your humble servant who tells this tale; yet, being better than his words, allowed that pious follower to lie down upon his digestive organs and with deep attention watch. There must have been great things to see, but to see them so was difficult. And if I huddle up what happened, excitement also shares the blame.

Pike had fashioned well the time and manner of this overture. He knew that the giant Crockerite was satiate now with May flies, or began to find their flavor failing, as happens to us with asparagus, marrow-fat peas, or strawberries, when we have had a month of them. And he thought that the first Yellow Sally of the season, inferior though it were, might have the special charm of novelty. With the skill of a Zulu, he stole up through the branches over the lower pool till he came to a spot where a yard-wide opening gave just space for spring of rod. Then he saw his desirable friend at dinner, wagging his tail, as a hungry gentleman dining with the Lord Mayor agitates his coat. With one dexterous whirl, untaught by any of the many books upon the subject, John Pike laid his Yellow Sally (for he cast with one fly only) as lightly as gossamer upon the rapid, about a yard in front of the big trout's head. A moment's pause, and then too quick for words was the thing that happened.

A heavy plunge was followed by a fearful rush. Forgetful of the current the river was ridged, as if with a plow driven under it; the strong line, though given out as fast as might be, twanged like a harp string as it cut the wave, and then Pike stood up, like a ship dismasted, with the butt of his rod snapped below the ferrule. He had one of those foolish things, just invented, a hollow butt of hickory; and the finial ring of his spare top looked out, to ask what had happened to the rest of it. "Bad luck!" cried the fisherman; "but never mind, I shall have him next time, to a certainty."

When this great issue came to be considered, the cause of it was sadly obvious. The fish, being hooked, had made off with the rush of a shark for the bottom of the pool. A thicket of saplings below the alder tree had stopped the judicious hooker from all possibility of following; and when he strove to turn him by elastic pliance, his rod broke at the breach of pliability. "I have learned a sad lesson," said John Pike, looking sadly.

How many fellows would have given up this matter, and glorified themselves for having hooked so grand a fish, while explaining that they must have caught him, if they could have done it! But Pike only told me not to say a word about it, and began to make ready for another tug of war. He made himself a splice rod, short and handy, of well-seasoned ash, with a stout top of bamboo, tapered so discreetly, and so balanced in its spring, that verily it formed an arc, with any pressure on it, as perfect as a leafy poplar in a stormy summer. "Now break it if you can," he said, "by any amount of rushes; I'll hook you by your jacket collar; you cut away now, and I'll land you."

This was highly skillful, and he did it many times; and whenever I was landed well, I got a lollipop, so that I was careful not to break his tackle. Moreover he made him a landing net, with a kidney-bean stick, a ring of wire, and his own best nightcap of strong cotton net. Then he got the farmer's leave, and lopped obnoxious bushes; and now the chiefest question was: What bait, and when to offer it? In spite of his sad rebuff, the spirit of John Pike had been equable. The genuine angling mind is steadfast, large, and self-supported, and to the vapid, ignominious chaff, tossed by swine upon the idle wind, it pays as much heed as a big trout does to a dance of midges. People put their fingers to their noses and said: "Master Pike, have you caught him yet?" and Pike only answered: "Wait a bit." If ever this fortitude and perseverance is to be recovered as the English Brand (the one thing that has made us what we are, and may yet redeem us from niddering shame), a degenerate age should encourage the habit of fishing and never despairing. And the brightest sign yet for our future is the increasing demand for hooks and gut.

Pike fished in a manlier age, when nobody would dream of cowering from a savage because he was clever at skulking; and when, if a big fish broke the rod, a stronger rod was made for him, according to the usage of Great Britain. And though the young angler had been defeated, he did not sit down and have a good cry over it.

About the second week in June, when the May fly had danced its day and died—for the season was an early one—and Crocker's trout had recovered from the wound to his feelings and philanthropy, there came a night of gentle rain, of pleasant tinkling upon window ledges, and a soothing patter among young leaves, and the Culm was yellow in the morning. "I mean to do it this afternoon," Pike whispered to me, as he came back panting. "When the water clears there will be a splendid time."

The lover of the rose knows well a gay voluptuous beetle, whose pleasure is to lie embedded in a fount of beauty. Deep among the incurving petals of the blushing fragrance, he loses himself in his joys sometimes, till a breezy waft reveals him. And when the sunlight breaks upon his luscious dissipation, few would have the heart to oust him, such a gem from such a setting. All his back is emerald sparkles, all his front red Indian gold, and here and there he grows white spots to save the eye from aching. Pike put his finger in and fetched him out, and offered him a little change of joys, by putting a Limerick hook through his thorax, and bringing it out between his elytra. *Cetonia aurata* liked it not, but pawed the air very naturally, and fluttered with his wings attractively.

"I meant to have tried with a fern web," said the angler; "until I saw one of these beggars this morning. If he works like that upon the water, he will do. It was hopeless to try artificials again. What a lovely color the water is! Only three days now to the holidays. I have run it very close. You be ready, younker."

With these words he stepped upon a branch of the alder, for the tone of the waters allowed approach, being soft and sublustrous, without any mud. Also Master Pike's own tone was such as becomes the fisherman, calm, deliberate, free from nerve, but full of eye and muscle. He stepped upon the alder bough to get as near as might be to the fish, for he could not cast this beetle like a fly; it must be dropped gently and allowed to play. "You may come and look," he said to me; "when the water is so, they have no eyes in their tails."

The rose beetle trod upon the water prettily, under a lively vibration, and he looked quite as happy and considerably more active, than when he had been cradled in the anthers of the rose. To the eye of a fish he was a strong individual, fighting courageously with the current, but sure to be beaten through lack of fins; and mercy suggested, as well as appetite, that the proper solution was to gulp him.

"Hooked him in the gullet. He can't get off!" cried John Pike, laboring to keep his nerves under. "Every inch of tackle is as strong as a bell pull. Now, if I don't land him, I will never fish again!"

Providence, which had constructed Pike, foremost of all things, for lofty angling—disdainful of worm and even minnow—Providence, I say, at this adjuration, pronounced that Pike must catch that trout. Not many anglers are heaven-born; and for one to drop off the hook halfway through his teens would be infinitely worse than to slay the champion trout. Pike felt the force of this, and rushing through the rushes, shouted: "I am sure to have him, Dick! Be ready with my nightcap."

Rod in a bow, like a springle riser; line on the hum, like the strong of Paganini; winch on the gallop, like a harpoon wheel, Pike, the head-center of everything, dashing through thick and thin, and once taken overhead—for he jumped into the hole, when he must have lost him else, but the fish too impetuously towed him out, and made off in passion for another pool, when, if he had only retired to his hover, the angler might have shared the baker's fate—all these things (I tell you, for they all come upon again, as if the day were yesterday) so scared me of my never very steadfast wits, that I could only holloa! But one thing I did, I kept the nightcap ready.

"He is pretty nearly spent, I do believe," said Pike; and his voice was like balm of Gilead, as we came to Farmer Anning's meadow, a quarter of a mile below Crocker's Hole. "Take it coolly, my dear boy, and we shall be safe to have him."

Never have I felt, through forty years, such tremendous responsibility. I had not the faintest notion now to use a landing net; but a mighty general directed me. "Don't let him see it; don't let him see it! Don't clap it over him; go under him, you stupid! If he makes another rush, he will get off, after all. Bring it up his tail. Well done! You have him!"

The mighty trout lay in the nightcap of Pike, which was half a fathom long, with a tassel at the end, for his mother had made it in the winter evenings. "Come and hold the rod, if you can't lift him," my master shouted, and so I did. Then, with both arms straining, and his mouth wide open, John Pike made a mighty sweep, and we both fell upon the grass and rolled, with the giant of the deep flapping heavily between us, and no power left to us, except to cry, "Hurrah!"

Chapter Twenty-Six

The River Sneak

by William Scrope

Like many readers of classic fishing stories, especially those from the UK decades ago, this editor and reader finds poaching stories to be irresistible. This is one of the best, from William Scrope (1772–1852), an English sportsman and amateur artist, known as a writer on sports.

IF I WERE TO WRITE AN ACCOUNT OF HALF THE POACHING STORIES that are common to all Salmon rivers, I should produce a book, the dimensions of which would terrify the public, even in this pen-compelling age.

In times when water bailiffs in Tweed had very small salaries, they themselves were by no means scrupulous about the observance of close time, but partook of the good things of the river in all seasons, lawful or unlawful. There is a man now, I believe, living at Selkirk, who in times of yore used certain little freedoms with the Tweed Act, which did not become the virtue of his office. As a water bailiff he was sworn to tell of all he saw; and indeed, as he said, it could not be expected that he should tell of what he did not see.

When his dinner was served up during close time, his wife usually brought to the table in the first place a platter of potatoes and a napkin; she then bound the latter over his eyes that nothing might offend his sight. This being done, the illegal salmon was brought in smoking hot, and he fell to, blindfolded as he was, like a conscientious water bailiff,—if you know what that is; nor was the napkin taken from his eyes till the fins and bones were removed from the room, and every visible evidence of a salmon having been there had completely vanished: thus he saw no illegal act committed, and went to give in his annual report at Cornhill with his idea of a clear conscience. This was going too near the wind, or rather the water; but what would you have?—the man was literal, and a great eater of salmon from his youth.

People who are not water bailiffs have not always so delicate a conscience. Let us examine the style and bearing of such marauders as have fallen under our notice.

In the first place, there is your man with a pout net, which resembles a landing net, only that it is very considerably larger, and is in shape only half of a circle; with this he scoops out foul salmon during floods, when, from weakness, they are unable to stem the current, and get close under the banks. This he transacts very snugly, under pretence of taking trouts; so indeed he does, and welcome too, if he would stop there; but this he is perfectly averse from.

Next in consequence comes your Triton, who walks the waters with a long implement in his hands, namely a leister, alias a waster; with this weapon, "quocunque nomine gaudet," the said deity, quick of eye and ready of hand, forks out the poor fish that are spawning on the streams; and this in close time. Vile, vile Triton!

Then comes your lawless band of black fishers, so called from their masks of black crape with which they disguise themselves: these men come forth in the darkness of the night to burn for salmon. When the winds are hushed, you may sometimes hear the dipping of oars and the clanking of a boat chain, and see at a distance a small light, like a glow-worm. In a little while the light blazes forth, and up rise a set of Othellos who are about to take a private benefit. These minions of the night are generally men of a desperate character, and it is not easy to collect water bailiffs sufficient in number or willing to encounter them; but if water bailiffs would fight, how very picturesque the attack would be! The rapids,—the blazing,—the leisters,—the combatants driven headlong into the river. Why, the battle of Constantine and Maxentius, and the affair of the bridge, as seen in the famous fresco, would be nothing to it. The only thing I should apprehend would be, that the bailiffs would eventually sport Marc Antony and run.

In contradistinction to these illuminati comes your plausible poacher, a sort of river sneak. This man sallies forth with apparent innocence of purpose; he switches the water with a trout-rod, and ambulates the shore with a small basket at his back, indicative of humble pretensions; but has a pocket in his jacket that extends the whole breadth of the skirts. He is trouting, forsooth, but ever and anon, as he comes to a salmon-cast, he changes his fly, and has a go at the nobler animal. If he hooks a salmon, he looks on each side with the tail of his eye to guard against a surprise; and if he sees any danger of discovery from the advance of the foeman, he breaks his line, leaves the fly in the fish's mouth, and substitutes a trout one;—said fish swims away, and does not appear in evidence.

I once came upon one of these innocents, who had hold of a salmon with his trout-rod in a cast a little above Melrose bridge, called *"The Quarry Stream."* He did not see me, for I was in the copsewood on the summit of the bank immediately behind him. I could have pounced upon him at once, I and my fisherman. Did I do so? I tell you, no. He would have broken his line as above, and have lost the fish; and I wanted a salmon, for it is a delicate animal, and was particularly scarce at that time.

So I desired Charlie to lie down amongst the bushes, and not to stir till the fish was fairly landed, and was in the capacious pocket, which has already been described. Then I counselled him to give chase, and harry the possessor. Judging, however, that if the man crossed the river at the ford a little below, which he was very likely to do, that he would have so much law of Charlie before he could descend the steep brae, that he might escape: I drew back cautiously, got into the road out of sight, and passed over Melrose bridge, taking care to bend my body so as to keep it out of sight behind the parapet; I then lay concealed amongst the firs in the opposite bank. Thus we had Master Sneak between us. I was at some distance from the scene of action to be sure, and somewhat in the rear, as I could advance no further under cover; but I had the upper ground, and was tolerably swift of foot in those days, which gave me confidence. I took out my pocket glass, and eyed my man. He was no novice: but worked his fish with great skill. At length he drew him on the shore, and gave him a settler with a rap of a stone on the back of his head; he then, honest man, pryed around him with great circumspection, and seeing no one, he took the salmon by the tail, and, full of internal contentment, deposited it in his well-contrived pocket: he then waded across to the south side of the river, with an intention, as it seemed, of revisiting his household gods and having a broil.

Charlie now arose from his lair, and scrambled down the steep. The alarm was given, but he of the salmon had a good start, with the river between him and his pursuer. So he stopped for a moment on the haugh to make out what was going forward on all sides, much after the fashion of an old hare, who runs a certain distance when she apprehends any thing personal, then rests for a moment or two, and shifts her ears in order to collect the news from all quarters of the compass. Even so did our friend, and having satisfied himself that he was a favoured object of attraction, he was coy, and took to flight incontinently; I now sprang up from the firs, the game being fairly afoot, and kept the upper ground. The pursuit became close and hot, but as the fugitive, like Johnny Gilpin, carried weight, I soon closed with him.

"You seem in a hurry, my good friend, your business must be pressing. What makes you run so?"

"Did ye no see that bogle there by the quarry stream, that garred me rin this gait, haud on for yer lives, sirs, for if he overtakes us, we are deid men."

"Why, the truth is, Sandy, that I do not choose to haud on at present, because I came forth in quest of a bonny salmon, and cannot go home without one; could you not help me to such a thing?"

At this Sandy took a pinch of snuff from his mull, and seeing my eyes fixed upon the length and protuberance of his pocket, answered quaintly enough,—

"Aye, that can I, and right glad am I to do ye a favour, ye shall no want for a salmon whilst I have one."

So saying, he pulled forth a ten pounder, which occupied all the lower regions of his jacket. "How the beast got here," said he, as he extracted him gradually, "I dinna ken, but I am thinking that he must have louped intill my pocket, as I war wading the river."

"Nothing more likely, and I will admit him to have done so for once, but, mark me, I will not admit of any salmon doing so in future without my permission in writing. You have been trouting, it seems, pray what sort of a fly do you use?"

"Whiles I use a wee ane, and while a muckle flee, ane for rough and deep water, and the ither for shallow streams. That is the way to trout, both in loch and river."

"True! I see you have some bonny little flies in your hat; take it off carefully, Purdie—you understand me,—and let me admire them."

Charlie advances, and taking off the man's hat with great care so as to keep the crown undermost, he pulls out from the inside six well tied salmon flies of the most approved colours, which he transferred to his own pocket. I actually saw *"Meg with the muckle mouth"* amongst them.

"Aye, ye are as welcome to the flees as ye are to the sawmont, and I am proud to do ye a good turn at ony gait."

"Well now, bear in mind, that I will never permit you to throw a fly wee or muckle in the Pavilion-water again; and if you darken the shores with your presence a second time, I will have you up at Melrose."

"I'm thinking I shall tak' your advice, for ye seem a sensible chiel. Will ye accept a pinch of snuff?"

"Good morning, good morning, get home to Selkirk as quick as ye can; we know ye well for a souter of that town. Run, run, the bogle is after you!"

"Run, aye that will I, and the deil tak' the hindmost," said he, and off he went at his best pace; leaving this blessing and the salmon to solace us.

CHAPTER TWENTY-SEVEN

Fishing with a Worm

by Bliss Perry

Every angler knows that fishing with a worm is a sure way to catch fish. But not all are willing to try it, and break the "sporting" code, much less write about it, as Bliss Perry (1860–1954) did in a book of the same title for Houghton Mifflin.

BELOW THE LOWER ROAD THE TAYLOR BROOK BECOMES UNCERTAIN water. For half a mile it yields only fingerlings, for no explainable reason; then there are two miles of clean fishing through the deep woods, where the branches are so high that you can cast a fly again if you like, and there are long pools, where now and then a heavy fish will rise; then comes a final half mile through the alders, where you must wade, knee to waist deep, before you come to the bridge and the river. Glorious fishing is sometimes to be had here, especially if you work down the gorge at twilight, casting a white miller until it is too dark to see. But alas, there is a well-worn path along the brook, and often enough there are the very footprints of the fellow ahead of you, signs as disheartening to the fisherman as ever were the footprints on the sand to Robinson Crusoe.

But "between the roads" it is "too much trouble to fish;" and there lies the salvation of the humble fisherman who disdains not to use the crawling worm, nor, for that matter, to crawl himself, if need be, in order to sneak under the boughs of some overhanging cedar that casts a perpetual shadow upon the sleepy brook. Lying here at full length, with no elbow room to manage the rod, you must occasionally even unjoint your tip and fish with that, using but a dozen inches of line, and not letting so much as your eyebrows show above the bank. Is it a becoming attitude for a middle-aged citizen of the world? That depends upon how the fish are biting. Holing a putt looks rather ridiculous also, to the mere observer, but it requires, like brook fishing with a tip only, a very delicate wrist, perfect tactile sense, and a fine disregard of appearances.

There are some fishermen who always fish as if they were being photographed. The Taylor Brook "between the roads" is not for them. To fish it at all is back-breaking, trouser-tearing work; to see it thoroughly fished is to learn new lessons in the art of angling.

To watch R., for example, steadily filling his six-pound creel from that unlikely stream is like watching Sargent paint a portrait. R. weighs two hundred and ten. Twenty years ago he was a famous amateur pitcher, and among his present avocations are violin playing, which is good for the wrist, taxidermy, which is good for the eye, and shooting woodcock, which before the days of the new Nature Study used to be thought good for the whole man. R. began as a fly-fisherman, but by dint of passing his summers near brooks where fly-fishing is impossible, he has become a stout-hearted apologist for the worm. His apparatus is most singular. It consists of a very long, cheap rod, stout enough to smash through bushes, and with the stiffest tip obtainable. The lower end of the butt, below the reel, fits into the socket of a huge extra butt of bamboo, which R. carries unconcernedly. To reach a distant hole, or to fish the lower end of a ripple, R. simply locks his reel, slips on the extra butt, and there is a fourteen-foot rod ready for action. He fishes with a line unbelievably short, and a Kendal hook far too big; and when a trout jumps for that hook, R. wastes no time in manoeuvring for position. The unlucky fish is simply "derricked" to borrow a word from Theodore, most saturnine and profane of Moosehead guides.

"Shall I play him awhile?" shouted an excited sportsman to Theodore, after hooking his first big trout.

"——no!" growled Theodore in disgust. "Just derrick him right into the canoe!" An heroic method, surely; though it once cost me the best squaretail I ever hooked, for Theodore had forgotten the landing net, and the gut broke in his fingers as he tried to swing the fish abroad. But with these lively quarter-pounders of the Taylor Brook, derricking is a safer procedure. Indeed, I have sat dejectedly on the far end of a log, after fishing the hole under it in vain, and seen the mighty R. wade downstream close behind me, adjust that comical extra butt, and jerk a couple of half-pound trout from under the very log on which I was sitting. His device on this occasion, as I well remember, was to pass his hook but once through the middle of a big worm, let the worm sink to the bottom and crawl along it at his leisure. The trout could not resist.

Once, and once only, have I come near equaling R.'s record, and the way he beat me then is the justification for a whole philosophy of worm-fishing. We were on this very Taylor Brook, and at five in the afternoon both baskets were two thirds full. By count I had just one more fish than he. It was raining hard.

"You fish down through the alders," said R. magnanimously. "I'll cut across and wait for you at the sawmill. I don't want to get any wetter, on account of my rheumatism."

This was rather barefaced kindness—for whose rheumatism was ever the worse for another hour's fishing? But I weakly accepted it. I coveted three or four good trout to top off with—that was all. So I tied on a couple of flies and began to fish the alders, wading waist-deep in the rapidly rising water, down the long green tunnel under the curving boughs. The brook fairly smoked with the rain, by this time, but when did one fail to get at least three or four trout out of his best half mile of the lower brook? Yet I had no luck. I tried one fly after another, and then, as a forlorn hope,—though it sometimes has a magic of its own,—I combined a brown hackle for the tail fly with a twisting worm on the dropper. Not a rise!

I thought of R. sitting patiently in the sawmill, and I fished more conscientiously than ever.

Venture as warily, use the same skill,
Do your best, whether winning or losing it,
If you choose to play!—is my principle.

315

Even those lines, which by some subtle telepathy of the trout brook murmur themselves over and over to me in the waning hours of an unlucky day, brought now no consolation. There was simply not one fish to be had, to any fly in the book, out of that long, drenching, darkening tunnel. At last I climbed out of the brook, by the bridge. R. was sitting on the fence, his neck and ears carefully turtled under his coat collar, the smoke rising and the rain dripping from the inverted bowl of his pipe. He did not seem to be worrying about his rheumatism.

"What luck?" he asked.

"None at all," I answered morosely. "Sorry to keep you waiting."

"That's all right," remarked R. "What do you think I've been doing? I've been fishing out of the sawmill window just to kill time. There was a patch of floating sawdust there,—kind of unlikely place for trout, any-way,—but I thought I'd put on a worm and let him crawl around a little." He opened his creel as he spoke.

"But I didn't look for a pair of 'em," he added. And there, on top of his smaller fish, were as pretty a pair of three-quarter-pound brook trout as were ever basketed.

"I'm afraid you got pretty wet," said R. kindly.

"I don't mind that," I replied. And I didn't. What I minded was the thought of an hour's vain wading in that roaring stream whipping it with fly after fly, while R., the foreordained fisherman, was sitting comfortably in a sawmill, and derricking that pair of three-quarter-pounds in through the window! I had ventured more warily than he, and used, if not the same skill, at least the best skill at my command. My conscience was clear, but so was his; and he had had the drier skin and the greater mag-nanimity and the biggest fish besides. There is much to be said, in a world like ours, for taking the world as you find it and for fishing with a worm.

CHAPTER TWENTY-EIGHT

Story-Telling on the Thames

by Jerome K. Jerome

Jerome Klapka Jerome (May 2, 1859–June 14, 1927) was an English writer and humorist, best known for the comic travelogue Three Men in a Boat *(1889).*

THE NEIGHBOURHOOD OF STREATLEY AND GORING IS A GREAT FISHING centre. There is some excellent fishing to be had here. The river abounds in pike, roach, dace, gudgeon, and eels, just here; and you can sit and fish for them all day.

Some people do. They never catch them. I never knew anybody catch anything, up the Thames, except minnows and dead cats, but that has nothing to do, of course, with fishing! The local fisherman's guide doesn't say a word about catching anything. All it says is the place is "a good station for fishing;" and, from what I have seen of the district, I am quite prepared to bear out this statement.

There is no spot in the world where you can get more fishing, or where you can fish for a longer period. Some fishermen come here and fish for a day, and others stop and fish for a month. You can hang on and fish for a year, if you want to; it will be all the same.

The Angler's Guide to the Thames says that "jack and perch are also to be had about here," but there the *Angler's Guide* is wrong. Jack and perch may be about there. Indeed, I know for a fact that they are. You can see them there in shoals, when you are out for a walk along the banks: they come and stand half out of the water with their mouths open for biscuits. And, if you go for a bathe, they crowd round, and get in your way, and irritate you. But they are not to be "had" by a bit of worm on the end of a hook, nor anything like it—not they!

I am not a good fisherman myself. I devoted a considerable amount of attention to the subject at one time, and was getting on, as I thought, fairly well; but the old hands told me that I should never be any real good at it, and advised me to give it up. They said that I was an extremely neat thrower, and that I seemed to have plenty of gumption for the thing, and quite enough constitutional laziness. But they were sure I should never make anything of a fisherman. I had not got sufficient imagination.

They said that as a poet, or a shilling shocker, or a report, or anything of that kind, I might be satisfactory, but that, to gain any position as a Thames angler, would require more play of fancy, more power of invention than I appeared to possess.

Some people are under the impression that all that is required to make a good fisherman is the ability to tell lies easily and without blushing; but this is a mistake. Mere bald fabrication is useless; the veriest tyro can manage that. It is in the circumstantial detail, the embellishing touches of probability, the general air of scrupulous—almost of pedantic—veracity, that the experienced angler is seen.

Anybody can come in and say, "Oh, I caught fifteen dozen perch yesterday evening;" or "Last Monday I landed a gudgeon, weighing eighteen pounds, and measuring three feet from the tip to the tail."

There is no art, no skill, required for that sort of thing. It shows pluck, but that is all.

No; your accomplished angler would scorn to tell a lie, that way. His method is a study in itself.

He comes in quietly with his hat on, appropriates the most comfortable chair, lights his pipe, and commences to puff in silence. He lets the youngsters brag away for a while, and then, during a momentary lull, he removes the pipe from his mouth, and remarks, as he knocks the ashes out against the bars:

"Well, I had a haul on Tuesday evening that it's not much good my telling anybody about."

"Oh! why's that?" they ask.

"Because I don't expect anybody would believe me if I did," replies the old fellow calmly, and without even a tinge of bitterness in his tone, as he refills his pipe, and requests the landlord to bring him three of Scotch,—cold.

There is a pause after this, nobody feeling sufficiently sure of himself to contradict the old gentleman. So he has to go on by himself without any encouragement.

"No," he continues thoughtfully; "I shouldn't believe it myself if anybody told it to me, but it's a fact, for all that. I had been sitting there all the afternoon and had caught literally nothing—except a few dozen dace and a score of jack; and I was just about giving it up as a bad job when I suddenly felt a rather smart pull at the line. I thought it was another little one, and I went to jerk it up. Hang me, if I could move the rod! It took me half-an-hour—half-an-hour, sir!—to land that fish; and every moment I thought the line was going to snap! I reached him at last, and what do you think it was? A sturgeon! a forty pound sturgeon! taken on a line, sir! Yes, you may well look surprised—I'll have another three of Scotch, landlord, please."

And then he goes on to tell of the astonishment of everybody who saw it; and what his wife said, when he got home, and of what Joe Buggles thought about it.

I asked the landlord of an inn up the river once, if it did not injure him, sometimes, listening to the tales that the fishermen about there told him; and he said:

"Oh, no; not now, sir. It did used to knock me over a bit at first, but, lor love you! me and the missus we listens to 'em all day now. It's what you're used to, you know. It's what you're used to."

I knew a young man once, he was a most conscientious fellow, and, when he took to fly-fishing, he determined never to exaggerate his hauls by more than twenty-five per cent.

"When I have caught forty fish," said he, "then I will tell people that I have caught fifty, and so on. But I will not lie any more than that, because it is sinful to lie."

But the twenty-five per cent plan did not work well at all. He never was able to use it. The greatest number of fish he ever caught in one day was three, and you can't add twenty-five per cent to three—at least, not in fish.

So he increased his percentage to thirty-three and a third; but that, again, was awkward, when he had only caught one or two; so, to simplify matters, he made up his mind to just double the quantity.

He stuck to this arrangement for a couple of months, and then he grew dissatisfied with it. Nobody believed him when he told them that he only doubled, and he, therefore, gained no credit that way whatever, while his moderation put him at a disadvantage among the other anglers. When he had really caught three small fish, and said he had six, it used to make him quite jealous to hear a man, whom he knew for a fact had only caught one, going about telling people he had landed two dozen.

So, eventually, he made one final arrangement with himself, which he has religiously held to ever since, and that was to count each fish that he caught as ten, and to assume ten to begin with. For example, if he did not catch any fish at all, then he said he had caught ten fish—you could never catch less than ten fish by his system; that was the foundation of it. Then, if by any chance he really did catch one fish, he called it twenty, while two fish would count thirty, three forty, and so on.

It is a simple and easily worked plan, and there has been some talk lately of its being made use of by the angling fraternity in general. Indeed, the Committee of the Thames Angler's Association did recommend its adoption about two years ago, but some of the older members opposed it. They said they would consider the idea if the number were doubled, and each fish counted as twenty.

If ever you have an evening to spare, up the river, I should advise you to drop into one of the little village inns, and take a seat in the tap-room. You will be nearly sure to meet one or two old rod-men, sipping their toddy there, and they will tell you enough fishy stories, in half an hour, to give you indigestion for a month.

George and I—I don't know what had become of Harris; he had gone out and had a shave, early in the afternoon, and had then come back and spent full forty minutes in pipeclaying his shoes, we had not seen him since—George and I, therefore, and the dog, left to ourselves, went for a walk to Wallingford on the second evening, and, coming home, we called in at a little river-side inn, for a rest, and other things.

We went into the parlour and sat down. There was an old fellow there, smoking a long clay pipe, and we naturally began chatting.

He told us that it had been a fine day to-day, and we told him that it had been a fine day yesterday, and then we all told each other that we thought it would be a fine day to-morrow; and George said the crops seemed to be coming up nicely.

After that it came out, somehow or other, that we were strangers in the neighbourhood, and that we were going away the next morning.

Then a pause ensued in the conversation, during which our eyes wandered round the room. They finally rested upon a dusty old glass-case, fixed very high up above the chimney-piece, and containing a trout. It rather fascinated me, that trout; it was such a monstrous fish. In fact, at first glance, I thought it was a cod.

"Ah!" said the old gentleman, following the direction of my gaze, "fine fellow that, ain't he?"

"Quite uncommon," I murmured; and George asked the old man how much he thought it weighed.

"Eighteen pounds six ounces," said our friend, rising and taking down his coat. "Yes," he continued, "it wur sixteen year ago, come the third o' next month, that I landed him. I caught him just below the bridge with a minnow. They told me he wur in the river, and I said I'd have him, and so I did. You don't see many fish that size about here now, I'm thinking. Good-night, gentlemen, good-night."

And out he went, and left us alone.

We could not take our eyes off the fish after that. It really was a remarkably fine fish. We were still looking at it, when the local carrier, who had just stopped at the inn, came to the door of the room with a pot of beer in his hand, and he also looked at the fish.

"Good-sized trout, that," said George, turning round to him.

"Ah! you may well say that, sir," replied the man; and then, after a pull at his beer, he added, "Maybe you wasn't here, sir, when that fish was caught?"

"No," we told him. We were strangers in the neighbourhood.

"Ah!" said the carrier, "then, of course, how should you? It was nearly five years ago that I caught that trout."

"Oh! was it you who caught it, then?" said I.

"Yes, sir," replied the genial old fellow. "I caught him just below the lock—leastways, what was the lock then—one Friday afternoon; and the remarkable thing about it is that I caught him with a fly. I'd gone out pike fishing, bless you, never thinking of a trout, and when I saw that whopper on the end of my line, blest if it didn't quite take me aback. Well, you see, he weighed twenty-six pound. Good-night, gentlemen, good-night."

Five minutes afterwards, a third man came in, and described how *he* had caught it early one morning, with bleak; and then he left, and a stolid, solemn-looking, middle-aged individual came in, and sat down over by the window.

None of us spoke for a while; but at length, George turned to the new comer, and said:

"I beg your pardon, I hope you will forgive the liberty that we—perfect strangers in the neighbourhood—are taking, but my friend here and myself would be much obliged if you would tell us how you caught that trout."

"Why, who told you I caught that trout!" was the surprised query.

We said that nobody had told us so, but somehow or other we felt instinctively that it was he who had done it.

"Well, it's a most remarkable thing—most remarkable," answered the stolid stranger, laughing; "because, as a matter of fact, you are quite right. I did catch it. But fancy your guessing it like that. Dear me, it's really a most remarkable thing."

And then he went on, and told us how it had taken him half an hour to land it, and how it had broke his rod. He said he had weighed it carefully when he reached home, and it had turned the scale at thirty-four pounds.

He went in his turn, and when he was gone, the landlord came in to us. We told him the various histories we had heard about his trout, and he was immensely amused, and we all laughed very heartily.

"Fancy Jim Bates and Joe Muggles and Mr. Jones and old Billy Maunders all telling you that they had caught it. Ha! ha! ha! Well, that is good," said the honest old fellow, laughing heartily. "Yes, they are the sort to give it to *me*, to put up in *my* parlour, if *they* had caught it, they are! Ha! ha! ha!"

And then he told us the real history of the fish. It seemed that he had caught it himself, years ago, when he was quite a lad; not by any art or skill, but by that unaccountable luck that appears to always wait upon a boy when he plays the wag from school, and goes way out fishing on a sunny afternoon, with a bit of string tied on to the end of a tree.

He said that bringing home that trout had saved him from a whacking, and that even his schoolmaster had said it was worth the rule-of-three and practice put together.

He was called out of the room at this point, and George and I again turned our gaze upon the fish.

It really was a most astonishing trout. The more we looked at it, the more we marvelled at it.

It excited George so much that he climbed up on the back of a chair to get a better view of it.

And then the chair slipped, and George clutched wildly at the trout-case to save himself, and down it came with a crash, George and the chair on top of it.

"You haven't injured the fish, have you?" I cried in alarm, rushing up.

"I hope not," said George, rising cautiously and looking about.

But he had. That trout lay shattered into a thousand fragments—I say a thousand, but they may have only been nine hundred. I did not count them.

We thought it strange and unaccountable that a stuffed trout should break up into little pieces like that.

And so it would have been strange and unaccountable, if it had been a stuffed trout, but it was not.

That trout was plaster-of-Paris.

CHAPTER TWENTY-NINE

On Lying Awake at Night
by Stewart Edward White

There are different kinds of lying awake at night—all of them bad and destined to leave you bleary-eyed the next day. No matter how good the fishing, the snoring of your companions, the excitement of anticipation, are tough to shut down when sleep eludes you.

Writer Stewart Edward White, introduced back in our musky story, describes the condition superbly in this story from his book The Forest.

What Mr. White tells you may not help you get a restful night, but at least you'll learn that the malady does not strike you alone.

ABOUT ONCE IN SO OFTEN YOU ARE DUE TO LIE AWAKE AT NIGHT. WHY this is so I have never been able to discover. It apparently comes from no predisposing uneasiness of indigestion, no rashness in the matter of too much tea or tobacco, no excitation of unusual incident or stimulating conversation. In fact, you turn in with the expectation of rather a good night's rest. Almost at once the little noises of the forest grow larger, blend in the hollow bigness of the first drowse; your thoughts drift idly back and forth between reality and dream; when—*snap!*—you are broad awake!

Perhaps the reservoir of your vital forces is full to the overflow of a little waste; or perhaps, more subtly, the great Mother insists thus that you enter the temple of her larger mysteries.

For, unlike mere insomnia, lying awake at night in the woods is pleasant. The eager, nervous straining for sleep gives way to a delicious indifference. You do not care. Your mind is cradled in an exquisite poppy-suspension of judgment and of thought. Impressions slip vaguely into your consciousness and as vaguely out again. Sometimes they stand stark and naked for your inspection; sometimes they lose themselves in the midst of half-sleep. Always they lay soft velvet fingers on the drowsy imagination, so that in their caressing you feel the vaster spaces from which they have come. Peaceful-brooding your faculties receive. Hearing, sight, smell—all are preternaturally keen to whatever of sound and sight and woods perfume is abroad through the night; and yet at the same time active appreciation dozes, so these things lie on it sweet and cloying like fallen rose leaves.

In such circumstance you will hear what the *voyageurs* call the voices of the rapids. Many people never hear them at all. They speak very soft and low and distinct beneath the steady roar and dashing, beneath even the lesser tinklings and gurglings whose quality superimposes them over the louder sounds. They are like the tear-forms swimming across the field of vision, which disappear so quickly when you concentrate your sight to look at them, and which reappear so magically when again your gaze turns vacant. In the stillness of your hazy half-consciousness they speak; when you bend your attention to listen, they are gone, and only the tumults and the tinklings remain.

But in the moments of their audibility they are very distinct. Just as often an odour will wake all a vanished memory, so these voices, by the force of a large impressionism, suggest whole scenes. Far off are the cling-clang-cling of chimes and the swell-and-fall murmur of a multitude *en fête* so that subtly you feel the gray old town, with its walls, the crowded marketplace, the decent peasant crowd, the booths, the mellow church building with its bells, the warm, dust-moted sun. Or, in the pauses between the swish-dash-dashings of the waters, sound faint and clear voices singing intermittently, calls, distant notes of laughter, as though many canoes were working against the current; only the flotilla never gets any nearer, nor the voices louder. The *voyageurs* call these mist people the Huntsmen, and look frightened. To each is his vision, according to his experience. The nations of the earth whisper to their exiled sons through the voices of the rapids. Curiously enough, by all reports, they suggest always peaceful scenes—a harvest field, a street fair, a Sunday morning in a cathedral town, careless travellers—never the turmoils and struggles. Perhaps this is the great Mother's compensation in a harsh mode of life.

Nothing is more fantastically unreal to tell about, nothing more concretely real to experience, than this undernote of the quick water. And when you do lie awake at night, it is always making its unobtrusive appeal. Gradually its hypnotic spell works. The distant chimes ring louder and nearer as you cross the borderland of sleep. And then outside the tent some little woods noise snaps the thread. An owl hoots, a whippoorwill cries, a twig cracks beneath the cautious prowl of some night creature—at once the yellow sunlit French meadows puff away—you are staring at the blurred image of the moon spraying through the texture of your tent.

The voices of the rapids have dropped into the background, as have the dashing noises of the stream. Through the forest is a great silence, but no stillness at all. The whippoorwill swings down and up the short curve of his regular song; over and over an owl says his rapid *whoo, whoo, whoo.* These, with the ceaseless dash of the rapids, are the web on which the night traces her more delicate embroideries of the unexpected. Distant crashes, single and impressive; stealthy footsteps near at hand; the sub-dued scratching of claws; a faint *sniff! sniff! sniff!* of inquiry; the sudden clear tin-horn *ko-ko-ko-óh* of the little owl; the mournful, long-drawn-out cry of the loon, instinct with the spirit of loneliness; the ethereal call-note of the birds of passage high in the air; a *patter, patter, patter* among the dead leaves, immediately stilled; and then at the last, from the thicket close at hand, the beautiful silver purity of the white-throated sparrow— the nightingale of the North—trembling with the ecstasy of beauty, as though a shimmering moonbeam had turned to sound; and all the while the blurred figure of the moon mounting to the ridge-line of your tent— these things combine subtly, until at last the great Silence of which they are a part overarches the night and draws you forth to contemplation.

No beverage is more grateful than the cup of spring water you drink at such a time; no moment more refreshing than that in which you look about you at the darkened forest. You have cast from you with the warm blanket the drowsiness of dreams. A coolness, physical and spiritual, bathes you from head to foot. All your senses are keyed to the last vibrations. You hear the littler night prowlers, you glimpse the greater. A faint, searching woods perfume of dampness greets your nostrils. And somehow, mysteriously, in a manner not to be understood, the forces of the world seem in suspense, as though a touch might crystallize infinite possibilities into infinite power and motion. But the touch lacks. The forces hover on the edge of action, unheeding the little noises. In all humbleness and awe, you are a dweller of the Silent Places.

At such a time you will meet with adventures. One night we put fourteen inquisitive porcupines out of camp. Near M'Gregor's Bay I discovered in the large grass park of my camp-site nine deer, cropping the herbage like so many beautiful ghosts. A friend tells me of a fawn that every night used to sleep outside his tent and within a foot of his head, probably by way of protection against wolves. Its mother had in all likelihood been killed. The instant my friend moved toward the tent opening the little creature would disappear, and it was always gone by earliest daylight. Nocturnal bears in search of pork are not uncommon. But even though your interest meets nothing but the bats and the woods shadows and the stars, that few moments of the sleeping world forces is a psychical experience to be gained in no other way. You cannot know the night by sitting up; she will sit up with you. Only by coming into her presence from the borders of sleep can you meet her face to face in her intimate mood.

The night wind from the river, or from the open spaces of the wilds, chills you after a time. You begin to think of your blankets. In a few moments you roll yourself in their soft wool. Instantly it is morning.

And, strange to say, you have not to pay by going through the day unrefreshed. You may feel like turning in at eight instead of nine, and you may fall asleep with unusual promptitude, but your journey will begin clear-headedly, proceed springily, and end with much in reserve. No languor, no dull headache, no exhaustion, follows your experience. For this once your two hours of sleep have been as effective as nine.

CHAPTER THIRTY

A Stream for Anglers

by W. H. H. Murray

Also known as "Adirondack Murray," William H. H. Murray (1840–1904) was an American clergyman and author of articles and books that popularized the Adirondack Mountains in upstate New York. His book Adventures in the Wilderness; or Camp Life in the Adirondacks *went through several printings, so popular was it among readers of Murray's time.*

I KNOW A STREAM AMONG THE HILLS, WHICH GLIDES DOWN STEEP declines, flows across level stretches and tumbles over rocky verges into dark ravines. Over it are white birches, and firs, and fragrant cedars, some spruces, tall and straight, and here and there an oak or mountain ash. The breezes, born of cool currents that pour downward from upper heights, where snow whitens yet, blow along this stream among the mountains full of ozone, brewed in the upper atmospheres, and which the nose of the climber drinks as the Homeric gods drank their wine, leisurely, because it is so strong and pure. In the spruces along this stream live two big, brown owls that doze through the day, and if you will sit for an hour and listen you will hear them mutter and murmur in their dreams; dreaming of mice in the meadow, and young chickens in the lowlands, I fancy. On the largest oak, old and gnarled, at the end of a dead bough, a white-headed eagle sits watchfully. Twenty feet below him his mate is hovering over four eggs in a huge nest made of dry sticks. Their eyes have seen more suns rise and set than mine, and will see the crimson long after mine are closed forever, doubtless. All men are their foes, yet they live on. All men are my friends, still I must die. Queer, isn't it?

There are anglers on this mountain stream, but only I know them. They fish each day, and each day fill their creels, and yet they use no rods, nor lines, nor hooks, nor flies, nor bait. It is because I have never fished this hidden stream myself that I have seen them fish it. Poachers? Nay. This brook is their preserve, and I would be a poacher on their rights should I cast line across it. Who are these strange anglers that angle so strangely?

The oldest of them is a snapping turtle, and a great angler he is in truth. I ambushed him as he lay asleep on a log one day, and on his back was written, A.D. 1710. That makes him one hundred and eighty years old—an age that all good anglers ought to live to. Do you tell me "That was a lie; he couldn't be so old?" It may be so—I won't quarrel with you, friend. Regard it as a bit of history, and I will agree with you. But he is a great angler, this old turtle, and has caught more trout than any angler who reads this passage—ten to one, I warrant.

The best angler of them all—better than the water-snake or the kingfisher, or the mountain cat, or the turtle, wise as he is—is an old brown mink. He is so old that his face is gray and his fur shabby, but he is a wise old angler. Six days I watched him come to the stream, and six good half-pound trout did I see the old gray veteran sit and eat on the cool, damp ledge against which the whirling bubbles ran. It was a sight to see him wash himself after his repast! And after he had thoroughly washed his mouth and cleansed his hands, he would stand and look into the deep, dark pool for a moment, contemplatively, as I fancied. Perhaps he is a deacon among the minks! Who knows? Isn't a good angler as good as a deacon, anyway?

There is a bit of meadow on the stream enclosed with a fringe of white birches and cedar growths; and amid the green grasses of it are cranberry vines, and bunches of beaver cups; white and blue flowers speck it with color, and the earth odors are strong over it. It is pleasant to stand in it and breathe in the aboriginal scents of wild roots and uncultivated mould. The untameable in me fraternizes so lovingly with this rare bit of untamed nature. This little mountain meadow, from whose stretch the beaver, with their sharp teeth, cut the trees centuries ago, is so real and genuine that it charges its influence to the very core of me. It is so natural that it makes me more so.

The old beaver dam is still there, and over it the water pours with soft noises into a deep and wide pool. On one side of this dark bit of water is a great rock. Its front is covered with thick mosses very rich in color. Across it wanders a vine with little red berries strung on it. Can you see the old beaver dam, the pool, the big rock, the moss, the running vine and the shining red berries? Yes? Very likely you can; but, oh, you who have such eyes to see—you cannot see the huge trout whose home that dark, deep pool is, and which I have seen so many times as he rose for the bug or grub that I tossed him. And once as I lay on the edge of the pool, hidden in the long grasses, I saw him at play, having a frolic all by himself, and, oh, he made that space of gloomy water iridescent as he flashed and flew through it. Where is he? Do you really wish to know? Well, I will be good and tell you. He is where I found him.

CHAPTER THIRTY-ONE

On Dry-Cow Fishing as a Fine Art

by Rudyard Kipling

World-famous novelist, poet, and journalist Rudyard Kipling (1865–1936) knew a great deal about many subjects, including trout fishing.

IT MUST BE CLEARLY UNDERSTOOD THAT I AM NOT AT ALL PROUD OF this performance. In Florida men sometimes hook and land, on rod and tackle a little finer than a steam-crane and chain, a mackerel-like fish called "tarpon," which sometimes run to 120 pounds. Those men stuff their captures and exhibit them in glass cases and become puffed up. On the Columbia River sturgeon of 150 pounds weight are taken with the line. When the sturgeon is hooked the line is fixed to the nearest pine tree or steamboat-wharf, and after some hours or days the sturgeon surrenders himself, if the pine or the line do not give way. The owner of the line then states on oath that he has caught a sturgeon, and he, too, becomes proud.

These things are mentioned to show how light a creel will fill the soul of a man with vanity. I am not proud. It is nothing to me that I have hooked and played seven hundred pounds weight of quarry. All my desire is to place the little affair on record before the mists of memory breed the miasma of exaggeration.

The minnow cost eighteenpence. It was a beautiful quill minnow, and the tackle-maker said that it could be thrown as a fly. He guaranteed further in respect to the triangles—it glittered with triangles—that, if necessary, the minnow would hold a horse. A man who speaks too much truth is just as offensive as a man who speaks too little. None the less, owing to the defective condition of the present law of libel, the tackle-maker's name must be withheld.

The minnow and I and a rod went down to a brook to attend to a small jack who lived between two clumps of flags in the most cramped swim that he could select. As a proof that my intentions were strictly honourable, I may mention that I was using a light split-cane rod—very dangerous if the line runs through weeds, but very satisfactory in clean water, inasmuch as it keeps a steady strain on the fish and prevents him from taking liberties. I had an old score against the jack. He owed me two live-bait already, and I had reason to suspect him of coming up-stream and interfering with a little bleak-pool under a horse-bridge which lay entirely beyond his sphere of legitimate influence. Observe, therefore, that my tackle and my motives pointed clearly to jack, and jack alone; though I knew that there were monstrous big perch in the brook.

The minnow was thrown as a fly several times, and, owing to my peculiar, and hitherto unpublished, methods of fly throwing, nearly six pennyworth of the triangles came off, either in my coat-collar, or my thumb, or the back of my hand. Fly fishing is a very gory amusement.

The jack was not interested in the minnow, but towards twilight a boy opened a gate of the field and let in some twenty or thirty cows and half-a-dozen cart-horses, and they were all very much interested. The horses galloped up and down the field and shook the banks, but the cows walked solidly and breathed heavily, as people breathe who appreciate the Fine Arts.

By this time I had given up all hope of catching my jack fairly, but I wanted the live-bait and bleak-account settled before I went away, even if I tore up the bottom of the brook. Just before I had quite made up my mind to borrow a tin of chloride of lime from the farm-house—another triangle had fixed itself in my fingers—I made a cast which for pure skill, exact judgement of distance, and perfect coincidence of hand and eye and brain, would have taken every prize at a bait-casting tournament. That was the first half of the cast. The second was postponed because the quill minnow would not return to its proper place, which was under the lobe of my left ear. It had done thus before, and I supposed it was in collision with a grass tuft, till I turned round and saw a large red and white bald faced cow trying to rub what would be withers in a horse with her nose. She looked at me reproachfully, and her look said as plainly as words: "The season is too far advanced for gadflies. What is this strange disease?"

I replied, "Madam, I must apologize for an unwarrantable liberty on the part of my minnow, but if you will have the goodness to keep still until I can reel in, we will adjust this little difficulty."

I reeled in very swiftly and cautiously, but she would not wait. She put her tail in the air and ran away. It was a purely involuntary motion on my part: I struck. Other anglers may contradict me, but I firmly believe that if a man had foul-hooked his best friend through the nose, and that friend ran, the man would strike by instinct. I struck, therefore, and the reel began to sing just as merrily as though I had caught my jack. But had it been a jack, the minnow would have come away. I told the tackle-maker this much afterwards, and he laughed and made allusions to the guarantee about holding a horse.

Because it was a fat innocent she-cow that had done me no harm the minnow held—held like an anchor-fluke in coral moorings—and I was forced to dance up and down an interminable field very largely used by cattle. It was like salmon fishing in a nightmare. I took gigantic strides, and every stride found me up to my knees in marsh. But the cow seemed to skate along the squashy green by the brook, to skim over the miry backwaters, and to float like a mist through the patches of rush that squirted black filth over my face. Sometimes we whirled through a mob of her friends—there were no friends to help me—and they looked scandalized; and sometimes a young and frivolous cart-horse would join in the chase for a few miles, and kick solid pieces of mud into my eyes; and through all the mud, the milky smell of kine, the rush and the smother, I was aware of my own voice crying: "Pussy, pussy, pussy! Pretty pussy! Come along then, puss-cat!" You see it is so hard to speak to a cow properly, and she would not listen—no, she would not listen.

Then she stopped, and the moon got up behind the pollards to tell the cows to lie down; but they were all on their feet, and they came trooping to see. And she said, "I haven't had my supper, and I want to go to bed, and please don't worry me." And I said, "The matter has passed beyond any apology. There are three courses open to you, my dear lady. If you'll have the common sense to walk up to my creel I'll get my knife and you shall have all the minnow. Or, again, if you'll let me move across to your near side, instead of keeping me so coldly on your off side, the thing will come away in one tweak. I can't pull it out over your withers. Better still, go to a post and rub it out, dear. It won't hurt much, but if you think I'm going to lose my rod to please you, you are mistaken." And she said, "I don't understand what you are saying. I am very, very unhappy." And I said, "It's all your fault for trying to fish. Do go to the nearest gate-post, you nice fat thing, and rub it out."

For a moment I fancied she was taking my advice. She ran away and I followed. But all the other cows came with us in a bunch, and I thought of Phaeton trying to drive the Chariot of the Sun, and Texan cowboys killed by stampeding cattle, and "*Green Grow the Rushes O!*" and Solomon and Job, and "loosing the bands of Orion," and hooking Behemoth, and Wordsworth who talks about whirling round with stones and rocks and trees, and "Here we go round the Mulberry Bush," and "Pippin Hill," and "Hey Diddle Diddle," and most especially the top joint of my rod. Again she stopped—but nowhere in the neighborhood of my knife—and her sisters stood moonfaced round her. It seemed that she might, now, run towards me, and I looked for a tree, because cows are very different from salmon, who only jump against the line, and never molest the fisherman. What followed was worse than any direct attack. She began to buck-jump, to stand on her head and her tail alternately, to leap into the sky, all four feet together, and to dance on her hind legs. It was so violent and improper, so desperately unladylike, that I was inclined to blush, as one would blush at the sight of a prominent statesman sliding down a fire escape, or a duchess chasing her cook with a skillet. That flopsome *abandon* might go on all night in the lonely meadow among the mists, and if it went on all night—this was pure inspiration—I might be able to worry through the fishing line with my teeth.

Those who desire an entirely new sensation should chew with all their teeth, and against time, through a best waterproofed silk line, one end of which belongs to a mad cow dancing fairy rings in the moonlight;

at the same time keeping one eye on the cow and the other on the top joint of a split-cane rod. She buck-jumped and I bit on the slack just in front of the reel; and I am in a position to state that that line was cored with steel wire throughout the particular section which I attacked. This has been formally denied by the tackle-maker, who is not to be believed.

The *wheep* of the broken line running through the rings told me that henceforth the cow and I might be strangers. I had already bidden good-bye to some tooth or teeth; but no price is too great for freedom of the soul.

"Madam," I said, "the minnow and twenty feet of very superior line are your alimony without reservation. For the wrong I have unwittingly done to you I express my sincere regret. At the same time, may I hope that Nature, the kindest of nurses, will in due season—"

She or one of her companions must have stepped on her spare end of the line in the dark, for she bellowed wildly and ran away, followed by all the cows. I hoped the minnow was disengaged at last; and before I went away looked at my watch, fearing to find it nearly midnight. My last cast for the jack was made at 6:23 p.m. There lacked still three and a half minutes of the half-hour; and I would have sworn that the moon was paling before the dawn!

"Simminly someone were chasing they cows down to bottom o' Ten Acre," said the farmer that evening. "'Twasn't you, sir?"

"Now under what earthly circumstances do you suppose I should chase your cows? I wasn't fishing for them, was I?"

Then all the farmer's family gave themselves up to jam-smeared laughter for the rest of the evening, because that was a rare and precious jest, and it was repeated for months, and the fame of it spread from that farm to another, and yet another at least three miles away, and it will be used again for the benefit of visitors when the freshets come down in spring.

But to the greater establishment of my honour and glory I submit in print this bald statement of fact, that I may not, through forgetfulness, be tempted later to tell how I hooked a bull on a Marlow Buzz, how he ran up a tree and took to water, and how I played him along the London-road for thirty miles, and gaffed him at Smithfield. Errors of this kind may creep in with the lapse of years, and it is my ambition ever to be a worthy member of that fraternity who pride themselves on never deviating by one hair's breadth from the absolute and literal truth.

CHAPTER THIRTY-TWO

A Bit of Luck

by Harry Plunket Greene

Harry Plunket Greene (June 24, 1865–August 19, 1936) was an Irish baritone who was most famous in the formal concert and oratorio repertoire. He also wrote Where the Bright Waters Meet *(1924), a classic book about* fly fishing.

I HAD AN EXPERIENCE WITH A TROUT ON THE KENNET, WHICH I ALWAYS associate, quite undeservedly, with "snatching." It was in 1922, and I was staying with Mr. Giveen, who had taken the Mill fishing from Col. Grove-Hills for the latter half of the season. He and I had often stood on the bridge at the top, where the water falls down from the lake of Ramsbury Manor, and hungrily objurgated the great fat three-pounders which laughed at us from beneath. These were rovers by profession, and never stayed long enough in one place to be fished for individually from below; and were up to every trick from above. They would lie with their noses on the ledge immediately underneath us, and dreamily watch the smoke from our pipes ascending to the blue; but the moment the top of a rod appeared over the edge, off they went. We tried concerted action many times, but as soon as ever one of the watchers disappeared from the bridge the pool was abandoned to two-year-olds. On this occasion I was passing by the sluice which forms a small side-carrier to the main fall and I put my head casually over the side, expecting nothing, and there right below me was a big golden trout tucked up under the boards, with his head down-stream and his tail up against the cracks where the water spurted through. He was doing no good there, so I felt it was my duty to get him.

It was an awful prospect. Immediately below him two planks ran across the sluice at intervals of about eight feet, and below them again in the fairway there was a veritable barricade of posts sticking up out of the stream in ragged profusion. There were three on the near side and two on the far side and a gaunt rubbing-post in the middle acting as a buoy, round which every sporting fish was in honor bound to double. Below these again there was another pole running right across the stream only four inches above the water, which swirled under it at a great pace. A more hopeless barbed-wire entanglement it would be hard to imagine to try and fish a fish out of, even if one hooked him. However, he was a beauty, and the fact that he was practically ungetable made it all the more exciting. I had up the ordinary tackle; by all the laws of caution I should have put up a ginger-quill with a No. 1 hook and a May-fly cast, but I reflected that if he got tangled up in the barriers a steel hawser would not hold him, and that if by some amazing fluke he ever came through, the fine tackle would be as good as anything else. Moreover, I should be able to swagger to the others about 4X casts and 000 hooks even more insupportably than before; so I stuck to what I had.

I stood well back where I could just see the tip of his nose and he could not see me, reeled in the line to within six inches of the cast, and gently dropped the fly on to him. It was at once carried out by the stream. I thought it was going to be hopeless, when to my intense delight the back eddy swirled it round at exactly the right moment and brought it over him again. It was then seized once more by the stream and carried off afresh. The process was repeated automatically without my having to do a thing, and there went my fly playing "last across" with him, rushing up the backwater, tweaking his nose and dashing off downstream before he could say a word. I was so delighted and laughing so hard that I could not help crawling up to see the fun, and put my head over to have a look. He was intently absorbed in the game and never saw me. He appeared to take no notice at first and treated it all with dignified unconcern, but as the impudent little beast dashed past him smothering him with insults he began to get impatient, and I saw his tail detach itself from the sluice-board and begin to wag. Then he began to shake his head and bunch himself to attack. But nothing happened for a long time and I was just going to give it up, as my arm was getting tired from the unnatural position, when I had a wonderful bit of luck. There was a twig sticking out from the wall on the far side over the back eddy, and the gut caught over it, and, before I knew it, there was the fly bobbing up and down in the water, right in front of him. This was too much. His enemy was delivered into his hands.

He leaped at it, seized it, knew in a moment what had happened, and dashed off down-stream under the planks and through the posts and out into the pool at the bottom. There I had to leave him for a long time to settle himself, with my rod bent double under the first plank. Then the fun began. I cautiously passed it under this with one hand and retrieved it with the other and did the same with the second plank. All idea of keeping the line taut was perforce abandoned. I still had the six upright posts and the flat pole beyond to negotiate. If he once got tangled up in these it would be all over. He was near the top of the pool now, and I lay flat on the ground with the point of the rod out in the space between me and the centre post, terrified lest he should swim up on the near side of A post, catch sight of me, and dash down on the far side or pay a visit to X, Y or Z post. I clung to Mother Earth like a tiger-skin on a polished oak floor. Sure enough, up he came. He swam through the near channel and roamed about under my eyes (or the corner of one of them) for about a fortnight apparently, and then swam slowly back to the pool the same way he had come!

It was almost too good to be true! But the crux was still to be faced—there was still the flat pole to get under. It ran across the top of the pool, with a space of about four inches between it and the water. It was a bare two inches thick and it was quite rotten. I had to get the rod under it somehow (for I could never risk letting him out of the pool again), and I could only just reach it with my hand by holding on to the bank above with my toes and descending apoplectically towards the water. It cracked loudly the moment I touched it. I had to lean hard on the horrible thing with my right hand, pass the rod under with my left, scrabble it out again somehow with my right on the other side, change hands and work myself back up the bank. It groaned and shivered its timbers and fired off shots like a machine-gun—but the little iron-blue had squared it and it held. It was not all over even then, for if the fish had caught sight of me he would have dashed up through the uprights again; so I backed slowly out of sight into a withy-bed and stayed there till there was not a kick left in him. As a matter of fact, he had done it all for me by returning through the posts the same way he had come. The only credit I can take is for keeping out of sight and performing gymnastics with an almost superhuman skill for one of my size and weight. He weighed 2¼ lbs.

CHAPTER THIRTY-THREE

A Fatal Salmon

by Frank Forester

Henry William Herbert (April 7, 1807–May 17, 1858), pen name Frank Forester, was a British-born American novelist, poet, historian, illustrator, journalist, and writer on sport.

IT WAS AS FAIR A MORNING OF JULY AS EVER DAWNED IN THE BLUE SUMmer sky; the sun as yet had risen but a little way above the waves of fresh green foliage which formed the horizon of the woodland scenery surrounding Widecomb Manor; and his heat, which promised ere mid-day to become excessive, was tempered now by the exhalations of the copious night-dews, and by the cool breath of the western breeze, which came down through the leafy gorges, in long, soft swells from the open moorlands.

All nature was alive and joyous; the air was vocal with the piping melody of the blackbirds and thrushes, carolling in every brake and bosky dingle; the smooth, green lawn before the windows of the old Hall was peopled with whole tribes of fat, lazy hares, limping about among the dewy herbage, fearless, as it would seem, of man's aggression; and to complete the picture, above, a score of splendid peacocks were strutting to and fro on the paved terraces, or perched upon the carved stone balustrades, displaying their gorgeous plumage to the early sunshine.

The shadowy mists of the first morning twilight had not been dispersed from the lower regions, and were suspended still in the middle air in broad fleecy masses, though melting rapidly away in the increasing warmth and brightness of the day.

And still a faint blue line hovered over the bed of the long rocky gorge, which divided the chase from the open country, floating about it like the steam of a seething caldron, and rising here and there into tall smoke-like columns, probably where some steeper cataract of the mountain-stream sent its foam skyward.

So early, indeed, was the hour, that had my tale been recited of these degenerate days, there would have been no gentle eyes awake to look upon the loveliness of new-awakened nature.

In the good days of old, however, when daylight was still deemed to be the fitting time for labor and for pastime, and night the appointed time for natural and healthful sleep, the dawn was wont to brighten beheld by other eyes than those of clowns and milkmaids, and the gay songs of the matutinal birds were listened to by ears that could appreciate their untaught melodies.

And now, just as the stable clock was striking four, the great oaken door of the old Hall was thrown open with a vigorous swing that made it rattle on its hinges, and Jasper St. Aubyn came bounding out into the fresh morning air, with a foot as elastic as that of the mountain roe, singing a snatch of some quaint old ballad.

He was dressed simply in a close-fitting jacket and tight hose of dark-green cloth, without any lace or embroidery, light boots of untanned leather, and a broad-leafed hat, with a single eagle's feather thrust carelessly through the band. He wore neither cloak nor sword, though it was a period at which gentlemen rarely went abroad without these, their distinctive attributes; but in the broad black belt which girt his rounded waist he carried a stout wood-knife with a buckhorn hilt; and over his shoulder there swung from a leathern thong a large wicker fishing-basket.

Nothing, indeed, could be simpler or less indicative of any particular rank or station in society than young St. Aubyn's garb, yet it would have been a very dull and unobservant eye which should take him for aught less than a high-born and high-bred gentleman.

His fine intellectual face, his bearing erect before heaven, the graceful ease of his every motion, as he hurried down the flagged steps of the terrace, and planted his light foot on the dewy greensward, all betokened gentle birth and gentle associations.

But he thought nothing of himself, nor cared for his advantages, acquired or natural. The long and heavy salmon-rod which he carried in his right hand, in three pieces as yet unconnected, did not more clearly indicate his purpose than the quick marking glance which he cast toward the half-veiled sun and hazy sky, scanning the signs of the weather.

"It will do, it will do," he said to himself, thinking as it were aloud, "for three or four hours at least; the sun will not shake off those vapors before eight o'clock at the earliest, and if he do come out then hot and strong, I do not know but the water is dark enough after the late rains to serve my turn a while longer. It will blow up, too, I think, from the westward, and there will be a brisk curl on the pools. But come, I must be moving, if I would reach Darringford to breakfast."

And as he spoke he strode out rapidly across the park toward the deep chasm of the stream, crushing a thousand aromatic perfumes from the dewy wild-flowers with his heedless foot, and thinking little of the beauties of nature, as he hastened to the scene of his loved exercise.

It was not long, accordingly, before he reached the brink of the steep rocky bank above the stream, which he proposed to fish that morning, and paused to select the best place for descending to the water's edge.

It was, indeed, as striking and romantic a scene as ever met the eye of painter or of poet. On the farther side of the gorge, scarcely a hundred yards distant, the dark limestone rocks rose sheer and precipitous from the very brink of the stream, rifted and broken into angular blocks and tall columnar masses, from the clefts of which, wherever they could find soil enough to support their scanty growth, a few stunted oaks shot out almost horizontally with their gnarled arms and dark-green foliage, and here and there the silvery bark and quivering tresses of the birch relieved the monotony of color by their gay brightness. Above, the cliffs were crowned with the beautiful purple heather, now in its very glow of summer bloom, about which were buzzing myriads of wild bees, sipping their nectar from its cups of amethyst.

The hither side, though rough and steep and broken, was not, in the place where Jasper stood, precipitous; indeed it seemed as if at some distant period a sort of landslip had occurred, by which the summit of the rocky wall had been broken into massive fragments, and hurled down in an inclined plane into the bed of the stream, on which it had encroached with its shattered blocks and rounded boulders.

Time, however, had covered all this abrupt and broken slope with a beautiful growth of oak and hazel coppice, among which, only at distant intervals, could the dun weather-beaten flanks of the great stones be discovered.

At the base of this descent, a hundred and fifty feet perhaps below the stand of the young sportsman, flowed the dark arrowy stream—a wild and perilous water. As clear as crystal, yet as dark as the brown cairngorm, it came pouring down among the broken rocks with a rapidity and force which showed what must be its fury when swollen by a storm among the mountains, here breaking into wreaths of rippling foam where some unseen ledge chafed its current, there roaring and surging white as December's snow among the great round-headed rocks, and there again wheeling in sullen eddies, dark and deceitful, round and round some deep rock-rimmed basin.

Here and there, indeed, it spread out into wide, shallow, rippling rapids, filling the whole bottom of the ravine from side to side, but more generally it did not occupy above a fourth part of the space below, leaving sometimes on this margin, sometimes on that, broad pebbly banks, or slaty ledges, affording an easy footing and a clear path to the angler in its troubled waters.

After a rapid glance over the well-known scene, Jasper plunged into the coppice, and following a faint track worn by the feet of the wild-deer in the first instance, and widened by his own bolder tread, soon reached the bottom of the chasm, though not until he had flushed from the dense oak covert two noble black cocks with their superb forked tails, and glossy purple-lustered plumage, which soared away, crowing their bold defiance, over the heathery moorlands.

Once at the water's edge, the young man's tackle was speedily made ready, and in a few minutes his long line went whistling through the air, as he wielded the powerful two-handed rod, as easily as if it had been a stripling's reed, and the large gaudy peacock-fly alighted on the wheeling eddies, at the tail of a long arrowy shoot, as gently as if it had settled from too long a flight. Delicately, deftly, it was made to dance and skim the clear, brown surface, until it had crossed the pool and neared the hither bank; then again, obedient to the pliant wrist, it arose on glittering wing, circled half around the angler's head, and was set fifteen yards aloof, straight as a wild bee's flight, into a little mimic whirlpool, scarce larger than the hat of the skilful fisherman, which spun round and round just to leeward of a gray ledge of limestone. Scarce had it reached its mark before the water broke all around it, and the gay deceit vanished, the heavy swirl of the surface, as the break was closing, indicating the great size of the fish which had risen. Just as the swirl was subsiding, and the forked tail of the monarch of the stream was half seen as he descended, that indescribable but well-known turn of the angler's wrist, fixed the barbed hook, and taught the scaly victim the nature of the prey he had gorged so heedlessly.

With a wild bound he threw himself three feet out of the water, showing his silver sides, with the sea-lice yet clinging to his scales, a fresh sea-run fish of fifteen, ay, eighteen pounds, and perhaps over.

On his broad back he strikes the water, but not as he meant the tightened line; for as he leaped the practised hand had lowered the rod's tip, that it fell in a loose bight below him. Again! again! again! and yet a fourth time he bounded into the air with desperate and vigorous *soubre-saults*, like an unbroken steed that would dismount his rider, lashing the eddies of the dark stream into bright bubbling streaks, and making the heart of his captor beat high with anticipation of the desperate struggle that should follow, before the monster should lie panting and exhausted on the yellow sand or moist greensward.

Away! with the rush of an eagle through the air, he is gone like an arrow down the rapids—how the reel rings, and the line whistles from the swift working wheel; he is too swift, too headstrong to be checked as yet; tenfold the strength of that slender tackle might not control him in his first fiery rush.

But Jasper, although young in years, was old in the art, and skilful as the craftiest of the gentle craftsmen. He gives him the butt of his rod steadily, trying the strength of his tackle with a delicate and gentle finger, giving him line at every rush, yet firmly, cautiously, feeling his mouth all the while, and moderating his speed even while he yields to his fury.

Meanwhile, with the eye of intuition, and the nerve of iron, he bounds along the difficult shore, he leaps from rock to rock, alighting on their slippery tops with the firm agility of the rope-dancer, he splashes knee-deep through the slippery shallows, keeping his line ever taut, inclining his rod over his shoulder, bearing on his fish ever with a killing pull, steering him clear of every rock or stump against which he would fain smash the tackle, and landing him at length in a fine open roomy pool, at the foot of a long stretch of white and foamy rapids, down which he has just piloted him with the eye of faith, and the foot of instinct.

And now the great Salmon has turned sulky; like a piece of lead he has sunk to the bottom of the deep black pool, and lies on the gravel bottom in the sullenness of despair.

Jasper stooped, gathered up in his left hand a heavy pebble, and pitched it into the pool, as nearly as he could guess to the whereabouts of his game—another—and another! Aha! that last has roused him. Again he throws himself clear out of water, and again foiled in his attempt to smash the tackle, dashes away down stream impetuous.

But his strength is departing—the vigor of his rush is broken. The angler gives him the butt abundantly, strains on him with a heavier pull, yet ever yields a little as he exerts his failing powers; see, his broad, silver side has thrice turned up, even to the surface, and though each time he has recovered himself, each time it has been with a heavier and more sickly motion.

Brave fellow! his last race is run, his last spring sprung—no more shall he disport himself in the bright reaches of the Tamar; no more shall the Naiads wreathe his clear silver scales with river-greens and flowery rushes.

The cruel gaff is in his side—his cold blood stains the eddies for a moment—he flaps out his deathpang on the hard limestone.

"Who-whoop! a nineteen-pounder!"

Meantime the morning had worn onward, and ere the great fish was brought to the basket, the sun had soared clear above the mist-wreaths, and had risen so high into the summer heaven that his slant rays poured down into the gorge of the stream, and lighted up the clear depths with a lustre so transparent that every pebble at the bottom might have been discerned, with the large fish here and there floating mid-depth, with their heads upstream, their gills working with a quick motion, and their broad tails vibrating at short intervals slowly but powerfully, as they lay motionless in opposition to the very strongest of the swift current.

The breeze had died away, there was no curl upon the water, and the heat was oppressive.

Under such circumstances, to whip the stream was little better than mere loss of time, yet as he hurried with a fleet foot down the gorge, perhaps with some ulterior object, beyond the mere love of sport, Jasper at times cast his fly across the stream, and drew it neatly, and, as he thought, irresistibly, right over the recusant fish; but though once or twice a large lazy Salmon would sail up slowly from the depths, and almost touch the fly with his nose, he either sunk down slowly in disgust, without breaking the water, or flapped his broad tail over the shining fraud as if to mark his contempt.

It had now got to be near noon, for, in the ardor of his success, the angler had forgotten all about his intended breakfast; and, his first fish captured, had contented himself with a slender meal furnished from out his fishing-basket and his leathern bottle.

Jasper had traversed by this time some ten miles in length, following the sinuosities of the stream, and had reached a favorite pool at the head of a long, straight, narrow trench, cut by the waters themselves in the course of time, through the hard schistous rock which walls the torrent on each hand, not leaving the slightest ledge or margin between the rapids and the precipice.

Through this wild gorge of some fifty yards in length, the river shoots like an arrow over a steep inclined plane of limestone rock, the surface of which is polished by the action of the water, till it is as slippery as ice, and at the extremity leaps down a sheer descent of some twelve feet into a large, wide basin, surrounded by softly swelling banks of greensward, and a fair amphitheatre of woodland.

At the upper end this pool is so deep as to be vulgarly deemed unfathomable; below, however, it expands yet wider into a shallow rippling ford, where it is crossed by the high-road, down stream of which again there is another long, sharp rapid, and another fall, over the last steps of the hills; after which the nature of the stream becomes changed, and it murmurs gently onward through a green pastoral country, unrippled and uninterrupted.

Just in the inner angle of the high-road, on the right hand of the stream, there stood an old-fashioned, low-browed, thatch-covered stone cottage, with a rude portico of rustic woodwork overrun with jasmine and virgin-bower, and a pretty flower garden sloping down in successive terraces to the edge of the basin. Beside this, there was no other house in sight, unless it were part of the roof of a mill which stood in the low ground on the brink of the second fall, surrounded with a mass of willows. But the tall steeple of a country church, raising itself heavenward above the brow of the hill, seemed to show that, although concealed by the undulations of the ground, a village was hard at hand.

The morning had changed a second time, a hazy film had crept up to the zenith, and the sun was now covered with a pale golden veil, and a slight current of air down the gorge ruffled the water.

It was a capital pool, famous for being the temporary haunt of the very finest fish, which were wont to lie there awhile, as if to recruit themselves after the exertions of leaping the two falls and stemming the double rapid, before attempting to ascend the stream farther.

Few, however, even of the best and boldest fishermen, cared to wet a line in its waters, in consequence of the supposed impossibility of following a heavy fish through the gorge below, or checking him at the brink of the fall. It is true, that throughout the length of the pass, the current was broken by bare, slippery rocks peering above the waters, at intervals, which might be cleared by an active cragsman; and it had been in fact reconnoitred by Jasper and others in cool blood, but the result of the examination was that it was deemed impassable.

Thinking, however, little of striking a large fish, and perhaps desiring to waste a little time before scaling the banks and emerging on the high-road, Jasper threw a favorite fly of peacock's herl and gold tinsel lightly across the water; and, almost before he had time to think, had hooked a monstrous fish, which, at the very first leap, he set down as weighing at least thirty pounds.

Thereupon followed a splendid display of piscatory skill. Well knowing that his fish must be lost if he once should succeed in getting his head down the rapid, Jasper exerted every nerve, and exhausted every art to humor, to meet, to restrain, to check him. Four times the fish rushed for the pass, and four times Jasper met him so stoutly with the butt, trying his tackle to the very utmost, that he succeeded in forcing him from the perilous spot. Round and round the pool he had piloted him, and had taken post at length, hoping that the worst was already over, close to the opening of the rocky chasm.

And now perhaps waxing too confident, he checked his fish too sharply. Stung into fury, the monster sprang five times in succession into the air, lashing the water with his angry tail, and then rushed like an arrow down the chasm.

He was gone—but Jasper's blood was up, and thinking of nothing but his sport, he dashed forward, and embarked, with a fearless foot, into the terrible descent.

Leap after leap he took with beautiful precision, alighting firm and erect on the centre of each slippery block, and bounding thence to the next with unerring instinct, guiding his fish the while with consummate skill through the intricacies of the pass.

There were now but three more leaps to be taken before he would reach the flat table-rock above the fall, which once attained, he would have firm foothold and a fair field; already he rejoiced, triumphant in the success of his bold attainment, and confident in victory, when a shrill female shriek reached his ears from the pretty flower-garden; caught by the sound, he diverted his eyes, just as he leaped, toward the place whence it came; his foot slipped, and the next instant he was flat on his back in the swifter stream, where it shot the most furiously over the glassy rock. He struggled manfully, but in vain. The smooth, slippery surface afforded no purchase to his gripping fingers, no hold to his laboring feet. One fearful, agonizing conflict with the wild waters, and he was swept helplessly over the edge of the fall, his head, as he glanced down foot foremost, striking the rocky brink with fearful violence.

He was plunged into the deep pool, and whirled round and round by the dark eddies long before he rose, but still, though stunned and half-disabled, he strove terribly to support himself, but it was all in vain.

Again he sunk and rose once more, and as he rose that wild shriek again reached his ears, and his last glance fell upon a female form wringing her hands in despair on the bank, and a young man rushing down in wild haste from the cottage on the hill.

He felt that aid was at hand, and struck out again for life—for dear life!

But the water seemed to fail beneath him.

A slight flash sprang across his eyes, his brain reeled, and all was blackness.

He sunk to the bottom, spurned it with his feet, and rose once more, but not to the surface.

His quivering blue hands emerged alone above the relentless waters, grasped for a little moment at empty space, and then disappeared.

The circling ripples closed over him, and subsided into stillness.

He felt, knew, suffered nothing more.

His young, warm heart was cold and lifeless—his soul had lost its consciousness—the vital spark had faded into darkness—perhaps was quenched for ever.

CHAPTER THIRTY-FOUR

A Gallant Poacher

by John Buchan

John Buchan (1875–1940) was a Scottish novelist, historian, and politician who did much of his writing while serving government posts in the UK and Canada. He was an avid outdoorsman, whose many works reflect that interest. His most famous novel was the thriller The 39 Steps, *reprinted many times and a popular movie.*

WHEN THE HISPANA CROSSED THE BRIDGE OF LARRIG, HIS MAJESTY'S late Attorney-General was modestly concealed in a bush of broom on the Crask side, from which he could watch the sullen stretches of the Lang Whang. He was carefully dressed for the part in a pair of Wattie Lithgow's old trousers much too short for him, a waistcoat and jacket which belonged to Sime the butler and which had been made about the year 1890, and a vulgar flannel shirt borrowed from Shapp. He was innocent of a collar, he had not shaved for two days, and as he had forgotten to have his hair cut before leaving London his locks were of a disreputable length. Last, he had a shocking old hat of Sir Archie's from which the lining had long since gone. His hands were sunburnt and grubby, and he had removed his signet-ring. A light ten-foot greenheart rod lay beside him, already put up, and to the tapered line was fixed a tapered cast ending in a strange little cocked fly. As he waited, he was busy oiling fly and line.

His glass showed him an empty haugh, save for the figure of Jimsie at the far end close to the Wood of Larrigmore. The sun-warmed waters of the river drowsed in the long dead stretches, curled at rare intervals by the faintest western breeze. The banks were crisp green turf, scarcely broken by a boulder, but five yards from them the moss began—a wilderness of hags and tussocks. Somewhere in its depths he knew that Benjie lay coiled like an adder, waiting on events.

Leithen's plan, like all great strategy, was simple. Everything depended on having Jimsie out of sight of the Lang Whang for half an hour. Given that, he believed he might kill a salmon. He had marked out a pool where in the evening fish were usually stirring, one of those irrational haunts which no piscatorial psychologist has ever explained. If he could fish fine and far, he might cover it from a spot below a high bank where only the top of his rod would be visible to watchers at a distance. Unfortunately, that spot was on the other side of the stream. With such tackle, landing a salmon would be a critical business, but there was one chance in ten that it might be accomplished; Benjie would be at hand to conceal the fish, and he himself would disappear silently into the Crask thickets. But every step bristled with horrid dangers. Jimsie might be faithful to his post—in which case it was hopeless; he might find the salmon dour, or a fish might break him in the landing, or Jimsie might return to find him brazenly tethered to forbidden game. It was no good thinking about it. On one thing he was decided; if he were caught, he would not try to escape. That would mean retreat in the direction of Crask, and an exploration of the Crask covers would assuredly reveal what must at all costs be concealed. No. He would go quietly into captivity, and trust to his base appearance to let off with a drubbing.

As he waited, watching the pools turn from gold to bronze, as the sun sank behind the Glenraden peaks, he suffered the inevitable reaction. The absurdities seemed huge as mountains, the difficulties innumerable as the waves of the sea. There remained less than an hour in which there would be sufficient light to fish—Jimsie was immovable (he had just lit his pipe and was sitting in meditation on a big stone)—every moment the Larrig waters were cooling with the chill of evening. Leithen consulted his watch, and found it half-past eight. He had lost his wrist-watch, and had brought his hunter, attached to a thin gold chain. That was foolish, so he slipped the chain from his buttonhole and drew it through the arm-hole of his waistcoat.

Suddenly he rose to his feet, for things were happening at the far end of the haugh. Jimsie stood in an attitude of expectation—he seemed to be hearing something far up-stream. Leithen heard it too, the cry of excited men . . . Jimsie stood on one foot for a moment in doubt, then he turned and doubled toward the Wood of Larrigmore. . . . The gallant Crossby had got to business and was playing hare to the hounds inside the park wall. If human nature had not changed, Leithen thought, the whole force would presently join in the chase—Angus and Lennox and Jimsie and Davie and doubtless many volunteers. Heaven send fleetness and wind to the South London Harrier, for it was his duty to occupy the interest of every male in Strathlarrig till such time as he subsided with angry expostulations in captivity.

The road was empty, the valley was deserted, when Leithen raced across the bridge and up the south side of the river. It was not two hundred yards to his chosen stand, a spit of gravel below a high bank at the tail of a long pool. Close to the other bank, nearly thirty yards off, was the shelf where fish lay of an evening. He tested the water with his hand, and its temperature was at least sixty degrees. His theory, which he had learned long ago from the aged Bostonian, was that under such conditions some subconscious memory revived in salmon of their early days as parr when they fed on surface insects, and that they could be made to take a dry fly.

He got out his line to the required length with half a dozen casts in the air, and then put his fly three feet above the spot where a salmon was wont to lie. It was a curious type of cast, which he had been practising lately in the early morning, for by an adroit check he made the fly alight in a curl, so that it floated for a second or two with the leader in a straight line away from it. In this way he believed that the most suspicious fish would see nothing to alarm him, nothing but a hapless insect derelict on the water.

Sir Archie had spoken truth in describing Leithen to Wattie Lithgow as an artist. His long, straight, delicate casts were art indeed. Like thistledown the fly dropped, like thistledown it floated over the head of the salmon, but like thistledown it was disregarded. There was, indeed, a faint stirring of curiosity. From where he stood Leithen could see that slight ruffling of the surface which means an observant fish. . . .

Already ten minutes had been spent in this barren art. The crisis craved other measures.

His new policy meant a short line, so with infinite stealth and care Leithen waded up the side of the water, sometimes treading precarious ledges of peat, sometimes waist-deep in mud and pond-weed, till he was within twenty feet of the fishing-ground. Here he had not the high bank for a shelter, and would have been sadly conspicuous to Jimsie, had that sentinel remained at his post. He crouched low and cast as before with the same curl just ahead of the chosen spot.

But now his tactics were different. So soon as the fly had floated past where he believed the fish to be, he sank it by a dexterous twist of the rod-point, possible only with a short line. The fly was no longer a winged thing; drawn away under water, it roused in the salmon early memories of succulent nymphs.

. . . At the first cast there was a slight swirl which meant that a fish near the surface had turned to follow the lure. The second cast the line straightened and moved swiftly up-stream.

Leithen had killed in his day many hundreds of salmon—once in Norway a notable beast of fifty-five pounds. But no salmon he had ever hooked had stirred in his breast such excitement as this modest fellow of eight pounds. "'Tis not so wide as a church-door," he reflected with Mercutio, "but 'twill suffice"—if I can only land him. But a dry-fly cast and a ten-foot rod are a frail wherewithal for killing a fish against time. With his ordinary fifteen-footer and gut of moderate strength he could have brought the little salmon to grass in five minutes, but now there was immense risk of a break, and a break would mean that the whole enterprise had failed. He dared not exert pressure; on the other hand, he could not follow the fish except by making himself conspicuous on the greensward. Worst of all, he had at the best ten minutes for the job.

Thirty yards off, an otter slid into the water. Leithen wished he was King of the Otters, as in the Highland tale, to summon the brute to his aid.

The ten minutes had lengthened to fifteen—nine hundred seconds of heart disease—when, wet to the waist, he got his pocket gaff into the salmon's side and drew it on to the spit of gravel where he had started fishing. A dozen times he thought he had lost, and once when the fish ran straight up the pool his line was carried out to its last yard of backing. He gave thanks to high Heaven, when, as he landed it, he observed that the fly had all but lost its hold and in another minute would have been freed. By such narrow margins are great deeds accomplished.

He snapped the cast from the line and buried it in mud. Then cautiously he raised his head above the high bank. The gloaming was gathering fast, and so far as he could see the haugh was still empty. Pushing his rod along the ground he scrambled on to the turf.

Then he had a grievous shock. Jimsie had reappeared, and he was in full view of him. Moreover, there were two men on bicycles coming up the road, who, with the deplorable instinct of human nature, would be certain to join in any pursuit. He was on turf as short as a lawn, cumbered with a telltale rod and a poached salmon. The friendly hags were a dozen yards off, and before he could reach them his damning baggage would be noted.

At this supreme moment he had an inspiration, derived from the memory of the otter. To get out his knife, cut a ragged wedge from the fish, and roll it in his handkerchief was the work of three seconds. To tilt the rod over the bank so that it lay in the deep shadow was the work of three more. . . . Jimsie had seen him, for a wild cry came down the stream, a cry which brought the cyclists off their machines and set them staring in his direction. Leithen dropped his gaff after the rod, and began running towards the Larrig Bridge—slowly, limpingly, like a frightened man with no resolute purpose of escape. And as he ran he prayed that Benjie from the deeps of the moss had seen what had been done and drawn the proper inference.

It was a bold bluff, for he had decided to make the salmon evidence for, not against, him. He hobbled down the bank, looking over his shoulder often as if in terror, and almost ran into the arms of the cyclists, who, warned by Jimsie's yells, were waiting to intercept him. He dodged them, however, and cut across to the road, for he had seen that Jimsie had paused and had noted the salmon lying blatantly on the sward, a silver splash in the twilight. Leithen doubled up the road as if going towards Strathlarrig, and Jimsie, the fleet of foot, did not catch up with him till almost on the edge of the Wood of Larrigmore. The cyclists, who had remounted, arrived at the same moment to find a wretched muddy tramp in the grip of a stalwart but breathless gillie.

"I tell ye I was daein' nae harm," the tramp whined. "I was walkin' up the waterside—there's nae law to keep a body frae walkin' up a waterside when there's nae fence—and I seen an auld otter killin' a saumon. The fish is there still to prove I'm no leein'."

"There is a fush, but you was thinkin' to steal the fush, and you would have had it in your breeks if I hadna seen you. That is poachn', ma man, and you will come up to Strathlarrig. The master said that any one goin' near the watter was to be lockit up, and you will be lockit up. You can tell all the lees you like in the mornin'."

Then a thought struck Jimsie. He wanted the salmon, for the subject of otters in the Larrig had long been a matter of dispute between him and Angus, and here was evidence for his own view.

"Would you two gentlemen oblige me by watchin' this man while I rin back and get the fush? Bash him on the head if he offers to rin."

The cyclists, who were journalists out to enjoy the evening air, willingly agreed, but Leithen showed no wish to escape. He begged a fag in a beggar's whine, and since he seemed peaceable, the two kept a good distance for fear of infection. He stood making damp streaks in the dusty road, a pitiable specimen of humanity, for his original get-up was not improved by the liquefaction of his clothes and a generous legacy of slimy peat. He seemed to be nervous, which, indeed, he was, for if Benjie had not seized his chance he was utterly done, and if Jimsie should light upon his rod he was gravely compromised.

But when Jimsie returned in a matter of ten minutes it was empty-handed.

"I never kenned the like," he proclaimed. "That otter has come back and gotten the fush. Ach, the maleecious brute!"

The rest of Leithen's progress was not triumphant. He was conducted to the Strathlarrig lodge, where Angus, whose temper and wind had alike been ruined by the pursuit of Crossby, laid savage hands upon him, and frog-marched him to the back premises. The head keeper scarcely heeded Jimsie's tale. "Ach, ye poachin' va-aga-bond. It is the jyle ye'll get," he roared, for Angus was in a mood which could only be relieved by violence of speech and action. Rumbling Gaelic imprecations, he hustled his prisoner into an outhouse, which had once been a larder and was now a supplementary garage, slammed and locked the door, and, as a final warning, kicked it viciously with his foot, as if to signify what awaited the culprit when the time came to sit on his case.

Early next morning, when the great door of Strathlarrig House was opened and the maids had begun their work, Oliphant, the butler—a stately man who had been trained in a ducal family—crossed the hall to reconnoitre the outer world. There he found an under-housemaid, nursing a strange package which she averred she had found on the doorstep. It was some two feet long, swathed in brown paper, and attached to its string was a letter inscribed to Mr. Junius Bandicott.

The parcel was clammy and Oliphant handled it gingerly. He cut the cord, disentangled the letter, and revealed an oblong of green rushes bound with string. The wrapping must have been insecure, for something forthwith slipped from the rushes and flopped on the marble floor, revealing to Oliphant's disgusted eyes a small salmon, blue and stiff in death.

At that moment Junius, always an early bird, came whistling downstairs. So completely was he convinced of the inviolability of the Strathlarrig waters that the spectacle caused him no foreboding.

"What are you flinging fish about for, Oliphant?" he asked cheerfully.

The butler presented him with the envelope. He opened it and extracted a dirty half-sheet of notepaper, on which was printed in capitals, "With the compliments of John Macnab."

Amazement, chagrin, amusement followed each other on Junius's open countenance. Then he picked up the fish and marched out of doors

359

shouting "Angus" at the top of a notably powerful voice. The sound brought the scared face of Professor Babwater to his bedroom window.

Angus, who had been up since four, appeared from Lady Maisie's pool where he had been contemplating the waters. His vigil had not improved his appearance or his temper, for his eye was red and choleric and his beard was wild as a mountain goat's. He cast one look at the salmon, surmised the truth, and held up imploring hands to Heaven.

"John Macnab!" said Junius sternly. "What have you got to say to that?"

Angus had nothing audible to say. He was handling the fish with feverish hands and peering at its jaws, and presently under his fingers a segment fell out.

"That fush was cleekit," observed Lennox, who had come up. "It was never catched with a flee."

"Ye're a leear," Angus roared. "Just tak a look at the mouth of it. There's the mark of the huke, ye gommeril. The fush was took wi' a rod and line."

"You may reckon it was," observed Junius. "I trust John Macnab to abide by the rules of the game."

Suddenly light seemed to break in on Angus's soul. He bellowed for Jimsie, who was placidly making his way towards the group at the door, lighting his pipe as he went.

"Look at that, James Mackenzie. Ay, look at it. Feast your een on it. You wass tellin' me there wass otters in the Largg and I said there wass not. You wass tellin' me there wass an otter had a fush last night at the Lang Whang. There's your otter and be damned to ye!"

Jimsie, slow of comprehension, rubbed his eyes. "Where wass you findin' the fush? Ay, it's the one I seen last night. That otter must be wrang in the heid."

"It's not wrang in the heid. It's you that are wrang in the heid, James Mackenzie. The otter is a ver-ra clever man, and its name will be John Macnab."

Slowly enlightenment dawned on Jimsie's mind.

"He was the tramp," he ingeminated. "He was the tramp."

"And he's still lockit up," Angus cried joyfully. "Wait till I get my hands on him." He was striding off for the garage when a word from Junius held him back.

"You won't find him there. I gave orders last night to let him go. You know, Angus, you told me he was only a tramp that had been seen walking up the river."

"We will catch him yet!" cried the vindictive head keeper. "Get you on your bicycle, Jimsie, and away after him. He'll be on the Muirtown road—There's just the one road he can travel."

"No, you don't," said Junius. "I don't want him here. He had beaten us fairly in a match of wits, and the business is finished."

"But the thing's no' possible," Jimsie moaned. "The skeeliest fisher would not take a saumon in the Lang Whang with a flee. . . . And I wasna away many meenutes. . . . And the tramp was a poor shilpit body—not like a fisher or any kind of gentleman at all—at all. . . . And he hadna a rod. . . . The thing's no' possible."

"I think it was the Deevil."

CHAPTER THIRTY-FIVE

Fish Are Such Liars

by Roland Pertwee

Roland Pertwee (1885–1963) was an English playwright, film and tele-vision screenwriter, director, and actor. We introduced Mr. Pertwee back in Chapter Twenty-Four with his story "The River God." This tale is from the book Fish Are Such Liars, *published in 1928. It was included in the Nick Lyons anthology* Hook, Line, and Sinker: Classic Fishing Stories *(2014).*

THERE HAD BEEN A FUSS IN THE POOL BENEATH THE ALDERS, AND THE small rainbow trout, with a skitter of his tail, flashed upstream, a hurt and angry fish. For three consecutive mornings he had taken the rise in that pool, and it injured his pride to be jostled from his drift just when the May fly was coming up in numbers. If his opponent had been a half-pounder like himself, he would have stayed and fought, but when an old hen fish, weighing fully three pounds, with a mouth like a rat hole and a carnivorous, cannibalistic eye rises from the reed beds and occupies the place, flight is the only effective argument.

But Rainbow was very much provoked. He had chosen his place with care. Now the May fly was up, the little French chalk stream was full of rising fish, and he knew by experience that strangers are unpopular in that season. To do one's self justice during a hatch, one must find a place where the fly drifts nicely overhead with the run of the stream, and natu-ral drifts are scarce even in a chalk stream. He was not content to leap at the fly like a hysterical youngster who measured his weight in ounces and

363

his wits in milligrams. He had reached that time of life which demanded that he should feed off the surface by suction rather than exertion. No living thing is more particular about his table manners than a trout, and Rainbow was no exception.

"It's a sickening thing," he said to himself, "and a hard shame." He added: "Get out of my way," to a couple of fat young chub.

"Chub indeed!"

But even the chub had a home and he had none—and the life of a homeless river dweller is precarious.

"I will not and shall not be forced back to midstream," he said.

For, save at eventide or in very special circumstances, trout of personality do not frequent open water where they must compete for every insect with the wind, the lightning-swift sweep of swallows and martins, and even the laborious pursuit of predatory dragon-flies with their bronze wings and bodies like rods of colored glass. Even as he spoke he saw a three-ounce leap at a dapping May fly which was scooped out of his jaws by a passing swallow. Rainbow heard the tiny click as the May fly's body cracked against the bird's beak. A single wing of yellowy gossamer floated downward and settled upon the water. Under the shelving banks to right and left, where the fly, discarding its nymph and still too damp for its virgin flight, drifted downstream, a dozen heavy trout were feeding thoughtfully and selectively.

"If only some angler would catch one of them, I might slip in and occupy the place before it gets known there's a vacancy."

But this uncharitable hope was not fulfilled, and with another whisk of his tail he propelled himself into the unknown waters upstream. A couple of strands of rusty barbed wire, relic of the war, spanned the shallows from bank to bank. Passing beneath them he came to a narrow reach shaded by willows, to the first of which was nailed a board bearing the words Pêche Réservée. He had passed out of the communal into private water—water running languidly over manes of emerald weed between clumps of alder, willow herb, tall crimson sorrel and masses of yellow iris. Ahead, like an apple-green rampart, rose the wooded heights of a forest; on either side were flat meadows of yellowing hay. Overhead, the vast expanse of blue June sky was tufted with rambling clouds. "My scales!" said Rainbow. "Here's water!"

But it was vain to expect any of the best places in such a reach would be vacant, and to avoid a recurrence of his unhappy encounter earlier in the morning, Rainbow continued his journey until he came to a spot where the river took one of those unaccountable right-angle bends which result in a pool, shallow on the one side, but slanting into deeps on the other. Above it was a water break, a swirl, smoothing, as it reached the pool, into a sleek, swift run, with an eddy which bore all the lighter floating things of the river over the calm surface of the little backwater, sheltered from above by a high shelving bank and a tangle of bramble and herb. Here in this backwater the twig, the broken reed, the leaf, the cork, the fly floated in suspended activity for a few instants until drawn back by invisible magnetism to the main current.

Rainbow paused in admiration. At the tail of the pool two sound fish were rising with regularity, but in the backwater beyond the eddy the surface was still and unbroken. Watching open-eyed, Rainbow saw not one but a dozen May flies, fat, juicy, and damp from the nymph, drift in, pause, and carried away untouched. It was beyond the bounds of possibility that such a place could be vacant, but there was the evidence of his eyes to prove it; and nothing if not a tryer, Rainbow darted across the stream and parked himself six inches below the water to await events.

It so happened that at the time of his arrival the hatch of fly was temporarily suspended, which gave Rainbow leisure to make a survey of his new abode. Beyond the eddy was a submerged snag—the branch of an apple tree borne there by heavy rains, water-logged, anchored, and intricate—an excellent place to break an angler's line. The river bank on his right was riddled under water with old rat holes, than which there is no better sanctuary. Below him and to the left was a dense bed of weeds brushed flat by the flow of the stream.

"If it comes to the worst," said Rainbow, "a smart fish could do a get-away here with very little ingenuity, even from a cannibalistic old hen like—hullo!"

The exclamation was excited by the apparition of a gauzy shadow on the water, which is what a May fly seen from below looks like. Resisting a vulgar inclination to leap at it with the violence of a youngster, Rainbow backed into the correct position which would allow the stream to present the morsel, so to speak, upon a tray. Which it did—and scarcely a dimple on the surface to tell what had happened.

"Very nicely taken, if you will accept the praise of a complete stranger," said a low, soft voice, one inch behind his line of sight.

Without turning to see by whom he had been addressed, Rainbow flicked a yard upstream and came back with the current four feet away. In the spot he had occupied an instant before lay a great old trout of the most benign aspect, who could not have weighed less than four pounds.

"I beg your pardon," said Rainbow, "but I had no idea that any one— that is, I just dropped in *en passant,* and finding an empty house, I made so bold—"

"There is no occasion to apologize," said Old Trout seductively. "I did not come up from the bottom as early to-day as is my usual habit at this season. Yesterday's hatch was singularly bountiful and it is possible I did myself too liberally."

"Yes, but a gentleman of your weight and seniority can hardly fail to be offended at finding—"

"Not at all," Old Trout broke in. "I perceive you are a well-conducted fish who does not advertise his appetite in a loud and splashing fashion."

Overcome by the charm of Old Trout's manner and address, Rainbow reduced the distance separating them to a matter of inches.

"Then you do not want me to go?" he asked.

"On the contrary, dear young sir, stay by all means and take the rise. You are, I perceive, of the rainbow or, as they say here in France, of the Arc-en-ciel family. As a youngster I had the impression that I should turn out a rainbow, but events proved it was no more than the bloom, the natural sheen of youth."

"To speak the truth, sir," said Rainbow, "unless you had told me to the contrary, I would surely have thought you one of us."

Old Trout shook his tail. "You are wrong," he said. "I am from Dulverton, an English trout farm on the Exe, of which you will have heard. You are doubtless surprised to find an English fish in French waters."

"I am indeed," Rainbow replied, sucking in a passing May fly with such excellent good manners that it was hard to believe he was feeding. "Then you, sir," he added, "must know all about the habits of men."

"I may justly admit that I do," Old Trout agreed. "Apart from being hand-reared, have in my twelve years of life studied the species in moods of activity, passivity, duplicity, and violence."

Rainbow remarked that such must doubtless have proved of invaluable service. It did not, however, explain the mystery of his presence on a French river.

"For, sir," he added, "Dulverton, as once I heard when enjoying 'A Chat about Rivers,' delivered by a much-traveled sea trout, is situated in the west of England, and without crossing the Channel I am unable to explain how you arrived here. Had you belonged to the salmon family, with which, sir, it is evident you have no connection, the explanation would be simple, but in the circumstances it baffles my understanding."

Old Trout waved one of his fins airily. "Yet cross the Channel I certainly did," said he, "and at a period in history which I venture to state will not readily be forgotten. It was during the war, my dear young friend, and I was brought in a can, in company with a hundred yearlings, to this river, or rather the upper reaches of this river, by a young officer who wished to further an entente between English and French fish even as the war was doing with the mankind of these two nations."

Old Trout sighed a couple of bubbles and arched his body this way and that.

"There was a gentleman and a sportsman," he said. "A man who was acquainted with our people as I dare to say very few are acquainted. Had it ever been my lot to fall victim to a lover of the rod, I could have done so without regret to his. If you will take a look at my tail, you will observe that the letter W is perforated on the upper side. He presented me with this distinguishing mark before committing me, with his blessing, to the water."

"I have seldom seen a tail more becomingly decorated," said Rainbow. "But what happened to your benefactor?"

Old Trout's expression became infinitely sad. "If I could answer that," said he, "I were indeed a happy trout. For many weeks after he put me into the river I used to watch him in what little spare time he was able to obtain, casting a dry fly with the exquisite precision and likeness to nature in all the likely pools and runs and eddies near his battery position. Oh, minnows! It was a pleasure to watch that man, even as it was his pleasure to watch us. His bravery too! I call to mind a dozen times when he fished unmoved and unstartled while bullets from machine guns were pecking at the water like herons and thudding into the mud banks upon which he stood."

"An angler!" remarked Rainbow. "It would be no lie to say I like him the less on that account."

Old Trout became unexpectedly stern.

"Why so?" he retorted severely. "Have I not said he was also a gentleman and a sportsman? My officer was neither a pot-hunter nor a beast of prey. He was a purist—a man who took delight in pitting his knowledge of nature against the subtlest and most suspicious intellectual forces of the wild. Are you so young as not yet to have learned the exquisite enjoyment of escaping disaster and avoiding error by the exercise of personal ingenuity? Pray, do not reply, for I would hate to think so hard a thing of any trout. We as a race exist by virtue of our brilliant intellectuality and hypersensitive selectivity. In waters where there are no pike and only an occasional otter, but for the machinations of men, where should we turn to school our wits? Danger is our mainstay, for I tell you, Rainbow, that trout are composed of two senses—appetite, which makes of us fools, and suspicion, which teaches us to be wise."

Greatly chastened not alone by what Old Trout had said but by the forensic quality of his speech, Rainbow rose short and put a promising May fly onto the wing.

"I am glad to observe," said Old Trout, "that you are not without conscience."

"To tell the truth, sir," Rainbow replied apologetically, "my nerve this morning has been rudely shaken, but for which I should not have shown such want of good sportsmanship."

And with becoming brevity he told the tale of his eviction from the pool downstream. Old Trout listened gravely, only once moving, and that to absorb a small blue dun, an insect which he keenly relished.

"A regrettable affair," he admitted, "but as I have often observed, women, who are the gentlest creatures under water in adversity, are a thought lacking in moderation in times of abundance. They are apt to snatch."

"But for a turn of speed, she would certainly have snatched me," said Rainbow.

"Very shocking," said Old Trout. "Cannibals are disgusting. They destroy the social amenities of the river. We fish have but little family life and should therefore aim to cultivate a freemasonry of good-fellowship among ourselves. For my part, I am happy to line up with other well-con-ducted trout and content myself with what happens along with my own particular drift. Pardon me!" he added, breasting Rainbow to one side. "I invited you to take the rise of May fly, but I must ask you to leave the duns alone." Then, fearing this remark might be construed to reflect adversely upon his hospitality, he proceeded: "I have a reason which I will explain later. For the moment we are discussing the circumstances that led to my presence in this river."

"To be sure—your officer. He never succeeded in deluding you with his skill?"

"That would have been impossible," said Old Trout, "for I had taken up a position under the far bank where he could only have reached me with a fly by wading in a part of the river which was in view of a German sniper."

"Wily!" Rainbow chuckled. "Cunning work, sir."

"Perhaps," Old Trout admitted, "although I have since reproached myself with cowardice. However, I was at the time a very small fish and a certain amount of nervousness is forgivable in the young."

At this gracious acknowledgment the rose-colored hue in Rainbow's rainbow increased noticeably—in short, he blushed.

"From where I lay," Old Trout went on, "I was able to observe the maneuvers of my officer and greatly profit thereby."

"But excuse me, sir," said Rainbow, "I have heard it said that an angler of the first class is invisible from the river."

"He is invisible to the fish he is trying to catch," Old Trout admitted, "but it must be obvious that he is not invisible to the fish who lie beside or below him. I would also remind you that during the war every tree, every scrap of vegetation, and every vestige of natural cover had been torn up, trampled down, razed. The river banks were as smooth as the top of your head. Even the buttercup, that very humorous flower that tangles up the bark cast of so many industrious anglers, was absent. Those who fished on the Western Front had little help from nature."

Young Rainbow sighed, for, only a few days before, his tongue had been badly scratched by an artificial alder which had every appearance of reality.

"It would seem," he said, "that this war had its merits."

"My young friend," said Old Trout, "you never made a greater mistake. A desire on the part of our soldiery to vary a monotonous diet of bully beef and biscuit often drove them to resort to villainous methods of assault against our kind."

"Nets?" gasped Rainbow in horror.

"Worse than nets—bombs," Old Trout replied. "A small oval black thing called a Mills bomb, which the shameless fellows flung into deep pools."

"But surely the chances of being hit by such a—"

"You reveal a pathetic ignorance," said Old Trout. "There is no question of being hit. The wretched machine exploded under water and burst our people's insides or stunned us so that we floated dead to the surface. I well remember my officer coming upon such a group of marauders one evening—yes, and laying about him with his fists in defiance of King's Regulations and the Manual of Military Law. Two of them he seized by the collar and the pants and flung into the river. Spinning minnows, that was a sight worth seeing! 'You low swine,' I heard him say; 'you trash, you muck! Isn't there enough carnage without this sort of thing?' Afterward he sat on the bank with the two dripping men and talked to them for their souls' sake.

"'Look ahead, boys. Ask yourselves what are we fighting for? Decent homes to live in at peace with one another, fields to till and forests and rivers to give us a day's sport and fun. It's our rotten job to massacre each other, but, by gosh, don't let's massacre the harmless rest of nature as well. At least, let's give 'em a running chance. Boys, in the years ahead, when all the mess is cleared up, I look forward to coming back to this old spot, when there is alder growing by the banks, and willow herb and tall reeds and the drone of insects instead of the rumble of those guns. I don't want to come back to a dead river that I helped to kill, but to a river ringed with rising fish—some of whom were old comrades of the war.' He went on to tell of us hundred Dulverton trout that he had marked with the letter W. 'Give 'em their chance,' he said, 'and in the years to come those beggars will reward us a hundred times over. They'll give us a finer thrill and put up a cleaner fight than old Jerry ever contrived.' Those were emotional times, and though you may be reluctant to believe me, one of those two very wet men dripped water from his eyes as well as his clothing.

"'Many's the 'appy afternoon I've 'ad with a roach pole on Brentford Canal,' he sniffed, 'though I've never yet tried m' hand against a trout.' 'You shall do it now,' said my officer, and during the half-hour that was left of daylight that dripping soldier had his first lesson in the most delicate art in the world. I can see them now—the clumsy, wet fellow and my officer timing him, timing him—'one and two, and one and two, and—' The action of my officer's wrist with its persuasive flick was the prettiest thing I have ever seen."

"Did he carry out his intention and come back after the war?" Rainbow asked.

"I shall never know," Old Trout replied. "I do not even know if he survived it. There was a great battle—a German drive. For hours they shelled the river front, and many falling short exploded in our midst with terrible results. My own bank was torn to shreds and our people suffered. How they suffered! About noon the infantry came over—hordes in field gray. There wire pontoons, rope bridges and hand-to-hand fights on both banks and even in the stream itself."

"And your officer?"

"I saw him once, before the water was stamped dense into liquid mud and dyed by the blood of men. He was in the thick of it, unarmed, and a German officer called on him to surrender. For answer he struck him in the face with a light cane. Ah, that wrist action! Then a shell burst, smothering the water with clods of fallen earth and other things."

"Then you never knew?"

"I never knew, although that night I searched among the dead. Next day I went downstream, for the water in that place was polluted with death. The bottom of the pool in which I had my place was choked with strange and mangled tenants that were not good to look upon. We trout are a clean people that will not readily abide in dirty houses. I am a Dulverton trout, where the water is filtered by the hills and runs cool over stones."

"And you have stayed here ever since?"

Old Trout shrugged a fin. "I have moved with the times. Choosing a place according to the needs of my weight."

"And you have never been caught, sir, by any other angler?"

"Am I not here?" Old Trout answered with dignity.

"Oh, quite, sir. I had only thought, perhaps, as a younger fish enthusiasm might have resulted to your disadvantage, but that, nevertheless, you had been returned."

"Returned! Returned!" echoed Old Trout. "Returned to the frying-pan! Where on earth did you pick up that expression? We are in France, my young friend; we are not on the Test, the Itchen, or the Kennet. In this country it is not the practice of anglers to return anything, however miserable in size."

"But nowadays," Rainbow protested, "there are Englishmen and Americans on the river who show us more consideration."

"They may show you consideration," said Old Trout, "but I am of an importance that neither asks for nor expects it. Oblige me by being a little more discreet with your plurals. In the impossible event of my being deceived and caught, I should be introduced to a glass case with an appropriate background of rocks and reeds."

"But, sir, with respect, how can you be so confident of your unassailability?" Rainbow demanded, edging into position to accept an attractive May fly with yellow wings that was drifting downstream toward him.

"How?" Old Trout responded. "Because—" Then suddenly: "Leave it, you fool!"

Rainbow had just broken the surface when the warning came. The yellow-winged May fly was wrenched off the water with a wet squeak. A tangle of limp cast lapped itself round the upper branches of a willow far upstream and a raw voice exclaimed something venomous in French. By common consent the two fish went down.

"Well, really," expostulated Old Trout, "I hoped you were above that kind of thing! Nearly to fall victim to a downstream angler. It's a little too much! And think of the effect it will have on my prestige. Why, that incompetent fool will go about boasting that he rose me. Me!"

For some minutes Rainbow was too crestfallen even to apologize. At last: "I am afraid," he said, "I was paying more heed to what you were saying than to my own conduct. I never expected to be fished from above. The fly was an uncommonly good imitation and it is a rare thing for a Frenchman to use Four-X gut."

"Rubbish," said Old Trout testily. "These are mere half-pound arguments. Four-X gut, when associated with a fourteen-stone shadow, should deceive nothing over two ounces. I saved your life, but it is all very provoking. If that is a sample of your general demeanor, it is improbable that you will ever reach a pound."

"At this season we are apt to be careless," Rainbow wailed. "And nowadays it is so hard, sir, to distinguish the artificial fly from the real."

"No one expects you to do so," was the answer, "but common prudence demands that you should pay some attention to the manner in which it is presented. A May fly does not hit the water with a splash, neither is it able to sustain itself in midstream against the current. Have you ever seen a natural insect leave a broadening wake of cutwater behind its tail? Never mind the fly, my dear boy, but watch the manner of its presentation. Failure to do that has cost many of our people their lives."

"You speak," said Rainbow, a shade sulkily, "as though it were a disgrace for a trout ever to suffer defeat at the hands of an angler."

"Which indeed it is, save in exceptional circumstances," Old Trout answered. "I do not say that a perfect upstream cast from a well-concealed angler, when the fly alights dry and cocked and dances at even speed with the current, may not deceive us to our fall. And I would be the last to say that a grasshopper skillfully dapped on the surface through the branches of an overhanging tree will not inevitably bring about our destruction. But I do most emphatically say that in such a spot as this, where the slightest defect in presentation is multiplied a hundred-fold by the varying water speeds, a careless rise is unpardonable. There is only one spot—and that a matter of twelve yards downstream—from which a fly can be drifted over me with any semblance to nature. Even so, there is not one angler in a thousand who can make that cast with success, by reason of a willow which cramps the back cast and the manner in which these alders on our left sprawl across the pool."

Rainbow did not turn about to verify these statements because it is bad form for a trout to face downstream. He contented himself by replying, with a touch of acerbity: "I should have thought, sir, with the feelings you expressed regarding sportsmanship, you would have found such a sanctuary too dull for your entertainment."

"Every remark you make serves to aggravate the impression of your ignorance," Old Trout replied. "Would you expect a trout of my intelligence to put myself in some place where I am exposed to the vulgar assaults of every amateur upon the bank? Of the green boy who lashes the water into foam, of the purblind peasant who slings his fly at me with a clod of earth or a tail of weed attached to the hook? In this place I invite attention from none but the best people—the expert, the purist."

"I understood you to say that there were none such in these parts," grumbled Rainbow.

"There are none who have succeeded in deceiving me," was the answer. "As a fact, for the last few days I have been vastly entranced by an angler who, by any standard is deserving of praise. His presentation is flawless and the only fault I can detect in him is a tendency to overlook piscine psychology. He will be with us in a few minutes, since he knows it is my habit to lunch at noon."

"Pardon the interruption," said Rainbow, "but there is a gallant hatch of fly going down. I can hear your two neighbors at the tail of the pool rising steadily."

Old Trout assumed an indulgent air. "We will go up if you wish," said he, "but you will be well advised to observe my counsel before taking the rise, because if my angler keeps his appointment you will most assuredly be *meunièred* before nightfall."

At this unpleasant prophecy Rainbow shivered. "Let us keep to weed," he suggested.

But Old Trout only laughed, so that bubbles from the river bed rose and burst upon the surface.

"Courage," said he; "it will be an opportunity for you to learn the finer points of the game. If you are nervous, lie nearer to the bank. The natural fly does not drift there so abundantly, but you will be secure from the artificial. Presently I will treat you to an exhibition of playing with death you will not fail to appreciate." He broke off and pointed with his eyes. "Over you and to the left."

Rainbow made a neat double rise and drifted back into line. "Very mellow," he said—"very mellow and choice. Never tasted better. May I ask, sir, what you meant by piscine psychology?"

"I imply that my angler does not appreciate the subtle possibilities of our intellect. Now, my officer concerned himself as vitally with what we were thinking as with what we were feeding upon. This fellow, secure in the knowledge that his presentation is well-nigh perfect, is content to offer me the same variety of flies day after day, irrespective of the fact that I have learned them all by heart. I have, however, adopted the practice of rising every now and then to encourage him."

"Rising? At an artificial fly? I never heard such temerity in all my life," gasped Rainbow.

Old Trout moved his body luxuriously. "I should have said, appearing to rise," he amended. "You may have noticed that I have exhibited a predilection for small duns in preference to the larger *Ephemeridae*. My procedure is as follows: I wait until a natural dun and his artificial May fly are drifting downstream with the smallest possible distance separating them. Then I rise and take the dun. Assuming I have risen to him, he strikes, misses, and is at once greatly flattered and greatly provoked. By this device I sometimes occupy his attention for over an hour and thus render a substantial service to others of my kind who would certainly have fallen victim to his skill."

"The river is greatly in your debt, sir," said Young Rainbow, with deliberate satire.

He knew by experience that fish as well as anglers are notorious liars, but the exploit his host recounted was a trifle too strong. Taking a sidelong glance, he was surprised to see that Old Trout did not appear to have appreciated the subtle ridicule of his remark. The long, lithe body had become almost rigid and the great round eyes were focused upon the surface with an expression of fixed concentration.

Looking up, Rainbow saw a small white-winged May fly with red legs and a body the color of straw swing out from the main stream and describe a slow circle over the calm surface above Old Trout's head. Scarcely an inch away a tiny blue dun, its wings folded as closely as the pages of a book, floated attendant. An upward rush, a sucking kerr-rop, and when the broken water had calmed, the dun had disappeared and the May fly was dancing away downstream.

"Well," said Old Trout, "how's that, my youthful skeptic? Pretty work, eh?"

"I saw nothing in it," was the impertinent reply. "There is not a trout on the river who could not have done likewise."

"Even when one of those two flies was artificial?" Old Trout queried tolerantly.

"But neither of them was artificial," Rainbow retorted. "Had it been so, the angler would have struck. They always do."

"Of course he struck," Old Trout replied.

"But he didn't," Rainbow protested. "I saw the May fly go down with the current."

"My poor fish!" Old Trout replied. "Do you presume to suggest that I am unable to distinguish an artificial from a natural fly? Are you so blind that you failed to see the prismatic colors in the water from the paraffin in which the fly had been dipped? Here you are! Here it is again!"

Once more the white-winged insect drifted across the backwater, but this time there was no attendant dun.

"If that's a fake I'll eat my tail," said Rainbow.

"If you question my judgment," Old Trout answered, "you are at liberty to rise. I dare say, in spite of a shortage of brain, that you would eat comparatively well."

But Rainbow, in common with his kind, was not disposed to take chances.

"We may expect two or three more casts from this fly and then he will change it for a bigger. It is the same program every day without a variation. How differently my officer would have acted. By now he would have discovered my little joke and turned the tables against me. Aye me, but some men will never learn! Your mental outfit, dear Rainbow, is singularly like a man's," he added. "It lacks elasticity."

Rainbow made no retort and was glad of his forbearance, for every word Old Trout had spoken was borne out by subsequent events. Four times the white-winged May fly described an arc over the backwater, but in the absence of duns Old Trout did not rise again. Then came a pause, during which, through a lull in the hatch, even the natural insect was absent from the river.

"He is changing his fly," said Old Trout, "but he will not float it until the hatch starts again. He is casting beautifully this morning and I hope circumstances will permit me to give him another rise."

"But suppose," said Rainbow breathlessly, "you played this game once too often and were foul hooked as a result?"

Old Trout expanded his gills broadly. "Why, then," he replied, "I should break him. Once round a limb of that submerged apple bough and the thing would be done. I should never allow myself to be caught and no angler could gather up the slack and haul me into midstream in time to prevent me reaching the bough. Stand by."

The shadow of a large, dark May fly floated cockily over the backwater and had almost returned to the main stream when a small iron-blue dun settled like a puff of thistledown in its wake.

The two insects were a foot nearer the fast water than the spot where Old Trout was accustomed to take the rise. But for the presence of a spectator, it is doubtful whether he would have done so, but Young Rainbow's want of appreciation had excited his vanity, and with a rolling swoop he swallowed the dun and bore it downward.

And then an amazing thing happened. Instead of drifting back to his place as was expected, Old Trout's head was jerked sideways by an invisible force. A thin translucent thread upcut the water's surface and tightened irresistibly. A second later Old Trout was fighting, fighting, fighting to reach the submerged apple bough with the full weight of the running water and the full strength of the finest Japanese gut strained against him.

Watching, wide-eyed and aghast, from one of the underwater rat holes into which he had hastily withdrawn, Rainbow saw the figure of a man rise out of a bed of irises downstream and scramble upon the bank. In his right hand, with the wrist well back, he held a light split-cane rod whose upper joint was curved to a half-circle. The man's left hand was detaching a collapsible landing net from the ring of his belt. Every attitude and movement was expressive of perfectly organized activity. His mouth was shut as tightly as a steel trap, but a light of happy excitement danced in his eyes.

"No, you don't, my fellar," Rainbow heard him say. "No, you don't. I knew all about that apple bough before ever I put a fly over your pool. And the weed bed on the right," he added, as Old Trout made a sudden swerve half down and half across stream.

Tucking the net under his arm the man whipped up the slack with a lightning-like action. The maneuver cost Old Trout dear, for when, despairing of reaching the weed and burrowing into it, he tried to regain his old position, he found himself six feet farther away from the apple bough than when the battle began.

Instinctively Old Trout knew it was useless to dash downstream, for a man who could take up slack with the speed his adversary had shown would profit by the expedient to come more quickly to terms with him. Besides, lower down there was broken water to knock the breath out of his lungs. Even where he lay straining and slugging this way and that, the water was pouring so fast into his open mouth as nearly to drown him. His only chance of effecting a smash was by a series of jumps, followed by quick dives. Once before, although he had not confessed it to Rainbow, Old Trout had saved his life by resorting to this expedient. It takes the strain off the line and returns it so quickly that even the finest gut is apt to sunder.

Meanwhile the man was slowly approaching, winding up as he came. Old Trout, boring in the depths, could hear the click of the check reel with increasing distinctness. Looking up, he saw that the cast was almost vertical above his head, which meant that the moment to make the attempt was at hand. The tension was appalling, for ever since the fight began his adversary had given him the butt unremittingly. Aware of his own weight and power, Old Trout was amazed that any tackle could stand the strain.

"Now's my time," he thought, and jumped.

It was no ordinary jump, but an aerial rush three feet out of the water, with a twist at its apex and a cutting lash of the tail designed to break the cast. But his adversary was no ordinary angler, and at the first hint of what was happening he dropped the point of the rod flush with the surface.

Once and once more Old Trout flung himself into the air, but after each attempt he found himself with diminishing strength and with less line to play with.

"It looks to me," said Rainbow mournfully, "as if my unhappy host will lose this battle and finish up in that glass case to which he was referring a few minutes ago." And greatly affected, he burrowed his nose in the mud and wondered, in the event of this dismal prophecy coming true, whether he would be able to take possession of the pool without molestation.

In consequence of these reflections he failed to witness the last phase of the battle, when, as will sometimes happen with big fish, all the fight went out of Old Trout, and rolling wearily over and over, he abandoned himself to the clinging embraces of the net. He never saw the big man proudly carry Old Trout back into the hayfield, where, before proceeding to remove the fly, he sat down beside a shallow dike and lit a cigarette and smiled largely. Then, with an affectionate and professional touch, he picked up Old Trout by the back of the neck, his forefinger and thumb sunk firmly in the gills.

"You're a fine fellar," he said, extracting the fly; "a good sportsman and a funny fish. You fooled me properly for three days, but I think you'll own I outwitted you in the end."

Rummaging in his creel for a small rod of hard wood that he carried for the purpose of administering the quietus, he became aware of something that arrested his action. Leaning forward, he stared with open eyes at a tiny W perforated in the upper part of Old Trout's tail.

"Shades of the war! Dulverton!" he exclaimed. Then with a sudden warmth: "Old chap, old chap, is it really you? This is red-letter stuff. If you're not too far gone to take another lease of life, have it with me."

And with the tenderness of a woman, he slipped Old Trout into the dike and in a tremble of excitement hurried off to the *auberge* where the fisherman lodged, to tell a tale no one even pretended to believe.

For the best part of an hour Old Trout lay in the shallow waters of the dike before slowly cruising back to his own place beneath the over-hanging bank. The alarming experience through which he had passed had made him a shade forgetful, and he was not prepared for the sight of Young Rainbow rising steadily at the hatch of fly.

"Pardon me, but a little more to your right," he said, with heavy courtesy.

"Diving otters!" cried Young Rainbow, leaping a foot clear of the water. "You, sir! You!"

"And why not?" Old Trout replied. "Your memory must be short if you have already forgotten that this is my place."

"Yes, but—" Rainbow began and stopped.

"You are referring to that little circus of a few minutes ago," said Old Trout. "Is it possible you failed to appreciate the significance of the affair? I knew at once it was my dear officer when he dropped the artificial dun behind the natural May fly. In the circumstances I could hardly do less than accept his invitation. Nothing is more delightful than a reunion of comrades of the war." He paused and added: "We had a charming talk, he and I, and I do not know which of us was the more affected. It is a tragedy that such friendship and such intellect as we share cannot exist in common element."

And so great was his emotion that Old Trout dived and buried his head in the weeds. Whereby Rainbow did uncommonly well during the midday hatch.

CHAPTER THIRTY-SIX

Retrospect

by Viscount Grey of Fallodon

Here's the way Nick Lyons introduced this story in his book Hook, Line, and Sinker: Classic Fishing Stories (2014): *'The passion in Viscount Grey of Fallodon's 'Retrospect' is of an entirely different stripe—reflective, deepened by years and layers of experience of the most diverse sort, redolent with precious memories, tempered by the intelligence of a wise and worldly man; it is like a fire of banked red coals, giving even more and steadier heat than the blazing fires of youth.'*

IN THE LATTER PART OF 1918 MY LAST BIT OF CENTRE VISION WAS obscured and I descended at once on to a lower plane of sight than I had yet experienced. Since then there has been very slow deterioration, which is now perceptible even as compared with 1918; but the great drop came when the centre vision went: after that the difference between a little more and a little less side vision is one of degree. It does not add to the number of total disabilities that are imposed by the loss of centre vision. By 1918 I had ceased to be able to see a small fly floating on the water. It was, however, possible to judge distance more accurately and to present a dry fly effectively to a rising trout more frequently than I should have supposed to be possible under such disadvantage. Nevertheless, it happened more than once in this season that I struck to the sound of a rise without seeing it, and found that I had hooked the trout for which I was trying. It had taken my fly on the surface and I had failed to see the rise, even though my eyes had been directed to the place where I knew the fish to be. It was evident that for me the end of dry-fly fishing was very near. It was so. When the season of 1919 came I could no longer see rises.

It would be possible still to get some trout on a dry fly with some one always in attendance to help me. The attendant would find a rising trout, would show me where to stand or to kneel: would describe the direction in and the distance to which the fly should be cast: would say when this had been done correctly: and finally would utter some exclamation when the fish took the fly, so that I might give the necessary strike. But the whole process would be intolerably cumbersome and clumsy, and I should bungle sadly. Skill in dry-fly fishing is denied to bad sight.

> *Nec vera virtus, cum semel exidit,*
> *curat reponi deterioribus.*

There remains wet-fly fishing for trout in still water and across or down stream. When there is no slack line, a certain proportion of trout—a good proportion when they are taking well—that come at an angler's fly will hook themselves. There is, of course, some bungling. With indistinct vision it is not easy to place the landing-net accurately under a trout, even when the fish is exhausted and can be held steady on the surface of the water, especially if this be a rippling stream. More than once recently, when wading in such water, where trout average four to the pound, has the mistake been made of placing the net carefully under a bit of foam, which, as the net was lifted, dissolved and disappeared like a mocking spirit. Nevertheless, the thing can be done still, independent and unaided, which is an essential part of the peculiar pleasure of trout fishing: and though my baskets are light there come bright gleams of success. The mere touch of a trout, even if it does not hook itself, gives a little thrill; the feel of a small, single-handed rod, its quick and delicate motion, and its response to the hand, are delightful: it is very pleasant to spend a day by rippling streams with a background of trees and the air lively with the songs of birds in April and May.

Salmon fishing is less difficult, though some of the pleasure is gone. It is twelve years since I have been able to see my fly fall on the water or to watch the line. These things were a matter of course in salmon fishing: not till I lost sight of them did I realize what an integral part of the interest of salmon fishing they were. The salmon angler watches the fall of his fly at each cast, and his eyes are ever on the draw of the stream on his line. To be deprived of the latter is an even greater loss than it is to be unable to see the fly fall on the water.

However good be the river or the beat on it, there must be many hours, and an occasional day, when the angler does not get a pull: and to fish hour after hour seeing only the rod and nothing of the line is a very blank business. On days of failure an angler may be said to go through four stages of feeling. He begins with Expectation: this is presently modified to Hope: after Hope has been long deferred the angler subsides into the stage of Resignation: finally as the day draws to a close he sinks into Despair. The angler who fishes without seeing his fly or line passes more quickly through the happier to the lower stages.

Every angler loses a certain proportion of the salmon that he hooks and plays. There are days of hard luck and of good luck in this matter, but taking figures over a period of days I used to estimate that my proportion of fish lost to fish landed was one in six. For example, in the ten good days on the Cassley, described in the preceding chapter, sixty salmon were hooked and fifty landed. Two of the ten salmon that escaped broke the line round rocks. As the hook had sufficiently firm hold to break a strong gut cast, it may be assumed that but for the exceptional misfortune of the rocks, these two fish would have been landed. Eight in sixty would thus have been the proportion of salmon lost owing to the hook coming out. This is not a proportion that should cause excessive annoyance, and I do not remember having suffered greatly from losing salmon before my sight was impaired. Since that time I have suffered very badly. In one black week on the Cassley a few years ago, out of twenty-two salmon hooked only seven were landed. None of those that escaped broke the line: the fly just came away unaccountably, often when the fish was almost within reach of the net.

In speaking of salmon "hooked" I include only the fish that have been actually played. Those that come to the surface immediately after being struck and splash themselves free are not counted; nor indeed are any salmon counted as "lost" if they have been held for quite a short time. In other words, only fish that have been not only hooked but played have been included in the calculation of fish lost. My experience that week was such as I hope no other angler may have to endure. A week that might have been happy and successful was turned to misery. My brother, who was fishing with me, hooked at least as many fish in those same six days, but did not lose an undue proportion and had a good week.

Things are, of course, not always so bad as in that week, or I should not be salmon fishing still. Nevertheless, the number of salmon hooked and played that I lose has been for the last twelve years very harassing. I cannot imagine why impaired sight should have caused this. It is not by sight, but by feel, that an angler strikes a salmon. In spring, salmon as a rule take the fly under water unseen: even if a fish does make a visible rise, the angler should not strike till the pull is felt. For this purpose it is an advantage not to see the rise. Why, then, should bad sight cause me to fail to hook fish securely? I can only suggest that the angler who watches the line coming round in the stream sees unconsciously, or half-consciously, the line tighten at the instant when he feels the pull of a fish: and that eyes and hands both being alert he strikes with more conviction than if he only felt and did not see. And to strike with conviction and not tentatively is necessary to hook salmon securely, especially with the big hooks that are used in spring.

Certainly since my sight was impaired I neither hook nor land as many fish as I used to do in comparison with others. The adverse change in this respect was very noticeable and persistent when my brother fished with me on the Cassley, where we could compare present with past experience on the same water. Some success still have, but the conclusion is irresistible that when a man ceases to be able to see what he is doing he does not do so well as he did before. The new method of salmon fishing with a greased line and comparatively small rod and fly presumably requires better sight than the ordinary method, and I have not tried it. It is by repute, and I dare say in practice, very effective, particularly in low water.

As long as there is a fair chance of getting fish the pleasure of fly fishing is to a very keen angler inexhaustible. It was, I think, Dr. Johnson who complained that he had never in his life had enough peaches. He therefore never knew, and we can never know, how many peaches would have satisfied him. In like manner, I shall never know for how many days I could fish continuously without wearying of it. Trout fishing has always been intermittent: of spring salmon fishing I have had, as a rule, from ten to twenty days in the season, and not more than ten days at a time. Would a keen golfer be satisfied if he played golf on from ten to twenty days only in the year? I suspect he would not, and I am sure that this allowance of salmon fishing is not satisfying. On the occasions when I have had a continuous spell of salmon fishing, I have quitted the river with as much regret at the end of the fifth or sixth week as I should have felt at the end of the first.

On the other hand, one does become more fastidious as to the kind of sport. To catch fresh run salmon spoils the interest in red or dark fish. The latter may give good sport, but to land a tarnished fish when an angler has been used to the brilliant excellence of fresh run spring salmon, gives a sense of dissatisfaction that blunts the edge of keenness.

Most men have to earn their own living and have little enough opportunity for indulging in pleasure, even if they have keenness. But any really keen angler who has not had to work from necessity, and yet has not spent the whole of each season in fly fishing, may say, as Clive said when he reflected on his opportunities of acquiring wealth in India, that he is astonished at his own moderation.

The moderation imposed on any one who undertakes important work in life may be very distressing. I recall, in particular, a certain bitter moment in the latter half of April, 1909. In 1906 and 1907 I had had no spring salmon fishing at all. In 1908 I had ten days, but the Cassley was low: I got only two salmon: in the whole time there was hardly any water in which to throw a fly. My days were spent walking about the moors in the April sunshine. "Not a bad way of spending a holiday," some one may say. True, but it was not the thing for which I had paid rent or which I had come to do, and it was not satisfying to a man who had not caught a spring salmon for three years.

In 1909 I came to the Cassley again and this time the river was in order. After three years of abstinence or failure, the prospect of good fishing was before me. On the first day I had five fish by four o'clock; this was equal to the best day I had ever had up to that time. The little post-office where I was staying was only a hundred yards from the river. I came in to see what the Foreign Office had sent me. There was an alarmist telegram about the state of things in Constantinople. I decided that I must return to London. It was then too late to get the evening train: I went back to the river and got one more salmon, making what was then a record for me. The next morning I left: the river was still in order; there was the prospect of a week of good sport if only I could stay: there was the certainty that I must wait a whole year before I could spring-salmon fish again. And there was not even the compensation of feeling a martyr to duty. If the disturbances at Constantinople became dangerous, British action must be limited to protecting British lives and property. The measures necessary for this would be taken by the diplomatic and naval authorities on the spot, whether I were at the Foreign Office or not. If I stayed at the Cassley till something really happened I could be at the Foreign Office in plenty of time to deal with political complications that might arise later on, the public interest would not suffer if I awaited developments. But the fear of what would be said in the House of Commons and in the Press, if something did happen and I were absent from my office, destroyed my equanimity: I went back to London feeling cowardly rather than noble, and not at all convinced that the sacrifice made was necessary. The event proved that it was unnecessary.

Such misfortune and disappointment leave a mark on memory, but it is an isolated incident. When the angler looks back he sees a long vista of happy days: by a special act of memory he can select individual days of outstanding success, but even these seem not to be exceptions; they are but contributory parts of an enjoyment that was greater than any single day could contain. For to an angler as he looks back, his angling days seem to belong to a world different from, and fairer than, the world in which he has worked. In retrospect the surroundings, the country, the beauty of river scenes are an inseparable part of the pleasure. The keen angler may indeed be comparatively indifferent to them when actively engaged in fishing. If a rare and beautiful bird had appeared in a Hampshire water-meadow when trout were rising and I was busy with them, what would the effect on my fishing have been? My impression is that I should have made a mental note of it, resolved to look for and watch the bird when the rise of trout was over, and have continued to fish without interruption. So intense is the interest and excitement of fly fishing when we are actively engaged in it. On the other hand, if I could again fish with a dry fly I should not now take a fishing, unless it was in beautiful country. The fact that the water meadows where I fished on the Itchen were one of the fairest spots in the world became an ever-increasing part in the enjoyment. This enhanced the anticipation of going thither; it made the days spent there radiant.

The cottage that I put up by the Itchen in 1890 was intended only as a fishing cottage; a place in which to get food, sleep, and shelter when I was not fishing. It became a sanctuary. The peace and beauty of the spot made it a sacred place. The cottage belongs to angling memories, but the fishing became a small part of the happiness that was associated with it. For thirty-three years the chosen spot remained a place of refuge and delight, not in the fishing season only. For the last four years, indeed, I had been unable to fish with a dry fly, and the original purpose for which the cottage had been put there had ceased to be. Great changes, however, had been taking place that were inseparable from a new epoch. For the first fifteen years there was little change and had been little change for many years before that time. I had seen the old mill at the village not far away replaced by a new building, and the dull, monotonous sound of a turbine had replaced the lively splashing of a waterwheel; but otherwise things remained as they were. The cottage was invisible from any road; it was approached by an old lime avenue, long disused, and the track down this was not suited for any wheels but those of a farm cart. There was a little wayside station on a single railway line close by; but the quickest route from London was to go by a fast train to Winchester, and thence to drive a distance between four and five miles to the nearest point to the cottage that was accessible by wheels. This was a drive of at least half an hour in a one-horse fly. Presently taxicabs took the place of the horse conveyance and reduced the time of the drive to a quarter of an hour. Was this an advantage? On balance, it was not. For escape from London meant that hurry, noise and bustle had been left behind: I had entered into leisure, where saving of time was no object, and often I would walk from Winchester to enjoy the country. There was a footpath way on each side of the river. By one of these one entered the cottage without, except for the momentary crossing of one road and of three secluded lanes, having had touch or sight of a road. There were thirty-three stiles on this path. It happened not infrequently that I could not get to Winchester till the latest train arriving there some time after eleven o'clock. The walk then lasted well into the midnight hour. In the dusk or dark it was easier to walk by the road than by the path. There was much charm in this midnight walk. Traffic had ceased, cottage lights had been put out, the inmates were all at rest or asleep. Now and then one heard, in passing, the song of a nightingale or a sedge-warbler, but in the main there was silence. It was pleasant after the hardness of London streets and pavements to feel the soft dust about my feet. On a still summer night there were sweet and delicate scents in the air, breathed forth from leaves and herbs and grass, and from the earth itself. It was as if one's own very being was soothed and in some way refined by the stillness, the gentleness and the sweetness of it all.

Then came the age of motors and tarred roads. Few people, I imagine, seek the smell of tar for its own sake. To me there is nothing unclean or nauseous in it, but it is a coarse, rough smell. The sweet and delicate scents of the night were obliterated by it, as if, overpowered and repelled, they had sunk back into the leaves and earth from which they had ventured into air. The strong smell of the tar seemed to disturb even the stillness of the night; the soft dust was no more, and the road was hard as a paved street. Not all, but much of the charm of the night walk was gone. There were other changes too; small houses of the villa type were built along the road that was nearest to the cottage: doubtless there are more of them now, for the cottage was accidentally destroyed by fire in January, 1923, and I have not seen the place for some years. The sense of change was in the air. It may be that change is for the good:

The old order changeth, yielding place to new,
And God fulfils himself in many ways,
Lest one good custom should corrupt the world.

It is not for us, who cannot forsee the future, who perhaps cannot rightly understand the present, to chide or to repine too much. Only it is impossible for us, who in our youth gave our affections to things that are passed or passing away, to transfer our affections to new things in which a new generation finds delight.

The beauty, however, of chalk-strewn valleys still remains wonderful. The river still waters meadows that are unspoilt and unchanged, and its clear purity is guarded and protected.

Still glides the stream and shall for ever glide,
The form remains, the function never dies.

Thus, as the angler looks back he thinks less of individual captures and days than of the scenes in which he fished. The luxuriance of water meadows, animated by insect and bird and trout life, tender with the green and gay with the blossoms of early spring: the nobleness and volume of great salmon rivers: the exhilaration of looking at any salmon pool, great or small; the rich brownness of Highland water: the wild openness of the treeless, trackless spaces which he has traversed in an explorer's spirit of adventure to search likely water for sea trout: now on one, now on another of these scenes an angler's mind will dwell, as he thinks of fishing. Special days and successes he will no doubt recall, but always with the remembrance and the mind's vision of the scenes and the world in which he fished. For, indeed, this does seem a separate world, a world of beauty and enjoyment. The time must come to all of us, who live long, when memory is more than prospect. An angler who has reached this stage and reviews the pleasure of life will be grateful and glad that he has been an angler, for he will look back upon days radiant with happiness, peaks and peaks of enjoyment that are not less bright because they are lit in memory by the light of a setting sun.

CHAPTER THIRTY-SEVEN

An Odyssey from *The Sun Also Rises*

by Ernest Hemingway

Published by Scribner's in 1926, Hemingway's breakout novel contains a trout-fishing episode that centers on two buddies fishing in the Spanish mountains. They have left the "running of the bulls" festivities at Pamplona and gone by bus to an inn near the streams. The narrator, Jake, is a newspaperman who works in Paris, and his friend is an aspiring writer. Jake was wounded somewhere in and around his testes (event never detailed) in World War I and cannot make love to his beloved Lady Brett Ashley. The story is remarkable in the sense of camaraderie it displays and the journey into the mountains and the fishing itself. The prose is sharp, crisp, and with a "felt life" few can equal.

WHEN I WOKE IN THE MORNING I WENT TO THE WINDOW AND LOOKED out. It had cleared and there were no clouds on the mountains. Outside under the window were some carts and an old diligence, the wood of the roof cracked and split by the weather. It must have been left from the days before the motor-buses. A goat hopped up on one of the carts and then to the roof of the diligence. He jerked his head at the other goats below and when I waved at him he bounded down.

Bill was still sleeping, so I dressed, put on my shoes outside in the hall, and went down-stairs. No one was stirring down-stairs, so I unbolted the door and went out. It was cool outside in the early morning and the sun had not yet dried the dew that had come when the wind died down. I hunted around in the shed behind the inn and found a sort of mattock, and went down toward the stream to try and dig some worms for bait. The stream was clear and shallow but it did not look trouty. On the grassy bank where it was damp I drove the mattock into the earth and loosened a chunk of sod. There were worms underneath. They slid out of sight as I lifted the sod and I dug carefully and got a good many. Digging at the edge of the damp ground I filled two empty tobacco-tins with worms and sifted dirt onto them. The goats watched me dig.

When I went back into the inn the woman was down in the kitchen, and I asked her to get coffee for us, and that we wanted a lunch. Bill was awake and sitting on the edge of the bed.

"I saw you out of the window," he said. "Didn't want to interrupt you. What were you doing? Burying your money?"

"You lazy bum!"

"Been working for the common good? Splendid. I want you to do that every morning."

"Come on," I said. "Get up."

"What? Get up? I never get up."

He climbed into bed and pulled the sheet up to his chin.

"Try and argue me into getting up."

I went on looking for the tackle and putting it all together in the tackle-bag.

"Aren't you interested?" Bill asked.

"I'm going down and eat."

"Eat? Why didn't you say eat? I thought you just wanted me to get up for fun. Eat? Fine. Now you're reasonable. You go out and dig some more worms and I'll be right down."

"Oh, go to hell!"

"Work for the good of all." Bill stepped into his underclothes. "Show irony and pity."

I started out of the room with the tackle-bag, the nets, and the rod-case.

"Hey! come back!"

I put my head in the door.

"Aren't you going to show a little irony and pity?"

I thumbed my nose.

392

"That's not irony."

As I went down-stairs I heard Bill singing, "Irony and Pity. When you're feeling . . . Oh, Give them Irony and Give them Pity. Oh, give them Irony. When they're feeling . . . Just a little irony. Just a little pity . . ." He kept on singing until he came down-stairs. The tune was: "The Bells are Ringing for Me and My Gal." I was reading a week-old Spanish paper.

"What's all this irony and pity?"

"What? Don't you know about Irony and Pity?"

"No. Who got it up?"

"Everybody. They're mad about it in New York. It's just like the Fratellinis used to be."

The girl came in with the coffee and buttered toast. Or, rather, it was bread toasted and buttered.

"Ask her if she's got any jam," Bill said. "Be ironical with her."

"Have you got any jam?"

"That's not ironical. I wish I could talk Spanish."

The coffee was good and we drank it out of big bowls. The girl brought in a glass dish of raspberry jam.

"Thank you."

"Hey! that's not the way," Bill said. "Say something ironical. Make some crack about Primo de Rivera."

"I could ask her what kind of a jam they think they've gotten into in the Riff."

"Poor," said Bill. "Very poor. You can't do it. That's all. You don't understand irony. You have no pity. Say something pitiful."

"Robert Cohn."

"Not so bad. That's better. Now why is Cohn pitiful? Be ironic."

He took a big gulp of coffee.

"Aw, hell!" I said. "It's too early in the morning."

"There you go. And you claim you want to be a writer, too. You're only a newspaper man. An expatriated newspaper man. You ought to be ironical the minute you get out of bed. You ought to wake up with your mouth full of pity."

"Go on," I said. "Who did you get this stuff from?"

"Everybody. Don't you read? Don't you ever see anybody? You know what you are? You're an expatriate. Why don't you live in New York? Then you'd know these things. What do you want me to do? Come over here and tell you every year?"

"Take some more coffee," I said.

"Good. Coffee is good for you. It's the caffeine in it. Caffeine, we are here. Caffeine puts a man on her horse and a woman in his grave. You know what's the trouble with you? You're an expatriate. One of the worst type. Haven't you heard that? Nobody that ever left their own country ever wrote anything worth printing. Not even in the newspapers."

He drank the coffee.

"You're an expatriate. You've lost touch with the soil. You get precious. Fake European standards have ruined you. You drink yourself to death. You become obsessed by sex. You spend all your time talking, not working. You are an expatriate, see? You hang around cafés."

"It sounds like a swell life," I said. "When do I work?"

"You don't work. One group claims women support you. Another group claims you're impotent."

"No," I said. "I just had an accident."

"Never mention that," Bill said. "That's the sort of thing that can't be spoken of. That's what you ought to work up into a mystery. Like Henry's bicycle."

He had been going splendidly, but he stopped. I was afraid he thought he had hurt me with that crack about being impotent. I wanted to start him again.

"It wasn't a bicycle," I said. "He was riding horseback."

"I heard it was a tricycle."

"Well," I said. "A plane is sort of like a tricycle. The joystick works the same way."

"But you don't pedal it."

"No," I said, "I guess you don't pedal it."

"Let's lay off that," Bill said.

"All right. I was just standing up for the tricycle."

"I think he's a good writer, too," Bill said. "And you're a hell of a good guy. Anybody ever tell you you were a good guy?"

"I'm not a good guy."

"Listen. You're a hell of a good guy, and I'm fonder of you than anybody on earth. I couldn't tell you that in New York. It'd mean I was a faggot. That was what the Civil War was about. Abraham Lincoln was a faggot. He was in love with General Grant. So was Jefferson Davis. Lincoln just freed the slaves on a bet. The Dred Scott case was framed by the Anti-Saloon League. Sex explains it all. The Colonel's Lady and Judy O'Grady are Lesbians under their skin."

He stopped.

"Want to hear some more?"

"Shoot," I said.

"I don't know any more. Tell you some more at lunch."

"Old Bill," I said.

"You bum!"

We packed the lunch and two bottles of wine in the rucksack, and Bill put it on. I carried the rod-case and the landing-nets slung over my back. We started up the road and then went across a meadow and found a path that crossed the fields and went toward the woods on the slope of the first hill. We walked across the fields on the sandy path. The fields were rolling and grassy and the grass was short from the sheep grazing. The cattle were up in the hills. We heard their bells in the woods.

The path crossed a stream on a foot-log. The log was surfaced off, and there was a sapling bent across for a rail. In the flat pool beside the stream tadpoles spotted the sand. We went up a steep bank and across the rolling fields. Looking back we saw Burguete, white houses and red roofs, and the white road with a truck going along it and the dust rising.

Beyond the fields we crossed another faster-flowing stream. A sandy road led down to the ford and beyond into the woods. The path crossed the stream on another foot-log below the ford, and joined the road, and we went into the woods.

It was a beech wood and the trees were very old. Their roots bulked above the ground and the branches were twisted. We walked on the road between the thick trunks of the old beeches and the sunlight came through the leaves in light patches on the grass. The trees were big, and the foliage was thick but it was not gloomy. There was no undergrowth, only the smooth grass, very green and fresh, and the big gray trees well spaced as though it were a park.

"This is country," Bill said.

The road went up a hill and we got into thick woods, and the road kept on climbing. Sometimes it dipped down but rose again steeply. All the time we heard the cattle in the woods. Finally, the road came out on the top of the hills. We were on the top of the height of land that was the highest part of the range of wooded hills we had seen from Burguete. There were wild strawberries growing on the sunny side of the ridge in a little clearing in the trees.

Ahead the road came out of the forest and went along the shoulder of the ridge of hills. The hills ahead were not wooded, and there were great fields of yellow gorse. Way off we saw the steep bluffs, dark with trees and jutting with gray stone, that marked the course of the Irati River.

"We have to follow this road along the ridge, cross these hills, go through the woods on the far hills, and come down to the Irati valley," I pointed out to Bill.

"That's a hell of a hike."

"It's too far to go and fish and come back the same day, comfortably."

"Comfortably. That's a nice word. We'll have to go like hell to get there and back and have any fishing at all."

It was a long walk and the country was very fine, but we were tired when we came down the steep road that led out of the wooded hills into the valley of the Rio de la Fabrica.

The road came out from the shadow of the woods into the hot sun. Ahead was a river-valley. Beyond the river was a steep hill. There was a field of buckwheat on the hill. We saw a white house under some trees on the hillside. It was very hot and we stopped under some trees beside a dam that crossed the river.

Bill put the pack against one of the trees and we jointed up the rods, put on the reels, tied on leaders, and got ready to fish.

"You're sure this thing has trout in it?" Bill asked.

"It's full of them."

"I'm going to fish a fly. You got any McGintys?"

"There's some in there."

"You going to fish bait?"

"Yeah. I'm going to fish the dam here."

"Well, I'll take the fly-book, then." He tied on a fly. "Where'd I better go? Up or down?"

"Down is the best. They're plenty up above, too."

Bill went down the bank.

"Take a worm can."

"No, I don't want one. If they won't take a fly I'll just flick it around."

Bill was down below watching the stream.

"Say," he called up against the noise of the dam. "How about putting the wine in that spring up the road?"

"All right," I shouted. Bill waved his hand and started down the stream. I found the two wine-bottles in the pack, and carried them up the road to where the water of a spring flowed out of an iron pipe. There was a board over the spring and I lifted it and, knocking the corks firmly into the bottles, lowered them down into the water. It was so cold my hand and wrist felt numbed. I put back the slab of wood, and hoped nobody would find the wine.

I got my rod that was leaning against the tree, took the bait-can and landing-net, and walked out onto the dam. It was built to provide a head of water for driving logs. The gate was up, and I sat on one of the squared timbers and watched the smooth apron of water before the river tumbled into the falls. In the white water at the foot of the dam it was deep. As I baited up, a trout shot up out of the white water into the falls and was carried down. Before I could finish baiting, another trout jumped at the falls, making the same lovely arc and disappearing into the water that was thundering down. I put on a good-sized sinker and dropped into the white water close to the edge of the timbers of the dam.

I did not feel the first trout strike. When I started to pull up I felt that I had one and brought him, fighting and bending the rod almost double, out of the boiling water at the foot of the falls, and swung him up and onto the dam. He was a good trout, and I banged his head against the timber so that he quivered out straight, and then slipped him into my bag.

While I had him on, several trout had jumped at the falls. As soon as I baited up and dropped in again I hooked another and brought him in the same way. In a little while I had six. They were all about the same size. I laid them out, side by side, all their heads pointing the same way, and looked at them. They were beautifully colored and firm and hard from the cold water. It was a hot day, so I slit them all and shucked out the insides, gills and all, and tossed them over across the river. I took the trout ashore, washed them in the cold, smoothly heavy water above the dam, and then picked some ferns and packed them all in the bag, three trout on a layer of ferns, then another layer of ferns, then three more trout, and then covered them with ferns. They looked nice in the ferns, and now the bag was bulky, and I put it in the shade of the tree.

It was very hot on the dam, so I put my worm-can in the shade with the bag, and got a book out of the pack and settled down under the tree to read until Bill should come up for lunch.

It was a little past noon and there was not much shade, but I sat against the trunk of two of the trees that grew together, and read. The book was something by A. E. W. Mason, and I was reading a wonderful story about a man who had been frozen in the Alps and then fallen into a glacier and disappeared, and his bride was going to wait twenty-four years exactly for his body to come out on the moraine, while her true love waited too, and they were still waiting when Bill came up.

"Get any?" he asked. He had his rod and his bag and his net all in one hand, and he was sweating. I hadn't heard him come up, because of the noise from the dam.

"Six. What did you get?"

Bill sat down, opened up his bag, laid a big trout on the grass. He took out three more, each one a little bigger than the last, and laid them side by side in the shade from the tree. His face was sweaty and happy.

"How are yours?"

"Smaller."

"Let's see them."

"They're packed."

"How big are they really?"

"They're all about the size of your smallest."

398

"You're not holding out on me?"

"I wish I were."

"Get them all on worms?"

"Yes."

"You lazy bum!"

Bill put the trout in the bag and started for the river, swinging the open bag. He was wet from the waist down and I knew he must have been wading the stream.

I walked up the road and got out the two bottles of wine. They were cold. Moisture beaded on the bottles as I walked back to the trees. I spread the lunch on a newspaper, and uncorked one of the bottles and leaned the other against a tree. Bill came up drying his hands, his bag plump with ferns.

"Let's see that bottle," he said. He pulled the cork, and tipped up the bottle and drank. "Whew! That makes my eyes ache."

"Let's try it."

The wine was icy cold and tasted faintly rusty.

"That's not such filthy wine," Bill said.

"The cold helps it," I said.

We unwrapped the little parcels of lunch.

"Chicken."

"There's hard-boiled eggs."

"Find any salt?"

"First the egg," said Bill. "Then the chicken. Even Bryan could see that."

"He's dead. I read it in the paper yesterday."

"No. Not really?"

"Yes. Bryan's dead."

Bill laid down the egg he was peeling.

"Gentlemen," he said, and unwrapped a drumstick from a piece of newspaper. "I reverse the order. For Bryan's sake. As a tribute to the Great Commoner. First the chicken; then the egg."

"Wonder what day God created the chicken?"

"Oh," said Bill, sucking the drumstick, "how should we know? We should not question. Our stay on earth is not for long. Let us rejoice and believe and give thanks."

"Eat an egg."

Bill gestured with the drumstick in one hand and the bottle of wine in the other.

"Let us rejoice in our blessings. Let us utilize the fowls of the air. Let us utilize the product of the vine. Will you utilize a little, brother?"

"After you, brother."

Bill took a long drink.

"Utilize a little, brother," he handed me the bottle. "Let us not doubt, brother. Let us not pry into the holy mysteries of the hen-coop with simian fingers. Let us accept on faith and simply say—I want you to join with me in saying—What shall we say, brother?" He pointed the drumstick at me and went on. "Let me tell you. We will say, and I for one am proud to say—and I want you to say with me, on your knees, brother. Let no man be ashamed to kneel here in the great out-of-doors. Remember the woods were God's first temples. Let us kneel and say: 'Don't eat that, Lady—that's Mencken.'"

"Here," I said. "Utilize a little of this."

We uncorked the other bottle.

"What's the matter?" I said. "Didn't you like Bryan?"

"I loved Bryan," said Bill. "We were like brothers."

"Where did you know him?"

"He and Mencken and I all went to Holy Cross together."

"And Frankie Fritsch."

"It's a lie. Frankie Fritsch went to Fordham."

"Well," I said, "I went to Loyola with Bishop Manning."

"It's a lie," Bill said. "I went to Loyola with Bishop Manning myself."

"You're cock-eyed," I said.

"On wine?"

"Why not?"

"It's the humidity," Bill said. "They ought to take this damn humidity away."

"Have another shot."

"Is this all we've got?"

"Only the two bottles."

"Do you know what you are?" Bill looked at the bottle affectionately.

"No," I said.

"You're in the pay of the Anti-Saloon League."

"I went to Notre Dame with Wayne B. Wheeler."

"It's a lie," said Bill. "I went to Austin Business College with Wayne B. Wheeler. He was class president."

"Well," I said, "the saloon must go."

"You're right there, old classmate," Bill said. "The saloon must go, and I will take it with me."

"You're cock-eyed."

"On wine?"

"On wine."

"Well, maybe I am."

"Want to take a nap?"

"All right."

We lay with our heads in the shade and looked up into the trees.

"You asleep?"

"No," Bill said. "I was thinking."

I shut my eyes. It felt good lying on the ground.

"Say," Bill said, "what about this Brett business?"

"What about it?"

"Were you ever in love with her?"

"Sure."

"For how long?"

"Off and on for a hell of a long time."

"Oh, hell!" Bill said. "I'm sorry, fella."

"It's all right," I said. "I don't give a damn any more."

"Really?"

"Really. Only I'd a hell of a lot rather not talk about it."

"You aren't sore I asked you?"

"Why the hell should I be?"

"I'm going to sleep," Bill said. He put a newspaper over his face.

"Listen, Jake," he said, "are you really a Catholic?"

"Technically."

"What does that mean?"

"I don't know."

"All right, I'll go to sleep now," he said. "Don't keep me awake by talking so much."

I went to sleep, too. When I woke up Bill was packing the rucksack. It was late in the afternoon and the shadow from the trees was long and went out over the dam. I was stiff from sleeping on the ground.

"What did you do? Wake up?" Bill asked. "Why didn't you spend the night?" I stretched and rubbed my eyes.

"I had a lovely dream," Bill said. "I don't remember what it was about, but it was a lovely dream."

"I don't think I dreamt."

"You ought to dream," Bill said. "All our biggest business men have been dreamers. Look at Ford. Look at President Coolidge. Look at Rockefeller. Look at Jo Davidson."

I disjointed my rod and Bill's and packed them in the rod-case. I put the reels in the tackle-bag. Bill had packed the rucksack and we put one of the trout-bags in. I carried the other.

"Well," said Bill, "have we got everything?"

"The worms."

"Your worms. Put them in there."

He had the pack on his back and I put the worm-cans in one of the outside flap pockets.

"You got everything now?"

I looked around on the grass at the foot of the elm-trees.

"Yes."

We started up the road into the woods. It was a long walk home to Burguete, and it was dark when we came down across the fields to the road, and along the road between the houses of the town, their windows lighted, to the inn.

We stayed five days at Burguete and had good fishing. The nights were cold and the days were hot, and there was always a breeze even in the heat of the day. It was hot enough so that it felt good to wade in a cold stream, and the sun dried you when you came out and sat on the bank. We found a stream with a pool deep enough to swim in. In the evenings we played three-handed bridge with an Englishman named Harris, who had walked over from Saint Jean Pied de Port and was stopping at the inn for the fishing. He was very pleasant and went with us twice to the Irati River. There was no word from Robert Cohn nor from Brett and Mike.

Sources

"A Fatal Salmon," by Frank Forester. Henry William Herbert (1807–1858), pen name Frank Forester, was a British-born American novelist, poet, historian, illustrator, journalist, and writer.

"A Gallant Poacher," by John Buchan (1875–1940), a Scottish novelist, historian, and politician. His most famous novel was the thriller *The 39 Steps*, reprinted many times and a popular movie.

"A President's Bass Fishing," by Grover Cleveland, from *Fishing and Shooting Sketches*, Outing Publishing, New York, 1906.

A Stream for Anglers, by W. H. H. Murray, from *Adventures in the Wilderness*, 1869.

A Wedding Gift, by John Taintor Foote, from the book of the same title, Appleton & Co., 1924.

Big Two-Hearted River, by Ernest Hemingway, from *In Our Time*, Boni & Liveright, New York, 1925.

Bright Rivers, by Nick Lyons, from the book of the same title, Lippincott, 1977, reprinted by permission of Nick Lyons.

"Fish Are Such Liars," by Roland Pertwee (1885–1963), an English playwright, film and television screenwriter, director, and actor. From the book of the same title, published in 1928. It was included in the Nick Lyons anthology *Hook, Line, and Sinker: Classic Fishing Stories*, 2014.

"Fishing Tips You Can Count On," by Lamar Underwood, from *1,001 Fishing Tips*, Skyhorse Press, 2010.

"Fishing with a Worm," by Bliss Perry (1860–1954), from the book of the same title for Houghton Mifflin. Nick Lyons included it in his anthology *Hook, Line, and Sinker: Classic Fishing Stories*, 2014.

Hemingway's Many-Hearted Fox River, by Nick Lyons, from *National Geographic* magazine, June 1997, and his book *Fishing Stories*, Skyhorse Publishing, 2014. Reprinted by permission of Nick Lyons.

Just for Openers and *Just Fishing,* by Tom Hennessey, from *Feathers 'n Fins*, Amwell Press, 1989. Reprinted by permission of Nancy Hennessey.

Little Rivers: Essay in Profitable Idleness and *A Leaf of Spearmint,* by Henry van Dyke Jr., from *Little Rivers*, 1895. *A Fatal Success,* by Henry van Dyke, from *Fisherman's Luck*, 1899.

Mid-Stream Crisis, by Lamar Underwood, *Sports Afield,* February 1983. Reprinted by permission of the author.

"On Dry-Cow Fishing as a Fine Art," by Rudyard Kipling, from the book of the same title, The Rowant Club, 1926.

"Retrospect," by Viscount Grey of Fallodon, Edward Grey, 1st Viscount Grey of Fallodon (1862–1933), better known as Sir Edward Grey. From *Fly Fishing,* 1920.

"Story Telling on the Thames," by Jerome K. Jerome. Jerome Klapka Jerome (1859–1927) was an English writer and humourist. Included by Nick Lyons in his anthology *Hook, Line, and Sinker: Classic Fishing Stories,* 2014.

The Angler, by Washington Irving, from *The Sketchbook of Geoffrey Crayon, Gentleman,* 1820.

"The Evening Rise" and "The Beginning of the Season," by John Waller Hills, from *A Summer on the Test,* first published in a limited edition in 1924 and reprinted in a popular edition with new chapters in 1930. The book was republished by Nick Lyons in 1983.

The Fighting Qualities of Largemouth Black Bass, by James A. Henshall, MD, from *Bass, Pike, Perch and Others,* Macmillan, 1903. *The Black Bass: Gamefish of the People,* from *Favorite Fish and Fishing,* Outing Publishing Co., 1908.

"The Finest Trout in the River" and "A Bit of Luck," by Harry Plunket Greene, excerpted from *Where the Bright Waters Meet,* first published in 1924, revised and enlarged in 1936, and published in the United States by Nick Lyons Books / Winchester Press.

The 'Lunge and *On Lying Awake at Night,* by Stewart Edward White, from *The Forest,* 1904.

The Night of Gytefisk, by Ernest Schwiebert, from *A River for Christmas and Other Stories,* 1988, The Stephen Greene Press, Penguin Putnam, reprinted by permission of Erik Schwiebert.

"The River God," by Roland Pertwee, *Saturday Evening Post,* July 7, 1928. It was reprinted in private editions. Nick Lyons included it in his anthology *Hook, Line, and Sinker: Classic Fishing Stories,* 2014.

"The River Sneak," by William Scrope (1772–1852), an English sportsman and amateur artist, known as a writer on sports.

The Royal Purple Game of the Sea and *A Bone-Fishing Pioneer,* by Zane Grey, from *Tales of Fishes,* 1919.

The Sun Also Rises, by Ernest Hemingway, excerpt from the original novel, Scribner's, New York, 1926.

"Thoughts in Coltsfoot Time," by Ernest Schwiebert, reprinted by permission of Erik Schwiebert.

"Thread of the River," by Odell Shepard, from his book *Thy Rod and Thy Creel,* first published in 1930 and had long been out of print when Nick Lyons republished it in 1984.